MIGHTY BY SACRIFICE

T0288270

Frontispiece: Mission No. 263, 2nd Bombardment Group, Fifteenth Army Air Force, August 29, 1944. Raid on Moravska Ostrava.

Mighty by Sacrifice

The Destruction of an American
Bomber Squadron, August 29, 1944

James L. Noles and James L. Noles Jr.

THE UNIVERSITY OF ALABAMA PRESS
Tuscaloosa

The University of Alabama Press
Tuscaloosa, Alabama 35487-0380
uapress.ua.edu

Copyright © 2009 by the University of Alabama Press
All rights reserved.

Hardcover edition published 2009.
Paperback edition published 2020.
eBook edition published 2015.

Inquiries about reproducing material from this work
should be addressed to the University of Alabama Press.

Typeface: AGaramond

Cover image: The sun sets on a B-17 Flying Fortress and its crew
at Langley Army Air Field, Virginia, July 1942; Library of Congress, Prints
and Photographs Division, LC-USW36-202

Cover design: Erin Kirk New

Paperback ISBN: 978-0-8173-5989-8
eBook ISBN: 978-0-8173-9017-4

A previous edition of this book has been catalogued by
the Library of Congress.

ISBN: 978-0-8173-1654-9 (cloth)

For Courtney Perry, Jennifer Perry, and all of the other grandchildren of the Fifteenth Air Force—this is what your grandfathers did for all of us

and

For Jackie and Elizabeth

So, at the threat ye shall summon—so at the need ye shall send
Men, not children or servants, tempered and taught to the end;
Cleansed of servile panic, slow to dread or despise,
Humble because of knowledge, mighty by sacrifice.
—Rudyard Kipling, *The Islanders*

Here we mark the price of freedom.
—World War II Memorial, Washington, D.C.

Contents

Acknowledgments

This book would have been impossible to write but for the support, encouragement, and assistance of an incredibly diverse and helpful group of people. At the great risk of forgetting or overlooking someone, the authors wish to thank the following, many of whom we are now fortunate enough to count among our friends.

Bill Tune, in his typically quiet and unassuming manner, was kind enough to share his story with us initially and help us to meet other veterans of the mission to Moravska Ostrava. Those men included his navigator, Loy Dickinson, who lent an incredible level of enthusiasm and energy to our efforts to locate and contact other survivors. Both Bill and Loy were also kind enough to allow us to quote freely from *Mission No. 263*, the book that they self-published, and coauthored with Frank Pindak, about the ill-fated mission.

Other survivors of the mission were equally helpful. They included Bill Garland, Jim Martin, Willard Netzley, Joe Owsianik, Duane Seaman, Albert E. Smith, Paul Sumner, and Leo Zupan. The same was true of their, and their comrades', descendants and relatives. Those ranks include Jeanette Ross, the niece of Ferris Joyner; Thomas Donahue, the son of Robert Donahue; Kati Netzley, the wife of Willard Netzley; William C. Bullock, the nephew of William Bullock; Fran Tune, the wife of Bill Tune; Charles Contrada, the son of Vincent Contrada (and who kindly allowed us to quote from his father's unpublished memoirs); Charles McVey Jr., the son of Charles McVey; Dorothy Fitzpatrick, the wife of John Fitzpatrick; Mary Huckstorff, the sister of Jim Weiler; Betty Reed, the sister of Russell Meyrick; Linda Gauger, Betty Reed's daughter; Vic Kreimeyer, who flew with

Russell Meyrick; and Fern Wagner, the sister of Joseph Sallings. In the Czech Republic, Jana Turchinkova, the granddaughter of Mojmir Baca, was an invaluable help as well as a voluntary translator, guide, and friend.

Dr. Richard Muller, professor of Military History, USAF Air Command and Staff College, Maxwell Air Force Base, also deserves copious credit. Without his professional guidance, suggestions, and, in a number of cases, careful editing, our book would have never passed historical or editorial muster. Thank you, Rich, and thanks also to the staff at the Air Force Historical Research Agency. The AFHRA and its archives are a national asset and essential to any book like ours. We are fortunate to have it here in Alabama.

Rebecca Roberts, at Berry College, helped us with respect to providing information on Berry College in the 1930s. The Burlington Historical Society assisted with information on Burlington, Wisconsin. So did John O'Connor, with the Springfield Museum, regarding Springfield, Massachusetts. Peter Kassak, a Czech historian, shared his helpful insight on AAF operations over Czechoslovakia during World War II and information that he had collected regarding the events of August 29, 1944. Likewise, Earl Martin, one of the authors of *Defenders of Liberty,* kindly shared his information on the mission and its aftermath. Ray Fowler, pilot of the restored B-17 *Liberty Belle,* was kind enough to share his practical insight on the operation of a B-17.

Thanks are also due to the staff and editorial board at The University of Alabama Press; to our manuscript editor, Debbie Self; and to the expert reviewers who took the time to examine and critique our initial manuscript. We deeply appreciate your faith in this project and the opportunity you provided us to tell this story. Similarly, thanks to Béverly Bashor, Kate McBride, and Denise Wright—friends, coworkers, and masters of the subtle nuances of Microsoft Word.

Finally, thank you to Jackie and Elizabeth. Without their own good-natured sacrifices of time and patience, we could have never even begun, much less finished, this book.

Prologue

A Long Way from Home

Staff Sergeant Robert D. Donahue—cold, hungry, cramped, and airsick—sped backward into harm's way at over 160 miles per hour. Such was the lot of a tail gunner on board a B-17G Flying Fortress bomber. Forced to half-kneel, half-sit on a bicycle seat-like saddle, a tail gunner rode blindly to wherever the Fortress's quartet of 1,200-horsepower Wright Cyclone engines dragged him.

Crammed uncomfortably in his bomber's tail, Donahue was unable to see where he was going. However, thanks to the square glass windows that surrounded his lonely perch and overlooked his pair of twin-mounted .50-caliber machineguns, he had a magnificent view of where his bomber, *Tail End Charlie*, had been. Before his eyes, long lines of white contrails streaked across the pale hazy blue of a late summer sky, trailing Donahue's group of bombers and pointing the way home to the American airfield at Amendola, Italy.

Four hours earlier, *Tail End Charlie* had lifted off from Amendola's runway and collected the other six planes that belonged to 20th Squadron, 2nd Bombardment Group (Heavy). With the squadron's other bombers echeloned tightly around it, *Tail End Charlie* had slid into position behind the three other squadrons that comprised the group and began the long journey north—across the Adriatic, over embattled Yugoslavia, across German-dominated Hungary, and into the hostile airspace of what was once Czechoslovakia.

So far, Group Mission Number 263 had been uneventful. No fighters, no unexpected flak nests, no mechanical problems—nothing to dispute the hope that the August 29, 1944, raid against the Czech city of Moravska Ostrava would be anything other than the "milk run" predicted by the optimists back at the air mission briefing that morning in Amendola. Nevertheless, the twenty-four-year-old Donahue had logged too many hours in the skies over the Third Reich to make the mistake of relaxing prematurely. In the past three months, he had flown missions against such notorious targets as Vienna; Blechhammer, Germany; and Ploesti, Romania. In a hard-fought raid against the oil refineries of Ploesti, Donahue had earned a Silver Star the previous month.[1]

Now, looking at the hands on his GI-issue wristwatch—strapped to the outside of his heavy leather flight gloves—Donahue knew that there was still plenty of time for trouble to raise its head up to 25,000 feet and take a malicious swipe at *Tail End Charlie* on today's mission. Donahue's watch showed 1040, which meant that they were still some twenty minutes from their target. At 1102, the first of the group's 250-pound bombs would tumble out of the bombers' open bays and smash into Moravska Ostrava's oil refineries and railway marshaling yards. Then, lightened of their payload, Donahue and his comrades would dash back to Amendola, where the welcoming warmth of a "medicinal" shot of whiskey at the mission's debriefing awaited him, as did the sanctuary of the rough stone and canvas hut Donahue called home.

Should he make it back to Amendola, Donahue could claim credit for his thirty-fourth combat mission. With that straightforward goal in mind, the tail gunner hoped the raid would indeed be the milk run his fellow aviators had forecasted. He was a good shot—as were most of the gunners that manned the critical tail position—but he felt no need to match his martial skills with the Germans today. Glancing down at the long black belts of thick .50-caliber bullets that passed him along the fuselage wall and into his machineguns, he hoped those bullets would remain unused.

Battling a bout of airsickness, Donahue shifted slightly on his uncomfortable perch, taking care not to dislodge the oxygen hose and intercom wires that kept him alive and in contact with the rest of the crew. He adjusted the steel helmet atop his head—a normally simple gesture now made challenging by his heavy cold-weather flying gear and bulky flak jacket—and, fighting off another wave of nausea, leaned forward as he peered through the window in front of him.

As Donahue's sharp eyes scanned the sky behind *Tail End Charlie,* he spotted a set of four black dots, approaching fast from the rear of the formation. The tail gunner knew that another set of escort fighters was due to arrive to take them over the target, and the quartet of dots formed the familiar stair-step formation of the bombers' "little friends"—their escort fighters. Nevertheless, he grabbed the yoke that controlled the machineguns' motorized Cheyenne turret. With a reassuring electrical buzz, it rotated slightly to point its twin guns at the approaching aircraft.

"Fighters coming up. Probably are friendly," Donahue announced calmly to First Lieutenant William S. "Bill" Tune, the bomber's pilot.[2] On board the squadron's other six bombers, Donahue's fellow tail gunners made the same observations to their own crews.

But before Tune could even reply, explosive puffs of smoke materialized beneath the wings of the oncoming aircraft. At that same instant, Donahue realized that the fighters were German Fw 190s.

"No, no—they're not!" Donahue yelled, desperately trying to correct his earlier mistake as a salvo of German wing-fired rockets slashed through the squadron's formation.[3] In an instant, his airsickness was forgotten. Peering into his reflector sight, Donahue squeezed off a long burst of bullets at the nearest fighter, even as more waves of German planes—Bf 109s and Fw 190s—speared straight toward the heart of the squadron from three different directions. Instantly, the sky seemed full of enemy aircraft. An after-action report later estimated their number as high as seventy.[4]

At the moment, however, there was no time to tally the attacking Germans. With a blink of the eye, the Bf 109s and Fw 190s scythed through the 20th Squadron, spraying the Flying Fortresses with machinegun and cannon fire. The German fighters sliced past the embattled B-17s with almost reckless abandon, lacerating their targets with cruel bursts of gunfire before slipping out of range to line up for another pass.

In response, Donahue and his fellow gunners blasted back at them, their .50-caliber guns pounding like jackhammers as lines of orange tracers strung across the violent sky. Spent shell casings rattled against the aluminum fuselage as Donahue whipped the tail turret back and forth, trying to lay a stream of bullets into the paths of the German fighters. Meanwhile, Tune and the other pilots wrestled their flight controls in their cockpits and fought to keep their seven bombers in formation. In an instant, their placid "milk run" to Morvaska Ostrava had degenerated into a desperate fight for their very lives—a fight too many of them were destined to lose.

I

Hometown Boys

By the end of World War II, approximately 2.2 million men and women were serving in the Army Air Forces (AAF) on six of the world's seven continents. But each officer's or airman's own story started somewhere else. Those stories began in large cities, small towns, or rural hamlets across America, converged, for some, on the 20th Squadron, 2nd Bombardment Group, and ended, for too many, in distant skies and fields far from home.

Bill Tune—Carbon Hill, Alabama

Carbon Hill huddles an hour northwest of Birmingham, hard alongside U.S. Highway 78 and the tracks of the Burlington Northern Santa Fe Railroad. Although the Alabama flag hangs above the modest town hall, the landscape surrounding the town rings truer to rocky Appalachia than to deep Dixie. Dark hills and ridges, some scarred with the remnants of defunct strip mines, crowd in against the town's small commercial district from the north. Like so many small American towns, Carbon Hill is a community fighting gamely for its economic survival, forgotten by the railroad and bypassed by the interstate.

Five miles to the north, the mining company town of Jagger has long since given up its ghost. It was never more than an outpost for the Brookside Coal Company anyway, a simple collection of six rough houses, a rudimentary one-room schoolhouse, and a company store. Today, Jagger is little more than the name of a rough two-lane road that winds past reclaimed strip mines, scraggly pine plantations, and the occasional cow pasture. Only the memories of former residents like William S. "Bill" Tune keep Jagger alive.

Tune's father, Tillman Tune, earned a living in Jagger as an independent contractor drilling dynamite blast holes for Brookside Coal. While Tillman worked the mines, his wife, Beulah, raised Tillman Jr. in a shotgun house rented from the company and lit by kerosene lamps. "We called them shotgun houses because their interiors were laid out in such a way that you could open the front door and fire a shotgun blast straight through the house and out the back door without ever hitting an interior wall," Tune explained.[1] Outside, Beulah kept a milk cow and a small cluck of chickens and tended a vegetable garden.

Tune entered that hardscrabble world in 1920 to share the house's second bedroom with Tillman Jr. Two other boys, Leon and Jim, followed. Despite their rough surroundings, Beulah had high hopes for her children. In the fall, she dispatched them to Carbon Hill to attend school with the town's children and, once a week, drove them to Jasper, 18 miles away, to take trumpet and saxophone lessons. Tune further sharpened his musical ear by escorting Mr. Winters, a blind piano tuner, on his Carbon Hill rounds.

But then Wall Street crashed. As the mining operations shut down, Tillman moved his family into Carbon Hill and bought a local grocery store. After school, when Tune was not delivering copies of the *Birmingham News* on a bike purchased from the Montgomery Ward catalog, Tune and his brothers helped his father in Tune's Grocery. Telephoned orders would be delivered in a grocery truck that ran, precariously, on a set of bald tires that were constantly being patched and re-inflated by the Tune boys.

"It never dawned on us that this was hard work—we just did what had to be done," Tune later reflected.[2] Additional hard work came in the form of railroad boxcars full of 100-pound bags of Purina cattle feed. Tune and his brothers faced the task of unloading the boxcars by hand for their father, who was a Purina cattle feed dealer. "My younger brother Leon thought it was an opportunity to build muscles," Tune recalled. "I can attest to the hard work but I do not remember any muscle-building."[3]

Starting a new business such as his grocery in the teeth of the Great Depression represented a remarkable leap of faith for Tillman Tune. Carbon Hill's economy was, by one estimate, 75 percent dependent upon the mining industry. Unfortunately, that industry had come to a complete standstill, throwing scores of miners out of work. Retail sales dropped to less than half of their previous levels, and the hoboes riding the rails of the Frisco Line through town provided stark evidence that life had grown tough all across the state. Just outside of Carbon Hill, abandoned mines and sinkholes filled with water, becoming breeding grounds for malaria-carrying mosquitoes. Before long, both of the town's banks failed, completely wiping out the Tunes' savings.[4]

As the town's economy worsened, Tillman Tune quietly looked the other way as friends and neighbors let their grocery bills go unpaid and continued to sell groceries to hungry families on credit. But eventually, financial reality caught up with Tune's Grocery. Tune's father reluctantly closed the store and returned to his contract work drilling blast holes for the few remaining strip miners. Meanwhile, Bill graduated from high school in Carbon Hill in 1937 and spent the next two years working odd jobs to help his parents stay afloat. Beulah Tune's dreams of a higher education for her sons seemed dashed against the hard reality of the Great Depression.

One day, however, the family's pastor told the Tunes of a possible opportunity at Berry College, in Rome, Georgia. At Berry, students could work for the college in lieu of paying tuition. It was no accident that the school's crest showed a cabin, the Bible, a lamp, and a plow. The cabin represented simplicity; the Bible, religion; the lamp, knowledge; and the plow, labor. With the pastor's recommendation backing him, Tune applied for admission and, in 1939, began classes at the college nestled in northwest Georgia's mountains.

Tune flourished at Berry, where he worked in the school's library. Hoping to become an architect, he majored in industrial arts while pursuing a minor in music and playing saxophone in the school's band. He also found time to meet and court Frances "Fran" Beggs, a pretty, bright-eyed fellow student from a farm outside of Royston, Georgia. The courtship presented its challenges—at the time, Berry was segregated by the sexes, and the girls' school was located a half mile from the men's college. The men and women were even separated in church, with men on one side and girls on the other. Only on Sunday afternoons could Tune and Fran meet, when they would sit and talk in the gym while holding hands. "We had one other method of seeing each other," Tune admitted. "When I was playing in the school band, Fran would sometimes sit in the band and turn the music sheets for me."[5]

In such a manner, three and a half years passed happily for Tune. Then, a Berry music professor invited Tune and several of his fellow students to her house on a Sunday afternoon to listen to CBS's Sunday broadcast of the New York Philharmonic Orchestra. The date was December 7, 1941, and before the concert was over, Tune and the others had learned from breathless announcers that the United States was at war. As they struggled to digest the news, a common question sprang from their lips.

"What are we going to do now?"[6]

Robert Donahue—Pittsburgh, Pennsylvania

As with Tune, the Great Depression shadowed the childhood of Robert D. Dona-hue. His father, an Irish immigrant, worked in Pittsburgh first as a trolley driver and later joined Pittsburgh's police force. In Pittsburgh, the Donahue family eventually grew to include five boys and three girls, with Robert, born in 1919, their eldest boy.

As a teenager, Donahue attended Oliver High School, on Pittsburgh's north side. But when the Great Depression hit, he realized that his parents could ill afford to feed a family of eight. Lying about his age, Donahue joined the Civilian Conservation Corps, or CCC. Sent to work in a series of camps in the western United States, Donahue lasted six months before the CCC realized that he was underaged. Yanking him from his work, his camp's cadre shipped him home.[7]

As soon as Donahue turned eighteen, he reenlisted in the CCC. This time, he found himself assigned to CCC Camp F-2-N, in Apache Creek, New Mexico. In a short period of time, he rose to become a crew chief, supervising small crews of men as they constructed roads, bridges, and stock tanks in the New Mexico wilderness.

"Very adaptable, alert, and industrious," the regional forester declared. "Possesses a pleasing personality." Writing back to Pittsburgh's chamber of commerce, he recognized Donahue as "one of the enrollees who had given unusually good service at the camp and is deemed most worthy of assistance in getting a job."[8]

The Japanese bombed Pearl Harbor the day after Donahue celebrated his twenty-second birthday back home in Pittsburgh. Shortly thereafter, a draft notice arrived at the Donahue home and, on March 14, 1942, at New Cumberland Army Depot, the AAF inducted Donahue into its ranks.

Loy Dickinson—Berkeley, California

On the other side of the country from Tune and Donahue, Loy Dickinson grew up in the city of Berkeley, California. He was only five days shy of his seventeenth birthday when he stepped out of his local Congregational Church on December 7, 1941, and learned of the attack on Pearl Harbor. With the Pacific Ocean lapping against his city's shores, the idea of a war with Japan resonated chillingly. Blackouts darkened Berkeley at night, while Dickinson's father, Lee, patrolled the streets as a block warden. "What really got people's attention more than [anything else] was the rationing," Dickinson remembered. "Food stamps, gas, tires, et cetera. That's when the word 'sacrifice' really meant something."[9]

Lee Dickinson, a World War I veteran with a battlefield commission, had come to Berkeley after leaving the army. He found work laboring as a press and slit operator for Western Waxed Paper Company and, in 1924, his wife, Pearl, gave birth to Dickinson. Four others, including a pair of twin girls, followed in regular succession.

For Dickinson, life on Otis Street, with five children tucked into a four-bedroom house, was a crowded one. Nevertheless, he had no complaints. A playground sat two short blocks away, and the local neighborhood swarmed with children playing basketball and stickball. He attended Abraham Lincoln Grammar School, a school populated at the time by a swirling mix of white, Japanese, Chinese, and black students. Today it is Malcolm X Grammar School.

In 1939, Dickinson entered Berkeley High School while, a half a world away, German *Panzers* were rolling across Poland. In high school, Dickinson was elected a freshman class officer, studied indifferently, and ran track in the winter and spring. Meanwhile, he worked a steady string of part-time jobs—delivering papers, mowing lawns, doing yard work, selling *Liberty* magazine, and hawking football programs at college football games at Memorial Stadium. He even cleaned the butcher shop at the local Piggly Wiggly every Saturday night for 35 cents. "The richest kid on the block," he joked—rich enough to afford his first bike for six dollars.[10]

Dickinson graduated in January 1943. Within three months, the military drafted him. "I have no clear recollection of what my parents thought except that they expected their son to do his duty for his country. For me, of course, it was a great adventure to be stepping out into a man's world."[11]

On April 5, 1943, Loy reported dutifully at San Francisco's Presidio with another complement of draftees. There, after he excelled at the battery of tests administered to his fellow draftees, an officer posed Loy an enviable question: "What would you like to do?"

Thinking of his girlfriend Barbara, who had grown up with missionary parents in Japan, Loy answered, "Japanese language school."

"That could happen," the officer admitted, "but there would be a ten-month wait. In the meantime, you'd be assigned to Camp Cook."

"What is Camp Cook?" Loy asked.

"Infantry," he replied.

"What are my other choices?" Loy quickly asked. Aviation cadet training was one of them and, as Loy put it simply, "This is how I ended up at Santa Ana, California."[12]

Jim Weiler—Burlington, Wisconsin

Unlike Dickinson, James A. "Jim" Weiler grew up squarely in America's heartland in the southern Wisconsin town of Burlington. Born in December 1921, Weiler was the son of Jacob and Nora Weiler. Jacob was a local veterinarian, and James—"Jim" to his family and friends, "Jimmie-Bird" to his sister Mary—shared the house on Burlington's McHenry Street with three brothers (Joe, Harold, and Phil) and sister Mary.

"I know it was during the Depression, but it was a great place to grow up," remembered Mary. "Money was short, but we got by." For her veterinarian father, "getting by" often meant working a barter system with local farmers. Small jobs would garner a bushel of vegetables. Larger efforts earned her father part of a hog due to be butchered.[13]

In Burlington, one of Weiler's earliest memories came from the time his family gathered around their radio to listen to news reports of Charles Lindbergh's epic solo transatlantic flight. Dr. Weiler supplemented the radio with readings from the newspaper and, when Lindbergh reached Paris, the whole Weiler clan celebrated. "What inspired Jim's love for flying? All I can think of is the 'Lone Eagle,' Charles Lindbergh," Mary surmised.[14]

Later, Weiler attended elementary and high school just down the street at St. Mary's, a pair of local Catholic parochial schools. He was an active student, known for his sense of humor and his skill at golf and archery. At some point during his adolescence, Weiler spotted the full-page newspaper ads for the Cal-Aero Technical Institute. Located at the Grand Central Air Terminal in Glendale, California, the institute was one of the premier training programs for pilots and aviation mechanics in the nation at the time. "When I graduate," Weiler told his family, "I want to go out to California and learn how to build airplanes. And then I want to learn how to fly them."[15]

In February 1941, still ten months shy of his twentieth birthday, Weiler said goodbye to his family and caught the train for California and the Cal-Aero Technical Institute. His educational investment soon proved to be a wise one. By the following summer, the Wisconsin veterinarian's son was working at the Lockheed plant in nearby Burbank.

But Weiler was not content to simply manufacture warplanes—as he had told his family, he wanted to fly them. In July 1942, he enlisted in the AAF and, by that November, was an aviation cadet at Santa Ana Army Air Base. In the months to follow, his three brothers would follow him into the military. Harold, an attorney, traded his law books for naval aviator wings. Joe, a reporter for the *Burlington Free Press,* was drafted into the army and became a tanker. Phil, the youngest, enlisted into the navy as soon as he was old enough. And back on McHenry Street, their mother hung a white flag with a red border and four blue stars—one for each of the Weiler boys—in the large front window of their home.[16]

Leo Zupan—Price, Utah

Leo Zupan's journey to the cockpit of a B-17 was a considerably less focused one than that of Weiler's. It also started in a far more different place—the wide-open mining town of Price, Utah. Price sits southeast of Salt Lake City in the arid country along the river that shares its name. The arrival of the railroad in 1883 transformed the town from a sleepy isolated farming community to the commercial and political hub of Castle Valley. It also sparked development of the region's coal mines, luring an influx of immigrant miners into the valley and surrounding hills. The chatter of Greek, Slav, German, Italian, and Japanese voices soon echoed through countless mining camps and in the dusty streets of Price, laying the foundation for their descendants to share no other identity but that of American.

Leo Zupan was one such child. His grandfather, a Croat immigrant, had followed the railroad to seek his fortune in Price, and his father had become one of the town's most successful construction contractors. Through years of hard work, Zupan built up both his business and his family. Eventually, the former numbered 120 employees, and the latter included his wife, a daughter, and two sons. The youngest was named Leo, born in 1920.

For a time, all was well in the Zupan home. But disaster struck when Zupan was only seven. His father died, the contracting business crumbled, and his mother took a job as a schoolteacher and began renting out the extra rooms in their house to boarders. Then the Great Depression struck. But somehow his mother kept the family fed, thanks in no small part to Zupan's own efforts. He ran a series of paper routes and worked for a year in the local JC Penney's department store. Still, he found time for fun. The neighborhood kids formed their own baseball team and waged a friendly rivalry with the north part of town, while a collection of local bands provided music at weekend dances. "We were a regular League of Nations," Zupan observed, "and, as far as the rest of Utah was concerned, we were a state of our own. Speakeasies, gambling, whorehouses, whatever—you name it and we had it."[17]

By the time Zupan was in high school, he had landed a steady part-time job working for a local dentist. After losing his savings and his house in the stock market crash, the dentist moved on to Moab, Utah, to open a new practice there. Zupan, at the age of sixteen, followed him to Moab, intent on keeping his job while finishing high school. He did so in 1937 and returned to Price.

Back in Price, Zupan found, as he put it simply, "there wasn't a heck of a lot to do." His sojourn in Price lasted long enough, however, for the town's first draft to select Zupan. He reported for his physical, where a doctor examined a chest x-ray and spied a spot on one of Zupan's lungs. Zupan's uncle had died of black lung disease, and the doctor quickly provided a description of Zupan's health that ensured he would be classified as "4-F"—medically unqualified. "I've often wondered about that," Zupan mused years later. "He was a local doctor, and everyone in Price looked out for each other. He knew my mother was a widow. Did I have a spot on that x-ray? I'll never know."[18]

Spared temporarily from the draft, Zupan learned of a job in Elko, Nevada, working at a JC Penney store. He took the job but, after wearying of working indoors, left it for an assignment grading roads in the mountains of northern Nevada and Idaho. Laid off at the end of the summer, he then learned of a job opening in a department store in Ashland, Oregon. Writing to the store's proprietor, Zupan secured a job and, using the last of his money, bought a one-way train ticket to Ashland in September 1941.

In Ashland, Zupan found a room at the Columbia Hotel. At two dollars a night, the room seemed cheap by modern standards. But the hotel bills were not going to leave much left over from Zupan's $100-a-month salary. As soon as he could, he moved into a local boardinghouse, where the $30-a-month bill for room and board was far more palatable. Now there was enough money for Zupan to take classes at the local college at night.

Even with work and classes, Zupan found time for fun. He typically spent weekend nights with a collection of bachelor friends and their dates at a chateau north of town. Saturday, December 6, 1941, was no exception, and he did not return to his boardinghouse abode until late in the night. After a night of drinking beer and dancing, he slept in late Sunday morning. When Zupan finally eased downstairs to scrounge any breakfast leftovers, he found the house abuzz with excited conversation. "We're at war!" a fellow boarder told him. For the first time in his life, Zupan heard the phrase "Pearl Harbor."[19]

In the wake of Pearl Harbor, Zupan struggled uncomfortably with his 4-F draft status. One Saturday night, he sat through a war movie about pilots. "I'd like to take a shot at that," he decided as the final credits rolled. That week, he wrote back to the Price draft board. "Can I enlist?" he asked. The board had no objection.[20]

With only a high school education under his belt, Zupan knew that he would need more than that to make it through flight school. Enlisting the aid of a local professor named Eliot McCracken, he began a crash course in algebra and calculus. Each morning, from 7:00 until 9:00, he studied under McCracken's tutelage. Then, at 9:00 A.M., he opened the department store and, after working a full day, studied until past midnight most nights.

After a successful physical examination, Zupan finally enlisted on May 22, 1942, only to be told to await his call-up orders for aviation cadet training. He finished the summer with the department store and returned to Price in September, where he discovered that the war effort had revived the coal industry. Zupan soon secured a job working a pair of diesel-powered air compressors. "It was a soft job," Zupan remembers, "and a union one. I was paid $3.45 an hour. I had more money than I knew what to do with. I worked shifts for other guys and saved enough money to buy $450 in war bonds."[21]

But the army had not forgotten about Zupan. Orders arrived directing him to Santa Ana and on November 11, 1942—Armistice Day, as Veterans' Day was called then—he reported for duty. On a day commemorating the veterans of the First World War, Zupan set out to become a veteran of the Second.

William Bullock—Roxboro, North Carolina

Commemoration and memory of the community's veterans never fell far from the minds of the citizens of Roxboro, North Carolina. In Roxboro, a statue of Confederate captain Fletcher Satterfield, 55th North Carolina Infantry, still stands proudly in the green grass beside the Person County Courthouse. At Gettysburg, Satterfield had fallen mortally wounded on Cemetery Ridge at a location North Carolinians long argued was the deepest penetration of the Union lines during that battle.

A generation later, William C. Bullock arrived in Roxboro and, in 1909, founded the Bullock Lumber Company. In Roxboro, he and his wife eventually raised four children—John, Nancy, Carr, and, finally, young William C. Bullock Jr. Nicknamed "Bitty," Bullock was a popular member of Roxboro High School who, upon graduating, departed for Wake Forest University to study medicine. Two years later, he decided his interests lay in business instead and transferred to the University of North Carolina. But when news of the Japanese attack rocked Chapel Hill, Bullock realized that a business career would have to wait.[22]

After graduating from the university in the summer of 1942, Bullock tried to enlist as a pilot in the navy. A broken elbow from childhood foiled that effort, however. Offended by the navy's refusal, Bullock signed up for the army instead.[23] Apparently, the army's standards for its pilots were not quite as high. In November 1942, Bullock found himself in route to Nashville, Tennessee, and the Army Air Force's classification center there.

Ed Smith—Findlay, Ohio

Like Bullock, Albert E. "Ed" Smith was another collegian turned aviator. In the fall of 1942, Smith had registered as a freshman at Ohio's Miami University. If he needed any reminder that his nation was now at war, he only had to look across the campus to the college's Fisher Hall and The Pines dormitories. Over the summer, the navy had turned that corner of the university into a naval reservation, complete with strategically placed sentry boxes, to host a radio training school. Scores of seamen fresh out of boot camp shared the campus with Smith and his fellow collegians, learning Morse code, typing, and radio operations instead of English, algebra, and economics.

Smith had come to Miami University from Findlay, Ohio, a small city in the northwestern part of the state. In Findlay, his father sold appliances while his mother raised Smith and his two brothers. He had been a senior at Findlay High School on the fateful Sunday afternoon the Japanese attacked Pearl Harbor. While playing board games at his next-door neighbor's house, Smith heard the news over the radio.

"It was a shock," he remembered. "I had figured we might well get into the war since we were already supplying England with equipment and supplies, but we certainly weren't expecting to get in at that level so quickly."[24]

Despite the nation's unexpected passage from peace to war, Smith stuck to his original plans of attending college. But soon after entering Miami University, he, along with many other Miami undergraduates, heeded duty's call. In November 1942, Smith rode to Wright Army Air Field near Dayton and, after taking the military's classification tests, scored high enough to qualify for the AAF's aviation cadet program. Excited about the prospect of flying, he returned to Miami as a member of the school's reserve unit to await orders.

Christmas came, but Smith's anticipated orders did not. After spending the holidays in Findlay, he returned to campus. Three weeks later, the army finally acted.

"Report for further classification at Kelly Army Air Base," the orders read. As February drew to a close, Smith caught a troop train bound for San Antonio—one of approximately 5,000 Miami University Redskins destined to serve in the military during the Second World War.[25]

Willard Netzley—Covina, California

Like Smith's, Willard Netzley's initial college career was an abbreviated one. After graduating from California's Covina Union High School in 1940, the short, good-humored Netzley entered nearby Citrus Junior College. For a young man from Covina, which sat 22 miles east of Los Angeles amid acres of orange and lemon trees, Citrus Junior College seemed a semantically logical progression in life. Netzley had grown up in a family of five boys and a girl and, like many residents of Covina, his parents owned an orange grove there. Netzley and his brothers spent their free time working the groves. "If we were poor during the Depression, so was about everybody," Netzley remembered simply.[26]

In the summer of 1941, the lure of high-paying wages in California's burgeoning aircraft industry proved too great for Netzley to remain in school. He traded Covina's orange groves for Lockheed's Hudson bomber assembly line in Burbank—the same plant where Weiler was destined to work. There, workers like Weiler and Netzley would eventually help produce some 2,900 Hudson bombers for various Allied air forces.

"I didn't work at Lockheed long before I knew that I was not cut out for factory work," Netzley admitted. "But from working for my dad where my cash pay was zero, I was delighted with the high wages of fifty-one cents per hour plus six cents night bonus."[27]

By the summer of 1942, nineteen-year-old Netzley's thoughts turned to military service. With a year of college under his belt, he considered his options.

"[AAF] recruiters mentioned that girls loved guys in the Air Force uniform and, anyway, in the Air Force you died with a clean shirt on," Netzley remembered. "So I joined the [AAF] at a little airfield in Chino, California."[28]

At the time, the Cal-Aero Academy operated a flight school under contract to provide primary flight training for AAF cadets. But Netzley only remained at Chino long enough to be inducted into the military. The AAF then directed the new recruit to return to Citrus Junior College and await further orders. Those orders came less than a year later and, in the spring of 1943, Netzley caught a train at Los Angeles's Union Depot. For him, the next stop would be Lincoln Army Air Base, in Lincoln, Nebraska, for basic training.

Charles McVey—Havelock, Nebraska

For Charles McVey, Lincoln, Nebraska, also represented a beginning, albeit in a far more traditional sense. There, he was born to Edward and Fayla McVey, the second of thirteen children in a sprawling Scots-Irish family. McVey grew up in the Lincoln suburb of Havelock, where, true to his Scottish roots, he developed an avid interest in golf. By the age of 12, McVey was caddying at the local public golf course and, by the time he graduated from Havelock High School, he was an accomplished golfer.[29]

In 1938, however, even the most gifted golfer's strokes and swings were unlikely to put food on the table in Depression-era Nebraska. The Tennessee Valley Authority offered far more promise, as well as a steady paycheck. Bidding his parents and siblings farewell, McVey responded to a newspaper advertisement and headed for Tennessee. In Tennessee, he not only found work but, in Nashville, met a young lady named Mildred Alene. McVey and Mildred married in August 1942.

Unfortunately, McVey's local draft board cut his honeymoon short. Drafted into the army, he completed boot camp and was then assigned to Fort Oglethorpe, a cavalry post nestled in the mountains of northern Georgia. At Fort Oglethorpe, McVey's typing skills landed him a job as a company clerk and, while, hammering away at his typewriter in the winter of 1942–1943, he learned of an opportunity to join the AAF. Perhaps McVey was growing tired of flying a desk or perhaps, like Netzley in distant California, he simply wanted to avoid a damp foxhole and cold rations. Whatever the reason, McVey volunteered for the AAF and soon shipped off to Florida for flight training. Determined to spend as much time with her new husband as possible, Mildred gamely followed.

Jim Martin—Harmon County, Oklahoma

James R. "Jim" Martin was the son of a farmer—in Martin's case, a sharecropper whose family first made the southern Oklahoma hamlet of Woodville home—long enough for his wife to give birth to James in 1924. Tenant farming, however, was a transient life, particularly as farmers like Martin's father struggled with falling prices and increasingly exhausted soil during the Great Depression. Martin moved his family west, into Harmon County, Oklahoma, in the state's southwestern corner across the Red River from Texas.

In Harmon County, life remained hard, particularly as the Dust Bowl began to manifest itself in the mid-1930s. Although several hundred thousand "Okies" eventually abandoned their Great Plains farms in the face of the ecological disaster, the Martins hunkered down in their rough corner of Oklahoma and hoped for the best. Years later, Martin remembered his father's struggles to scratch out a living growing cotton and maize.

"He worked from first light to last light and earned about 75 cents a day," Martin recalled. "Oklahoma was a tough place for farmers. I can remember dust storms so thick that it was dark in the middle of the day, so dark that the chickens would go to roost. One day the real estate would all blow north and the next day it would blow back."[30]

In such times, the diversions for Martin were simple ones. On Saturday afternoons, for example, his father would take Martin, his four brothers, and his sister into Hollis, where he shopped and had his tools sharpened. "He always gave us kids each a quarter," Martin recalled. "A triple dip of ice cream was five cents, a movie was ten cents, and popcorn was five cents. That left a whole nickel for us to blow."[31]

Working alongside his father in the cotton and maize fields, Martin managed to make his way through grade school in Hollis. Eventually leaving home in 1940 at the age of 16, he enrolled in the National Youth Administration (NYA) in Enid, Oklahoma. The NYA was, like the CCC, a New Deal program designed to teach job skills and offer employment to alleviate the ravages of the Great Depression. It specifically targeted unemployed youths like Martin and, by 1940, was focusing its efforts on training its participants in the kinds of skills needed by the country's growing military industry. Not coincidentally, Martin trained to be a welder, earning $15 a month plus room and board.

In Martin's case, the NYA worked just as the government hoped it would. Martin first put his new welding skills to use with the aircraft manufacturer Boeing in Wichita, Kansas, and then, hearing that Kaiser Shipbuilding was paying welders a dollar an hour on the West Coast, caught a train to San Francisco in 1941 and landed a job at the shipyards. But by April 1943, Martin and several of his friends had grown tired of their work on Kaiser's Liberty Ships. Instead, they decided, they wanted to become tankers in the U.S. Army. A sergeant at the recruiting station on Market Street assured them that a spot in the tank corps was theirs for the asking.

"Well, I tell you I never saw a tank," Martin later said good-humoredly. "They sent us directly to the Presidio of San Francisco, put us in uniform, and it was no time until I was in basic training in Fresno, California."[32]

Bill Garland—Vancouver, British Columbia

The childhood of William T. "Bill" Garland was a far cry from the dusty, hardscrabble existence of Jim Martin. Born in Seattle, Washington, Garland grew up as a young expatriate north of the border. In 1923, when Garland was seven, his father moved his family from Seattle to Vancouver, the largest city in the Canadian province of British Columbia. In the "Roaring Twenties," Vancouver's economy hummed along, primed, in some of the city's less wholesome quarters, by a thriving bootlegging business during Prohibition but fueled primarily by the province's shipping, fishing, mining, and lumber industries. Garland's father found work in the latter industry, where he ran a sawmill.[33]

The Great Depression struck Canada just as hard as it did the United States. The country's western provinces, heavily dependent upon natural resource and agricultural exports, were particularly vulnerable. Vancouver's problems were exacerbated by its relatively moderate climate, which attracted hundreds of unemployed men and their families from the other western provinces. Within this simmering cauldron, labor unrest plagued the city throughout much of the 1930s while the government kept the city's dockyards under control only through three years of martial law. Despite the economic turmoil, Garland's father had managed to keep his family afloat as he transitioned from a sawmill operator to an equipment salesman. Later, he founded his own company that built portable sawmills.

Meanwhile, Garland completed his high school education, graduating in 1934. An active athlete, he played basketball and rowed four- and eight-man crews in the waters of Burrard Inlet and the Fraser River. With his school days behind him, his focus turned to work and his father readily welcomed the tall, strapping teenager into the family business.

By 1938, however, Garland had decided to trade the scenic but damp Northwest for much drier climes. He moved to Phoenix, Arizona, where he found work in a local steel mill. Three years later, on Sunday, December 7, 1941, he took a car into the desert outside of town for a picnic with some friends. The car did not have a radio and so it was not until they returned to town that evening that they learned Pearl Harbor had been attacked. By then, many of his former classmates and school chums from Vancouver were already in uniform and deployed overseas.

Volunteering for military service, Garland chose the AAF. "I wanted to fly," he stated laconically, "and it seemed the best force to do so."[34] He enlisted in Phoenix on July 27, 1942, and received orders for preflight training at Santa Ana, California. There, after a childhood growing up under the Canadian flag, Garland was destined to begin serving his country under the Stars and Stripes.

Joe Owsianik—South Plainfield, New Jersey

If Garland's childhood had an international flair to it, so did that of Joseph "Joe" Owsianik. In Owsianik's hometown of South Plainfield, New Jersey, the Lehigh

Valley Railroad provided a conduit for the coal shipments to fuel new factories and the new immigrants to labor in them. Hungarians, Poles, Irishmen, and Italians carved out their slice of the American dream in the neighborhood originally called New Brooklyn.

Those immigrants' ranks included Paul Owsianik. He arrived in New Jersey from Krakow, Poland, in 1889, married a fellow immigrant named Mary, and joined a predominantly Irish workforce tending to the tracks of the Lehigh Valley Railroad. Meanwhile, the neighborhood's population—and the Owsianik's family—grew. Paul and Mary's first child was a boy, followed in steady succession by five girls and, finally, in 1924, a second son they christened Joseph and nicknamed Joe. Tragedy struck, however, two years after Joe Owsianik's birth when his mother died, leaving her husband with seven children. Then in 1936, Joe's father died. Now the fate of the young Owsianik clan rested in the hands of Joe's older brother Victor. Victor responded faithfully and, through the depths of the Great Depression, kept Joe and his five sisters clothed and fed.[35]

As those hard years passed, Joe literally grew up with nearby Hadley Field. The airfield opened in 1924, the same year as his birth, and grew steadily into an important airport. Its significance was underscored on July 1, 1925, when the nation's first night airmail flight took off from Hadley Field, bound for the distant West Coast. The flight arrived triumphantly in California thirty-three and a half hours later.

With such excitement blossoming two miles from his home, Owsianik could not resist the urge to visit the airfield whenever he had a chance. One day, the airfield's owner spotted the young teenager eyeballing one of his aircraft.

"You like airplanes?" the owner asked in a not unfriendly tone.

"Yes, sir!" Owsianik responded.

"You want a job?"

"Yes, sir!"

"I can pay you five dollars a week, and I'll teach you how to fly. You interested?"

"Yes, sir!"[36]

Owsianik found his true passion working at Hadley Field. He oiled and gassed airplanes, logged the planes out for rental and checked them back in, washed them, and generally helped in whatever way he could. "I just loved it," Owsianik recalled. "I'd start at 4:30 A.M. and would have been there even earlier if there had been any work to be done at that hour."[37] For his part, the airfield's owner kept his word and taught Owsianik to fly.

When Owsianik was not at Hadley Field, he attended vocational school in nearby New Brunswick, where he labored to learn the printing trade. The siren's call of the airfield, however, was a seductive one, and Owsianik progressed inter-mittently through the school. "I spent too much time with those airplanes," he ad-mitted later with a laugh.[38] Eventually, while still a teenager, he took a job driving a delivery truck for the Sealtest Milk Company.

In South Plainfield, Owsianik's pleasures were simple ones. In the wintertime, they included ice skating at a nearby pond. On December 7, 1941, the seventeen-year-old returned from a Sunday afternoon of skating. With his blades slung over his shoulder, he stepped back into his house. In the parlor, he could hear a radio an-nouncer speaking in excited tones. The Japanese, the announcer warned, had at-tacked the territory of Hawaii.

"Oh, boy," Owsianik thought to himself as a sickening wave of anxiety washed over him. "They are going to call up Victor. Who will take care of the family?"[39] For his part, Owsianik was in no hurry to get into uniform, despite a gaggle of friends who rushed to enlist in the wake of Pearl Harbor. For him, the only uniform in which he was interested at the moment was that of the Sealtest Milk Company.

But even Owsianik's work driving the milk van provided daily reminders of a nation at war. His daily rounds took him to nearby Camp Kilmer, a staging area for the port of New York. "Troop trains would roll in and out all the time," Owsianik remembered. "One day the camp would be bulging at the seams, and the next day it would be empty. And when they were gone, you knew they were going to war."[40]

Eventually, Owsianik's own turn came. A draft notice arrived and, after a physi-cal examination and other bureaucratic indignities at the Newark National Guard Armory, he was inducted into the AAF on March 23, 1943. A week at Fort Dix fol-lowed before orders shipped him off to Miami Beach for basic training. Mean-while, his older brother Victor received a medical deferment due to an eardrum in-jured in childhood. Despite Owsianik's earlier fears, he, and not his older brother, was destined for combat overseas.

Joseph Sallings—Luttrell, Tennessee

Some men, such as Owsianik, were destined for fighting. Others, such as Joseph Sallings, seemed to have been born fighting. That was certainly the case if one was, like Sallings, a descendant of those restless Scots-Irish pioneers who had crossed the Great Smoky Mountains and carved out freeholds in the dusky hollows, rocky meadows, and fertile river and creek bottoms of northeastern Tennessee. Most farmed—primarily corn, tobacco, and some cotton—although others earned their livings logging timber or mining the surrounding hills in what would one day be called Union County. An uncommon streak of independence and self-reliance remained a common virtue among such men, even as small communities such as Luttrell began to coalesce.

A railroad finally reached Luttrell in 1887, turning the small hamlet into the market center for the rest of the county. For years to come, Luttrell was the key link to the outside world for small farmers like Willett Sallings and his wife, Mamie. Willett raised tobacco and hogs—sometimes as many as 300 at a time—while Mamie raised their children, Joseph and Fern. Another sibling died in infancy.

For the Sallings family, it was a simple life. The family had no car, three-mile walks to school were an accepted hardship, and their community life centered on the local Baptist church. The Sallings attended church every Sunday—and every wedding and funeral in the interim. In Luttrell, there simply wasn't much else to do.[41]

Fern was only seven when her brother Joseph's attendance at Horace Maynard High School drew to a close in the spring of 1942. Soon thereafter, the postman delivered a draft notice for the wiry farmboy. The Union needed Union County's men, and Sallings was no exception. He bade farewell to Luttrell without complaint and, with a light suitcase in hand, caught a bus for Fort Oglethorpe, Georgia. There, on November 7, 1942, within a stone's throw of Chickamauga—one of the bloodiest battles of the Civil War—Sallings became one of over ten million draftees inducted in the U.S. military during World War II.

Russell W. Meyrick—Springfield, Massachusetts

Russell W. Meyrick's hometown of Springfield, Massachusetts, was as distinctly American as that of Sallings. Nestled on the Connecticut River, Springfield has witnessed James Naismith invent basketball, George Washington establish the first national armory, and Smith & Wesson begin manufacturing handguns in 1852.

As far as young Meyrick was concerned, however, Springfield was simply home to his parents, William and Kathryn, and his three younger siblings, Elizabeth, Jeanette, and Donald. Meyrick's father owned a restaurant in town in which he cooked as the chef. "It was a simple family restaurant," Meyrick's younger sister Elizabeth (Meyrick) Reed remembered. "That was back when you could get a blue plate special for a quarter."[42]

Recalling Springfield in the 1930s, Reed described it as "sort of a good time—I have to admit. It was during the Depression, but everyone was in the same boat. In our neighborhood, the kids would play in the streets and the parents would sit on the porches and talk and watch them. You don't see that much anymore."[43]

Meyrick attended Springfield's Technical High School, co-opting in his later years at the school with the Wico Electric Manufacturing Company in West Springfield. After graduation, Meyrick joined the company as a tool designer. Wico made quality ignition systems for stationary motors and for the engines of John Deere, Case, and Wisconsin tractors. As women began to fill the ranks of the plant's workers, many of the new female employees suffered cuts on their hands when screwing in the various wires and magnetos of the unfamiliar ignition assemblies. Displaying his usual flair for innovation and invention, Meyrick invented a tool with a hand-guard that put an end to such lacerations.

Such attributes made Meyrick an indispensable part of Wico's operation, and Wico was considered a vital war industry. Accordingly, the Springfield draft board deferred Meyrick from the draft and local recruiters blocked his efforts to enlist voluntarily. Frustrated, he embarked upon a letter-writing campaign, even pleading his case in a letter to President Roosevelt.[44] Successful at last, Meyrick enlisted in the army on April 15, 1942, at the age of twenty-one, signing up for a term of service that his papers described as "the duration of the War or other emergency, plus six months, subject to the discretion of the President or otherwise according to law."[45]

For Meyrick, it was the most open-ended of commitments in a particularly dark time. The previous week, U.S. and Filipino forces on Bataan surrendered to the Japanese—arguably the largest capitulation of American forces in the nation's history. Meanwhile, in Asia, British and Chinese forces reeled before a Japanese onslaught in Burma. In North Africa, Rommel finished preparations to unleash his rejuvenated *Afrika Korps* against British and Commonwealth forces weakened by diversion of troops to the Far East. On the Eastern Front, the *Wehrmacht,* having weathered the Red Army's winter offensive, readied for a counteroffensive that would lead to some of the war's bloodiest battles yet. In short, "the duration of the War" threatened to be unlimited—at least for the foreseeable future.

⤸

All told, Meyrick and his comrades formed a disparate bunch—Yankees and Southerners, city slickers and Okies, truck drivers and high school students, college graduates and high school dropouts. But they were all about to be swept up in an industrial and organizational juggernaut of leviathan proportions. In terms of both uniformity and efficiency, that juggernaut's creation of flying machines and the men to man them would leave much to be desired. In terms of sheer magnitude, however, it represented an undertaking and an accomplishment of unprecedented effort that would leave none of its participants the same again—regardless of whether or not they survived "the duration of the War."

2
Silver Wings

"Massed, Angered Forces"

The idea that Japan's attack on Pearl Harbor pushed the United States—the pro-verbial "sleeping giant"—from peaceful indolence onto a war footing practically overnight is among the most enduring myths in America's popular memory. The total truth is far more complex. In reality, the United States had, by the closing years of the 1930s, already begun taking steps to forge a lethal war machine. These prescient steps, though dangerously delinquent, set America's military along a path of growth and development that would enable it to weather the calamity of Pearl Harbor and stagger vengefully into the fray.

For the U.S. Army's aviators, 1938 was a seminal year in such growth. That September, Hitler's *Wehrmacht* marched into Czechoslovakia's Sudetenland shielded by a swarming umbrella of *Luftwaffe* fighters and dive-bombers. It was a sobering spectacle and, in the United States, the Army Air Corps (as it was then called) took stock of its own limited capabilities. To its dismay, it counted only 1,700 tactical and training aircraft, manned and serviced by 1,600 officers and 18,000 enlisted men.[1] Of those officers, if they attended the Air Corps Tactical School as late as 1935, they spent more hours on horseback than in the classroom studying such topics as air logistics.[2] This was hardly the stuff of hemispheric defense. Some went so far as to call it "utterly inadequate."[3]

Accordingly, General Henry H. "Hap" Arnold, chief of the Army Air Corps, argued eloquently and successfully for a force of 7,000 warplanes in the wake of the

Sudetenland debacle. Convinced by Arnold, President Roosevelt directed the War Department to draft an organizational and armament program for an Air Corps of 10,000 aircraft and, on January 12, 1939, requested the necessary funding from Congress.[4]

On April 3, 1939, Congress responded by authorizing the expenditure of $300 million for an Air Corps of no more than 6,000 airplanes.[5] Although Roosevelt and Arnold had requested more, and despite the fact that many aircraft would be redirected to Great Britain and other allies, Congress's action increased the number of military aircraft being produced nearly fivefold and set a course toward a greatly expanded Air Corps of 24 groups. Such an increase was especially significant since, at the time, the only modern four-engine heavy bombers the United States possessed were thirteen Boeing B-17 Flying Fortresses.[6]

At the time, the B-17's storied history was scarcely five years old. In 1934, the Army Air Corps had solicited bids for a new multiengine bomber, which, it assumed, simply meant two engines rather than one. Specifically, the Air Corps wanted a bomber capable of carrying 2,000 pounds of bombs 2,000 miles at a speed of at least 200 miles per hour, and it initially wanted as many as 220 of them.[7] Such planes would be able to reinforce such regions as Hawaii, Alaska, and the Panama Canal Zone by means of a direct flight from the continental United States and, once in position, could defend those possessions against even more distant land and naval threats.

Despite the stern requirements of the bid proposal, Boeing, Douglas, and Martin gamely pursued the contract. Boeing, determined to capitalize on the success of its revolutionary Boeing 247 commercial airliner, boldly devoted $275,000 of the company's own capital to finance the design of its prototype heavy bomber, powered it with four engines, and christened its effort "Project 299."[8]

Project 299 flew for the first time on July 28, 1935—"a beautifully designed, streamlined, gleaming giant of a plane."[9] At the time, the Project 299 prototype, with four engines crowning a 104-foot wingspan, was the heaviest land-based plane yet built in the United States (at the time, the title of "largest" still belonged to the World War I–era Witteman-Lewis XNBL-1 Barling bomber, which boasted a wingspan of 120 feet). Project 299's gleaming girth, coupled with an unprecedented five machinegun positions, inspired Richard L. Williams of the *Seattle Times* to declare the new aircraft a "15-ton flying fortress."[10] Thanks to the newspaperman's hyperbole, Project 299 had a new name.

In the initial competition, however, the "Flying Fortress" was bested by Douglas's twin-engine B-18. Nevertheless, the Air Corps was impressed enough during the trials to acquire thirteen of Boeing's bombers, designate the aircraft the Y1B-17 (with the "Y1" indicating that the aircraft was still undergoing service testing), and assign a dozen of them to the 2nd Bombardment Group at Langley Field, Virginia. The 2nd Group crewed its bombers with handpicked men and embarked upon a campaign of record-breaking flights intended to garner national attention to the Flying Fortress. The steady, rugged, and dependable Fortress quickly became popular with her pilots and, in the wake of several record-breaking transcontinental flights and two high-profile missions to South America, the army deemed the bomber's service testing complete. It dropped the "Y" designation and ordered 39 B-17Bs from Boeing in 1938.[11]

Nevertheless, the War Department seemed hesitant to commit wholeheartedly to the heavy bomber concept. The order for the third version of the Flying Fortress (the B-17C) numbered only thirty-eight; orders for the fourth version (the B-17D, which cost $202,500 a plane) totaled only forty-two.[12] By now, Boeing had upped the bomber's engines to nearly 1000 horsepower each and armed it with six .50-caliber machineguns and one .30-caliber machinegun. As more and more B-17s arrived on the flight lines of American airfields, the military's appetite for them—and for their fellow heavy bomber, the Consolidated B-24 Liberator—grew at what seemed to be an insatiable pace. "The pattern of prewar expansion of the Air Corps," the air force's official history concluded, "was . . . one of repeated upward revisions of goals, with each objective rendered obsolete before it had been realized."[13]

The historical record underscores that observation. For example, in March 1940, encouraged by Roosevelt's requested for $1.8 billion for national defense, the War Department adopted plans for a 41-group Air Corps. But two months later, when Hitler turned west and punched into the Low Countries and France, the War Department realized the need for a 54-group Air Corps to fulfill what it coined the "First Aviation Objective." Less than a year later, the ultimate goal shifted to the "Second Aviation Objective"—a force of 84 groups. Such a force meant producing 36,500 aircraft and 30,000 new pilots annually. America's aviation industry and the Army Air Corps —and subsequently the AAF, into which the Air Corps had evolved on June 20, 1941—labored to meet those goals.[14]

If there were any doubts regarding the urgency of the Second Aviation Objective, the Pearl Harbor disaster of December 7, 1941, dispelled them. A month after the Japanese attack, President Roosevelt delivered 1942's State of the Union speech to a grim Congress and underscored the production needs that America's global conflict demanded. With unflappable confidence, he committed American industry to a war production effort the likes of which the United States—or, for that matter, the world—had never seen.

In his familiar nasal cadence, the president rattled off a remarkable litany of production goals to the gathered congressmen and a listening nation—45,000 tanks, 20,000 antiaircraft guns, 6 million tons of new merchant shipping, and, perhaps most remarkable, 60,000 new aircraft. "We must raise our sights all along the production line," he declared. "Let no man say it cannot be done . . . These figures and similar figures for a multitude of other implements of war," Roosevelt declared, "will give the Japanese and Nazis a little idea of just what they accomplished . . . The militarists of Berlin and Tokyo started the war, but the massed, angered forces of common humanity will finish it."[15]

To help Roosevelt fulfill his martial vision, Boeing teamed with Douglas Aircraft and the Vega division of Lockheed Aircraft. The resulting joint effort allowed the three erstwhile competitors to work together in what became known as the B-V-D (Boeing-Vega-Douglas) Pool and to eventually produce 12,731 Flying Fortresses.[16] As they did, the B-17 underwent a constant evolution of design. The B-17D model quickly led to versions bearing the suffix E. On the B-17E, Boeing replaced the rather conventional vertical tail fin with a larger, swooping fin—thus creating a tail so big that airmen began calling the Fortress the "Big Ass Bird."[17] It also increased the span of the tail elevator, which delivered greater stability for higher altitude bombing runs, and lengthened the fuselage by six feet to a total length of nearly 74 feet. The additional length enabled it to add a twin .50-caliber mount in the bomber's tail—the so-called stinger. The design also included a pair of .50-caliber guns in a powered turret atop the fuselage; another pair bristled in the ball turret mounted underneath the plane. These were in addition to two .50-caliber waist guns mounted in windows on each side of the fuselage and the .30-caliber machinegun in the plane's nose.[18]

The B-17F soon followed the E Model. Its modifications included a frameless Plexiglass nose, paddle-blade propellers, and some 400 other more subtle improvements. Finally came the B-17G.[19] The G model benefited from the addition of a chin turret position and a number of other improvements.[20] In addition to its role as a bomber, the Flying Fortress in its various versions and configurations also served as a tanker, an aerial gunship, a long-range reconnaissance and air-sea rescue aircraft, an electronic countermeasures platform, and even as a remotely controlled flying bomb.[21] In the end, the B-17 became one of the most iconic aircraft of the Second World War.

"The Boys in the Flying Fortresses"

Manning so many bombers with trained crewmen, however, proved to be just as challenging as building the aircraft themselves. Fortunately, just as in the case of aircraft production, the personnel spigot had been cracked open in just the nick of time. With respect to pilots, the Air Corps's 1939 plan for a 24-group force required 1,200 flight school graduates a year.[22] In light of the high elimination rates associated with flight training, that requirement meant the Air Corps needed to recruit 12,000 applicants annually if it hoped to find 2,200 qualified candidates to undertake flight training. Only half of those, the Air Corps expected, would complete such training.[23] Subsequent leaps to a 41-group and then a 54-group Air Corps required annual graduations of 7,000 and 12,000 pilots respectively.[24] Then came the adoption of the 84-group goal—the so-called Second Aviation Objective—in early 1941. It required the production of 30,000 new pilots each year.[25] For the Air Corps's three regional training centers, the Second Aviation Objective translated to a need to graduate 455 single-engine pilots, 808 twin-engine pilots, 358 cadet bombardiers, 100 observers, and 656 gunners every five weeks, in addition to 133 cadet navigators every six weeks.[26]

The attack on Pearl Harbor jolted the ongoing expansion to even greater efforts. In January 1942, the War Department directed the newly christened AAF to expand from 350,000 to 998,000 personnel within the year—a remarkable goal for an organization that had barely numbered 20,000 four years earlier.[27] The following month, in one of his signature "fireside chats," President Roosevelt warned the Axis of what was to come.

"Ever since this nation became the arsenal of democracy—ever since enactment of Lend-Lease—there has been one persistent theme through all Axis propaganda," the president warned. "This theme has been that Americans are admittedly rich, and that Americans have considerable industrial power—but that Americans are soft and decadent, that they cannot and will not unite and work and fight. From Berlin, Rome and Tokyo we have been described as a nation of weaklings—playboys—who would hire British soldiers, or Russian soldiers, or Chinese soldiers, to do our fighting for us."

"Let them repeat that now!" Roosevelt challenged, his voice rising. "Let them tell that to General MacArthur and his men. Let them tell that to the sailors who today are hitting hard in the far waters of the Pacific. Let them tell that to the boys in the Flying Fortresses. Let them tell that to the Marines!"[28]

The AAF answered such exhortations with relish. By the end of 1942, it had 1.6 million men and women in uniform.[29] By 1945, the AAF counted some 2.2 million men and women in its ranks—approximately one-third of the U.S. Army.[30] Of course, not all of those 2.2 million were pilots or even members of aircrews. A massive logistical tail—ground crewmen, mechanics, jeep and truck drivers, staff officers, medics and doctors, mechanics, cooks, weathermen, radiomen, personnel and supply clerks, intelligence and operational personnel—followed and supported every aircraft that took to the skies.

With respect to America's heavy bomber force, however, it was the pilots, bombardiers, navigators, and aircrewmen—the boys in the Flying Fortresses, the B-24s, and the B-29s—that represented the tip of the AAF's spear. But if there was a common thread running throughout the AAF's training of those men—whether the training of officer or enlisted man—one could say, with considerable fairness, that the only common thread was that there was no common thread at all. In an organization devoted to order and uniformity, each man's tale was surprisingly unique—as the young men destined for the 20th Squadron, 2nd Bombardment Group would discover.

Bill Tune

Bill Tune's military career began in the spring of 1942, while he was still a senior at Berry College. Taking a break from his studies, he traveled to Atlanta and volunteered for the AAF. After his initial induction, the army dispatched Tune back to Berry to finish college and await further orders. Although graduation at Berry College came, his expected set of orders did not. Spring turned to summer and Tune knew he had to earn a paycheck somewhere. Returning to Alabama, he took a job with the engineering firm of J. W. Goodwin and E. B. Van Keuren, which had just landed a contract building the new army airfield at Courtland, Alabama.

Relieved at his good fortune, Tune traveled the next day to Courtland, an antebellum town surrounded by the cotton fields of Alabama's Tennessee Valley. In Courtland, Tune discovered that the hardest part of his new job would be finding a place to live. Fortunately, the site's construction manager convinced the couple running his boardinghouse to make room for one more guest, enabling Tune to enjoy several months of home-cooked meals and rides with the manager to and from the work site. The rides were particularly welcomed—private cars were already an increasingly scarce commodity as manufacturers turned their attention to jeeps, trucks, and even aircraft.[31]

In the meantime, Tune proposed to his Berry College sweetheart Fran Beggs. She accepted, but the two decided to postpone their wedding until Tune completed his military service. While Tune worked at Courtland, Fran transferred to Georgia State College for Women, when she completed her studies in Home Economics. She later taught similar courses before landing a job as a home economist with a local electric utility.

Tune's anticipated orders finally arrived in November 1942, scarcely a month before the airfield began operations. Those orders directed him to AAF Classification Center Nashville, one of the AAF's newest classification centers. The pell-mell rush to complete the center had been so hurried that the local Red Cross had had to beg Nashville's civilians to donate spare coat hangers to the center. Despite such challenges, the $5 million, 560-acre center became the largest of the AAF's classification centers, with 10,000 future aviators and airmen passing through its gates annually.[32] For his part, Tune was less than impressed with the center. He found the center, located near the city's rail yard, to be cold, muddy, dreary, and "overrun with raw recruits."[33]

The center, however, had not been designed for comfort or aesthetics. Its main goal was to take the AAF's would-be officers and determine how best to utilize them—as pilots, bombardiers, or navigators. By 1942, the AAF had already eliminated its prewar requirement that aviation cadets possess two years of college education and dropped the enlistment age from 21 to 18 years.[34] Nevertheless, even with the relaxation of education and age standards, a set of common hurdles remained. Those included intensive physical examinations, a series of psychological interviews, and the Aviation Cadet Qualifying Examination, or ACQE. An individual's ACQE results, derived after several days of testing, not only assured the AAF that he was qualified to enter its ranks but also enabled it to channel him into the appropriate specialty—pilot, bombardier, or navigator.

In the ACQE's system of evaluation and classification, would-be pilots were found to demonstrate not only interest in aviation but also superior aptitude in such examination areas as perception, reaction times, coordination, discrimination between visual objections, and visualization of mechanical movements. Tune, a steady fellow with four years of practical industrial and engineering studies under his belt, took the ACQE and other examinations in stride and drew an assignment for pilot training. He spent eight weeks in Nashville, however, waiting for assignment to a Preflight training course. When the coveted orders finally arrived, Aviation Cadet Tune caught the train south to Montgomery, Alabama, and Maxwell Field, where he arrived in January 1943 and embarked upon Preflight training with the Class of 43-H.[35]

During peacetime, the AAF had deemed nine weeks of Preflight necessary. The war's exigencies shortened its duration to six. During those six weeks, cadets such as Tune honed basic military skills—marching, saluting, spit-shining shoes, and making a tight bunk—while also learning to handle a rifle, tie a tourniquet, and send and receive a message in Morse code. In addition, Preflight offered an introduction to the principles of flight.

After completing Preflight at Maxwell, Tune again boarded a train, this time bound for Arcadia, Florida, and for "Primary"—the first of three stages of flight training. Assigned to one of the field's whitewashed wooden barracks, he dropped off his duffel bag in his spartan living quarters and, with a quick round of handshakes, met his three new roommates. Fellow Alabamian Bill Starcher hailed from Prattville, just north of Montgomery. The other two men called Tennessee and Florida home. Before the year was out, Starcher would be killed learning to fly a fighter plane. The other two washed out during training.[36]

For cadets Tune and his roommates, Primary—also called "elementary flight training," or, less respectfully, "kite flying"—marked their first time in a cockpit. With as many as fifty-six Primary programs in operation around the country, the AAF had to rely on civilian instructor pilots to provide the knowledge and instruction, while the military supplied the aircraft, facilities, and syllabi. For the student pilots' part, they would spend half the day flying and half the day in ground school classes.

The instructors at Dorr Field wasted little time in introducing their students to the cockpit. On the first day of Primary, Tune and his class assembled on the airfield's tarmac. Amid neat rows of Stearman PT-17 Kaydet biplanes, the cadets met their instructor pilots for the first time. In later years, Tune would look back on his military service and conclude that he had been very lucky at times. His assignment of an instructor pilot—or "IP" in airfield jargon—was one such moment for, at Dorr, Tune and five other cadets fell under the personal tutelage of an instructor pilot named Blair.

Blair, a tall, slightly graying southerner, was all that his students could have hoped for in an instructor pilot. Some IPs were what students called "screamers," but not Blair. Calm, patient, wise, and experienced, he had a knack for calmly sharing his own considerable flying skills with his students. In his seven weeks at Dorr, Tune never heard a negative word uttered about Blair. Years later, he would still remember his IP's quiet admonitions to always watch his altitude—advice that served him well in the months to come.

That first day, Blair wasted no time introducing his new charges to the PT-17. It was a fabric-covered biplane that lacked instruments, a radio, or even an intercom system. To communicate with Tune once the noisy engine was running, Blair had to yell through a plastic funnel device—the so-called "Gosport"—connected to Tune's leather flight helmet. At a time when Nazi Germany was on the verge of producing its first jet aircraft, one might have thought the PT-17 was hopelessly archaic. But the little biplane awed Tune nevertheless as he settled into a cockpit for the first time.

Tune and Blair took to the air for the first time together on March 4, 1943. Although the flight only lasted 35 minutes, Tune could still remember the bright, clear day years later. Quickly and effectively, Blair demonstrated how to taxi, take off, maintain straight and level flight, and initiate—and then recover from—a stall. He even showed Tune some of the more complex maneuvers he would have to master, such as spins and loops. Blair then brought the biplane in for a landing. As they shut down the aircraft and pushed chocks under the plane's wheels, Blair casually warned Tune that his first solo flight would come within eight hours of training. The syllabus allowed for no more time.

Blair was absolutely correct. On March 17, Blair and Tune flew out to one of Dorr's auxiliary fields. The field was little more than a runway carved out of the Florida countryside, but a ring of fields like it around Dorr allowed the school to disperse its infant aviators to less congested airspace for their day's flights. Once Tune taxied off the runway and pulled to a halt on the field's tarmac apron, Blair unbuckled his seatbelt. He climbed out of the backseat onto the wing and patted Tune reassuringly on his shoulder.

"It's all yours, Mr. Tune. Take it up," Blair said.[37] He then hopped to the ground and walked to the side of the runway. Tune was on his own.

Craning his head left, right, and up, Tune checked for other aircraft traffic in the area. There was none. Edging the plane's throttle forward, he taxied up to the end of the runway, lined up for takeoff, and looked for incoming planes. Still clear, he saw. Reassured, Tune advanced the throttle all the way and, with a slight frisky jolt, the biplane began rolling down the runway. Seconds later, the PT-17 arced off the runway. Tune was airborne.

Thanks to Blair's careful instruction, the next few moments all seemed to come automatically to Tune. Manipulating the flight controls gently but firmly, he eased the biplane into a tight oval-shaped pattern around the airfield. Then, banking to the right and easing back on the throttle, he lined up with the field's runway and brought the plane in for a smooth landing. His first solo flight was a success.

In the weeks that followed, Blair interspersed more instruction with Tune's solo bouts in the air—reinforcing earlier instruction on such topics as engine start-up procedures, normal and forced takeoffs and landings, stall and spin recoveries, and climbing and gliding turns and also providing training on more complicated tasks such as figure eights and chandelles, cross-wind landings, maximum performance glides, precision landings and approaches, and power-off and short-field landings. Primary ended with work on night flying, navigation, and sessions in Link simulators.[38]

Although Tune progressed steadily through the syllabus, he never quite embraced flight training's more daring maneuvers—particularly recovering from spins or stalls. "When it came to doing stall and spins, I would fly my whole hour's flying time before I was able to talk myself into doing them. It was always a frightening thing for me," he explained years later. Reflecting on his solo flight experiences and his apprehensiveness, Tune decided that he was more suited to be a bomber pilot.[39]

Such decisions, however, were out of Tune's hands—at least for the immediate future. First he had to master flight school's Basic phase. In May 1943, Tune reported to Bainbridge Army Air Field in southwestern Georgia. Bainbridge was another airfield hastily constructed in 1942 to serve the needs of an expanding AAF—in particular, the need to put aviation cadets through their increasingly intense paces in Basic. "Primary can make mistakes," observed the commanding officer of the Basic Flying School at California's Moffett Field, "Basic will correct them; Basic cannot make mistakes because Advanced has no time to fiddle with corrections of technique."[40]

Tune's training at Bainbridge included acrobatics, instrument flying (both in the air under a hood and, depending upon availability, on the ground in the box-like Link flight simulators, which the student pilots labeled "the Jeep"), cross-country training, and night flying. Toward the end of the Basic stage came formation flying. When they were not on the flight line or in the air, cadets attended ground school and pursued other, more traditional, military training. The former included classes in engine and aircraft operations, navigation, weather, and wireless telegraphy.

On the flight line at Bainbridge, Tune faced seven weeks in the cockpit of the the Vultee BT-13A Valiant. The Valiant was larger, faster, and more demanding than the PT-17 and the plane's tendency to shake violently as it approached stall speed was especially disconcerting—thus its nickname the "Vultee Vibrator." But Tune survived his brush with the Vibrator and completed Basic at Bainbridge on June 26, 1943. Looking back on the experience, two memories dominated his recollection of training in southern Georgia. "One, the habit the instructor had of jerking the throttle back during the landing approach for an emergency landing exercise," he recalled. "Two, my nose was a solid blister from the sun throughout the full training period."[41]

At the end of Basic, Tune received orders for Advanced—his next stage of flight school training—at Moody Army Air Field in Valdosta, Georgia. Tune was well pleased with the assignment to Moody; it was a training field for twin-engined aircraft, which meant that he was still on track for a bomber cockpit. At Moody, he trained in the Beech AT-10 Wichita, logging his first twin-engine flight on July 6, 1943. Approximately half of the AAF's future bomber and transport pilots during the Second World War completed their twin-engine transition training in the AT-10—which proved to be an excellent example of American industry's adaptation to wartime production needs. In order to conserve scarce metals for warplane construction, Beech Aircraft Company constructed the AT-10 primarily out of plywood, with only the engine cowlings and cockpit enclosure made of aluminum. The aircraft's heavy use of wood enabled Beech to contract out the plane's component construction to furniture companies and other nontraditional manufacturers.[42]

At Moody, the pace of training proceeded at a rapid clip. In five days of July and then in August 1943, Tune accumulated 20 hours in daytime dual flight instruction, eight hours of dual night flight instruction, 22 hours of solo daytime flight, 12 hours of solo night flying, and 22 hours of instrument flying.[43]

For cross-country training, the students paired up with partners. Tune's was an aviation cadet from California, with whom Tune narrowly avoided disaster on a cross-country jaunt that took them to Charlotte, North Carolina, Selma, Alabama, and back to Moody Field. Somewhere past Stone Mountain, Georgia, they became lost and, as they struggled to find a landing field, almost ran out of gas. "We were told after landing that we only had fumes left in the tank," Tune recalled.[44]

Such close calls notwithstanding, Tune finished his training at Moody on August 30, 1943. Although he had hoped to become a B-17 pilot, the AAF had other ideas. Orders directed him to attend B-24 Liberator training at Montgomery's Maxwell Field. Eight weeks of learning to manhandle the stubborn controls of a Liberator followed. By the end of November 1943, Tune had logged 122.4 hours behind the controls of the B-24—enough to qualify as a pilot and bringing his total military flight training to 337.35 hours.[45]

"This student is well above average," Major C. F. Adams, the commanding officer of the 610th Training Squadron, wrote of Tune when he completed his training at Maxwell. "He learns rapidly and retains instruction. He is quiet and slightly unaggressive but has confidence in himself and will command respect through his flying ability. His flying ability is above average. His landings are exceptionally good. Instrument work is only average, formation and all other phases are above average."[46] Despite such kudos, a long train ride, rather than his own aircraft, took him to his next duty assignment: Gowen Field, a B-24 training base in Boise, Idaho.

At Idaho's Gowen Field, Tune met the other officers of his B-24 crew. Second Lieutenant Fred P. Markowitz, a Brooklyn native, occupied the B-24's copilot seat. First Lieutenant Leon H. Leigh, another New Yorker, was a veteran of the prewar army but, despite his rank, was the aircraft's bombardier. Rounding out the officers, Flight Officer Ralph T. Mooney, a farmboy from Nebraska, flew as the bomber's navigator.[47]

Tune and the other officers worked diligently together to weather three months of intensive operational training in Idaho. They then traveled to Kansas, where

Topeka Army Air Field served as a training base to prepare bomber crews for their upcoming journey to distant theaters of war. At Topeka, Tune and his fellow officers picked up the rest of their crew. Staff Sergeant Lloyd H. Allen, from Florida, joined Tune as the bomber's flight engineer. Staff Sergeant Angelo J. Cirigliano, of New York, was the B-24's radio operator. Sergeant Paul J. Ryan, of Delaware, was its armorer as well as one of its gunners. Other gunners were Sergeant Rex V. Phinney, of Nebraska; Sergeant Richard P. Rasmussen, of Iowa; and a sergeant named Palmer, who, like Tune, was from Alabama.[48]

Crew training took the form of cross-country jaunts, dummy bombing runs, and aerial gunnery practice. The latter was fun, if not necessarily realistic, according to Tune, who remembered flying 30 to 50 feet above the ground while the gunners blasted at targets along the way. "In combat we never did anything like this," Tune admitted, "[but] it was fun and a legal way to buzz the ground."[49]

At the same time, Tune gleaned important lessons that would stand him in good stead later in his career as a bomber pilot. Once, curious to see how his enlisted crewmen were faring during a formation flight, he left the cockpit in the hands of his copilot and worked his way through the fuselage to the tail gunner's position. Swaying and bouncing in the tail, a nauseated Tune struggled with his first and only bout of airsickness. "This made me realize that formation flying had to be done smoothly and evenly," he remembered. "If that was done, then the other planes in the formation did not have to fight the controls so hard to stay in formation."[50] In the months to come, Tune would appreciate the value of a tight, well-disciplined formation of bombers more than he had ever imagined possible.

Leo Zupan and Bill Garland

Leo Zupan reported for his own classification at Santa Ana Army Air Base on November 11, 1942. Santa Ana was a sprawling training facility in Orange County, California, that subjected Zupan to the ACQE and its accompanying round of physical tests, mental examinations, and interviews.

"Do you smoke?" one interviewer asked Zupan.

"A cigar now and then," he answered.

"Do you drink?"

"Some."

"Do you gamble?"

"Yes."

"Well, that's probably a good thing," the interviewer assured him dryly.[51]

Zupan completed both his ACQE exams and his Preflight training at Santa

Ana. "What do I remember about Santa Ana? A lot of running and marching," he recalled. "And we learned some Morse code, shot rifles, and studied identification of aircraft and ship silhouettes. We also pulled KP in the mess halls but, since we were aviation cadets, they called it 'mess management'—you couldn't have cadets doing KP."[52]

The moment of truth came for Zupan at the end of Santa Ana's Preflight training. His class of aviation cadets fell into formation and faced a lone officer sitting behind a table. One by one, each aviation cadet stepped forward, stated their name, and received a white envelope in return. Inside each, a piece of paper read either "pilot," "navigator," or "bombardier." Zupan's read "pilot."[53]

In the meantime, Zupan followed the completion of his Preflight training at Santa Ana with a quick three days of leave. He left the training base with a smile and a set of folded orders directing him to Eagle Field in California's San Joaquin Valley. Even a head cold failed to dampen his spirits. But each morning of leave heralded a day of increasing illness. When the time arrived to catch the train to the small South Dos Palos station, Zupan knew he was sick. Nevertheless, he had no intention of letting anything interfere with his date for flight school. Steeling himself, he managed to report to the train and complete the journey without anyone in authority realizing how ill he was.

Zupan's train pulled into Dos Palos in the midst of a winter rainstorm. "Raining like hell," he remembered. "We piled into the back of a pickup truck and they hauled us to our barracks. It was a beautiful stucco place."[54] Later historians agreed with Zupan's opinion. "A soda fountain, bowling alley, landscaping and a recreation hall made Eagle Field the country club of training bases," one historian wrote.[55]

Zupan, however, was in no shape to fully appreciate his surroundings. He managed to make it to only his first class before being dispatched to sick call. At the airfield's infirmary, the doctor diagnosed pneumonia. Zupan spent ten days in the hospital, where a gas mask dangling from the foot of his bed reminded him that he was still in the military. Fortunately, a round of sulfa drug treatments managed to get him back with his class.

At Dos Palos, Zupan flew, most of the time, in the PT-19 Cornell. Initially designed and built by Fairchild, the PT-19 had become so popular as a trainer that, as the AAF expanded, Fairchild contracted with such manufacturers as Howard Aircraft, Fleet Aircraft, Aeronca, and the St. Loius Airplane Company to meet the AAF's demands. Eventually, 7,742 of the aircraft were built, making it the most widely used of the Allied trainers. Unlike its counterpart the Stearman PT-17, the

PT-19 was a monoplane, since Fairchild had reasoned that the AAF's pilots would be flying monoplanes rather than biplanes. With a maximum speed of 128 miles per hour, the PT-19 was speedier than the PT-17 and, with a wider landing gear arrangement, easier to land.[56]

Behind the controls of the PT-19, Zupan survived Primary and advanced to Basic, in his case at California's Lemoore Army Air Field. Although Lemoore was also located in California's San Joaquin Valley, it compared poorly to Eagle Field to its north. Lemoore, with its triangular pattern dirt runway and rough facilities, was certainly no country club. There was little time to complain, however. Zupan soon found himself, like Tune, in the cockpit of the "Vultee Vibrator." And like Tune, he mastered the challenging trainer. Not all of his comrades were so fortunate. One day, Zupan returned from his day's flight to find a classmate named McCool sitting dejectedly on his bunk.

"Kopecki got killed," McCool told Zupan flatly. "He crashed on approach."

"Oh, God," thought Zupan. Kopecki had been the best pilot in Primary. Now he was simply another statistic. "It was a dangerous business," Zupan reflected years later.[57]

At the end of Basic, Zupan welcomed the orders that directed him to Advanced at Luke Army Air Field outside of Phoenix, Arizona. Luke was home to single-engine training, which meant that the AAF had marked Zupan for eventual duty in a fighter plane. Now he found himself in the cockpit of an AT-6 Texan, the AAF's preeminent Advanced trainer. "Man, that was a neat plane," Zupan recalled of his trainer, impressed with both its 1600-horsepower engine and its retractable landing gear.[58]

In addition to mastering a more powerful aircraft such as the Texan, Zupan also honed his instrument flying skills at Luke, flying under the so-called hood with an instructor in the backseat of the AT-6. As Zupan leveled off somewhere between 6,000–7,000 feet, the IP would give him a heading to fly. At that point, it became Zupan's task to determine his location while relying on the sound from nondirectional beacons. "If the sound started fading away, you'd know you were flying away from the beacon," Zupan remembered. "We'd cut through the quadrants, listening for 'da-da' and 'da-dit' over the radio to guide us where we were going."[59]

Zupan graduated from Advanced on December 5, 1943. With his new silver wings shining brightly, the new pilot hoped for an assignment with an operational fighter squadron. Instead, the AAF slotted Zupan for duty as an instructor pilot. "I guess they figured I would be a good IP because I was a little bit older than the other student pilots—a little more conservative," he reasoned.[60] But Zupan's career as an instructor pilot was a short one. After ten days at San Antonio's Randolph Army Air Field, new orders dispatched him to Carlsbad, New Mexico. Apparently, the AAF needed more bomber pilots.

Zupan's brief sojourn at Carlsbad soon led to an assignment to Nevada's Indian Springs. At the airfield outside of Las Vegas, Zupan flew the B-17 for the first time while, in the same aircraft behind him, gunnery students learned their own craft with their .50-caliber machineguns.

"The B-17 seemed awfully big," Zupan remembers. "After all, I had always flown single-engine planes. But you get what you get with the B-17. It was a very easy plane to fly, very stable. That was important with formation flying, which could be bad enough even if you had a good plane. But, generally, I liked to fly formation, so it didn't bother me."[61]

In addition to the plane's size, there was another significant difference to flying a bomber. "Now, as a bomber pilot, I was responsible for nine other guys," Zupan recalls. "For example, you had to worry about their oxygen, so you were always calling for oxygen checks, especially from your ball turret gunner. That was something a fighter pilot did not have to worry about. He was just on his own and responsible for himself."[62]

After Zupan completed his training at Indian Springs, another set of orders directed him to Salt Lake City's Hill Army Air Field to join what would be his combat crew for further training and eventual overseas deployment. At Hill, the AAF operated a massive aviation supply and repair depot named, somewhat ominously, for Major Ployer Peter Hill, who had been killed in the crash of the B-17's Model 299 prototype. It was yet another reminder of the dangers associated with Zupan's new line of work.

At Hill, Zupan joined with Bill Garland, who had grown up in Canada but was now serving in the armed forces of his native land. Garland had also learned to fly in Primary at Dos Palos and, again like Zupan, he completed Basic at Lemoore. Remaining in California, he finished Advanced at Stockton Army Air Field—an airfield that, thanks to its prewar dedication date of January 11, 1941, could claim to be one of the oldest army airfields on the West Coast. Upon graduation from Stockton, the newly minted Second Lieutenant Garland received orders for B-17 training at Roswell, New Mexico. "I always wanted to fly a B-17," he remembered. "I thought it was the best plane the air force had."[63]

With his training at Roswell completed, Garland joined Zupan and the rest of his combat crew in Salt Lake City. Twenty-eight years of age, Garland stood nearly six feet, four inches tall and towered over his five-foot, eight-inch copilot. "We looked like Mutt and Jeff," Zupan admitted.[64] Nevertheless, the two men took a quick liking to each other. "Leo Zupan was one of the best," Garland declared.[65]

Second Lieutenant Albert E. Novak, a married officer from St. Louis, Missouri, drew duty as the bomb crew's bombardier. Like Garland and Zupan, he was older than the fresh-out-of-college lieutenants typical of the AAF at the time. "Very serious and worked hard at his job," Garland remembered.[66] The crew's navigator, though, did not stick around long enough to make much of an impression. He was Jewish and, worried about the prospects of falling into Nazi hands should he be shot down, successfully applied for a slot with a Pacific-bound bomber crew.[67]

The new crew's enlisted men included Staff Sergeant Irving D. Katz, from Chicago, who served as the crew's flight engineer and top turret gunner. "A great guy and an outstanding engineer," in Zupan's words.[68] "A fine engineer," Garland echoed.[69] Like the navigator, Katz was also Jewish. Whether by choice or otherwise, however, he remained with Garland's crew and ran the risk of potentially dealing with Nazi captors.

Staff Sergeant Jesse L. Barker, of Quitman, Georgia, drew duty as the bomber's ball turret gunner. "A clean-cut, nice guy," according to Zupan, "but always struck me as a little big for a ball turret gunner."[70] Barker was twenty-four—relatively old for a gunner. "He did a good job in a difficult assignment," Garland added.[71] Sergeant Ralph E. DeWitt, a Minnesota farmboy with a wife in Egan, Illinois, reported for duty as one of the two waist gunners—"a good gunner," according to Garland.[72] Sergeant Russell Payne, a "real nice kid," in Zupan's memory, stood at the other waist gunner position. His newly wed wife, Helen, waited for him back in Maryland. "A fine man," in Garland's estimation.[73]

Sergeant Robert C. Hoadley, a Californian, arrived for duty as the bomber's tail gunner. "He was a classy guy," Zupan remembers, "and was always well dressed. For example, he had bought a pair of English flying boots trimmed in fur. That was typical of Hoadley. He was a dapper fellow, but a damn good tail gunner."[74] Garland agreed, at least with respect to the latter quality.[75] Staff Sergeant Charles "Charley" Griffin, a New Yorker with a wife back in Hartsdale, rounded out the crew. Griffin was the crew's radio operator. "A very good radio operator," Garland recalled.[76] "He was another nice guy," Zupan remembered. "They were all nice guys. It was a good crew."[77]

After ten days in Salt Lake City, the crew shifted to Dalhart Army Air Field in Texas, a training field for aircrews heading overseas. "Dalhart was a cow town out in the middle of the desert," Zupan recalled. "It was a rough place. It was the only place I've ever been where you would open the door, jump out over a snow bank, and land in sand. But the townspeople treated us well and, since there were so many stockyards around, you could buy a steak for 75 cents. And they were big steaks, too. The waitress would bring it and it would be hanging off every side of your plate."[78]

After several weeks, Garland, Zupan, and crew traded dusty Dalhart and its war-weary training fleet for MacDill Field, near Tampa, Florida. They honed their operational skills at MacDill, in addition to drawing a set of personal sidearms and a wealth of K-rations. Their new .45-caliber pistols provided a sobering reminder that their first day of combat flying was not far away.[79]

Jim Weiler

Jim Weiler weathered Preflight training on the West Coast at Santa Ana, not far from where he had once worked at the Lockheed plant in Burbank. After Santa Ana, he completed Primary at Thunderbird Field in Phoenix, Arizona. Before leaving Thunderbird in May 1943, Weiler shared some thoughts with a reporter from a hometown newspaper. At the time, his brother Joseph was a tanker in the army; eldest brother Harold had already earned his wings as a naval aviator.

"Plans on getting married after the war, not before; after the war would like to fly, live in Wisconsin; his idea of a good time on pass is relaxing, dining, dancing," the newspaper reported. "Jim's favorite food is steak. He needs eight hours of sleep and right now he's not getting quite enough. He's had 82 hours of flying experience with Porterfield 65s and PT-17s. What does he like about flying? Everything. He thinks the war will be long because the stakes are plenty high. He likes the living conditions and the keen competition of training, dislikes athletics before the flight line."[80]

After Thunderbird, Weiler completed Primary at dusty Pecos Field, deep in west Texas. Advanced training followed in Texas's Big Bend country at Marfa Army Air Field. With a shiny pair of new aviator's wings gleaming on his uniformed chest, Weiler traded Marfa for Roswell Army Air Field. In New Mexico, he completed his transition to the B-17. Combat crew training in Florida would come next.

Loy Dickinson

The AAF needed officers other than pilots and copilots to crew the AAF's bombers. In particular, it required navigators and bombardiers. In the summer of 1943, Training Command calculated that it would have to produce one navigator for nearly every five pilots, and one bombardier for approximately every six pilots.[81]

Unfortunately, by then, the AAF had much lost ground to recover. For example, although the First Aviation Objective had called for training 4,888 navigators, that effort had, by the summer of 1941, only produced a mere 339 of them.[82] From that shaky start, however, the AAF eventually trained over 50,000 navigators during the war years—an accomplishment that the historian Rebecca Cameron christened "a triumph of numbers." But, as she also noted, that accomplishment was both slow and arduous in coming.[83]

Previously, in the prewar expansion years, the Air Corps had acquired its navigators (and bombardiers) from the ranks of pilot training "eliminees" (or, less politely, "washouts"). However, this system for procuring navigators and bombardiers was far from perfect. At its very heart, it intimated that those crewmembers were inferior to the pilots that had successfully completed their flight training. For some men relegated to a bombsight or navigator's table, lower morale was the inevitable result. Furthermore, reliance on flight school washouts to provide future navigators and bombardiers created a procurement system that wasted both valuable time and precious training resources.

As its expansion escalated, the AAF recognized the problems associated with staffing its ranks of navigators and bombardiers with flight school washouts. In response, it relied increasingly on the ACQE to identify would-be navigators and bombardiers with a ready understanding of maps and charts, an interest in science, and their mathematical aptitude, accuracy in using tables and instruments, strong reasoning facilities, and quick comprehension of verbal material. One cynical pilot summed up the classification system rather succinctly: "Pilots were chosen from those who gave quick and correct answers; bombardiers were chosen from those who gave quick and erroneous answers; navigators were those who gave slow and correct answers." In reality, however, the navigator candidates usually tested the highest.[84]

For Loy Dickinson, however, the path to a navigator assignment was simply a matter of "some slight near-sightedness, and bad night vision."[85] Nevertheless, his eyesight was adequate enough for a navigator. After Dickinson finished his Preflight training in the spring of 1943, the AAF dispatched him to Las Vegas for gunnery school to occupy his time while a slot at navigator school became available.

In gunnery school, Dickinson attempted to master a variety of weapons and firing techniques. He met with an equally varying degree of success. Early in the gunnery training, the cadets shot skeet in an effort to help them learn to lead their targets. "I did quite well with that," Dickinson reflected. "But when we were in the air shooting at moving targets . . . well, that was a different story. It was just beyond me."[86]

After gunnery school, Dickinson attended radio school, where he struggled with Morse code as mightily as he had struggled with aerial gunnery. Emerging triumphant, he then proceeded to the navigator's school at Hondo Army Air Field in Medina County, Texas. Hondo Field, located 40 miles west of San Antonio, provided another example of the massive mobilization effort required by the United States' sudden entry into the Second World War. First authorized in March 1942, the base opened scarcely three months later and eventually grew to contain more than 600 buildings, streets and sewers, electricity and water utilities, an airdrome with runways, taxiways, and parking aprons crowded with B-34s, B-18 Bolos, AT-7s, and AT-11 Kansans. The frantic 89-day construction effort had cost $7.25 million, but it seemed well worth the cost. Hondo quickly became the AAF's largest navigation school, graduating its first class of navigators in November 26, 1942. In all, 14,158 navigators trained at the airfield during the war.[87]

The training at Hondo impressed Dickinson—"very well done," he recalled.[88] Dickinson's syllabus proved typical of the 18-week training course completed by most navigation students, who learned to navigate using the methods of dead reckoning, pilotage, and radio and celestial navigation. Dead reckoning called for a navigator to take the best information available—previous positions, time elapsed, airspeed, headings, and wind drift—and to approximate his position. Pilotage used a compass in conjunction with maps and visible terrain features. Radio navigation relied on bearings derived from the aircraft's reception of signals from radio beacons. Celestial navigation required a navigator to use a sextant to identify the positions of the moon and certain stars and then, relying on a set of almanacs and tables, to convert the acquired data and obtain a "fix" for his aircraft. Although somewhat archaic, celestial navigation was particularly useful on transoceanic flights or night bombing missions.

Putting theory to practice, the student navigators typically flew in crews of three students paired with a single instructor, although the shortage of instructors presented a challenge to maintaining such ratios, as did the availability of adequate training aircraft. Dickinson remembered flying in groups of three to four students on board aircraft such as the Douglas B-18 Bolo and the Beech AT-11 Kansan. Completing such training, Dickinson graduated from navigation school in the winter of 1943, earning both his second lieutenant's commission and his navigator's wings.[89]

Normally, assignment to an operational crew would have followed immediately but, in Dickinson's case, the brand-new navigator contracted tonsillitis. Sidelined by the resulting operation, he bided his time in Hondo while he honed his navigational skills in the school's Link flight simulators. In the spring of 1944, however, the AAF was not going to let a trained navigator go unused for long. Orders eventually arrived for Dickinson that directed him to MacDill Army Air Field in Tampa, Florida, to join a crew bound for overseas duty. That crew proved to be Garland's and Zupan's, now in need of a new navigator. Garland quickly recognized the young Californian's professional expertise. "He was the youngest member of the crew but very competent," Garland declared.[90] Dickinson felt equally comfortable about his new crewmates—or at least as comfortable as one could hope to feel about an untested crew destined for the air war against Hitler's Germany.

Ed Smith and William Bullock

Despite the AAF's increasing emphasis on the ACQE, Ed Smith, the former Miami University student, became a navigator via the "eliminee" route. Originally, he had harbored hopes of becoming a pilot. Indeed, the classification center in San Antonio had tabbed him as such. Pleased with the prospect, he completed Preflight training in San Antonio, although a bout with the mumps delayed his graduation.[91] Once finished with Preflight, Smith reported to Hicks Field, just outside of Forth Worth, Texas, for Primary. Under the tutelage of civilian instructor pilots, he mastered the PT-19 Cornell monoplane and his Primary course of instruction. But then came Basic.

For Basic, the AAF dispatched Smith to Independence, Kansas. There, in the summer of 1943, he shared a tarpaper-covered barracks with 40–50 other student pilots. The showers and latrines were located in a separate facility. More troubling than the accommodations, however, was the BT-14 in which Smith now found himself flying. Built by North American, the BT-14 was one of the later iterations of the company's famed line of trainers nicknamed Texans.

"It was a good airplane," Smith admitted, "but it had rather narrow landing gear. The BT-13 and the BT-15 had wider landing gear. If I had been anywhere else, with any other aircraft, I might have been all right. My flying was okay, but my landings in the BT-14 weren't. I failed a couple of check rides and, when I went before the elimination board, requested navigation school. I had always been good at math, so I thought that would be a good alternative."[92] The board members thought likewise, and new orders directed Smith to San Marcos, Texas. There, in September 1943, he began training as a navigator. "It was a very intensive course," Smith remembered. "In our particular echelon, we had between 30–40 students and eight or nine instructors. We learned different aspects of navigation—celestial, pilotage, dead reckoning, and a little radio beacon work—in the classroom and then put it to practice in AT-11s."[93]

If Smith's navigation training was intense, his gunnery training was anything but. "Gunnery training?" he laughed when asked about it. "None whatsoever," he scoffed. "We went out to a gunnery range and fired a Thompson submachinegun and a .45 pistol. I fired a half a dozen rounds and the instructor said, 'yeah, yeah, you're qualified.'"[94]

Smith graduated from navigator school in mid-February 1944. Two weeks of leave back in Findlay, Ohio, followed. The days passed quickly, however, and he soon bade his family goodbye and caught a train for Sioux City, Iowa. There, upon arriving at the city's train station, two other AAF officers disembarked with him and stepped into the cold morning of an Iowa winter. Instantly, all of their thoughts turned to the closest place to get a warm breakfast before reporting. A passerby directed them to a nearby diner where, over a cup of coffee, Smith made the acquaintance of fellow officers Bill Simon and Frank Smith.

"Simon was destined to be shot down on his first mission over Ploesti," Smith remembered. "Frank Smith, on the other hand, completed all fifty of his missions and returned safely to the States. I guess that pretty much summed up what was ahead of any three bomber crews at that time."[95]

Later that day, after signing in at the airfield, Smith met his crew. For the past several days, they had been filtering in to Sioux City and he was the last man to join the aircraft. The crew's pilot, he learned, was William Bullock, formerly of the University of North Carolina. "He was an excellent pilot," Smith recalled. "A bit of a North Carolina redneck, but I had a lot of confidence in him."[96]

Second Lieutenant Howard "Howie" I. Season, from Cannon Falls, Minnesota, flew as Bullock's copilot. "He was a Minnesota Swede," Smith explained. "If you called him a Norwegian, he'd get mad at you."[97] Second Lieutenant John C. Quinn, from Long Island, New York, rounded out the officers as the crew's bombardier. Technical Sergeant Joseph H. "Whitey" Morien, of Rockland, Michigan, served as the bomber's flight engineer. After converging in Sioux City, Bullock's and Smith's crew departed for Sebring, Florida, for further operational training.[98]

Russ Meyrick

Russ Meyrick, who had embarked upon a frantic letter-writing campaign in order to be allowed to enlist back in Springfield, Massachusetts, was rewarded with a slot for bombardier training. Happy at last, he reported to Victorville Army Air Field in California's San Bernardino Valley.

In Victorville, Meyrick, as a bombardier in training, embarked upon a highly technical syllabus of ground training. His subjects would have included such topics as physics, electricity, theory of bombing and bombsights, instruments, use of computers and bombsights, elementary navigation, gyroscopes, bomb rack control, bombs and fuses, tactics, bombing in formation and in overcast conditions, and pedagogy. Course work also included such topics as antiaircraft defenses, aerial photography, maps, codes, and an orientation to ground and naval forces.[99]

As far as their aerial training was concerned, Meyrick and his fellow bombardier students completed both dry bombing runs and dozens of actual bomb releases (using 100-pound black powder and sand-filled practice bombs)—all the while battling a lack of both bombsights and aircraft. Even when bombsights were available, they were not necessarily the type found in operational bombing squadrons. In a similar vein, the student bombardiers relied on such aircraft as the twin-engine Boeing B-18 and the Beech AT-11 Kansan—a far cry from the B-17s and B-24s from which so many of the bombardiers would operate in the future.[100]

At Victorville, Meyrick excelled at his training—so much so, in fact, that, for a time, he was relegated to instructor duty at Victorville. Only another round of letter-writing freed him of that assignment and garnered him a new set of orders for assignment to Rapid City Army Air Base, South Dakota. There he joined Second Lieutenant Vic Kreimeyer, his new copilot; Clyde Raynor, of Riverside, California, would be their pilot; Second Lieutenant Robert C. Matthews would be their navigator.[101]

"Russ was an excellent bombardier," Kreimeyer, who had left school at Iowa State College to join the AAF, remembered. "He was very likeable, very intelligent, and very agreeable. At the same time, he felt very strongly about the war and was intent on doing his job as best as he could. In fact, our whole crew got along great. We were all very close and all very compatible."[102]

Despite his intensity and focus on his mission, Meyrick did find time in Rapid City to marry his girlfriend, Eleanor "Ellie" Sheridan. Meyrick and Ellie invited the crew to the wedding, and Matthews even squired one of Ellie's friends to the festivities.[103] It was a happy occasion but, despite the festivities, overseas combat beckoned—as they all well knew.

Willard Netzley and Charles McVey

Like Meyrick, Willard Netzley was also destined for duty as a bombardier. Slotted for flight officer training, he received a rudimentary education in navigation with the University of Nebraska's college training detachment in Lincoln, Nebraska. Netzley then completed Preflight training at Santa Ana, California, and underwent gunnery training at Kingman Army Air Field in the northwestern corner of Arizona.

"Gunnery training in Kingman, Arizona, was excellent," Netzley recounted.

"We would man the waist gun of a B-17 and a tow plane would tow a target by. The bullets had paint on the tips and a count was kept of our hits. The empty cartridges were kicked out and lay on the floor. One cadet slipped on a cartridge on the floor and hung onto his machine gun with his finger on the trigger to gain his balance, and the gun swung around and shot down the tow plane. They washed out that cadet and we were all sorry. He was the only cadet with shooting down a plane to his credit before he got out of gunnery school."[104]

By then, the army had already tabbed Netzley for training as a bombardier. For many aviation cadets, a diversion away from a pilot's coveted cockpit seat was a bitter disappointment—but not for the young Californian. Netzley accepted his assignment with equanimity. "I was small in stature in high school, too small to engage in varsity sports," Netzley explained. "Many cadets had been sports heroes in high school and college and had all the physical coordination that a pilot needs, and all the self-confidence. [I had a] 'I'll take what they give me' approach."[105]

Netzley eventually graduated from the AAF's bombardier course at Deming Army Air Field, a rough, dusty airfield in southwestern New Mexico shadowed by the Florida Mountains. A generation earlier, at what was then called Camp Cody, thousands of U.S. cavalry troopers and artillerists had trained to battle Pancho Villa among Camp Cody's jackrabbits, rattlesnakes, and tumbleweed. Now the encampment had a new mission for a new generation. "This was to be a school for bombardiers," the airfield's commander, Colonel Milton M. Murphy, wrote in 1943. "Those Vikings of the sky whose skilled hands and beautifully coordinated bodies were to drop tons of destruction and eventual defeat on the ramparts of our enemies."[106]

Netzley completed the hurried three-week-long bombardier course at Deming—and perhaps endured such purple prose from Colonel Murphy—before proceeding to Ardmore, Oklahoma, to be assigned an operational crew. Before he did, however, he pinned on the badge of a bombardier and the insignia of a flight officer. It was a gold bar with two separated halves of a blue oval in the middle. "They referred to our bar as the 'Order of the Blue Diaper Pin,'" Netzley remembered. "We took some razzing."[107]

Any "razzing" Netzley suffered as a flight officer, though, would soon be offset by a welcomed vagary of the military's pay scale. "Second lieutenants' monthly earnings were base pay of $150 and flight pay of $75. Everyone not a commissioned officer [i.e., flight officers] also earned $22.50 in 'overseas pay,' so I earned $22.50 per month more than the other officers in the crew."[108]

Netzley's status as a flight officer was the result of the army's pell-mell buildup in the months preceding Pearl Harbor that had created too many pilot seats and not enough pilots. In response, Congress enacted the Aviation Student Act on June 4, 1941, to enable a select group of enlisted men to be trained as "aviation students" in what became known as the "flying sergeants" program. At the time, the army had restricted pilot training to candidates with two years of college or its equivalent. These requirements did not apply to the enlisted pilots who, upon graduation, would receive a warrant as a "staff sergeant pilot." For these men, lower age and education requirements applied.

The flying sergeants program faced challenges as soon as the first class of 200 students began training at Randolph Field on August 23, 1941. The army, with its strong collective memories of only officers serving as pilots during the First World War, struggled to find a niche for staff sergeant pilots exercising command in an aircraft's cockpit. Congress had legislated a compromise solution the following summer by creating the rank of "flight officer" for such pilots.[109]

In Ardmore, Netzley met his new navigator, Charles McVey, the Tennessean who had traded the TVA for the AAF. "McVey was a wonderful crew member and a wonderful man," Netzley recalled in later years. Netzley also met Second Lieutenant Robert "Bob" McCloskey, of Porterville, California, the crew's pilot and soon to be Netzley's best friend. The two men were close to the same age and, like Netzley, McCloskey had grown up on a California farm. "He was easy-going, confident, and our crew was like a family."[110]

Other members of their crew included copilot Second Lieutenant Hugh L. Baynes; tail gunner Sergeant Elmer J. Pruitt Jr., of Clair Shores, Michigan; and flight engineer and upper turret gunner Staff Sergeant James A. Jones, of Sheridan, Arkansas. Left waist gunner Sergeant Harold Schirmer, of Southgate, Kentucky; right waist gunner Sergeant Charles A. Munden, of Dallas, Texas; ball turret gunner Sergeant Luther L. Durrette, of Bowling Green, Kentucky; and radio operator Staff Sergeant Edwin R. Everett, of Scranton, Pennsylvania, rounded out a team that, after Ardmore, flew to Lincoln, Nebraska, for further stateside training.[111] Meanwhile, Netzley continued to hone his bombardier skills as best he could. The day he would be called upon to put those deadly skills to the test would soon be at hand.

Robert Donahue

After leaving Pittsburgh, Robert Donahue joined a torrent of enlisted recruits that flooded Miami Beach—an unusual military destination that, in the end, was a happy one for most concerned. For Miami Beach, the influx of recruits such as Donahue represented the city's economic salvation. Back in 1942, the government had imposed rationing on gasoline, oil, and tires. It also froze railroad schedules at the October 1942 levels, thus preventing the railway's normal seasonal increases in trains plying the tourist trade south. For Miami's tourism industry, it was a brutal one-two punch. Rationing dealt a blow to those tourists who typically drove to Florida, while the absence of passenger trains prevented the railways from providing alternative transportation. Deprived of tourists in the winter of 1942–1943, Miami Beach faced economic ruin.[112]

Fortunately, the hotel owners now had one thing the military needed—an ample supply of vacant rooms. Rather than building even more new bases, the army and navy saw a far more economical answer in the quiet hotels and streets fronting Miami Beach. In short order, hotels became barracks (or, in the case of the Nautilus and Biltmore, hospitals), restaurants became mess halls, movie theaters became classrooms, and golf courses became parade fields and obstacle courses. For monthly rent of $20 a head, the hotels helped house the 600,000 servicemen and women who trained in southern Florida during the war.[113]

In Miami, Donahue endured Basic Training—a thirteen-week impersonal amalgamation of orientation, indoctrination, harassment, and training in rudimentary military skills such as drilling, military etiquette, marksmanship, and first aid. Welding school at Chanute Army Air Field followed. Chanute Field, the headquarters of the AAF's Technical Training Command, was located in east-central Illinois outside of Champaign. At Chanute, Donahue joined hundreds of young airmen training to maintain aircraft and life-support equipment, weld and work metal, assist in meteorology, and otherwise keep the AAF's pilots and aircraft in the air. Once he learned how to repair metal airframes shredded by enemy flak or mangled by crash landings, Donahue headed for the distant Aleutian Islands.[114]

At an airfield in the frigid, foggy Aleutians, Donahue found there was no need for his newly acquired skills with a welding torch. In fact, while stationed there, he never welded a single piece of metal. "Isn't that like the army?" he marveled sarcastically.[115]

After a year of no action, Donahue became determined to, in his words, "get into the war." He volunteered for gunnery school. "This was a chance to see some action. I did not want to go home after the war and say I did not see any of the action."[116] Obligingly, the AAF sent Donahue to gunnery school in Las Vegas in October 1943.

Surprisingly, despite the notion that bomber formations could be self-defending, formal aircraft gunner training was practically nonexistent prior to Pearl Harbor. Nevertheless, schools in Panama City and Buckingham, Florida; Las Vegas, Nevada; Kingman and Yuma, Arizona; and Harlingen and Laredo, Texas, were soon turning out gunners prepared to battle enemy fighters.

Generally speaking, the 300,000 gunners produced by the AAF during World War II underwent a six-week training course. After orientation to various machineguns and their nomenclature, students took courses in sights and sighting, ballistics and bore sighting, basic tactics, turret maintenance and drill, malfunctions, and aircraft and warship recognition. They fired BB guns and .22 caliber rifles at stationary and moving targets, rode in trucks across skeet and trap ranges while shooting shotguns at clay pigeons, and eventually advanced to firing .30- and .50-caliber machineguns. Such gunnery training utilized simulators, ground ranges, and air-to-air gunnery exercises during both day and night.

For a time, certain gunnery schools focused on training gunners specialized in certain turret and gun configurations. Laredo and Harlingen Fields in Texas trained B-24 gunners in the Martin upper, Sperry ball, and Consolidated tail turrets. Tyndall trained men specializing in B-25 and B-26 medium bombers. Las Vegas and Arizona's Kingman Field trained B-17 gunners in the Sperry upper and ball turrets and in the so-called Cheyenne tail turret.[117] In addition to training tail gunners, the latter two airfields even served as the location for the filming, in the summer of 1942, of the Warner Brothers propaganda film *Rear Gunner*. "We've got enough pilots to fly every plane in the world," the AAF had reportedly told Warner Brothers. "But we need rear gunners . . . Can you put something together in a hurry . . . and give it some romantic appeal?" Warner Brothers responded with *Rear Gunner*, which paired Ronald Reagan with Burgess Meredith and which boasted such lines as "They know that the fire from your guns is the fire of freedom." Well pleased with its effort, Warner Brothers later contended that the film had convinced thousands of men to enlist.[118]

Trained at Las Vegas, Donahue indeed drew duty as a B-17 tail gunner. When he joined his future crew in Salt Lake City and proceeded with them for operational training in Ardmore, Oklahoma, he quickly realized that he had had the good fortune to join a tight, cohesive group. The bomber was skippered by Lieutenant Thomas H. Hancock, of Pocatello, Idaho. Hancock's copilot, Flight Officer Irving Thompson, was from Poughkeepsie, New York. The navigator, Lieutenant Arnold A. Witoff, was a native of Brooklyn, while the bombardier, Flight Officer Roswell P. Pierce, hailed from Chicago.[119]

Donahue's fellow enlisted crewmembers included John E. Butler, the flight engineer, from Atlanta, Georgia; Joseph A. Bernard, a gunner and the crew's armorer, from Manchester, New Hampshire; gunner and assistant flight engineer Charles C.

Watson, from Jacksonville, Alabama; and ball turret gunner William D. Winston, from Freeport, Louisiana. Technical Sergeant Robert R. Kirsch, the bomber's radio operator, had, like Donahue, grown up in Pittsburgh.[120] Together, these men would man the B-17's aluminum ramparts.

Joe Owsianik and Joseph Sallings

Owsianik, the New Jersey truck driver, joined the AAF a year after Donahue's entry. After the usual round of examinations and paperwork at the induction center at New Jersey's Newark Armory, Owsianik reported to Fort Dix. A week's sojourn at Dix followed before orders dispatched him south to Miami Beach. "I had never been out of New Jersey, and never further south than South Plainfield," Owsianik remembered. "For me, Miami Beach was something else."[121]

Not all was rosy, however, in the resort town. A week after arriving in Miami, Owsianik paused from scrubbing pots and peeling potatoes to take a break outside the mess hall. Sitting near a coal bin, Owsianik enjoyed a quick cigarette. As he smoked, a lieutenant walked by. Owsianik simply looked up at the officer as he strolled past.

"Soldier, what's your name?" the lieutenant demanded, spinning around in his tracks.

"It's Joe Owsianik," Owsianik answered politely, but neglecting to stand.

The officer stomped back to Owsianik. "Soldier," he demanded, "get up and salute the American uniform."

"What do you mean?" Owsianik asked in reply. So far, during the course of his two weeks in uniform, he had been taught to march and to scrub pots. Somehow, the finer points of military courtesy had been overlooked.

"Soldier, I want your name, your army serial number, and the hotel where you're staying," the lieutenant ordered. Chastened, Owsianik replied and the lieutenant continued on his rounds.

Owsianik finished his day of KP duty and returned to his hotel. There, to his dismay, he found his name posted on the company bulletin board. "One week of KP duty for not saluting officer," the typed paper read.

"Man, I nearly crapped a brick," Owsianik remembered, reliving the moment. "I get a charge out of it now, but it sure wasn't funny at the time."[122]

Thousands of the AAF's future mechanics, armorers, radio operators, ordnance specialists, supply clerks, and gunners joined Donahue and Owsianik at Miami Beach, turning the strip of brightly painted Art Deco hotels and apartment buildings along the wide swath of beach into one vast military training camp. So did

Joseph Sallings. If Miami Beach was an eye-opening experience for Owsianik, it is difficult to imagine what the farmboy from the mountains of Union County, Tennessee, must have thought of his visit to Miami. He soon traveled even further afield—first to Santa Ana, California, where he completed armorer training, and then on to Laredo, Texas, for gunnery school.[123]

Meanwhile, Owsianik proceeded to Buckley Field, near Denver, Colorado, for what seemed to be an abbreviated gunnery familiarization course. A subsequent assignment to nearby Lowery Field followed. Then came orders for Kingman Field and a more focused and formalized syllabus of instruction. Orders for Salt Lake City's Hill Army Air Field followed, where Owsianik climbed into his first B-17 to join his operational crew.[124]

Owsianik's crew spent little time at Hill. They soon departed for Waco Army Air Field in Texas. At the airfield an hour south of Dallas, the gunners honed their skills firing at target sleeves towed by other planes, and the bombardier manipulated his bombsight on dummy bomb runs.

Jim Martin

Like Florida, the West Coast shouldered its own burden of molding boot recruits into airmen. Jim Martin, the sharecropper's son from Oklahoma who had left his job in a San Francisco shipyard hoping to become an army tanker, found himself at California's Fresno Army Air Base in April 1943 for his own Basic training. From there, he progressed through training at Buckley and Lowery Army Air Fields, near Denver, Colorado, before, like Sallings, heading to Laredo, Texas, for aerial gunnery training.

"I thought our training was very good," Martin declared simply. "I can still handle a shotgun. They started us out on shotguns and I learned a lot about shooting."[125]

After completing gunnery training in Laredo, Martin received orders to report to Sioux City, where he joined Ed Smith's and William Bullock's crew as a gunner. He had also, however, received a ten-day furlough in the interim. Making the most of the opportunity, he returned to Oklahoma and married a local Harmon County girl, Jewel "Judy" Rogers. Only nineteen at the time, Martin had to get his parents to give him permission to marry before the local justice of the peace could tie the proverbial knot.

The justice completed the ceremony at 6:00 that evening. Two hours later, however, before Martin could even enjoy his honeymoon night, a telegram arrived ordering him to report back to duty and proceed immediately to Sioux City to join his crew.

"We did not get to sleep together for over fourteen months," Martin recalled, reflecting on his abbreviated honeymoon. "But Judy was an exceptional person. She took everything in stride."[126]

Martin has equally fond memories of his pilot Bullock. "Lieutenant Bullock was a very good pilot," Martin remembered. "He was a good person who was looking after his men."[127] Bullock, Smith, Martin, and crew trained throughout March and most of April as they awaited orders for deployment overseas. Martin did not know it, but it would be a long time before he saw Judy again.

3
Into the Fray

Bill Tune

As Tune's crew completed their operational training at Topeka Army Air Field, the question of their eventual destination was never far from their minds. They still did not know if they were destined to fight the Japanese or the Nazis. Given the B-24's longer range, duty in the Pacific seemed a distinct possibility, although Tune knew that Liberators were also serving with the Fifteenth Army Air Force based in Italy. A set of sealed orders, entitled "Movement Orders, Heavy Bombardment Crew Number FV-070-BQ 27, To Overseas Destination" and marked "Restricted," ended the discussion on March 19, 1944.

"You are assigned to Shipment FV-070-BQ, as Crew No. FV-070-BQ 27, and to B-24 airplane 42-94950, on Aircraft Project Number 9058R," the orders directed. "You are relieved from attached, unassigned, 3rd Heavy Bombardment Processing Headquarters, this station, and will proceed via military aircraft and/or rail to Morrison Field, West Palm Beach, Florida, or such other Air Port of Embarkation as the Commanding General, Air Transport Command, may direct, thence to the overseas destination of Shipment FV-070-BQ."[1] It was a pretty good bet, the crew decided, that the commanding general would not send them via rail to Morrison Field. It looked like they would be flying south.

"This is a PERMANENT change of station," the orders stated. "You will not be accompanied by dependents; neither will you be joined by dependents en route to, nor at, the Air Port of Embarkation. You will not discuss this movement except as may be necessary in the transaction of *official* business."[2]

"In lieu of subsistence a flat per diem of seven dollars ($7.00) is authorized for Officers and Flight Officers for travel and for periods of temporary duty en route to final destination, when necessary, in accordance with existing law and regulations," the orders continued. Just in case there was any doubt, the subsequent sentence declared that "[p]ayment of mileage is not authorized."[3]

Further inquiry revealed that Shipment FV-070-BQ was bound for Italy's Fifteenth Army Air Force. At the time, U.S. aircrews flying their bombers to Europe relied on one of two general routes. They took either a northern route from Canada to North Africa via the Azores Islands or a southern route across the Caribbean, to Brazil, across the Atlantic to West Africa, and then northeast across the Sahara and Mediterranean. Tune's orders' reference to Morrison meant that he would be taking the southern route.

On March 21, 1944, in the midst of a snowstorm, Tune took off from Kansas City, Kansas, in a brand-new B-24. With Markowitz in the copilot's seat and Leigh sitting idly at his bombardier's station, Mooney set a course for Morrison Field. One of the gunners, Palmer, had fallen ill and was left behind. A last-minute replacement, Sergeant Louis Kenner, rode in his place.[4]

Relying on his instruments, Tune took off into the swirling snow. Heeding the admonitions of instructor pilots such as the sage Mr. Blair, he labored to get as much distance between the bomber and the unforgiving earth below as possible. It proved to be a prescient decision. As the bomber climbed past 10,000 feet, the controls in Tune's hands became sluggish. It was never easy to manhandle a B-24's notoriously stubborn controls, but now Tune suddenly found himself struggling to keep the bomber aloft. Meanwhile, the cockpit dash's airspeed indicator stopped registering changes in airspeeds. The needle seemed frozen.

Worried about stalling the fully loaded bomber, Tune pushed forward on the control yoke, putting the bomber in a shallow dive to try to gain some airspeed. The airspeed indicator remained frozen in place. Fortunately, instincts honed by months of flight training now took over. With a flash of recognition, Tune realized that ice had been forming on the bomber, increasing its weight, hampering the flight controls, and interfering with the proper measuring of airspeed.

Responding to a mental emergency checklist drilled into him through a series of talented instructor pilots, he flipped on the pitot heater and the wings' de-icer boots. Almost immediately, the airspeed indicator—which relied on the now-thawing pitot tube for accurate readings—began to reflect an accurate air speed and, as the wings started melting through the ice, the plane's controls became responsive once again. Relieved, Tune flew on. "This was only one of the occasions where my earlier training by Mr. Blair proved to be excellent," he reflected.[5]

As conditions improved, Tune could focus on more trivial matters—such as an aerial visit to his hometown. Carbon Hill lay, more or less, en route to Palm Beach, and Tune directed Mooney to set a course that would bring them over the town. But when they cut across northwest Alabama and Tune spotted a familiar bridge along Highway 78 traversing the Warrior River, he knew that his navigator was approximately thirty miles off-course. It was an inauspicious way to begin a career as an operational combat crew. Success on a bombing raid would be measured in terms of feet, not miles. Trying not to let the navigator's performance bother him, Tune pressed on for Florida.

"It was probably for the better," Tune reflected on his inadvertent bypassing of Carbon Hill. "I was going to go right down the front street. If I had done that the display window glass in each store would probably have vibrated out and broken. I could have awakened the town of 1,500 people, though, and they would have seen a new B-24."[6]

Later that day, Tune's Liberator arrived at Palm Beach's Morrison Field. Coincidentally, Tune's oldest brother, Tillman, was stationed at the airfield, but duty prevented Tune from contacting him during the crew's brief stay there. As his orders warned, he was not to discuss his overseas movement with anyone—not even his brother. Tune took his job and his orders seriously. Besides, preparation for his first over-water flight demanded his full attention. Once over the Caribbean Sea, there would be precious little margin for error.

On March 23, 1944, at 4:25 A.M., the wheels of Tune's Liberator left Morrison Field's cool tarmac. For two hours, he flew through the predawn darkness, then watched the sun creep up on the eastern horizon. Four hours later, the B-24 landed on the wide, well-maintained concrete runways of Borinquen Field, Puerto Rico, where ground crews quickly topped off the bomber's fuel tanks. Within an hour, Tune and crew were aloft once more, this time heading for Trinidad. Upon reaching the island, he flew inland, tracking toward Waller Field. Angling around the 4,000-foot, jungle-covered mountains to the north and south of the airfield, Tune set down in the soft dusk of a Caribbean twilight.

The next morning, Tune departed Waller Field and, with Mooney calling out course headings over the intercom, set a course for Belem, Brazil. As Tune soon realized, however, Mooney's course left much to be desired. After reaching the South American coastline, Mooney directed Tune to continue flying south. Tune complied but, after a short while, grew increasingly concerned. As they roared along at an altitude of 2,000 feet, all he could see below him was miles of swampland and the occasional village of curious villagers looking skyward.

"Mooney, do you know where we are?" Tune asked.

"I have no idea," Mooney answered honestly.

"Then let's turn around and get out of this swamp," Tune replied.[7]

As he spoke, Tune banked the Liberator into a wide left turn and pointed its nose north for the coastline. Once there, Mooney managed to get an accurate navigational fix. Reassured, Tune turned around once more and flew for Belem.

After an eight-hour flight, Tune and his crew found the airfield at Belem to be an unsettling outpost of civilization, a former Pan American Airlines field stuck on the southern edge of the Amazon River's massive delta. It was little more than a collection of huts and an airstrip, surrounded by what the young pilot from Carbon Hill, Alabama, remembered as primeval jungle. He spent an uneasy night listening to the cacophony of jungle noises just beyond the airfield's perimeter.

The next morning, Tune completed the next leg of their journey—a five-hour hop to the city of Forteleza, Brazil. Located on the northern edge of South America's protrusion into the Atlantic Ocean, Forteleza offered a practical jumping-off point for the intimidating hop across the Atlantic to West Africa. Tune's crew spent nearly three days in Forteleza before departing for Dakar, Senegal.

"We took off at 2200 hours and headed across the Atlantic Ocean," Tune recounted. "After flying some four hours, with the plane trimmed up and engines synchronized, I let Markowitz, who had been sleeping, take over while I grabbed a few minutes of sleep."

"This did not work too well," Tune admitted, "because shortly thereafter Sergeant Cirigliano, the radio operator, woke me and asked if I would stay awake and take over the controls. It seems that the copilot made them nervous because he would not let the plane fly itself but kept changing the controls after they had been trimmed up. We did as the fellows asked and did not sleep anymore during the whole flight. My concern was if our navigator was going to hit Dakar."[8]

Fortunately, 11 hours later, Mooney's navigation on this critical leg proved to be flawless. "As we approached the African coast, it was a wonderful feeling to see land in the distance along with a beautiful sunrise," Tune wrote. "Mooney announced that straight ahead of us should be Dakar and, to everyone's delight, it turned out to be just that."[9]

The crew spent the night of March 28–29 in Dakar and, the next day, pressed north for Marrakech, in French Morocco. It was a lengthy flight across the Western Sahara and over the Atlas Mountains, and a weary crew arrived in Marrakech at

4:30 that afternoon. Delayed in Marrakech for two days awaiting further orders, they did not depart until April 1, when they flew on to El Aouina, Tunisia.

In Tunisia, Tune stayed close to his aircraft. Not everyone on the crew, however, was so circumspect. The more adventurous portion of the crew, including Mooney, "ended up in a bar," Tune recalled. "Before they left the bar Mooney got into a fight with a colonel and was arrested. He was to be court-martialed but the powers-that-be released him to go on with us to Italy."[10]

Retrieving Mooney from jail cost the crew another day. With his liberated navigator safely on board, Tune departed Tunisia, angled across the Mediterranean Sea and, after skirting the island of Sicily, reached Manduria, Italy, four hours and 40 minutes later. Tune, his crew, and their B-24H were now part of the 720th Squadron, 450th Bombardment Group—the so-called Cottontails.

As Tune taxied to a stop and Markowitz ran through the postflight checklist, Tune reflected on the remarkable journey he had just completed. In the span of less than a week, he had set foot on four continents. He had weathered blizzards in the midwestern United States, visited Caribbean isles and airfields hacked out of jungle and swamp, weathered the Atlantic, traversed the Sahara, and crossed the Mediterranean. Now, he was in Italy, presumably days away from his first combat mission as a bomber pilot and ready for assignment to an operational squadron. The date was April 3, 1944, and, according to his personal logbook, he had 519 hours of training under his belt.[11] Would that be enough when he drew duty for that first mission? Only time would tell.

Tune and his crew, however, were only ten tiny drips in a gushing pipeline of planes and personnel streaming overseas in early 1944. Scores of other bomber crews, married up with one another in the winter and spring of 1943–1944, offered their own contribution to the flow. And for what one might have expected to be a uniform process of replacement and reinforcement, it was, in practice, anything but uniform.

Bill Garland, Leo Zupan, and Loy Dickinson

After MacDill, Garland's crew relocated to Hunter Field, in Savannah, Georgia, for a brief stay before continuing up the Atlantic coast to Bangor, Maine. From Bangor, it was an easy flight to Goose Bay, Labrador. Poised to enter a combat theater of operations, Garland's crew decided the time had come to confer a nickname on their plane. They named it *In the Bag* and, after a careful preflight inspection and round of route planning and weather checks, took off in the middle of the night bound for the Azores.

"Bill said I fell asleep on that flight," Zupan said of the overseas flight. "I probably did, and he did too. So Loy, who was our navigator and only 19 at the time, was flying through the night for us."[12]

Eventually awaking from their slumber, Garland and Zupan called for their navigator.

"Loy, get up there and check the sun and see where we are," Garland ordered. Banks of clouds obscured the sea below. As far as Garland could tell, they could be anywhere. And so, with sextant in hand, Dickinson obeyed. After a quick round of observations, calculations, and referencing his tables, the young navigator reported that they were right on course. And a few moments later, the mountainous Azores slipped into view, their peaks piercing the clouds. "God, it was great to see those peaks coming out of the clouds," Zupan remembered.[13]

In the Bag landed at the Azores' Lajes Field—a rough collection of tents bordering a set of metal-strip runways and taxiways. As the aircraft refueled, Zupan took a walk to stretch his legs. As he strolled, a B-24 taxied alongside him. Looking into the plane's cockpit, Zupan saw his old flight school friend McCool sitting at the controls. At that same moment, he suddenly remembered that McCool still owed him from a wager back at Dos Palos. Yelling and gesturing, he tried to catch McCool's attention—to no avail. The B-24 taxied onto the runway and took off, leaving the unpaid debt in its dusty wake.[14]

In the Bag soon followed, leaving the Azores and winging to Marrakech, Morocco. After a brief stay among stucco buildings that looked like they had been occupied by the French Foreign Legion, Garland and his crew pressed on for Italy, arriving in the summer of 1944 several weeks after Tune's arrival. They drew duty with the 2nd Bombardment Group's 20th Squadron and settled in to the airfield at Amendola.

Joe Owsianik and Robert Donahue

After completing their training at Waco, Owsianik and his crewmates traveled to Kearny, Nebraska, where they expected to pick up a bomber to take overseas. Instead, they soon found themselves on a troop train rolling east to Langley Field, Virginia. Then came another train ride to New York's LaGuardia Airport. At LaGuardia, Owsianik's crew boarded a civilian charter aircraft for a flight to Gander, Newfoundland. Once refueled, their plane that took them through the Azores, Casablanca, and Tunis and on to Italy. Owsianik reached Amendola and the 20th Squadron, 2nd Bombardment Group, on June 6, 1944, at about 4:00 P.M., just as the group's aircraft were returning from the day's mission. The Fifteenth Air

Force had dispatched hundreds of aircraft that day to aid in disrupting the German response to the Normandy landings that morning. "What a fantastic sight," Owsianik reflected. "The sky was full of B-17s and B-24s. They just filled the air. I'll never forget it."[15] Six days later, Donahue and his crew arrived in Amendola as well. Within a month, both he and Owsianik would join those bombers on similar combat missions.

Willard Netzley and Charles McVey

Netzley, McVey, and their crew stayed in Lincoln, Nebraska, for only a short time—barely long enough to sign for a brand-new B-17G. Then, just as summer was beginning to warm the Midwest, they left Nebraska. Flying east, McVey charted a course to New Hampshire's Granier Field. Then, following the well-worn path blazed by scores of other bombers flying to do battle with the Third Reich, they made their way to Italy by way of the Azores, Marrakech, and Tunisia.[16] Netzley and McVey joined the 2nd Bombardment Group's 20th Squadron at Amendola, Italy, in time to draw their first combat assignments in July 1944.

Russ Meyrick and Jim Weiler

The arrival of Netzley and McVey in Amendola coincided with the arrival of newlywed bombardier Russ Meyrick. Like Netzley and McVey, Meyrick's crew had flown the northern route from Newfoundland to the Azores and North Africa to join the 20th Squadron. By then, Jim Weiler, the Wisconsin veterinarian's son, had been with the squadron for approximately a month after completing his own operational training stateside at Tampa's Drew Field and Savannah's Hunter Army Airfield. Since arriving in Italy, he had piloted a raid against occupied France and a pair of assaults on the refineries of Ploesti, Romania.[17] The mission tallies of navigators and bombardiers such as McVey, Netzley, and Meyrick would waste little time in catching up with Weiler's count, however. Ongoing aerial attrition in the grueling bombing campaign against the Third Reich meant that the sharp minds and steady hands of such specialists were an increasingly essential commodity.

Ed Smith and Jim Martin

Ed Smith, Jim Martin, and the rest of William Bullock's crew trained throughout March and most of April before leaving their bomber behind and reporting to Grand Island, Nebraska, to prepare for overseas assignment. After a week in Grand

Island, they departed by train for Norfolk, Virginia. A week later, they joined 40 other aircrews on board an old converted United Fruit Company freighter, the *Sea Perch,* at Newport News and then spent the next eleven days as passengers in a troop convoy transiting the Atlantic to Oran, Algeria. *Sea Perch* was short of crewmen, and gunners like Martin took turns manning the guns on the transport's decks for the Atlantic passage.[18]

After a brief interlude in a holding camp in Oran, Smith, Bullock, and Martin boarded a British passenger ship, the *Dublin Castle,* on the afternoon of June 5, 1944. The next day, when they awoke, they discovered that the ship had already stood out of Oran's harbor. They also learned that, in the wee hours of that same morning, the Allies had stormed ashore Normandy on D-Day.

Smith also made another discovery—life for an officer on board an English-crewed ship was quite pleasant. On board the old fruit freighter that had taken them across the Atlantic, he had slept in a rack of hard bunks six high in the ship's hold. Now, he and his fellow officers slept on freshly laundered linens in immaculate staterooms, paired with only one other roommate. Every meal was five or six courses, usually with steak following fish. Martin and the enlisted men, however, had a much tougher time. For them, the shipboard fare was barely enough to stave off the pangs of hunger. Realizing their airmen's dilemma, Smith and the officers began sneaking food out of the well-stocked galleys to supplement their meager rations.[19]

A few days later, sometime during the second week in June, the ship arrived in Naples. The Allies had captured the port seven months earlier but it still bore the marks of air raids and an enthusiastic effort by the retreating Germans to destroy any useful facilities. Underscoring the destruction, a half-sunk ship lay in the muck by one of the piers, tilting precariously to one side. Undeterred, the British skipper of Smith's ship moored alongside the wrecked vessel. Within a few minutes, a series of gangplanks were in place, allowing Smith and the other passengers to disembark, cross the other ship's sloping decks, and step ashore Italy.

Even though it had reached Italy, Bullock's crew's transportation odyssey was not yet over. At the docks' rail yard, Bullock, Smith, and the others boarded a box car and, using their stuffed overseas bags as cushions, tried to make themselves as comfortable as possible as the train lurched into motion. By evening, they had arrived in Foggia, where an army truck picked them up for delivery to Amendola. Deposited unceremoniously at the darkened airfield, Bullock led his tired crew on foot to the 20th Squadron's headquarters.

At headquarters, they met the squadron's first sergeant, Master Sergeant Clyde "Tiny" Atkerson. Bespectacled, sporting a crew-cut, and built like a linebacker, the cigar-chomping Atkerson was anything but tiny. He was, however, an efficient and dedicated noncommissioned officer—just what a wartime outfit like the 20th Squadron needed. He talked the incoming crew through an initial round of paperwork before focusing on Smith, the crew's navigator.

"Oh, you're a navigator," Atkerson commented. Before Smith could say anything else, the first sergeant continued. "That's good. We've been losing a lot of them."[20]

Atkerson, as Smith soon learned, was not speaking idly. Within a week, the operations staff had Smith assigned to fly his first mission. It would be Smith's initial contribution to a gargantuan strategic undertaking the Allies had christened the Combined Bomber Offensive, or CBO. And as Smith quickly realized, in the summer of 1944, the CBO was just reaching its bloody, destructive zenith.

4
The Combined Bomber Offensive

In the spring and early summer of 1944, the Allies' strategic bombing campaign was, like a pair of giant claws, throttling Nazi Germany from two different directions. Flying from England, the Eighth Air Force and the RAF formed one pincher. Based in southern Italy, the Fifteenth Air Force and their British and Commonwealth comrades formed the other. Scarcely a day passed without some corner of the Third Reich trembling under Allied bombs.

Monday, April 3, 1944, for example, marked more than simply the date of Bill Tune's arrival in Italy. That same day, although the Eighth Air Force was still regrouping in England following an abortive raid against Ludwigshafen, Germany—a confused affair that mistakenly bombed the Swiss city of Schaffhausen—the AAF's Italian air bases were busy. The Twelfth Air Force's medium bombers destroyed the railway bridges north of Orvieto, Italy; its light bombers wrecked the railroad at Attigliano; and its fighters struck the Sesti Bagni railway station, a German supply dump and bivouac area, and the towns of Pignataro Interamna and Itri. For its part, the Fifteenth Air Force dispatched over 450 B-17s and B-24s to bomb the aircraft factory and railway marshaling yard in Budapest, Hungary, and other marshaling yards at Knin, Brod, and Drnis.[1]

Despite such frenetic activity, the Combined Bomber Offensive—as Allies called the U.S.-British bomber war against Germany—was at a critical conceptual crossroads in April 1944 when Tune landed in Italy. For those officers blessed with higher pay grades than Tune's, the offensive's arrival at such a crossroads should not have been surprising—after all, the history of the Allies' bombing strategy was one of constant evolution, conflict, and compromise.

The roots of that strategy's evolution grew out of Air War Plans Division Plan 1, or AWPD/1. As the official Army Air Forces history of the war admitted drolly, "irrespective of the intrinsic merits of AWPD/1, the views expressed therein were not wholly consistent with those of the War Department."[2] Modern aviation writer Stephen Budiansky's assessment was far more blunt. The war plan's "sheer chutzpah," he declared, "has rarely been equaled in military staff work."[3]

AWPD/1, for its part, traced its genesis to July 9, 1941, when President Roosevelt called for "an estimate of overall production requirements required to defeat our potential enemies."[4] Sensing a golden opportunity, General Henry "Hap" Arnold, chief of what was then the Army Air Corps, volunteered his Air War Plans Division estimate of the aviation requirements and turned to officers who, prior to joining Arnold's staff, had honed their doctrinal skills as instructors at the Army Air Corps Tactical School at Maxwell Field, Alabama. Led by Lieutenant Colonel Harold L. George, the staff capitalized boldly on the opportunity. Rather than simply provide the requested production figures to complement the War Department's existing Rainbow 5 war plan, they submitted "nothing less than a plan for defeating Germany by means of aerial bombardment."[5]

In order to knock Nazi Germany out of the war, AWPD/1's tabbed pages detailed the careful buildup of an overwhelming American bomber force based in Great Britain. Flying high, flying fast, and protected by on-board aerial gunners wielding lethal defensive firepower, the bombers would strike against Hitler's air power, electric generation capabilities, transportation, and fuel oil facilities, while, more controversially, remaining alert for an opportunity to turn its attention to Berlin to deliver the quick *coup de grace* against the German capital's civilian morale.[6]

Later, a subsequent amended plan, AWPD/42, deleted enemy morale as an explicit potential target and replaced it with submarine pens and synthetic rubber production facilities.[7] The destruction of such priority targets, the AAF believed, could be achieved by daylight precision bombing. For its planners, "daylight precision bombing was an article of faith," particularly after studies of the *Luftwaffe*'s unsuccessful blitz against the United Kingdom seemed to repudiate the presumed effectiveness of night bombing.[8]

Reflecting on the American bombing strategy, Wesley Craven and James Cate, who compiled the U.S. Air Force's official history of its participation in the Second World War, listed several factors that buttressed such faith in precision bombing. Practically speaking, the workhorse B-17 could only carry a relatively small payload of bombs—approximately 6,000 pounds. That compared poorly to Britain's Avro Lancaster, with a payload capacity of 14,000 pounds of bombs, and so the AAF valued precision bombing as a way of maximizing the B-17's capabilities. Such bombing complemented what Craven and Cate described as Americans' "traditional reverence for marksmanship which went back to the squirrel rifle of frontier days when scarcity of powder and shot put a premium on accuracy."[9] The two historians also identified a carry-over from the U.S. military's prewar stress on heavy long-range bombers providing the best defense against enemy ships—a utilization that, naturally, required precision bombing. Finally, they noted that precision bombing offered an "antidote to widespread antipathy" toward attacks on civilian targets.[10]

Nevertheless, "daylight precision bombing," as another pair of historians concluded, "was a misleading phrase . . . It was certainly daylight and it was certainly bombing, but it was hardly precise." The United States Strategic Bombing Survey's postwar review of the bomber offensive, they noted, had examined the efficiency of attacks on oil refineries. The results were hardly impressive. For every hundred bombs dropped against such targets, one hit oil pipelines, two hit production facilities, two failed to explode, three hit decoy plants, eight landed in open terrain inside the target area, and eighty-four missed the target altogether.[11] Of course, such disparagement benefits from hindsight—a luxury Allied strategists lacked in 1942. Instead, confident in its strategic vision, the AAF unleashed its bombers for its first strike against occupied Europe.

On the evening of June 11, 1942, thirteen B-24 Liberators took off from a Royal Air Force (RAF) base near the Suez Canal and, after flying all night, appeared in the skies over the Romanian city of Ploesti the next morning. Capitalizing on the surprise, they left a burning oil refinery in their wake. A month later, on July 4, 1942, six A-20A Havoc medium bombers of the 15th Bombardment Squadron (Light) attacked German airfields in Holland. The following month, a dozen Eighth Air Force B-17s bombed a railway marshaling yard at Rouen-Sotteville, France, on August 17. American bomb strikes on Germany itself would not occur for another five months.

In the end, however, the goals of AWPD/1 and AWPD/42, and the idea that air power alone could deliver an Allied victory, proved unrealistic. With respect to Germany, one of their key presumptions was that Hitler had already stretched his economy to the breaking point in order to finance his campaigns of conquest. In reality, however, only 49 percent of Germany's gross national product in 1941 had been devoted to supporting the Nazi war effort.[12] Furthermore, Operation Bolero, the build-up of Allied forces in England in 1943 for a cross-Channel invasion of

France, hinted that the American bombing campaign might not have enough time to produce strategic results. In the meantime, the decision to invade North Africa diverted precious resources from England to the North African and Mediterranean theaters of operation. Similar diversions of men and material to the Pacific further exacerbated the Eighth Air Force's logistical challenges.

Compounding its problems, the Eighth Air Force failed to pursue the war plans' strategic prioritization with the bomber squadrons that remained in England. Supreme Headquarters Allied Expeditionary Force, the U.S. Embassy in London, the U.S. Navy, the Joint Strategic Survey Committee, and the British air staff all weighed in with their orders, arguments, and opinions on how to best employ the American B-17s and B-24s. The result was a haphazard series of missions against ports, shipyards, and U-boat pens in "a nightmare of conflicting and ill-defined objectives for strategic bombardment."[13] Such missions were not only of limited strategic value but costly as well, particularly at a time when the bombers lacked long-range fighter-escorts and did not carry the improved defensive weapons arrangements of later versions of the B-24 and the B-17.

As 1942 progressed, the increasing American losses in the skies over Europe brought the difference in U.S. and British strategic bombing strategy into sharp focus. The RAF believed that general area attacks would achieve such widespread urban destruction that any critical industrial activity would be stymied if not destroyed.[14] Accordingly, the RAF had used its heavy bombers under the cover of darkness since March 1942 and embraced the benefits of a night bombing campaign—the lower costs of constructing lighter, less armed night bombers, and those bombers' greater bomb payloads, smaller crews, and fewer operational losses.[15]

"My, we admire you chaps for going up against Jerry during the day," an RAF pilot told one American bombardier shortly after he arrived at Amendola. The Americans shared the airfield with several British bomber units. "Heck," the bombardier admitted years later, "we admired *them* for going up against the Germans at night."[16]

Faced with such conflicting views on how best to implement an effective bombing campaign, Allied war planners agreed to a compromise solution in the spring of 1943. The solution was a simple one—the RAF would bomb Europe by night and the AAF would bomb by day. Christening the cooperative strategic effort the Combined Bomber Offensive, the strategists ordered it to focus on six priority target categories—submarines, the aircraft industry, ball bearing production, oil, synthetic rubber, and military transport—to pave the way for an Allied invasion of Europe. This would, as one American strategist indelicately put it, "soften the Hun for the land invasion and the kill."[17] According to the agreement, the Eighth Air Force, complemented by the RAF's night attacks, was to implement the strategy by initiating Operation Pointblank in the summer of 1943.

Pointblank's objectives, however, required the AAF to be able to field a strategic bombing force of 51 heavy bombardment groups within a year. It was an optimistic requirement at a time when the Eighth Air Force only possessed a dozen such groups. Stymied by poor reconnaissance and strategic intelligence, a misplaced belief in the ability of unescorted bombers to make it to the target, and inadequate numbers of bombers and maintenance crews, Pointblank ran headlong into Germany's increasingly effective web of radars, lethal flak batteries, and aggressive fighter pilots.[18]

Nevertheless, the AAF pursued Pointblank's objectives gamely. American bombers—stacked in tight box-like defensive formations to provide the maximum protection against the marauding German fighters—painted Europe's skies with their white contrails. Forty-one percent of the missions they flew targeted the *Luftwaffe's* ability to wage war. They raided airfields, aircraft depots, training centers, final assembly plants, testing facilities, essential raw material industries such as aluminum, oil, and rubber, and the factories that manufactured such aircraft components as engines, ball bearings, air frames, and instruments. From July 24 to 30, 1943, AAF bombers flew over 1,000 sorties against targets in occupied Europe in what it called "Blitz Week." But although Blitz Week managed to put a sizable (albeit temporary) dent in Germany's aircraft production capability, it did so at the cost of almost 100 American bombers and, less quantifiably, of the surviving air crews' morale. For their part, the Germans simply accelerated the dispersal of their key industries.

In increasing frustration, Allied air planners cast about for a series of targets that would represent the *Luftwaffe's* critical choke point. In the late summer of 1943 the AAF settled on a series of four targets: the Romanian oil refineries of Ploesti, the ball bearing plants of Schweinfurt, Germany, and the aircraft factories of Regensburg, Germany, and Wiener-Neustadt, Austria. It was a bold—and, in hindsight, reckless—selection of targets, for each lay well beyond the range of the AAF's escort fighters. The bombers would be going after some of the most heavily defended targets in the Third Reich painfully alone.

First came the raid on Ploesti, where oil refineries produced some 60 percent of Hitler's crude oil. On August 1, 1943, 177 B-24s took off from Libya to strike Ploesti in a daring low-level raid code-named Operation Tidalwave. Bad weather and the loss of the lead navigator's aircraft, however, denied the bombers the close coordination and split-second timing necessary for success. Instead, the valiant crews roared over the target in piecemeal groups scarcely 100 feet off the ground.

The result was little short of a massacre as the B-24s tried desperately to avoid German fighters and flak batteries while searching for their targets amid the dense black plumes of smoke. In the end, the Americans lost 54 aircraft. The awarding of five Medals of Honor to airmen flying the mission attested to the courage of the bomber crews. But even though they knocked out 42 percent of the refineries' production capability for a period of time, few dared to call it a victory.[19]

Attacks on Schweinfurt, Regensburg, and Wiener Neustadt followed. Again, the bombers flew in alone, suffered from operational mishaps, and paid an appalling cost. Five hundred and fifty-seven bombers braved German and Austrian airspace to bomb the aircraft factories and ball bearing plants; 117 failed to return. Back in England, as the survivors watched Graves Registration Units clear out the quarters of shot-down crews, they began to wonder if they had fallen into a war of attrition not unlike the one that had been fought on France's battlefields 25 years earlier.

Little did they know that the worst was yet to come.

Bad weather kept the Eighth Air Force grounded in England for much of September, preventing it from following the Schweinfurt-Regensburg raids with missions capable of destroying the mangled factories completely. It was not until the second week in October that the Eighth Air Force could mount another major offensive. Once again, its B-17s and B-24s returned to Regensburg and Schweinfurt in an infamous weeklong series of raids. The resulting carnage caused the week to be forever known to the air force as "Black Week."

Approximately 1,140 bombers participated in Black Week. The Germans downed 148 of them—a loss rate of nearly 13 percent. The worst day came on October 14, when 229 B-17s raided Schweinfurt. Over a quarter of them failed to make it home.[20] Their melted and mangled carcasses stretched across the European countryside in a grim ribbon of blazing funeral pyres clearly visible to the surviving aircrews racing for home. "The perception of a self-defending bomber force perished on 'Black Thursday,' the day of the second Schweinfurt attack," one air force historian noted.[21]

Understandably, the losses suffered during Black Week shook the AAF's confidence badly. Determined to protect their own pilots while keeping the pressure on the *Luftwaffe*, Allied planners decided to supplement Operation Pointblank with what they christened Operation Argument. Operation Argument would be an all-out bombing offensive against Germany's production of fighter aircraft, building on a groundswell of improvements to the AAF's operational capabilities. The Allies' development of long-range fighter escorts, coupled with the arrival of the B-17G in ever-increasing numbers, signaled more trouble for the Germans. With its chin turret, the B-17G was far more capable of foiling the bold head-on assaults of daring *Luftwaffe* pilots.

Operation Argument, however, faced more than opposition from Germany's fighter pilots and flak batteries. The operation could not commence until forecasts predicted three uninterrupted days of acceptable flying weather, but Europe's skies refused to cooperate. From mid-October of 1943 onward, an ugly gray overcast of cloud and fog had stubbornly blanketed the Continent, mocking the AAF's notions of decisive precision bombing.

As October slipped into November, Allied aircrews, still tied to Operation Pointblank while they waited for the break in the weather deemed necessary to implement Operation Argument, endured the tense frustration of mission after mission being canceled because of bad weather. Actual missions, of course, were even worse. White-knuckled bomber pilots, straining at the controls of their B-17s and B-24s, struggled to maintain formation in the murky gray skies without slamming into one another. Ice-laden wings made control of the bombers even more cumbersome. At the gunners' positions, the sergeants battled frostbite and hypothermia.

Meanwhile, the H2X radar systems came into operational use on the American bombers. Derived from the British H2S system, it initially offered some hope of increasing the AAF's bombing tempo. Nevertheless, the technique quickly encountered its own challenges. Indoctrinated into the superiority of their Norden bombsights, the AAF's commanders resisted the new bombing method. When forced to provide crews for H2X training to become their units' would-be pathfinders, they often sent their poorest—and thus least missed—personnel or installed the radar sets in substandard aircraft. Even when the trained crews and equipment were in place, they suffered from poor maintenance, lack of spare parts, and overwork.[22] Too often, the bombardiers found themselves releasing their payloads blindly over cloud-obscured targets. But even then, the AAF resisted referring to such efforts as "blind bombing." "Overcast bombing technique" or "bombing through overcast" were Hap Arnold's preferred euphemisms.[23]

Confronted with such poor weather plaguing northern Europe, the Allies' Combined Chiefs of Staff began considering basing some of the strategic bombing effort at airfields other than England. Southern Italy, for example, offered the promise of better weather conditions. Bombers based in Italy could also bring half of Hitler's fighter aircraft production—hereto untouched—within range of Allied air strikes.

Accordingly, on November 1, 1943, the AAF activated the Fifteenth Air Force in Tunis. Wasting no time, 112 of its bombers took to the sky the next day in a 1,600-mile round-trip raid against aircraft factories in Wiener Neustadt, Austria.

A month later, in December, the Fifteenth Air Force relocated to Bari, Italy. It ensconced its bomber and fighter groups in a swath of airfields across southern Italy. Most centered on the airfield complex constructed by Mussolini around Foggia. In an ironic twist of fate, the Fascist dictator's own runways were now being used against his ally Hitler. By the time Tune's crew joined it, the Fifteenth Air Force consisted of 21 heavy bomber and seven fighter groups.

Despite high hopes for opening another aerial front against the Third Reich, the Fifteenth Air Force faced a daunting set of challenges. Inevitable calls for strategic air strikes against targets in the Mediterranean theater of operations distracted it from Operation Argument's prerogatives. So did tactical operations in support of the Allied advance north through Italy and the landings at Anzio and Salerno. More bad winter weather, muddy Italian airfields, and the daunting Alpine barrier whittled further at the Fifteenth Air Force's effectiveness in the winter of 1943–1944.

The year 1944 arrived in the wake of organizational changes for the AAF as well. Hap Arnold, by now the commanding general for the United States Army Air Forces, created the United States Strategic Air Forces. The USStAF, based in England and commanded by Lieutenant General Carl A. Spaatz, would wield operational control over the Eighth and the Fifteenth Air Forces and administrative control of the tactical Ninth Air Force. Administrative control of the Fifteenth Air Force rested with Lieutenant General Ira C. Eaker as commander of the Mediterranean Allied Air Forces. The original commander of the Fifteenth Air Force, Lieutenant General James "Jimmy" Doolittle, took command of the Eighth Air Force, while Lieutenant General Nathan F. Twining became the commanding officer of the Fifteenth Air Force.

In England, Doolittle brought with him an aggressive attitude and a new vision for how fighters could best protect his bombers that eventually filtered throughout USStAF. Upon taking command, he found a sign in his fighter commander's office that announced, "THE FIRST DUTY OF THE EIGHTH AIR FORCE FIGHTERS IS TO BRING THE BOMBERS BACK ALIVE." Doolittle ordered it taken down and replaced with another that proclaimed, "THE FIRST DUTY OF THE EIGHTH AIR FORCE'S FIGHTERS IS TO DESTROY GERMAN FIGHTERS."[24]

In response, AAF fighter groups escorting bomber missions began designating one of their three squadrons as the "bouncing squadron" to be bounced against enemy fighter formations as soon as they were detected. Thus, rather than remaining tied to the bomber formations, the fighters began to offer wide-ranging area coverage. They surged ahead of the bombers, seeking out German fighters as soon as they were spotted or, even better, while they were still in the vulnerable stage of forming up after takeoff. The results bore out the new tactics. On January 29 and 30, 1944, for example, AAF fighters claimed record numbers of aerial victories against *Luftwaffe* interceptors.

In the days to come, while the AAF waited for the weather to break to unleash Operation Argument, the fighters added to their tallies by seeking out targets of opportunity on the way home from the air raids. Enemy airfields, railroads, and troop positions fell victim to their strafing and rocketing attacks. To a large extent, the fighters, complemented by the stalwart gunners manning the .50 calibers of the B-17s and B-24s, began to achieve Argument's objectives in a far more direct way than the air planners had envisioned. Every German pilot shot down was an increasingly tough blow for the *Luftwaffe* to stomach, especially as the AAF changed its rotation system that, previously, had rotated airmen home to the States automatically after they had completed 25 missions. Now, heavy bomber crews became eligible to rotate home after completing 30 missions. That number would eventually increase to 35 and then 50. Fighter pilots had to log 200 combat hours to become eligible. No matter how unpopular the decision might have been to men trying to survive their tour of duty in the skies over Europe, it helped keep experienced crews on hand and in the wings as the build-up for Operation Argument continued.

By February, military meteorologists predicted a week-long break in the inclement winter weather. Operation Argument's time had arrived. The RAF began what became known as "Big Week" with a 730-bomber raid against Leipzig, Germany, on the night of February 19–20. A loss rate of 11 percent hinted at Operation Argument's looming cost and reminded observers of an AAF report that had declared grimly that strategic bombing efforts had to intensify even if such an effort meant "attriting U.S. forces at a greater rate than replacements are available."[25] Undaunted, the Eighth Air Force sent 1,000 bombers aloft the next day for a series of raids in the Leipzig area. The Fifteenth Air Force attacked Regensburg on the twenty-second.

Big Week drew to a close on the evening of February 26, 1944. By then, the AAF and the RAF had flown some 6,200 bombing sorties, dropping more than 19,000 tons of bombs on 18 airframe and two ball bearings manufacturing centers. They lost 370 heavy bombers and 38 fighters, but *Luftwaffe* losses fell somewhere between 230 and 600.[26] An aerial battle of attrition was now fully joined and, to some extent, the *Luftwaffe*'s fate was sealed. Among the most telling statistics was the VIII Fighter Command's ability, thanks to a recent influx in replacements, to end Big Week with 90 percent *more* fighter pilots than at its beginning.[27] The Germans had no hope of matching such a juggernaut of fresh, well-trained pilots. The influence of the attacks on Hitler's ball bearing manufacturing base might have been debatable—his industrial minister, Albert Speer, later claimed that even after Big Week, "not a tank, plane, or other piece of weaponry failed to be produced because of a lack of ball bearings"—but the loss of experienced *Luftwaffe* pilots was becoming far more critical.[28]

Meanwhile, Allied air planners pressed their advantage home. Seeking to lure the *Luftwaffe* into more costly battles it could not afford to fight, they dispatched the next wave of bombers against Berlin. On March 6 and 8, the Eighth Air Force struck the Nazi capital. Ironically, the heavily defended enemy capital was not so much the target as the contested airspace above it. German fighters downed 69 bombers on the first day of the so-called Battle of Berlin, but the *Luftwaffe* lost 120 fighters in the span of two days.[29] The Germans were already stripping other fronts for fighters, rushing students through flight training, deploying night fighters during the day, and throwing bomber and transport pilots into fighter cockpits. It could ill afford the loss of 120 fighter pilots, and the absence of fighter opposition in the skies of Berlin on March 9 underscored that reality. In the spring of 1944, both Argument and Pointblank seemed to be paying rich dividends.

A pair of strategic diversions, however, dulled Argument's effectiveness. First, the threat of Hitler's impending use of his self-proclaimed "terror weapons"—the V-1 and V-2 rockets, possibly carrying chemical or biological payloads—against British cities caused the Allies to assign an "over-riding priority" to the bombing of enemy facilities associated with design, manufacture, or launch of those weapons. In the end, some 6,100 sorties that could have been flown against other strategic targets as part of Operations Pointblank or Argument sallied forth against the V-1 and V-2 sites instead. The Allies called this effort Operation Crossbow. In months to come, as Operation Crossbow continued, Hitler would admit that the Nazi rockets were a better defensive weapon than offensive weapon. Each bomb dropped on a rocket site, he reasoned, was one less dropped on Germany.[30] Many Allied bomber pilots would have agreed with the Fuhrer.

The second diversion came as Operation Overlord—the cross-Channel invasion of Normandy—approached. To support the invasion, some members of the Allied staff supported the so-called transportation plan, which called for air strikes against German bridges, marshaling yards, and locomotive and railroad repair facilities to prevent a rapid counterstroke against the Normandy beachhead. Others argued for the "oil plan," which envisioned air raids against the Nazis' oil refineries and similar facilities. Such attacks, officers such as Spaatz stressed, would mortally threaten the weakest link in the enemy's economy and force a final climatic battle of attrition with the *Luftwaffe*. Not coincidentally, the *Luftwaffe* was, at the time, increasingly relying upon undertrained pilots whose flight school experience had suffered from a lack of aviation fuel.

Among the Allied staff, the strategic argument soon reached a fever pitch. "The air problem has been one requiring a great deal of patience and negotiations," General Dwight D. Eisenhower warned as he prepared to lead the gathering Allied expeditionary force into France. "Unless the matter is settled at once, I will request relief from this command."[31]

Shortly thereafter, on March 26, 1944, Eisenhower cut the Gordian knot and opted for the transportation plan. He refused, however, to place Spaatz's strategic bombers under the command of his ambitious deputy, Air Chief Marshal Arthur Tedder of Britain. That decision left Spaatz with a degree of flexibility he exploited while adhering to the strictures of the transportation plan. He was not above "resort[ing] to subterfuge," as one historian noted, to go after his preferred oil targets.[32] A broad interpretation of Eisenhower's subsequent April 17 directive to maintain pressure on the German air force—which Spaatz reasoned could be most readily applied by challenging the *Luftwaffe* with attacks on its prized oil installations—provided him with further rationalization for air raids on the refineries and synthetic oil facilities that he preferred to target.[33] But it was not until June 8, 1944, however, that Spaatz could clearly dictate that his bombers "primary strategic aim henceforth would be to deny oil to the enemy's armed forces."[34]

Tune and his crew had no way of knowing it at the time, of course, but Spaatz's reputed subterfuge was about to have a direct effect on their immediate future. When they arrived at Manduria on April 3, 1944, their new squadron mates greeted them enthusiastically. Tune soon realized, however, that the real reason for the warm welcome was the brand-new B-24H he had just delivered and a new feature that it boasted—a protective sheet of 3/8" steel around the cockpit's seats. In two days, the squadron and the rest of the 450th Group were to raid a target of legendary peril—the Romanian oil refinery complex of Ploesti.

On April 5, Tune watched 28 of the group's bombers take off for the eight-and-a-half-hour round-trip flight to Ploesti. At the time, the AAF was supposed to be focusing on transportation targets, so the mission nominally targeted the Romanian city's railway marshaling yard. Still, Spaatz knew "full well that the pattern of the bombing would include some of the oil refineries."[35] Tune's recently delivered bomber, commandeered by another crew for this mission, would help stitch that destructive pattern. Its journey, however, was not destined to be a round trip.

In all, the Fifteenth Air Force dispatched 230 bombers against Ploesti that day. Before the 450th Group's squadrons even reached the target, a dozen Bf 109s ambushed the formation from the cover of clouds. Diving through the group's lead squadron, they then swept up through the second echelon. Blasting with rockets, cannon, and machineguns, the Bf 109s shot three of the B-24s out of formation.

Undeterred, the group soldiered on, only to come under a larger attack by 112 enemy fighters as the bombers approached the target. At this point, the group encountered heavy flak, which proved to be a mixed blessing. The flak kept the enemy fighters at a respectful distance but damaged practically every bomber in the group. Two other bombers were lost to enemy fighters, and another five were damaged. Technical Sergeant Milburn Riddle, a flight engineer assigned to the 2nd Group's 96th Squadron, recalled the day's mission.

"Ploesti was spectacularly frightening," Riddle remembered. "They threw everything at us. You could barely make out the other formations through the anti-aircraft fire. It was dark as night. Fighters did not hit our formation but were all over the B-24s. . . . We left Ploesti with huge columns of smoke filling the sky. It really was a piece of work, but I didn't want to go back to that place."[36]

The army agreed with Riddle's assessment of the mission's damage. "Despite the persistence of the fighter attacks, the intense barrage of enemy flak, and partial concealment of the target by a smoke screen, the group continued through for a highly successful bombing run, inflicting grave damage to vital enemy installations, supplies, and equipment," a Unit Citation awarded to the group declared.[37]

Back in Manduria, however, it was apparent that the successful delivery of some 85 tons of bombs on Ploesti came at a heavy cost. Not only had five of 28 bombers been lost, but nearly every one of the aircraft that managed to return were damaged by flak. For the immediate future, as ground crews worked to repair the mangled survivors, it seemed as if there would be too many crews and not enough aircraft.

Apparently, the 2nd Bombardment Group stationed at Amendola Field did not suffer that same problem. Rather, it had plenty of B-17s, but it needed fresh crews—and it was not too picky about what kind of crews they were. Accordingly, the Fifteenth Air Force headquarters dispatched Tune and his crew north to join the 2nd Bombardment Group, where Tune would become a B-17 pilot with a unit that called itself "Defenders of Liberty."

5
"Defenders of Liberty"

Bill Tune and his fellow refugees from Manduria's carnage left the 450th Group sometime in the middle of April. A shuffle of orders dispatched them to *Staz Di Amendola* Landing Ground or, as the airmen simply called it, Amendola. Their new home, located twelve miles northeast of the city of Foggia, was one of a series of airfields that arced to the west and north of the city. Several squadrons of RAF night bombers were based at the airfield. So were U.S. heavy bombardment groups of B-17 Flying Fortresses—the 97th Bombardment Group and the 2nd Bombardment Group. Tune's orders directed him to the latter, a unit of 319 officers, 1,498 enlisted personnel, and 58 B-17 bombers divided among the group headquarters and its four subordinate squadrons.[1]

As Tune eventually discovered, the 2nd Bombardment Group boasted one of the most storied lineages in the AAF. The group traced its history to 1918 and the 1st Day Bombardment Group, which had served with distinction in the First World War. In 1921, the army redesignated the unit as the 2nd Group (Bombardment). Assigned to Virginia's Langley Field, the group operated under the motto "Death and Destruction." Only later, in the course of several goodwill missions to South America in 1940, did the army decide that "Defenders of Liberty" was a more appropriate slogan for the group. The group's motto remains "Defenders of Liberty" to this day.

The insignia of the group's 20th Squadron—a shadowy, derby-hatted character poised to hurl a round bomb—also evolved for the sake of good public relations. For many people, the image of a sinister bomber was a far too disturbing one during the Red Scare of the early 1920s. The squadron's irreverent christening of their mascot as the "Mad Bolshevik" did not help matters. Before long, a new insignia—depicting a swashbuckling character standing on a flying bomb and throwing a bomb of his own—replaced the Mad Bolshevik. With the same irreverence, the squadron's aviators nicknamed the new mascot "Pineapple Pete."[2]

After weathering the initial blows of the Great Depression (and seeing half of its officers assigned as cadre to Civilian Conservation Corps units), the 2nd Bombardment Group began flying the twin-engined Martin B-10B and the Douglas B-18 Bolo in the mid-1930s. They were popular aircraft but, with limited ranges and payloads, of limited strategic value. It would take the arrival of the YB-17 to herald the coming of a strategic bombing force and the group's pilots would be the new era's heralds. In 1937, the 2nd Bombardment Group took possession of a dozen YB-17s and became the first operational unit in the Army Air Corps to be equipped with the Flying Fortress.

For the next four years, the group helped prove the B-17's capabilities. Pilots logged cross-country jaunts to California, undertook goodwill flights to several South American nations, and participated in a much-publicized training exercise involving the at-sea location and interception of the battleship USS *Utah* and the passenger liner SS *Rex* on the high seas. On a lighter note, the group's crews even helped MGM film *Test Pilot* with Spencer Tracy and Clark Gable.

Ford J. Lauer served as one of the 2nd Bombardment Group's pilots on many such prewar missions. Therefore, when, as a colonel, he received command of the newly formed 304th Bombardment Group, he wasted little time in calling upon General Robert C. Olds, the commanding general of the Second Air Force. Olds was not only a former commander of the 2nd Bombardment Group but also an old friend of Lauer's. Lauer managed to convince Olds to redesignate the 304th as the 2nd Bombardment Group, a change that went into effect on November 10, 1942. Its four squadrons became the 429th, the 49th, the 96th, and the 20th Squadron. In one fell swoop, Lauer had masterminded a genealogical coup and, thanks to a stroke of a pen, his infant unit boasted one of the most distinguished lineages in the AAF.[3]

Lauer's group began its operational training in remote Ephrata Army Air Base in eastern Washington. Subsequent training phases occurred in Great Falls, Montana, at a collection of surrounding airfields, and, finally, a train-up for the unit's impending overseas deployment in Kearny, Nebraska. Orders then dispatched the group's bombers to Morrison Field, West Palm Beach, Florida, their so-called point of aerial embarkation.

On March 10, 1943, the aircrews' journey really began. From Morrison Field, the 2nd Bombardment Group's B-17s flew across the Caribbean Sea, skirted the northeastern coast of South America, made a final refueling stop in Natal, Brazil, and then either flew directly to Dakar, Senegal, or hopped into Africa via Ascension Island. All of the bombers rendezvoused in Marrakech, French Morocco, and then continued on to Algeria. On May 30—a month and a half after its bombers left the States—the last of the group's ground echelon finally caught up with their aircrews following a difficult Atlantic sea voyage and a series of train and truck journeys across North Africa.

Even in the absence of its full complement of staff and ground crews, the group's bombers flew their first combat mission on April 28—an abortive effort to bomb Axis shipping in Sardinia's Terranova harbor. Finding the target obscured by clouds, all of the group's bombers returned with full payloads. It was an anticlimactic welcome to the air war in Europe, but only the first of 412 combat missions to come during the group's operations in the Second World War.

For the next seven months, the 2nd Bombardment Group operated out of airfields in North Africa, bombing targets in Tunisia, Sicily, Italy, France, Greece, and even Austria. The Allied landings in Italy, however, opened new possibilities for the group and the AAF as a whole. Following the creation of the Fifteenth Air Force, the group deployed to Amendola, Italy, on December 10, 1943, in a rushed wartime movement. At the time, the front lines were only 45 miles away and the distant rumble of artillery guns could be heard at night. Looking back on the hectic move to the group's new Italian base, participants declared that "it was so confused a Philadelphia lawyer could not have untangled it."[4]

History does not record if any Philadelphia lawyers were present with the group, but its officers and men managed nevertheless to reorganize at Amendola quickly enough to be able to fly its first mission from its new home four days later. On December 14, the group's bombers, now under the command of Colonel Herbert E. Rice, struck at the Hassani airdrome in occupied Greece. Battling enemy fighters and accurate flak, the Defenders of Liberty returned from the mission with the loss of one plane. It was their one hundred and seventh mission of the war.

Meanwhile, back in Amendola, the group's staff, ground crews, and airmen battled to carve a home out of the Italian mud and mire. Actually, as far as most Italian airfields were concerned, Amendola was better than most. Although the airfield bore the marks of Allied air raids, two parallel runways, constructed of interlocking steel mats, offered relatively stable landing strips even in the mud and muck of an Italian winter.

A collection of low, rugged hills rose four miles to the north of the airfield, separated from the field by the Foggia-Manfredonia highway. In the intervening space, the brown, brushy ground provided forage and shelter for herds of sheep and their shepherds. Occasionally, a hapless sheep would wonder on to the runway, where it would meet an untimely and gruesome end at the hands of a speeding bomber.

The hills' high ground provided a bivouac area for the airmen. The group's staff took over a large farmhouse and its several outbuildings, turning the villa into the group's headquarters and adding a Quonset hut to fulfill the need for a near-term location to hold pre-mission briefings. Taking advantage of the unusual proximity of all four squadrons to one another, the group soon had a well-organized, well-staffed medical station operational as well—four squadron dispensaries and a group infirmary.[5]

Around the villa complex, a rough tent city began to grow up among the scraggly remnants of once-productive olive tree groves and ancient stone walls. Before long, rows of canvas tents, or rough stone huts roofed with canvas, marked the low-lying plateau with the unmistakable olive-drab imprint of an American military operation. Meanwhile, back on the flight line, wooden shacks rose to house the group's spare parts, equipment lockers, and parachute rigging operations.

"It seemed very well organized to me," Tune remembered. Apparently, life had settled into a deceptively mundane routine on the ground for the 2nd Group in the four months since it moved to Amendola. "They had lost several crews and, after we signed in, they told us to just go and select a set of quarters. We found a stone hut that had been built by local Italian labor. The walls were five feet high and we had the canvas from a tent for a roof. It even had a small porch, also under a section of canvas."[6] Taking a paintbrush and a small tin of black paint in hand, Tune's co-pilot, Fred Markowitz, painted "Wee Bit O'Brooklyn" across the edge of the hut's canvas roof near its wooden frame door in honor of his home town.

"Wee Bit O'Brooklyn" was larger than most, and his crew soon found themselves sharing it with four officers from another crew. Second Lieutenant Harold T. "Tommy" Tomlinson, a pleasant Californian, led this second group of rookies, which arrived in Amendola at approximately the same time as Tune. Tomlinson and Tune had trained together back in the States in flight school, where their surnames had caused them to often find themselves standing together in formation or in line. Now, stuck in close quarters with Tomlinson and the others—three officers named Allen, Barnett, and Watson—to endure the airfield's monotony, Tune became fast friends with Tomlinson. Tune found another friend in Lester Brasfield, a fellow pilot who had grown up just down the road from Tune in Jasper, Alabama, the county seat of Walker County. Such friendships helped to pass the time at the Italian air base. Otherwise, "chow, sleep, fly missions, hope for mail—those things pretty much summed up life at Amendola," Tune recalled.[7]

"The impression that I had when we arrived was that of a well-organized Boy Scout camp," Loy Dickinson added. "The four officers of our crew (Garland, Zupan, Novak and me) had a decent place to keep our stuff and a good bed. As I recall, it was a concrete slab with canvas covering that was probably quite adequate for the summer time that we were there. Not sure what winter conditions were like. Food is and was food. I just remember that I was excited to be there and to be among so many diverse and talented men."[8]

Willard Netzley took a broader view of life in Amendola and its environs. Foggia, he observed, had been heavily damaged in its capture from the Germans the previous fall. "In the summer of 1944," he wrote, "there was not a store, restaurant, or theater open in Foggia except a theater with part of its roof blown off, which was used for USO-type performances. Except for the buildings used by the Allied military, Foggia was a dead city. All of the young ladies had apparently migrated to Rome. The climate was like Southern California, and on a day when we were not flying a practice or combat mission we would browse around the countryside or go fishing in sailboats with Italian fishermen who took us along for company or for a few cigarettes, a bar of candy, or a handful of Italian *lira* represented by paper one-cent notes."[9]

Back at the airfield, random perks helped to keep up morale. A B-17 made a weekly trip to Cairo to keep the bars stocked with beer and wine. The men chilled their beers by soaking the cans in aviation fuel and then hanging them in a sock on a clothesline. As the fuel evaporated, it cooled the cans and their contents. Even more Yankee ingenuity was displayed when, shortly after the group's arrival, curious airmen had discovered a set of cave-like limestone quarries. Previously, the Italians had used them for wine cellars before the Germans turned them into horse stables and POW cells. Now, after a thorough cleaning, one became the group's enlisted men's club, the other the Group Theater. A sergeant dubbed the entertainment complex the "Rock Fella Social Center." It was a dark trek down a 50-foot long passageway, with flashlight in hand and bats flitting around one's ears, to get to the club's bar, but the atmosphere dissuaded few visitors. Nor did it stop the Group Chaplain from claiming a corner of the caves for the group's chapel.

Other than respites created by bad weather, there was little time, however, to enjoy the Rock Fella Social Center or visits into Foggia. For the rest of that wet winter and spring, whenever the weather permitted, the group flew missions against Axis targets in northern Italy, Germany, Austria, Greece, Yugoslavia, Bulgaria, and southern France. For two of those missions—raids on Steyr, Austria, and Regensburg, Germany—the group received a remarkable pair of two back-to-back Presidential Unit Citations on February 24 and February 25, respectively.

Visits to the nearby city of Foggia provided a welcome break from such operations. There, an American with ten dollars in hand could find an Italian family willing to treat him and three friends to a complete spaghetti dinner. A visit to the local Red Cross club, staffed by American volunteers and serving coffee and dough-nuts, provided a more familiar taste of home. Occasionally, Madeleine Carroll, the beautiful British actress Bob Hope once called "his favorite blonde," joined the men there. After losing a sister in the Germans' bombing of London, Carroll had put her movie career on hold to serve as a Red Cross volunteer in Italy.

But booze flown in from Cairo, spaghetti dinners, and even Bob Hope's fa-vorite blonde could only hold the group's officers' attention for so long. Eventu-ally, they wanted a club of their own. After an informal meeting, all agreed to chip in ten dollars each to finance the construction of a club. Italian laborers, using stone from local quarries and wood from fragmentation bomb crates, managed to complete a reputable building by March—one destined to spark envy throughout southern Italy. The club, complete with pristine white table cloths, formally opened on April 4, 1944. The evening consisted of a floor show and dancing, music from two bands and an Italian orchestra, and a visit by the Fifteenth Air Force's com-manding officer, Major General Nathan Twining.

"At least we had class," one of the 20th Squadron's bombardiers remembered, comparing the officers' club to Amendola's rough tents, uncomfortable army cots, and slit-trench latrines. "For the evening meal, we would often wipe the ever-present Italian mud from our shoes, put on our Class A uniforms, and go to the of-ficers club as 'officers and gentlemen' . . . it was an incongruous setting to say the least," he reflected. "As the dignified waiter poured another glass of Chianti and as the ensemble softly played, it was hard to believe that just a few hours before we were getting our asses shot off over some stinking German oil refinery."[10]

The group's medical history, however, provided a more jaded observation re-garding such creature comforts. "Combat crews often have to be treated with 'kid gloves'; they expect much and at times their requests or complaints are unreason-able and selfish in the eyes of the ground personnel," the history declared. "The majority of those who fly combat have but one thing in mind and that is to fly their required number of missions and get back to the U.S. They protest any major or minor discomforts. They are the first to complain. They have been the 'fair haired' boys ever since they got their wings."[11]

"A sensible way of keeping peace and harmony is to give those who fly every re-quest and at the same time give the same benefits to the ground echelon," the his-tory continued. "Ground personnel are kept reasonably happy as long as they have good food, good living quarters, and ample privileges. However, the morale of the flying personnel is more complex since the fatigue and hazards of combat affect them in various ways. After exceptionally difficult raids we will invariably have anxieties appearing in certain men. Our group has had its share of anxiety neurosis among combat crews. With experienced and understanding flight surgeons using devious methods we have had few who could not finish their fifty missions. Occasionally a firm hand and voice accomplishes more than subtle psychotherapy."[12]

In March 1944, however, even a "firm hand and voice" could not prevent the weather from causing many missions to be aborted or limited in range. Nevertheless, the "fair haired boys" bombed targets in the Italian cities of Rome, Anzio, Padua, Turin, San Giorgio, Cassino, Villaorba, and Verona. On longer ranging missions, they struck Klagenfurt, Austria, and Sofia, Bulgaria. Losses were suffered, but certainly not as many during the brutal string of missions endured in February.

April brought slightly better, if still unusually wet and cool, weather, more opportunities for deep-strike strategic targets in support of the Combined Bomber Offensive, and the arrival of Tune and his crew. According to the group's official history, Tune's crew found a group enjoying "very good" morale, despite a series of false alarms of air raids during the middle of the month. "This can be attributed to the relatively few personnel losses, decreased enemy resistance—flak and particularly fighters, good food, increase in PX rations, notably candy, beer, and cokes, and the clubs, both officers and enlisted."[13] Reports of venereal diseases declined, mosquito nets and atabrine tablets kept malaria under control, and competition in the softball league among the group's squadrons was "keen."[14]

The 20th Squadron's official history, penned by Captain James A. Clark, the squadron's intelligence officer, offered a chattier look at the latter half of April as he shared personal insights about life on the ground at Amendola in addition to reports on the squadron's missions in hostile skies elsewhere. The following are some of the entries he penned in the squadron's "War Diary" for the middle and latter part of the month.

"April 8. Non-operational. The highlight of the day was music coming over a loud-speaking system that has been set up by communications. We can now hear music all over our area."

"April 10. Non-operational. A very rainy day. The mess hall personnel are trying their skill at a few pies, and they aren't doing badly. We haven't had any pies in some time. However, it would take a master-mind to create a masterpiece from this dehydrated stuff that we are issued."

"April 12. The 176th mission was to Fishamend A/C Factory, Austria. Good coverage of target, many fires and much smoke were observed. Only a few fighters were encountered. The flak was heavy but our Group did not encounter any, the other groups seemed to be getting [their] share. Today the USO put on a stage show for the Group. The Officer's Club imported an Italian orchestra to play at their Club, the orchestra was from Naples. For four straight nights we have had RED alerts, no aircraft sighted or bombs dropped."

"April 14. Non-operational due to inclement weather. The Group flew a practice mission led by Lt. Col. Ryan. Today the personnel were issued mosquito netting and have been taking Atabrine tablets the last few days. We are in the HOTTEST malaria spot in this theatre."

"April 16. Target, Brosov A/C Factory, Rumania. Target completely covered over and bombs jettisoned in the Adriatic. We are not having any fresh meat these days. Some say the reason is lack of ice for storage, some say lack of ships because of invasion plans. No matter what we are on the short end."

"April 18. The Group today had a practice mission for 7 a.m. briefing. Weather is very nice. A softball league among the different Sqdns. of the Group has been formed and games will get under way soon. The communication's loud speaker has plenty of volume, we will know by heart the few records they have managed to secure."

"April 20. Mission for today, Castilfranco M/Y's, Italy. Target overcast and no bombs were dropped. During the evening a B-17 of the 97th Bomb Group caught fire on the line. It was loaded with bombers at the time. Luckily no one was injured as they had time to get away before the ship exploded."

"April 24. Operational, Ploesti M/Y's, Rumania, fair pattern in the target area, it was clear en route and over the target for a change. There were 49 to 50 ME 109's in the air but they were not very aggressive. Over the target a large amount of smoke was observed. In the line of sports, today the 20th Officers' soft-ball team was beat, however, the 20th Squadron enlisted men's team is still undefeated."

"April 26. Non-operational, it started raining early in the day and never let up. Only routine office duties carried out."

"April 27. Today again a mission was scheduled but called off due to bad weather. The rain again today was an all-day affair."

"April 30. Operational. Reggio Emilia A/D, Italy, all the bombs fell to the left of the briefed target area. Here in the camp area we have had more high winds, these winds seem to come from no where."[15]

All in all, as far as Tune could tell, the war seemed to be going rather well at Amendola in April 1944. Then again, he still had yet to fly his first combat mission. But even with the time needed for the former B-24 pilot to find his way into the cockpit of a B-17, that first mission was only days away.

6
Mortal Arithmetic

Bill Tune

In the spring of 1944, when the Fifteenth Air Force welcomed Bill Tune to its fold, it required its pilots and aircrews to complete 50 combat missions. Initially, whether a mission was a so-called milk run against a nearby soft Italian target or a nerve-wracking long-distance raid against a flak-encircled fortress such as Vienna, each mission had counted for one credit. The conferral of such credit assumed that the mission was completed successfully. Aborted missions, whether caused by individual maintenance difficulties or operational obstacles such as bad weather, did not count toward a crew's total.

Not surprisingly, the stress of such a calculus threatened to weigh heavily on the men called upon to complete it. The group medical history, penned in June 1944, candidly recognized such stress. "Probably the greatest chores for the flight surgeons have been those combat men who have required psycho-therapy in order that they might complete a reasonable period of combat duty," the history recorded. "Our chief objective has been to keep the flying personnel physically and mentally fit so that maximum bombing effort could be maintained at all times."[1]

"We believe 50 combat missions is a fair goal for combat men to shoot at," the report continued. "By giving them a certain number of missions to complete gives them more incentive than flying them for an indefinite period. Also, fewer men will bother the flight surgeon if he knows the flight surgeon expects him to fly 50 missions. A certain few cannot complete 50 missions because of anxiety or for physical reasons."[2] By June, the group could tally approximately 2,600 men and officers who had flown on combat missions. Eleven had been sent to the Medical Disposition Board for physical reasons; another 20 were boarded for anxiety neurosis.[3]

Shortly after Tune arrived in Italy, he benefited from a compassionate shift in the local arithmetic. Starting in May of that year, the Fifteenth Air Force began granting double credit for long-distance raids on targets located above the 47th parallel of north latitude and/or east of the 23rd line of east longitude. This new calculus meant that crews received two-for-one credit for missions against such despised targets as Munich, Vienna, Budapest, and Ploesti and, with fifty missions complete, would be able to return home.

Tune's first step toward his fiftieth mission came on April 30, 1944. Surprisingly, his first combat mission was also the first time he sat behind the controls of a B-17. Given the exigencies of wartime operations at Amendola, there was no time or resources to devote to a more formal transition or to even allow Tune to make some local, noncombat training flights. "It was obvious that they had a critical need for pilots," Tune noted philosophically. "My first flight in a B-17 was my first combat mission. But that was okay—I had been requesting to fly B-17s at every step through flight school. I guess I finally got my wish."[4]

Fortunately, fate smiled on the inexperienced pilot that day. The group drew a milk run for Tune's combat debut—a raid on the enemy airdrome at Reggio Emelia, some 72 miles northwest of Florence. The 2nd Group's recently promoted group operations officer, Lieutenant Colonel Donald H. Ainsworth, led the 37 bombers that the group sent aloft to join their comrades in the 97th Group. For his part, Tune flew as copilot at the right hand of the 20th Squadron's commander, Major James G. Ellis.

Neither enemy flak nor hostile fighters challenged the group as it winged over Reggio Emilia at 23,350 feet. While German crewmen and pilots, interrupted mid-lunch, sprinted to their air raid shelters, Tune's bombardier joined with 34 others (two planes had developed maintenance problems and aborted) to rain 50.28 tons of 20-pound fragmentation bombs across the airfield complex. An after-action review was unimpressed with respect to the group's accuracy that day but the group's historian still managed to capture the bright side of the mission.

"One would have thought that the war was over, for there wasn't even the slightest resistance of any kind and all the combat crews returned with broad smiles on their faces," he wrote.[5]

Back safely at Amendola, as he worked the bomber's throttles to steer the big beast, Ellis maneuvered the bomber off the runway and onto its parking stand. He then killed the engines in rapid succession with quick twists of his wrist and turned to Tune.

"Tune, you were lucky—you had a good first trip," the squadron commander said. "But don't kid yourself—they won't all be like this one."[6]

Ellis was absolutely correct, as Tune discovered on his next mission. In the meantime, he garnered an additional local training flight. Still, with his group raining blows against targets ranging from the Romanian oil refineries to the German army headquarters at Monte Sorate, Italy, Tune knew that it would not be long until his next combat mission. Official word of that mission came on May 17, when the lieutenant read his name on the squadron headquarters' alert board. His typed name on the white piece of typewriter paper declared that he would be flying into combat the next day.

Another milk run, he wondered?

No such luck.

The next morning, when the group's operations officer pulled back the curtain concealing the oversized map of Europe hanging in the mission briefing room, the pilot sitting on the bench next to Tune gasped and, in one simple phrase, captured the feelings of every airman in the room.

"Oh, God, Ploesti."

Wasting little time, the briefers confirmed everyone's worst fears. The day's target was Romania's Ploesti railroad marshaling yards, where tanker cars full of refined oil and petroleum congregated. Flak would be heavy, enemy fighters likely, and the weather probably poor. Adding to the bombers' difficulties, the defenders would probably set afire a collection of large oil-filled pots arrayed around Ploesti's outskirts. Once aflame, the pots would mask the target in thick, black, impenetrable smoke.

Fortunately, ever since April, a select number of the Fifteenth Air Force's bombers were equipped with the H2X "Mickey" pathfinder radar system. The H2X system was a self-contained system transmitter-receiver, operated by a specially trained crewman. It transmitted a beam that scanned the ground in front of the aircraft and produced a map-like image of the terrain on a cathode-ray tube that could be used to guide the bomber onto target. Once the radar operator confirmed that they were over the target, his bombardier would simply toggle the payload. The aircraft flying in trail would, as soon as they spotted the falling bombs, do likewise. The Americans called this bombing method "pathfinder force" bombing, or PFF. It lacked the precision of the vaunted Norden bombsight, of course, but, when faced with targets such as Ploesti, strategic necessity trumped precision.

Once again, Tune flew as a copilot, and once again Ainsworth led the group. On this particular mission, however, Tune flew with Second Lieutenant John J. Janicek. Janicek's entire crew from the States, with the exception of his bombardier who had been flying in the lead plane that day, had perished in a midair collision seven weeks earlier on a mission against Sofia, Bulgaria. Janicek had fallen ill that morning and was thus not with the rest of his crew when another B-17, caught in another bomber's prop wash as they maneuvered through the IP, smashed down on top of them. Both planes disintegrated, leaving 20 unidentifiable bodies to be buried in a mass grave in Kasbarevo, Bulgaria. Now, like so many other orphaned pilots and crewmen, Janicek was working toward his 50-mission total flying with whomever the squadron assigned.

Today, Janicek's luck held once again. About one hour into the flight, the formation received a change in mission. Ploesti, a terse radio message reported, was completely clouded over. Instead, the group winged toward its alternate target of Belgrade, Yugoslavia, and the city's railroad marshaling yards. Tune imagined scores of airmen sighing with relief at the change in plans.

The cloud cover remained unbroken as the formation approached Belgrade. "Mickey" would have to be used here as well to put the bombers' payloads on—or at least near—their targets. As the stream of bombers passed the IP and straightened out into their bomb run, Bill saw flashes sprinkling the sky in the distance. Almost instantly, each flash morphed into an ugly black ball of smoke.

"Congratulations, Tune," Janicek barked, "you are going to experience your first flak." "But believe me, this is light."[7]

Undeterred by the flak, Janicek kept his bomber locked in formation. Fortunately, no shells burst near them and, a few moments later, Tune heard the bomb bay doors open. Then a tumbling line of bombs stringed out of the group's lead bomber, signaling for Tune's bombardier to toggle his own payload. The B-17 bucked upward as the 500-pound bombs fell toward the unseen Yugoslavian capital below. Then came the dash for home.

After Tune and Janicek maneuvered the B-17 into its parking position and completed the postflight checks, Tune climbed down out of the Fortress. Rather than climb in the jeep waiting to take him to the group's debriefing, he strolled over to examine the commotion surrounding a nearby bomber. Two trucks parked alongside the aircraft while the ground crew, swarming like ants, clambered atop and around it.

As Tune walked closer, he noticed a swath of jagged holes that pocked the bomber's aluminum fuselage. Those sporadic holes, he realized, were the handiwork of the German flak gunners around Belgrade. If any one of the pieces of flak that caused those holes had struck an engine, a fuel or hydraulic line, or the cockpit, the results would have been catastrophic. And there was not a thing the pilot or crew could have done about it. Pure chance seemed to separate the quick and the dead—just as Janicek had learned the morning sickness had grounded him. An experienced, talented pilot, Tune reflected, could stay tucked up tight in the formation, make a perfect bomb run, and count on the most alert crewmembers in the world to fend off enemy fighters. But at the end of the day, he decided, it mattered little if a silver-dollar-sized piece of flak shrapnel cut through that pilot's bomber at the wrong place and at the wrong time. It was a sobering thought but, nevertheless, Tune had completed his second mission. Now he had 48 to go.

Tune flew his next mission the very next day, bombing railway and highway bridges near the Italian city of Rimini in an effort by the Fifteenth Air Force to disrupt the German supply lines feeding their forces arrayed against the advancing Allies. Another local training flight followed and then, in his fourth combat mission, the group took off to raid enemy troop formations near Avezzeano, Italy, on May 22. They had to abort, however, when they found the target covered in clouds. Disappointed, the Flying Fortresses returned home after several unsuccessful passes over the target, leaving only the flutter of 10,000 propaganda leaflets in their wake. Aborted missions, as they all knew, did not count toward their 50 missions.

The Avezzeano mission did, however, prove that Tune was capable of commanding his own bomber. That opportunity came the very next day when, on May 23, the group sallied forth to attack German columns in the vicinity of Ferentino. Heavy cloud cover concealed the German units fleeing from the Cassino battle zone, however, and once again the group's bombers had to be content with carpeting the vicinity in thousands of propaganda leaflets.

May 24 brought Tune his third mission in three days—this time against an aircraft factory in Atzgerdorf, Austria, a suburb of Vienna. The factory at Atzgerdorf symbolized how Austria was, in the wake of devastating raids on the Wiener Neustadt complex, dispersing its aircraft manufacturing, assembly, and repair facilities. Dispersed did not mean undefended, however, as the group soon discovered.

Thirty-two of the group's B-17s arrived over the cloud-covered target guided by a radar-equipped Pathfinder aircraft. A dense cloud of bursting flak challenged the incoming bombers' passage. Flak hit 19 of the B-17s, damaging two of the planes severely. Flights of *Luftwaffe* fighters menaced the formation from afar but, thanks to the presence of the P-51 Mustangs flying in escort, kept their distance. Tune returned from the mission—which lasted nearly seven hours—unscathed and, thanks to the distance to the target, able to claim two-for-one credit for the mission.

The month of May ended in a flurry of four more missions for Tune. He accompanied the group's bombers on strikes against the Venissieux railway marshaling yards at Lyon, France, the St. Etienne marshaling yards, the Avignon locomotive repair facilities, and the Wollersdorf Airdrome near Wiener Neustadt, Austria, where the Germans staged their newly assembled fighters. Flak was heavy but relatively inaccurate over Wiener Neustadt. Perhaps, the American pilots dared hope, their raids were beginning to take their toll on the Germans.

Meanwhile, back in Amendola, sporadic episodes of entertainment provided welcome breaks from the press of missions. An almost Biblical onslaught of grasshoppers in mid-May had sparked a counteroffensive by Amendola's pesticide-spraying, boot-crunching American residents so organized and energetic that it warranted mention in the group's official history.[8] Movies in the Cave Theater kept the men entertained, as did the start of regular excursion's to nearby Manfredonia's beach.

June began on a relaxed note for Tune, if not necessarily for all of his comrades in the group. From June 2 through June 11, the 2nd Bombardment Group participated in Operation Frantic, a series of "shuttle" missions that allowed the U.S. bombers to bomb enemy targets deep in eastern Europe and then fly on to refuel and rearm at Soviet bases in the Ukraine. Although Tune did not participate in Frantic, he took full advantage of the break in normal operations to log local training flights. Thanks to seven local training flights between May 30 and June 10, Bill accumulated another 20 hours in the cockpit.[9] In the interim, Amendola received the heartening news that Rome had fallen on June 4 and, that, on June 6, the Allies had landed in Normandy to begin the long-awaited liberation of France.

The end of Operation Frantic brought a return to a more regular operational tempo for the group. In the latter half of June, Tune flew missions against the Oberpfaffenhoffen airfield outside of Munich, Germany; the large Koolaz and Fante crude oil refineries near Budapest; and the railway marshaling yards in Parma, Italy. The Budapest mission proved a difficult one, complete with heavy flak and aggressive enemy fighters. Several B-17s were damaged and one from the 49th Squadron was shot down.

At the morning air mission briefing of June 23, Tune again heard the dreaded word "Ploesti." Although the Fifteenth Air Force had been pounding Ploesti since April, the Germans and Romanians still defended it gamely. This day's raid proved no different. As the group approached the city, it found it was covered by smoke screens and blanketed with clouds of flak. Unable to locate its primary target, the Dacia Romano Oil Refinery, the group dropped its bombs on targets of opportunity within the city proper. Wheeling around, the bombers raced for home, keeping wary eyes on the small groups of Bf 109s prowling the periphery and ready to pick off stragglers. But none straggled, and all made it home.

Meanwhile, life on the ground at Amendola settled into what passed for routine. The group's medical section dutifully filed a medical history for the unit that month. It provided an informative perspective on life at the air base.

"Clothing and medical supplies are satisfactory," the report read. "PX rations are excellent, including some four or five candy bars weekly, gum, beer, Coca-Cola, toiletries, cigarettes, and cigars. Movies are shown three days a week with four performances each day. Some films are old, some new. Boxing bouts two times weekly, frequent softball and volleyball games, target practice, and horse-shoes. Frequent dances for officers and enlisted men with nurses, WAC(s), and Italian girls attending—but always too few in number."[10]

Combat missions, however, were plentiful in mid-1944. For Tune, the final week of June brought missions against oil storage facilities in Sete, France, the Schwechat oil refinery in Vienna, and Budapest. The latter degenerated into an aerial battle with nearly 40 aggressive German fighters—more than Tune had ever seen. The enemy fighters and Budapest's flak batteries damaged three bombers and downed one of the 49th Squadron's Flying Fortresses. All in all, however, the group counted itself lucky to escape with such light casualties. It also gave as good as it received, shooting down nearly a quarter of the *Luftwaffe* pilots that took to the air in Budapest's defense.[11]

The month ended with a failed mission to Blechhammer, Germany, aborted for bad weather as the group neared Hungary's Lake Balaton. But even as Tune rested on a rare day without flying on June 28, he could not escape from the reminders of his work's occupational hazards. An errant P-38 Lightning fighter slammed into the ground just south of camp, leaving little more than a scorched patch of earth on a dusty Italian hillside.

July brought better flying weather, more missions, and, on the ground back in Amendola, hotter temperatures. Although the discovery and reactivation of a local ice cream factory added a taste of home at Amendola, ice cream could only do so much. A sympathetic chain of command, faced with a canceled mission and record highs on the first of the month, issued each man in the group four cans of warm, weak beer. But even after nearly two years in the AAF, Tune still had not acquired a taste for alcohol. Thirsty friends ensured that his four cans did not go to waste.

July brought more than ice cream and beer, of course. For Tune, first came a mission against the Almas Fuzito oil storage and refinery complex in Hungary, diverted due to bad weather to Gyor's railway marshaling yards. Then came raids on railway car repair shops in Arad, Romania, and, on July 4, 1944, against an oil refinery in Brasov, Romania.

As if the heavy flak over Brasov refinery was not enough, the group erupted into a spontaneous celebration of the Fourth of July at approximately 2200 that evening. Only threats from the group commander over the camp's loudspeakers succeeded in extinguishing the revelry. A nearby wheat field, set ablaze by falling shells, was the only casualty of the holiday.[12]

Fourth of July festivities aside, the Brasov mission marked a particularly noteworthy milestone for Tune. Not only had he survived two months in the combat theater but, with the double-credit awarded for the Brasov raid, he now had over half of the missions completed necessary for rotating home. Twenty-six down, and 24 to go.

At the time, Tune's concern for or understanding of the strategic rationale behind those previous targets' selection could be summarized very simply—"not at all," he said. "We barely even knew the squadron and group commanders and staff."[13] But from an academic perspective, a review of Tune's logbook reveal a pattern of missions that underscored the strategic debate being waged between the Transportation Plan advocates and the AAF strategists who believed oil was what one French statesman termed "the blood of victory."

Tune flew against 19 targets from April 30 through July 4, 1944. Some were aborted, while others garnered him two-for-one credit. In the sense of general categorization, those targets could be summarized as follows. Two missions were flown against an enemy airfield. Five targeted railroad marshaling yards (although the original targets for two of those missions were oil related). One targeted railway bridges. Two were flown against enemy troop movements or positions. Two missions struck aircraft factories. Another mission bombed a railroad locomotive factory. Five struck oil refineries or oil storage facilities.

As July progressed, Tune kept at it, leaving strategic considerations to be debated at loftier levels than his hut at Amendola while he steadily added to his number of completed missions. He flew missions against railway marshaling yards in Verona, Italy; Vienna's Vosendorf oil refinery; Budapest's Fanto oil refinery; and Ploesti. The month ended with a raid on the Manfried Weiss armament works near Budapest and then, once again, Ploesti. Other squadrons in the group suffered casualties on the Ploesti raid, but Tune's 20th Squadron seemed to be leading a charmed life. In fact, in the entire time he had been flying combat missions, the squadron had only lost two aircraft, downed on a single mission against well-defended Blechhammer, Germany, on July 7, 1944.

Nevertheless, the Blechhammer mission struck close to home to Tune. Although Tune did not draw duty on that particular mission, his tent mate and friend Harold Tomlinson did. So did Tune's navigator, Ralph Mooney, who joined the crew of Second Lieutenant William Nabinger for the mission. Tomlinson's and Nabinger's crews were but two in the 2nd Group tasked with attacking the city's South Oil Refinery. Although still under construction, the synthetic oil plant was producing 500,000 tons of oil annually, making it the third most productive oil facility in the Third Reich. If the American bombers could knock out the refinery's gas generators, the plant would be inoperative for at least six months.[14]

The Germans, of course, intended to put up a stout fight to protect such a precious target. While the group was still 34 minutes away from the target, a force of between 40 and 60 German fighters attacked the oncoming bombers. After unleashing a salvo of rockets at the American formation, they closed boldly with the Flying Fortresses. Hammering volleys of .50-caliber fire from the bombers' gunners met their onslaught and, for a few brief moments, each side traded machine-gun rounds and cannon shells.

Swooping past Tomlinson's B-17, the German fighters blasted his bomber's tail section, raking it with machinegun and cannon fire. Kneeling at his position behind the tail gun, Corporal Joseph B. Cash Jr. never had a chance. His first combat mission became his last. Other shells claimed Sergeant Philip J. McQuaid in the ball turret and killed the bomber's radio operator, Staff Sergeant Henry F. O'Neal. The waist gunners barely had time to report massive damage to the tail section before another fusillade of German gunfire killed them. In the cockpit, Tomlinson knew that his badly damaged plane, now on fire, was practically defenseless. He ordered his crew to bail out and, after being helped into his parachute by his copilot, did the same. Before the day was over, he was a prisoner of war but nevertheless counted himself lucky to be alive.[15]

Nearby, a Flying Fortress from the 429th Squadron met a similar fate. The other bombers—Mooney's included—soldiered on.

Reaching Blechhammer, the bombers found the target obscured by smoke and the sky above it thick with exploding flak shells. Nevertheless, they stayed on course, dropping some 68 tons of 500-pound bombs on the city. Unfortunately, most missed the target.

The German gunners on the ground, however, enjoyed slightly better accuracy. One crew managed to place a flak shell right into Nabinger's cockpit, blowing off the front of the aircraft in an ugly, violent explosion. Almost immediately, the decapitated B-17 nosed over, stalled, and plummeted to the ground. Some observers claimed to have spotted three chutes emerge from the wreckage. Others saw none.

At any rate, none of Nabinger's crew—to include Mooney—survived. According to German records, Mooney, Nabinger, and two other crewmen were buried initially in Freiderau, Germany, near the mangled bomber's crash site, although Mooney's remains were exhumed following the war and rest today at Zachary Taylor National Cemetery in Louisville, Kentucky.[16]

Tune followed his tent mates to Germany on August 3, 1944, when his thirty-seventh mission took him to the Ober Raderach chemical works in Friedrichshafen, Germany. A last-minute diversion dispatched his squadron's bombers against a target of opportunity—a local highway bridge. Four days later, he returned to Germany to raid one of Blechhammer's oil refineries. Those two raids cost the group two bombers and 20 men. One bomber, damaged by flak over Friedrichshafen, limped into Switzerland and was interned. The other bomber, hit over Blechhammer, crashed in southern Germany. Fortunately, all but one of its crew survived, although they spent the rest of the war in a German *Stalag*.

Other missions for Tune during the first half of August included a raid on German tactical positions near Savona, Italy, gun emplacements outside of Toulon, France, and most dramatic of all, a predawn bombardment of the Cote d'Azur landing beaches in support of the Allied invasion of southern France on August 15, 1944. Major James Ellis flew as his copilot that day. The squadron commander had last flown with Tune on the pilot's first mission back in April. Nevertheless, the lieutenant had plenty to worry about besides Ellis's presence on that particular mission. The need to bomb the beaches between 0700 and 0730 meant that the group would have to take off in the early morning darkness—a nerve-wracking proposition on a crowded runway with 2,780 gallons of high-octane aviation fuel and between 6,000 and 8,000 pounds of bombs on each aircraft.

In the end, the mission—partially fueled by Benzedrine tablets prescribed by the flight surgeons to keep the flight crews awake and alert—was a successful one. It not only provided key air support for the Allied landings but marked a milestone in Tune's own progression as a pilot. Satisfied with the lieutenant's performance, Ellis tasked him to be the squadron's lead pilot. That designation meant that, in future missions, Tune would fly the lead plane and be responsible for keeping all seven of the squadron's Flying Fortresses in formation, on time, and on target.

Tune's first mission as squadron leader came a week later, in a strike against the Wiener Neustadt aircraft factory near Vienna. Braving heavy and accurate flak, Tune's bombers unloaded their payloads high above the smoke-obscured target and hoped for the best. Two days later, on August 26, his squadron of B-17s successfully bombed a bridge and viaduct near Venzone, Italy, blanketing the targets with a lethal carpet of high explosives.

After his safe return from the Venzone raid, Tune completed the routine mission debriefing with the group's intelligence staff. Then, with the late Italian summer sun still hanging high in the sky, he hitched a ride in a weathered jeep bound for the mess hall. With any luck, he thought, he might still be able to catch lunch.

As the jeep bounced along the rutted path and powdered its passengers in fine brown dust, Tune allowed himself to think about the future. For Tune, the Venzone raid marked his forty-seventh mission. Three more missions and he would be able to return home. So far, August had proved to be a very promising month for the 2nd Bombardment Group. In the entire month, enemy gunners and fighters downed only six of the group's bombers. Those numbers, although they represented the loss of sixty men, were less than half of the group's losses in the previous month.

"Group morale . . . was believed to be as high as it could possibly get," declared the group's historical records for August. "This can be attributed mainly to the rapid progress of the ground units on all fighting fronts in the European conflict, particularly in France, where Paris fell on 23 August. Most everyone is tired of the war and wants to go back home (not via India) and these recent successes actually were shots in the arm rejuvenating everyone till you could almost see, written on their faces, 'I'll be home for Christmas.'"[17]

If Tune's luck continued to hold he could be back in Carbon Hill well before then—perhaps even this time next month. But the prospect almost seemed too enticing to consider. Ever the practical pragmatist, Tune quickly pushed those thoughts to the back of his mind. In Amendola, it did not pay to think too far into the future. One never knew what tidings the evening's mission board would bring.

Willard Netzley

For his part, Willard Netzley's memories of the air war reflected a youthful bravado. "When it was a combat mission day," the young bombardier from the California orange groves wrote, "we were all ready and willing to go slug it out with the Nazis until they called it quits."[18]

That was not to say, however, that Netzley was fearless. On the contrary— Netzley had a healthy respect for every mission. "Some [missions] took us over the Maritime Alps," he recalled, "solid granite mile-high plus slabs with hardly a crag or bush, except maybe a tiny cliff dweller's house clinging to the granite. I remember praying, 'Don't dump us on that uninhabitable surface.'"[19]

The ugly black barrages of enemy flak were even more feared. "When the Germans fired their anti-aircraft ack-ack, they made three mid-air separate explosions," Netzley explained. "If the second was further away than the first, you were okay. If they were coming toward you, forget about watching and hit the floor!"[20]

On August 25, Netzley teamed with Robert McCloskey for a mission against an aircraft factory in Brno, Czechoslovakia. The raid was deemed a success, with good coverage of the target and no losses or injuries on the part of the attacking aircraft. After feasting on a dessert of peaches and ice cream that evening, Netzley penned a buoyant letter to his parents and brothers.

"Well, I guess combat is pretty rough," Netzley wrote, tongue firmly in cheek. "Both our co-pilot and tail gunner landed up in the hospital yesterday. The co-pilot hurt his back riding to town on the back of a truck; strained a muscle somewhere around a kidney. The tail gunner shot himself in the leg with his .45 caliber automatic. He was lizard hunting and luckily he was using bird-shot instead of ball ammunition or he would have broken his leg for sure. The medics have all the buck-shot picked out so he should be O.K. in a few days."[21]

"I've completed 18 missions now, the navigator [Charles McVey] is only one ahead of me, he has nineteen," Netzley continued. "I'm hoping the war will be over before I get around to finishing my 50 but if it should last that long I should be finished in a couple more months anyway."[22]

For Netzley, that would soon prove to be wishful thinking.

Joseph Sallings

For his part, Joseph Sallings soon found himself in a different kind of war altogether. On June 16, 1944, the farmboy from eastern Tennessee drew duty for an air strike against the Florisdorf oil refinery in Vienna, Austria. Temporarily leaving the 2nd Squadron to team up with a 49th Squadron crew piloted by First Lieutenant Shelby F. Vaughn on board B-17 No. 42-38089, Sallings took his position as 089's right waist gunner.

The 49th Squadron flew as the group's trail squadron on the mission. It was an unenviable position—particularly when, just north of Hungary's Lake Balaton, between eight and 12 German fighters intercepted the group. Darting and swooping like hungry kestrels, they plagued Sallings and his comrades for nearly an hour as the bombers labored on toward Vienna. Then, as the formation neared the oil refinery, its bombardiers found the target obscured by clouds. A steady barrage of antiaircraft fire from the ground, however, hinted that the B-17s were right on target. Clinging grimly to their course through the ugly black bursts of flak, the Flying Fortresses showered the refinery and the adjacent railway marshaling yards with their bombs and hoped for the best.

Somewhere over Vienna, one of the German flak shells burst too close to Salling's bomber. It knocked out one engine, and Vaughn quickly feathered it. But another engine was damaged as well, and the crippled bomber limped further and further behind the formation as the 49th Squadron raced for home. By the time 089 reached the Yugoslavian border, she was all alone and beginning to lose altitude. The prospect of making it across the Adriatic Sea back to Italy seemed faint, and Vaughn decided to crash-land the bomber some 100 kilometers east of Zabgreb. Sallings and the rest of the crew rode it down with him into an open field.

Vaughn's crew weathered the crash landing without injury and walked to a nearby village for water. In it, they soon came face-to-face with a well-disciplined band of men, most armed with old bolt-action German army rifles.

"Are you English?" the band's leader asked.

"No, we are Americans," Vaughn answered for his crew. Immediately, he could see that the answer was well received.

"We will take you to safety," the leader answered. He soon explained that his men were part of Marshal Tito's partisan force battling the Germans.[23]

For the next two weeks, the partisans led the downed crew through Yugoslavia's mountains. "They were a very efficient outfit, although armed with old German army rifles," Sallings reported. "We stayed with them for 15 days and met many units of Marshal Tito's armies during that time but we never did see him. I liked them very much."[24]

Escorted by their partisan allies, Sallings's crew reached a secret airfield near the Adriatic coast used by the Office of Strategic Services—the World War II precursor to today's Central Intelligence Agency—for supply missions to the partisans. An American transport plane soon shuttled them back from the OSS airfield to Italy.

By July 1, 1944, Sallings and his comrades were safely back in their bunks at Amendola and, before long, they were flying once more. Sallings quickly logged 11 more missions, twice returning home to Amendola in a flak-riddled bomber. Nevertheless, his luck held—for the time being.

Robert Donahue

Upon Robert Donahue's arrival at Amendola, the former CCC worker was quickly immersed in an operational tempo that accelerated throughout the summer. But it was July 9, 1944, against dreaded Ploesti that he always remembered. Years later, over a fish sandwich and a cold beer back in his native Pittsburgh, Donahue recounted the story of his mission against the city's Xenia Oil Refinery to his son.[25] It was, as Donahue recalled, his thirty-fourth mission as a tail gunner and, this time, his bomber sported an experimental 20 mm cannon in the tail rather than its usual .50-caliber machinegun.

For Donahue's crew, the mission began on an ominous note. With the crew late to arrive at their bomber on the flight line that particular morning, they lacked the time to say their usual pre-mission prayer. On this day, it had to wait until they were already airborne. Other aspects of the flight, however, remained true to form for Donahue. As always, he wore a religious medallion under his flight suit for luck and protection. And as always, he became airsick. Donahue admitted that he never flew a combat mission without throwing up.

As the bomber, piloted by Second Lieutenant Thomas H. Hancock, headed for enemy territory, its crew quickly and methodically prepared for the upcoming combat. Crewmen hung parachutes by one clip onto their harnesses, laid first aid kits and flak helmets in convenient locations, and pulled extra ammunition boxes out of storage and placed them near their guns. When the order came to test fire those guns over the Adriatic, Hancock's crew was ready.

No amount of preparation, however, could protect the bomber from sheer bad luck. Mechanical problems began plaguing the bomber's No. 2 engine en route. By the time it reached Ploesti, Hancock could barely keep his B-17 in formation. With their bomber buffeted violently by flak, Donahue and the other gunners could only huddle in their flak helmets and jackets and hope that three engines would be enough to get them over the target. But just before the bomb release point, the No. 3 engine sputtered and quit.

Hopelessly underpowered, the B-17 struggled faithfully over the target. Once over the refinery, bombardier First Lieutenant Edward G. MacCollister, of Syracuse, New York, dropped his payload. He then hurriedly raised the bomb bay doors, hoping to keep the bomber as streamlined as possible. Meanwhile, Hancock pushed the throttles on the remaining two engines forward, redlining the massive Pratt & Whitney engines as he coaxed every bit of power out of them as he strained to keep up with the rest of the group. It was, however, to no avail. The rest of the bombers pulled steadily away, heading for the rally point, or RP, on the far side of the city. Once at the RP, the group would collect its stragglers, turn around, and head for home. Anyone left behind would be easy pickings for the ravenous enemy fighter pilots circling outside the flak barrage—as Hancock well knew.

In the cockpit of his ailing B-17, Hancock made a snap decision. Rather than trailing after the rest of the group toward the RP, he elected to turn and, in effect, cut the corner of the flowing bomber stream's route home. By striking out laterally from the bomber stream, he might be able to catch up with his group after it had circled back around at the RP and was heading for home.

It was a perilous tactic, however. Once Hancock made his turn, he abandoned whatever protection had existed in the wake of the bomber stream. Now his B-17 was truly on its own. It only took a moment for the enemy fighters to capitalize on the opportunity. As if by magic, they materialized to the front of the bomber, sliding past MacCollister's barking chin turret gun as they raked Hancock's plane. Jerking and twisting the controls, he took whatever evasive action he could while his upper turret gunner, Staff Sergeant John E. Butler, of Atlanta, Georgia, sawed a Bf-109 in half with a well-placed sustained burst. The German's comrades stayed in the fight, though, peppering the Flying Fortress with gunfire.

Meanwhile, in the tail of the aircraft, Donahue carefully worked his 20 mm cannon. He waited patiently as the unsuspecting fighters rolled in on the tail and pulled into range. As soon as they did, he opened fire, driving off the shocked enemy pilots with each thunderous burst.

Nevertheless, one Bf 109 pressed home its attack, raking the entire length of the fuselage with devastating cannon fire. Both waist gunners, Sergeant Joseph H. Bernard, of Manchester, New Hampshire, and Sergeant Charles C. Watson, of Jacksonville, Alabama, were wounded in the assault. After being knocked to the deck, the two helped each other back into position and continued the fight. In the meantime, another cannon shell smashed into the gun sight in the ball turret and exploded in the face of gunner Staff Sergeant William D. Winston. Other shells exploded underneath the flight deck, destroying the radios and many of the flight controls. Fragments peppered the navigator's, Second Lieutenant George W. Shuster, of Cleveland, Ohio, flak suit and wounded Butler in the upper turret. Fortunately for Hancock, his stowed parachute shielded him from much of the blast's effects.

Such luck, Hancock realized, was running low. By now, it was clear to him and his crew that their bomber was doomed. A final, fatal blow seemed inevitable. One more pass by the enemy fighters would, without a doubt, bring such a blow.

Before that blow could fall, though, a miracle appeared in the skies over Romania. It came in the form of a streaking formation of P-38 Lightning fighters—what the German pilots fearfully called "the fork-tailed devils." With machineguns and cannons blasting, the American fighter pilots drove off Hancock's tormentors and bought him enough time to intercept the rest of his squadron as it headed back for home. His gamble—for the moment—had paid off.

There was still, however, a long way to go before they reached the safety of Amendola, particularly for the bomber's wounded men. With heating systems shot out and the plane's oxygen system failing, their ordeal was just beginning.

Staff Sergeant Robert R. Kirsch, the radio operator from Pittsburgh, Pennsylvania, worked to apply tourniquets to the wounded waist gunners while he ignored his own wounds. Meanwhile, Donahue pulled Winston out of the mangled ball turret and began to apply first aid to him. Butler, limping on his own hastily bandaged leg, soon joined them, as did the navigator and bombardier.

In the cockpit, Hancock battled to keep up with the rest of his squadron, which had, for its part, faithfully slowed down to keep him in its protective fold. All seemed well until Butler noticed black oil seeping through the cowling on the No. 4 engine. Shortly after the bomber crossed the Yugoslav coast and began to transit the Adriatic, that engine sputtered and died.

Almost immediately, Hancock's bomber began to lose altitude. With only one engine straining to keep the B-17 aloft, a ditching in the sea seemed unavoidable. Desperate to avoid such a disaster, Hancock and Butler tried to restart the No. 3 engine. They had little faith in the effort but, miraculously, it coughed back to life. As it gradually gained power, it managed to help arrest the bomber's descent. Now, the Flying Fortress was skimming the waves, but it was at least holding level.

After a gut-wrenching hour, Hancock piloted the wounded bomber over the Italian coast. He spotted Amendola but, before he could even breath a sigh of relief, No. 3 quit once more. Already so low, Hancock had no hope of trading altitude for time. His only hope was to get the No. 3 engine running again. Once again, his prayers were answered. No. 3 coughed back to life, keeping the B-17 tenuously aloft.

As the Flying Fortress approached the airfield, Butler began firing off every flare he could find to signal their oncoming approach. Meanwhile, Hancock's copilot, Flight Officer Irving Thompson, of Poughkeepsie, New York, frantically cranked down the bomber's landing gear by hand. Moments later, the bomber smacked down hard on Amendola's runway. The emergency brake managed to slow the B-17 down enough for it to survive the wrenching ground loop that capped the fateful flight. In an explosive cloud of dirt and dust, Donahue's thirty-fourth mission came to an end. The following month, he and the rest of his crew received Silver Stars for their gallant fight.

Shortly thereafter, Donahue and his best friend, a ball turret gunner named Frank Rapley, thumbed their way into nearby Foggia. In the wake of missions like the raid on Ploesti, they were not about to forgo a night on the town if opportunity presented itself. And if the opportunity for a good-natured battle with local MPs arose, Donahue and Rapley took it as well.[26]

That evening, after returning from Foggia, an exhausted Donahue immediately flopped into his bunk. Rapley, however, carefully undressed, hung his uniform with care, and crawled contentedly into his bed. He was still snoring comfortably the next morning when Donahue arose to fly as a last-minute replacement on a mission. It wasn't until the next mission—on July 21, 1944—that Rapley flew. This time, Donahue stayed behind while Rapley's mission took him to Brux, Czechoslovakia. In the skies of Central Europe, Rapley's plane fell victim to German fighters. Rapley lost his life, and Donahue had lost a close friend.[27]

Ed Smith

Ed Smith, the former Miami University freshman, flew his first combat mission on June 16, 1944, less than a week after arriving in Italy. He wore the wings of a navigator, and navigators were a scarce commodity at Amendola. Often, bombardiers who possessed rudimentary navigational training had to fly as navigators, leaving the bomb-dropping duties to enlisted crewman appointed as "toggeliers" for a particular mission. A bona fide navigator such as Smith, therefore, could count on flying early and often.

Smith's inaugural flight took him to Vienna, Austria, to strike the Florisdorf Oil Refinery. As the group's trailing squadron fought off the attack of eight to 12 enemy fighters, the rest shouldered their way through heavy flak, only to find the target concealed by clouds. They dropped 42.8 tons of 250-pound bombs through the overcast, hoped for the best, and headed for home. Twenty-eight of the 29 bombers made it back to Amendola, although over half were damaged by flak.[28]

Within the last two weeks of June, Smith logged missions against Ploesti; Sete, France; Vienna; and Budapest, and Blechhammer, Germany. In July and August, his tally continued: Arad, Romania; Brasov, Romania; Montpelier, France; Verona, Italy; Vosendorf, Austria; Ploesti; Verona again; Ploesti again; Munich; Brux, Czechoslovakia; Linz, Austria; Wiener Neustadt, Austria; Budapest; Ploesti two more times; Portes le Valence, France; Le Pouzin, France; Blechhammer again; Gyor, Hungary; Toulon, France; St. Valier, France; Ploesti once again; and one more trip to Vienna.

"On that first mission, you are just sort of ignorant, to say the least," Smith remembered, thinking back to his first raid against Vienna. "You are just waiting. There is tension, but not a lot of fear or fright. But after a few missions, and after hearing about and seeing other crews go down, you realize that it is a dangerous playing field out there."[29]

One of Smith's initial missions to Ploesti underscored how dangerous that playing field could be. As his bomber approached the target, a series of flak shells bracketed the B-17. The storm of shrapnel knocked out one engine and damaged another.

"It was just like someone put on the brakes," Smith remembered. "The rest of the group surged ahead and left us all alone."[30]

Smith's pilot realized that a lone bomber, struggling along on two engines, stood little chance of surviving in the skies above Ploesti. He ordered his bombardier to jettison their bomb payload and, with a sharp bank, headed for home. Even then, everyone on board knew that making it home to Amendola would now take luck more than anything else.

Fortunately, Lady Luck was flying with Smith that day, and she came in the form of a squadron of P-38 Lightnings. "It was the best feeling I ever had, to see those P-38s arrive. It's the one thing I always remember."[31]

The fighter squadron spotted the wounded bomber and moved to cloak it in a protective screen. Flying lazy, sweeping S's through the sky, the fighter pilots managed to stay with the plodding bomber and escorted it all the way to the Yugoslav coast without incident. Once over the Adriatic, Smith's B-17 struggled mightily but, ultimately, safely to reach Amendola. Despite the narrow escape, there was scarcely time for the navigator to catch his breath before being dispatched aloft once again.

Ed Smith, still bouncing from crew to crew, also flew in the group's last mission against Ploesti on August 18. He found himself paired with his regular copilot, Second Lieutenant Howard "Howie" I. Season, while his regular pilot and bombardier, Bill Bullock and John Quinn, manned another aircraft. His regular enlisted crew was enjoying a well-earned respite at rest camp.

"I kicked the night before because Howie and I couldn't fly with Bill and Johnny but it didn't do any good," Smith recalled.[32]

The next morning, with Flight Officer Robert H. Rogers at the controls flying his first mission as a pilot, Smith winged toward Ploesti. Just as Rogers passed the IP and began his bomb run, the first wave of stomach-churning nausea rolled over Smith. For the first time since flight school, he became airsick. The array of charts and tables on his small navigator's table swam fuzzily in and out of his vision as he struggled not to vomit in his oxygen mask.

Meanwhile, Rogers piloted the B-17 over Ploesti. As nearby flak bursts rattled the aircraft, First Lieutenant William E. Chalcroft togglied his payload. Chalcroft's stick of bombs tumbled down into the smoky pall covering the refineries before exploding with ugly orange flashes in the shadowy gloom.

Rogers kept the bomber on a steady course as they cleared the target and then, once past Ploesti, turned for home. The bomber labored faithfully across western

Romania and Yugoslavia and then over the Adriatic Sea. "Well," thought Smith, "another mission over. Every time I had been to Ploesti something always happened, but I guess this is going to be uneventful."[33]

Smith guessed wrong. Seventy-five miles south of Trieste, at an altitude of 15,000 feet, trouble flared both literally and figuratively. A fire broke out in the No. 4 engine, which was the outer engine on the right wing. Smith spotted it at the same time as Staff Sergeant Charles J. Armstrong, the right waist gunner. Both men yelled into their intercoms, warning the pilots of the fire.

Immediately, Rogers responded by nosing the bomber into a steep dive, hoping to extinguish the flames. For 3,000 feet, the B-17 screamed down toward the sea. The fire, however, only burned brighter. By the time Rogers's altimeter registered 12,000 feet, a large hole had burned through the right wing. He considered trying to ditch but, with the wing aflame, he did not want to risk the bomber exploding in midflight. "Abandon ship!" he yelled.

In the navigator's compartment, Smith pulled off his heavy flying boots and reached for the escape hatch. With a violent tug, he yanked its handle to knock out the door pins. As soon as the door was loose, the slipstream ripped it away from the aircraft, pulling Smith with him. In a split second, he found himself tumbling head over heels, some 7,000 feet over the Adriatic, as he struggled to deploy his chest-pack parachute.

Plummeting through the air, Smith yanked at his ripcord—to absolutely no effect. Looking down, he realized that he had been pulling the pack's carrying handle. Relieved, he yanked once more—this time on the rip cord's handle. But still nothing happened.

Scanning his chute pack quickly, Smith realized that his left arm was draped firmly across the top of the chute, thus preventing the pack's spring snaps from opening. He pulled his arm away and gave the pack a solid hit with his right arm. This time, the chute popped open.

"This sounds like a long time but all this happened in a matter of seconds," Smith recalled.[34]

As he floated down, he watched the unmanned bomber plummet downward, its right wing ablaze. As it fell, the wing bent back and broke away from the fuselage, mere seconds before the B-17 smashed into the Adriatic. With a thunderous boom, it detonated on impact, scattering chunks of aluminum and flaming debris across the ocean swells.

As he watched the demise of his bomber, Smith struggled to loosen his clothing, knowing that he would soon be swimming for his life. He began unbuttoning his coveralls while kicking off his shoes and socks. Then, as he neared the water, he tried to unbuckle his chute's leg straps—to no avail. By the time he hit the water, everything seemed to go wrong—an unsurprising outcome in light of the minimal parachute training aviators such as Smith had received. Still affixed to his harness, he found himself being pulled backward through the water as the chute sailed in the wind. In frustration, Smith recalled that a brief training lecture had suggested completing a water landing so that the chute would pull a parachutist forward through the waves.[35]

"I think landing backwards helped save my life," Smith reflected in retrospect. "My feet hit the water and I fell backwards. I unfastened my left leg strap because my right one was still tight. I then unfastened my chest strap. This loosened my right leg and I unbuckled in a hurry. The wind was strong enough to billow up part of my chute and blew me along the water all this time. If I had been facing forward, I could have been pulled along the water face down and probably drowned."[36]

After he struggled out of his chute pack's straps, Smith yanked the cords of his Mae West vest, expecting it to inflate automatically. To his shock, it did not. Instead, the yellow vest remained limply plastered to his flight clothes.

Treading water in the rolling swells, Smith pulled off the vest, slipped out of his heavy flight jacket, coveralls, and electric suit and clothes. "All this time I was swallowing half the sea," he remembered. "I really thought I was going to drown, but I gasped for air when I could. Half the time I gasped for air a wave would come along and I'd get a mouthful of sea water."[37]

Finally disrobed, Smith pulled on his Mae West once more. This time, he began to inflate it manually with puffs of his own breath. After a few exhalations, however, he realized that the vest's valves had been left open inadvertently—which was why the vest had not inflated automatically. Closing them, he resumed his puffing, occasionally glancing up at three B-17s circling overhead. He knew that, in those planes, radio operators were calling back to base and enabling Air-Sea-Rescue operations to fix on the downed crew's position.

As the bombers circled, their waist gunners threw out pairs of inflatable one-man rafts. None fell close enough for Smith to use and, realizing that he was, for the moment, on his own, he ripped open the packet of sea marker attached to his Mae West. The dye turned the water around him a yellowish green and Smith paddled to stay within its boundaries.

After a short but lonely period of time adrift, Smith heard one of his fellow crewmen yelling across the water. He shouted back and, a few minutes later, one of the inflatable rafts bobbed into view. One survivor lay awkwardly in the raft while another clung to its side. Smith paddled over to it—"by then I was pretty well pooped," he recalled—and clutched its side.[38] The raft's buoyancy kept both

Smith and his spirits afloat. The three men began rotating in and out of the raft to give each one a break from the seawater. It was not a perfect vessel, however—the raft had two holes in it—and the trio spent much of their time huffing and puffing to keep the raft inflated.

Eventually, the three B-17s banked away and winged west for the Italian coast. To Smith's relief, a lone twin-engined medium bomber soon arrived on station in their stead. It dropped a larger raft, which fell out of sight. Smith and his comrades began paddling toward where it had dropped as the bomber circled overhead.

Then a PBY Catalina arrived on station, dropped a smoke bomb to signal its landing zone, and splashed down in an open-sea landing barely a hundred feet from Smith's raft. The Catalina's crew threw a rope to Smith and pulled his raft alongside the amphibian aircraft. Smith and his mates clambered on board to join a fourth who had been plucked from the sea individually. In total, they had spent almost two hours in the water.

Meanwhile, another Catalina arrived and rescued the flight engineer, Technical Sergeant Willis M. Church, and two other crewmen. They were the lucky ones. Rogers, Season, and Staff Sergeant John J. Bradley, the plane's left waist gunner, did not survive.[39] Everyone had made it out of the burning plane and successfully deployed their parachutes, but the loss of three of the bomber's ten men was a sobering reminder of the dangers of bailing out over water.

Leaving the scene of Smith's crash, the Catalina then searched for a downed fighter pilot. Unsuccessful and running low on gas, the Catalina headed for Amendola. Arriving at 1830 in a driving rainstorm, it splashed down on the flooded runway. An ambulance met the Catalina and, driving through water up to its hubcaps, took Smith, Chalcourt, and the other survivors to the base hospital, where they spent the next 24 hours under observation. A brief interview by an army newsreel crew followed. Then it was back to the war for Smith.

Loy Dickinson

Loy Dickinson was another navigator who soon discovered that his skills were in high demand in Amendola. Accordingly, the former Boy Scout from Berkeley soon found himself bouncing from aircraft to aircraft with each mission, filling in with different crews as the need for trained navigators arose. He flew his first mission on July 18 against Memmingen, Germany, in a B-17 piloted by First Lieutenant Lawrence S. Grennell.

A week later, Dickinson again flew with Grennell. By then, he had already logged four missions in six days. This day's mission took the squadron to Linz,

Austria, an important center for the manufacture of the Third Reich's *Panzers*. As the bombers winged their way north, Dickinson saw the squadron's lead bomber waggle its wings to signal that it was dropping out of its lead position. Later, he learned that it had developed mechanical problems. The pilot of the bomber flying in the squadron's No. 2 slot dutifully slipped his B-17 into the lead as the erstwhile leader fell away from the squadron.

As the two aircraft orchestrated this maneuver, however, the original lead pilot ordered his bombardier to jettison the bomber's payload. By now, the squadron was past the IP but still short of Linz. Presumably, the pilot wanted to lighten his aircraft's weight so that its laboring engines could keep up with the rest of the squadron as they approached the target. Dutifully, his bombardier jettisoned the bombs.

"Several, shall we say, alert bombardiers saw this as the lead to drop their bombs," Dickinson reported sarcastically. "I recall hitting the bombardier on his shoulder with the heel of my hand and yelling that we were not over the target. He reacted appropriately and did not drop his bombs immediately, but he could see that everyone else was doing so."[40]

"Everyone else" included most, if not all, of the remaining 27 bombers flying for the group that day. With varying degrees of hesitancy, they dropped their bombs—not on the tank works, but in the vicinity of the towns of Pregarten and Hagenberg. Berta Kurz was a 21-year-old Austrian fraulein living with her parents in a small village called Klingerwehr. Five decades later, she recounted the morning's events:

"About 11:00 a.m.—I had just left the shop [in Pregarten] and was on my way home—the siren began to scream. So I turned and went back to the shop, since no one was supposed to be in the street during an air raid. Just after a few minutes I saw the enemy bombers coming in against the blue sky. They could be well seen. First I was not frightened, but suddenly the ground began to tremble, window panes clattered, and heavy detonations were heard . . . from the direction of Hagenberg. Black clouds of dust and smoke rose from there, and they soon covered the sunlight, it got dark like in the evening."[41]

Leaving Pregarten, Kurz scampered down a series of paths into the valley where her parents' village lay. As she ran, she could still hear the noise of plane engines in the sky above her. On the ground, however, all was silent. There was no sound of human life. Not even a bird chirped.

"I was deeply worried about my parents and their house," Kurz remembered. "Luckily there was no one killed or injured in my family. The air pressure had broken all window panes and pushed in all doors. The roof was heavily damaged. Our neighbor's home was nothing but rubble [and] Mrs. Karlinger was dead. Mr. Karlinger [stayed] with us for a while until he moved away from the area. Quite many of the houses that were damaged were not repaired before the end of the war."[42]

Even though the bombers had made it within 15 miles of their target, the premature drop essentially aborted the mission. The abort meant that no mission credit would be granted. For men—particularly the group's enlisted personnel—who had braved the morning's mission only to see it fail through no fault of their own, the lack of credit was a bitter pill to swallow. "After our return several of the pilots went to the group commander to appeal for mission credit for the enlisted crewmen who had no culpability at all," Dickinson reported. "The entreaties fell on deaf ears."[43]

At the time, the airmen's concern for the citizens of Pregarten, Hagenberg, and other bombed cities and villages rated second to the ongoing tally of completed missions. "I did not really think about it," Dickinson candidly admitted years later when asked about the possibility of his missions causing civilian casualties. "When I did think about it, I told myself that we were bombing military targets. We were bombing the enemy. In looking in the rear view mirror, I would think that an older more mature person would certainly consider it. As the saying goes, this was a war of necessity."[44]

In the meantime, Dickinson soldiered on. On August 18, 1944, he flew against Ploesti. Twenty-five B-17s from the group found the Romano-American Oil Refinery, despite the smoke billowing some 15,000 feet into the air from the fires set by a preceding wave of bombers. After Dickinson's bombardier dropped his load of 500-pound bombs through heavy flak, their pilot headed for home, relieved to still be in one piece.

Arriving back at Amendola, Dickinson's pilot guided the weary B-17 onto the runway. Seconds after touching down, however, the plane's right tire blew out. With a wrenching lurch, the bomber edged toward the side of the runway and bore down on a collection of parked aircraft. Dickinson and the navigator, sitting in the chin of the Fortress, watched the unfolding scene in mute terror.

"You could feel the blood draining out of every pore in your body," Dickinson remembered. "There are three missions that I think of every once in a while," he said 62 years later. "This was one of them."[45]

Meanwhile, in the cockpit, the two pilots manhandled their control yokes, trying desperately to keep the bomber on the runway while, with rigid legs, they stomped on brakes. Outside, the wheels squealed in protest as the stench of burning rubber trailed the speeding bomber down the runway.

In the nose, a white-faced Dickinson watched as the group of parked aircraft loomed closer and closer. A fiery crash seemed inevitable—at least until he realized that, almost imperceptibly, the B-17 seemed to be slowing down. But was it an illusion? Before he could decide, the bomber slowed even further, its 36,000 pounds straining forward against the stubborn brakes. The brakes, Dickinson realized, were working. But would they be enough?

In the end, the brakes saved the day. But just barely. The B-17 squeaked to a stop a few feet short of the other parked bombers. From the crew, a collective sigh of relief echoed through its aluminum fuselage as the two pilots finally dared to relax their legs and lift their booted feet off the brake pedals. Disaster had been averted—for now.

⌐⌐

Although Dickinson and Smith did not know it at the time, their mission of August 18 was the last mission that the 2nd Bombardment Group flew against Ploesti. Other AAF groups hit the city the following day, with the RAF adding to the destruction that evening. In the final summation, 59,834 airmen (if one does not count repeat missions) had managed to drop 13,469 tons of bombs on the Romanian city, paying the price of 350 lost bombers to do so. By the time the sun rose on August 20, oil production in Ploesti was less than 10 percent of its original capacity. Within days, invading Red Army troops administered the *coup de grace*.[46]

The impending fall of Ploesti to the Soviets, however, did not even warrant mention in the official histories of the 2nd Bombardment Group or the 20th Squadron. It may have even attracted less attention in the officers' club, mess halls, and tents of Amendola. There still seemed to be plenty of targets elsewhere. On August 20, the group launched a deep strike against the synthetic oil and rubber works of Oswiecim, Poland, garnering the praise of the Fifteenth Air Force's commander the next day for its bombing accuracy. "Close study of bomb strike photos and photo reconnaissance photographs of yesterday's attack show that outstanding success was achieved in destroying these targets," Major General Nathan F. Twining declared. "The attacks of yesterday were the best that this air force has ever achieved. My congratulations to you, your staff and all personnel for this superb performance."[47]

Two days later, determined to repeat the success against Oswiecim, the group hit the oil refineries in Odertal, Germany. A partial smokescreen forced the group to make two passes across the target. Heavy flak claimed one bomber from the 96th Squadron. Then, on the return flight, a swarm of eight Bf 109s pounced on *Big Twidget,* lagging a half mile behind the rest of the formation. The German fighters downed the bomber, although eight of its crew managed to bail out safely. Overall, the bombing results were uncertain, although the group believed optimistically that most of its bombs fell in the target area.[48]

Undeterred by the loss of the two crews over Odertal, the rapid tempo of missions continued for the rest of the month. On August 23, the group raided the Wiener Neustadt aircraft factory in Vienna and, the next day, an airdrome complex in Pardubice, Czechoslovakia. Enemy fighters failed to claim any of the group's bombers and two subsequent missions, against an aircraft factory in Brno, Czechoslovakia, and a railroad viaduct in northern Italy, encountered even less resistance.

On August 27, the group weathered heavy flak to hit the oil refineries of Blechhammer, Germany. Heavy, accurate flak damaged several planes and seriously wounded four men from the 96th Squadron. The following day, on August 28, the refineries of Moosbierbaum, Austria, felt the group's wrath on its 262nd combat mission of the war. Flak gunners managed to damage several more aircraft and wound three men. A fourth, a flight engineer with the 429th Squadron, suffered a fatal heart attack.[49]

Painful as those casualties were to suffer, they paled in comparison to the grim days of the previous winter. The 20th Squadron in particular seemed to be enjoying a lucky streak. With the exception of the loss of Smith's bomber on the final Ploesti mission, the squadron had not lost a single aircraft in the month of August.

Little did the squadron realize, though, that its run of good fortune was hurtling to a calamitous conclusion. For seven of its bombers and 70 of its men, their luck would run out before the month was over, on a mission the 2nd Group simply called "Mission 263," and on a raid against a Czech city of which few had ever heard—Moravska Ostrava.

7

Cry Havoc . . .

"Lieutenant Tune, time to wake up, sir."

Bill Tune opened his eyes cautiously as an unseen hand gently nudged his shoulder. A shadowy figure, standing beside his cot, loomed behind the glare of a flashlight. He could not see the man's face, but he presumed it was one of the operations sergeants from squadron headquarters. Tune knew it was still early in the morning—or late in the night, depending upon how one looked at things—and his head cleared slowly. Some men struggled to sleep before a mission, but the anticipation never bothered Tune. He had slumbered soundly, even on his canvas army-issue cot.

"Thanks, sergeant. I'm up," Tune said. Glancing down at his watch, he saw its luminous hands read 3:00 A.M. The date was August 29, 1944. "Yeah, I'm up."[1]

Content that Tune was indeed awake, the sergeant slipped out of the door with a quick creak of wood. In the darkness, he continued his rounds through Amendola's winding rows of huts and tents. Meanwhile, in his own crude stone hut, Tune pulled his legs out of his blanket, parted the mosquito netting cloaking his cot, and swung his feet onto the floor. Rubbing his eyes, he reached for his flashlight. He shared the canvas-roofed hut with two other officers from his crew, and with three survivors of another crew, but this morning Tune was the only man awake. Having completed 47 missions, he had been selected as the lead pilot for the seven B-17s that the 20th Squadron would send aloft today. That assignment pulled him from his own crew and cobbled him together with another nine aviators for the pending mission. It was far from the best of circumstances for a pilot simply trying to finish his tour and go home, but Tune knew that worrying would not change anything.

Grabbing the olive drab steel helmet he kept under his cot, Tune partially filled it with cold water, drawing the water from a faucet soldered to a P-38's drop tank. It was a crude arrangement, but such was the indoor plumbing at Amendola, and Tune had no complaints. Balancing his flashlight on his cot, the young Alabamian sat on his footlocker at the end of his cot. With the helmet between his legs and a handheld mirror in his left hand, he scraped at his whiskers with a razor. There were few sticklers for military "spit & polish" in the 20th Squadron at this point in the war, but Tune did not want his oxygen mask chaffing against his whiskers throughout the upcoming flight.

As he shaved, he thought of the mission he would soon be flying. The crew and aircraft scheduling board, updated with information last night, had shown that the bombers would be carrying a full load of fuel. That meant a long flight, and generally the longer the flight, the uglier the mission. Nevertheless, that was not always the case. With any luck, today's target would be a milk run and he would return in the late afternoon with his forty-eighth combat mission to his credit. That would leave only two more to complete before he could rotate back to the States.

Tune's good fortune to date seemed to mirror that of the Allies in general. In western and southern Europe, the Germans were being hammered by General Patton's tanks in Normandy, the Allied landings in southern France, and the assault on Gothic Line north of Florence, Italy. The situation was even worse for the *Wehrmacht* on the Eastern Front, where a Red Army offensive in the Carpathian Mountains capitalized on Romania's sudden defection from the Axis camp and threatened to break through the battered German lines into Slovakia and Hungary. In Romania itself, hard-riding Cossacks and Red Army tankers already had the oil derricks and refinery towers of Ploesti in sight.

"Russian Armies Nearing Ploesti As Enemy Totters," headlines from the *Birmingham News* promised its readers back home on August 29. "Historic Chateau-Thierry and Soissons Are Seized," even larger headlines declared. "Yankees Occupy Scenes of Great Battles in 1918."[2]

Not to be outdone, DeWitt MacKenzie, an Associated Press "war analyst," offered his own prognostications. "The speed at which the Allied mechanized forces are advancing and cutting the Germans to pieces in France, in a warfare of amazing fluidity, is impressing observers with the possibility that the retreating Nazis may arrive on their own frontiers in such disorganized state as to precipitate chaos within the Reich itself," he warned gleefully.[3]

Such prognostications were, however, far from Tune's mind. His immediate goal was to make it through the day's mission. To that end, Tune continued with his daily morning ritual. Trying not to disturb his sleeping comrades, he pulled two pairs of woolen socks onto his feet. Then came his long underwear over his underwear and t-shirt, followed by his cotton flight suit. Tune knew that it would likely be another hot, dusty, late summer day in southern Italy. In a few short hours, however, he would be flying above 20,000 feet over the Alps, where the temperature would plummet to 20 to 50 degrees below zero Fahrenheit in his unpressurized aircraft. Tune intended, therefore, to dress accordingly. He would don his fleece-lined flight trousers and jacket at the equipment shed near the flight line.

Next, Tune emptied his pockets, leaving his wallet and other miscellaneous personal effects in a small pile on his cot. This was a standard operating procedure for the group's pilots. They did not want any additional intelligence falling into enemy hands should they be shot down and captured. Besides, a German soldier shouldn't profit from Tune's misfortune. Thinking of such things, he made sure he had his .45-caliber automatic pistol he carried in his leather shoulder holster. But if he needed that pistol, he admitted to himself, he was in deep trouble.

Sitting back down on the edge of his cot, Tune tugged on a pair of GI brogans and laced them in the dark. Once clothed, he grabbed his scarf and cap and, taking the helmet of water in hand, stepped out of the hut and into the heavy darkness of the predawn. Tune emptied the helmet by the side of the hut away from the door, returned it underneath his cot, and then stepped back outside once again. The camp operated under a blackout in the unlikely event of a German air raid, but Tune didn't need lights to find his way to the latrine and then to the mess hall.

The group's mess hall was a wooden structure, crowded but comfortable. Once inside, Tune stepped into a quiet line of men. He shuffled forward to receive an unappetizing dollop of powdered eggs accompanied by toast and fried Spam. Tune poured himself a glass of orange juice and found a seat at one of the tables.

For the next few moments, Tune sipped on his orange juice and pushed the eggs and Spam around his plate. He knew that the Italians outside the airfield's gates would envy such a meal, but he hesitated to eat or drink too much before a flight. Peeling off layers of clothes to relieve oneself in a freezing aircraft was never an easy affair. He took a few more sips of juice, nibbled on some toast, and finally stood up. He deposited his tray and plates with the KPs standing by the steaming kitchen, stepped back outside, and hiked over to the group's operations room.

The group's staff had placed its operations room in a cave-like limestone quarry carved out of one of the low-lying hills near the bivouac area. Stepping through the cave's steel door, Tune flashed his ID card to a bleary-eyed MP. The MP nodded perfunctorily, waved him through the entrance, and checked his name off a roster on a clipboard.

Squinting his eyes against the harsh glow of the light bulbs, Tune entered the cave. A fetid locker-room odor assailed his nostrils as he stepped inside. It was the smell of nervous fear numbed by bleary-eyed exhaustion. Too many unwashed men had sweated through their pre-mission briefings while sucking on Pall Mall and Lucky Strike cigarettes in the cave. Not all, Tune knew from experience, had returned.

As his squadron's lead pilot, Tune took a seat on one of the front benches, a makeshift affair constructed of planks laid across stacked bricks. He sat with his back to a few dozen fellow pilots, copilots, navigators, bombardiers, and staff officers. A simple wooden platform occupied the end of the cave. A closed curtain at the back of the platform shielded what everyone knew to be a wall-sized map of Italy, the Balkans, and Central Europe. In a moment, that map would answer the morning's great question: "What's the target today?"

From the back of the room, a staff officer announced formally that all officers were present or otherwise accounted for. The cave fell silent as the metallic click of the MP closing the door echoed across the cavern's hewn stone walls.

As soon as he did, another officer called the group to attention. Tune and the other men rose to their feet as Colonel John D. Ryan, the group commander, mounted the platform in front of them. Ryan was a 1938 graduate of the United States Military Academy at West Point, where he had lettered in football. Although not yet 30, Ryan was responsible for four squadrons of B-17 bombers, their aircrews, and their maintenance teams. "We all looked up to him," one 20th Squadron bombardier later remembered. "He was our idea of what a commander should be."[4]

Ryan ordered the silent officers to take their seats. The clock hanging on the wall showed 0415. But rather than eyeing the clock, every man in the room focused on the curtain behind Ryan. With a nod from Ryan, a staff officer tugged at a drawstring and parted the curtains, revealing the map. A series of red lines, written in grease pencil on the massive map, traced a route from Amendola north across the Adriatic, over northern Yugoslavia, into Hungarian airspace, and then into Czechoslovakia.

"Today's target," Ryan intoned in a time-honored format familiar to such briefings, "is Moravska Ostrava, Czechoslovakia." Technically, Moravska Ostrava now lay in what its German overlords had christened the Reich Protectorate of Bohemia and Moravia. Today, known as Ostrau, it is located in the Czech Republic. But prior to Hitler's invasion of Czechoslovakia in 1939, the historic Moravian city sat in eastern Czechoslovakia. Thus, in the lexicon of the Allied crusade to liberate occupied Europe and defeat Hitler, it was still identified as part of Czechoslovakia.

Such political details, however, fell far from the minds of Tune's comrades. To them, Moravska Ostrava was simply a target benign enough to have never warranted an attack until today—and that, as far as they were concerned, was a very good sign. It certainly lacked the infamous reputation of Munich, Ploesti, or Vienna. Tune even heard some men behind him mutter "milk run." Personally, he wasn't so sure. It would be a long flight, with the first leg over a sea spotted with German picket boats ready to radio a warning ahead to their comrades.

Running through the mission's basics, Ryan identified the group's targets as the Privoser Oil Refinery and the Moravska Ostrava railway marshaling yard. Alternate targets were the city's industrial area, the Szolnck marshaling yard, the Szajol yard, and the Ozegled yard. Reading from the operations order transmitted from 5th Wing headquarters the previous evening, Ryan explained the mission's importance.

"Yesterday's most successful attacks put both Blechhammers out for some time," he recited. "Photographs also showed Ploesti virtually destroyed. Thus all major oil installations within our range with possible exception of Brux appear immobilized. Apart from counter air defensive attacks, the primary objective now is to destroy the maximum amount of ground force equipment at closest point to its possible use in the front lines, particularly tanks and motor transport known to be in short supply. These may be found in assembly shops and factories, at depots, and in large central European marshalling yards. Plan for [today] concentrates bulk of force in Moravska Ostrava, where two small refineries clean up bulk of Czech production."[5]

The Fifteenth Air Force, Ryan explained, would be putting over 500 aircraft into the air this particular morning, with the majority hitting Moravska Ostrava. The 2nd Bombardment Group was only one of several tasked with a strike on the Czech city. Within the group itself, the 429th Squadron would take the lead, with Lieutenant Colonel John S. Cunningham flying the lead aircraft. The 96th was to fly right echelon, with the 49th on the left. The 20th would bring up the rear thereby creating what amounted to an aerial box of aircraft.[6]

Tune tried to keep a straight face, but this assignment was not good news for his squadron. The trailing position in the formation—called "Tail End Charlie" by the air crews—was a bad draw. The inevitable straggling of a four-group formation meant that the end of the formation would be ragged and difficult to maintain— the perfect target for *Luftwaffe* fighter pilots.

Completing his portion of the briefing, Ryan directed the officers' attention to the weather officer, who shared his meteorological prognostications with the assembled group. Layers of broken clouds in route and over the target were predicted.[7] His words stoked a low rumble of mumbles. Those clouds could conceal not only the target but also any *Luftwaffe* fighters lurking in ambush among them. On a happier note, the group's intelligence officer predicted limited fighter opposition and reported that only 40 heavy flak guns protected the Czech target.[8]

Major Jacob W. Bigham Jr., the group's operations officer, followed the intelligence officer's briefing. Jabbing at the map with a thin stick of wood, Bigham tapped out a series of waypoints along the group's route to Moravska Ostrava: Pitomaga, Ersekujvar, and Hor Lidec, all eventually leading to Neutitschein, the raid's IP. Navigators scrawled the points into their notebooks, noting the relevant latitudes and longitudes. The bombardiers in the room took particular notice of Neutitschein. At the IP, they would take control of their bombers and guide them in onto the target. Continuing, Bigham announced the bombing altitude would be 26,500 feet, with a time over target at 1102 and an expected return to base by 1420.[9]

With respect to fighter cover, Bigham explained that the 306th Fighter Wing would be providing six groups of P-51 fighters for penetration, target, and withdrawal cover. The 49th Bombardment Wing would attempt to create a diversion for the morning's raid by flying first toward Vienna and Budapest to flush enemy fighters into rising to defend those cities. Rather than proceed on to them, however, the 49th would turn and strike Szeged, Hungary.[10] In the 2nd Group, Bigham continued, the radio call sign for the group would be "Freezol 16," on VHF Channel B, with internal communications within the group on Channel A. Crews were to be on station at their aircraft on the flight line at 0545, taxiing at 0615, and taking off at 0625.[11]

The briefing concluded with a prayer led by the group chaplain. Then Ryan took center stage once more and, after a few quick words of encouragement, called for a time hack. Together, they all pulled back on the stem of their wristwatches and, with a countdown from "10," synchronized their watches with the group commanders.

After the briefing, the pilots and officers checked the crew boards posted along the cave's wall. Tune confirmed that he would be flying aircraft number 42-97159, a Boeing B-17G Flying Fortress, with a crew pieced together from the rest of the squadron. His copilot, he noted with satisfaction, was First Lieutenant Francis W. "Ike" Flynn, an experienced and capable officer. Flynn had been grounded with the flu back in June when the rest of his crew had been blasted out of the skies over Blechhammer, Germany, by a well-aimed burst of flak. Now the orphaned pilot filled in with whatever crews needed a pilot. He had flown with Tune on four previous occasions. Tune and Flynn would be paired with Loy Dickinson, who was now flying as the squadron's lead navigator, with Russell Meyrick as their bombardier. Tune was acquainted with Dickinson, whom he knew to be a thoroughly competent navigator, and had flown with Meyrick on the bombardier's first combat mission. "A wonderful fellow with an excellent personality," Tune later wrote of the bombardier.[12]

The two pilots tracked down the navigator and bombardier in the bustling crowd and exchanged a quick round of handshakes. Together, they stepped back outside the cave, where the sky was still dark, to catch a ride to the aircraft.

Out on the flight line, the ground crewmen's day had already started as well. In the words of one of the group's postwar historians, "If the air war in the Mediterranean was under-sung, then the work of those who toiled long in the grit and grime as members of a ground echelon must be the lost chord in the chorus for unsung heroes."[13] In the early morning darkness, the ground crew responsible for 42-97159—or simply "159," in the crew's abbreviated jargon—conducted a pre-flight inspection of the bomber, test-started its engines, and checked the myriad engine gauges to ensure all was as it should be. In the wrench-wrestling, piston-popping world of the maintenance crew, an aircraft abort due to a mechanical failure on the flight line was the ultimate black mark of shame. Tune knew, therefore, that he would find on the flight line a B-17 in as good a condition as could be coaxed from its weary metal frame.

On the dusty road outside of the cave's entrance, Tune, Flynn, Dickinson, and Meyrick clambered into an empty truck for the bumpy ride out to the squadron's equipment shed on the flight line. A few moments later, the truck turned off the dirt track and alongside the equipment shed. There, sleepy supply sergeants handed out the heavy fur-lined leather jackets, trousers, gloves, and boots that B-17 aviators needed to keep warm at altitude. They also distributed parachutes and escape kits. Each kit contained some chocolate candy bars, a silk map of Europe, a compass, and a shot of morphine. As with his pistol, Tune hoped he would never need it.

A short truck ride followed, this time rumbling along Amendola's steel-matted runway. The aircraft of the 20th Squadron were parked on metal-matted hard stands along the left of the runway; the bombers of the 97th Squadron sat on the runway's right side. Crunching into a lower gear, the truck's driver slowed to a stop alongside the B-17 bomber bearing the tail number 97159 in neat black letters.

This particular Fortress was a battered aluminum beast, accented with black rudders, elevators, wing tips, and rubber de-icing boots. A black "Y" in a circle on her tail fin marked her as one of the 2nd Group's planes. Tune knew she had been shot up rather badly in an earlier mission, but it looked like the ground crews had done their usual yeoman repair work on her, as evident by the carefully crafted square and rectangular patches of metal that dotted her fuselage and wings. A previous crew had painted *Tail End Charlie* on the fuselage underneath the pilot's window.

"Well, they got that right," Tune thought.[14]

Tune and the other three officers piled out of the truck. As they did, the rest of the bomber's crew—a collection of six sergeants charged with flight engineer duties, radio communications, or simply manning the Fortress's machineguns—rolled to their feet. They had been resting under the bomber's wing waiting for the officers' arrival.

In a few short sentences, Tune described the upcoming mission to the assembled crew. They took the news without comment. Instead, they simply nodded before pulling themselves up through hatches in the bombers' fuselage or climbing up the metal frame ladders to the side doors. Dickinson and Meyrick followed to attend to their own preflight tasks, with Meyrick paying a quick visit to the bomb bay to ensure that the payload of twenty 250-pound bombs was secure. Meanwhile, Flynn pulled the massive propellers on each of the bomber's four engines through a complete rotation, ensuring that any water in the fuel lines worked its way through the system.

For his part, Tune and the ground crew chief walked carefully around the aircraft. With each step, the two men eyeballed the bomber. Inside, they could hear the metallic clicks and snaps of the gunners checking out the B-17's thirteen .50-caliber machineguns. The walk-around inspection of the B-17 revealed no problems to Tune's trained eye. He clambered up into the bomber—never an easy job in the heavy flight gear—and squeezed into the cockpit, where he stashed his parachute behind his seat. By then, Flynn was already in the cockpit working through the preflight checklist. He spoke quietly to himself as he checked off items on the list.[15]

"Tail wheel—locked."

"Gyro—set."

"Generators—on."

Tune settled in beside him in the cast-iron seat on the cockpit's left. He slipped his flight helmet onto his head and plugged the helmet's radio plug into the aircraft's intercom system.

"Can you hear me?" he asked into the intercom mike as he tugged on his gloves. He strapped his wristwatch to the outside of the left one.

"Loud and clear," Flynn responded.

Tune pulled out his own checklist. He knew that, in the unseen recesses of the bomber, his crew was completing checklists of their own. After a quick confirmation of the plane's weight and balance calculations, he handed his checklist to Flynn.

"Read them out to me, Ike," Tune said. He was a careful pilot and never did the checklist from memory.

"Controls and seats," Flynn began.

Tune adjusted his seat slightly to his satisfaction. "Check," he responded.

"Fuel transfer valves and switch," Flynn said.

"Off."

"Intercoolers."

"Cold."

"Gyros."

Tune pulled the black knob by the plane's attitude indicator. For a moment, it bobbled wildly but quickly settled. "Uncaged," he confirmed.

"Fuel shut-off switches."

"Open."

And so on.

Meanwhile, as the officers worked, Joseph Sallings took the bomber's right-side waist gunner position. There, he checked the workings of his .50-caliber machine-gun and inspected his oxygen connections. For the former Tennessee farmboy, this was his thirteenth mission. Behind him, Joe Owsianik took position as the left-side waist gunner. Having also drawn duty as the squadron's cameraman for this particular mission, Owsianik had caught an early ride out to the aircraft in a jeep. As the jeep pulled up alongside *Tail End Charlie,* the aircraft's ground crew chief had stepped forward to greet him. The two men were acquaintances.

"Where are you going?" the crew chief had asked Owsianik.

"Can't tell you that," Owsianik had answered.

"That's all right, but if I were you I wouldn't go today. This plane is going down."

"How do you know that?" the airman had challenged.

"I've been working with B-17s since Africa and every one of my planes has gone down after being shot up on its previous mission. No. 97159 was shot up several weeks ago—its last mission."

"This mission looks like it will be a milk run," Owsianik had replied with as much bravado as he could muster. The crew chief could only shrug in reply.[16]

A few moments after Owsianik's arrival, Robert Donahue, the tail gunner, and Staff Sergeant Robert Kirsch, the radio operator, reached the aircraft. The loss of three wounded men over Ploesti from their original crew the previous month had effectively broken up their crew. Now they found themselves assigned to fill out random crews as the squadron's operational needs dictated.

The remaining two men of *Tail End Charlie*'s crew had joined Donahue, Kirsch, and the others at the aircraft shortly before the officers arrived. Technical Sergeant Thomas C. Coogan, the bomber's flight engineer, hailed from New Orleans. Sergeant Joseph Marinello, the ball turret gunner, called Brooklyn home.[17] Coogan, as flight engineer, would man the upper turret guns in flight. For takeoff, however, he pulled himself up into the cockpit and, with watchful eyes glued on the array of gauges in front of Tune and Flynn, assessed the preparations for engine run-up.

In the cockpit, once the initial items on the checklist were completed, Tune confirmed with Kirsch that all the radio frequencies were set. Then a quiet moment of relaxation descended on the cockpit—but only for a moment. With a glance at his wristwatch, Tune confirmed it was time to start the engines.

"Okay, let's go," he told Flynn. Without being asked, Flynn started again with the checklist.

"Alarm bell," Flynn began.

Tune rang it. It worked. "Check."

"Wheel chocks."

Tune look to his left underneath the left wing. The chocks were still snugly against the fat black tires. "In place," he said.

"In place on the right," Flynn added. "Fire guard and call clear."

Tune stuck his arm out the window, his thumb up, and gestured at the ground crew chief. He was standing in front of the plane with a fire extinguisher in hand. "Clear," Tune yelled.

The crew chief returned the call with a shout of "clear" and a thumbs-up signal. Flynn continued.

"Master switches."

Tune quickly flipped the switches across the top of the control panel pedestal forward. "On," he declared.

"Battery switches and inverters."

Again, more quick flicking of switches. "On." Tune confirmed the readings on his voltmeters. "Checked," he added.

"Parking brakes—hydraulic check—on," Flynn read.

"On," Tune said.

"Booster pumps—pressure."

"On and checked."

"Carburetor filters." Flynn answered this one, as per the checklist's requirements. "Open," he said aloud. Then he read the next item.

"Fuel quantity."

"What do you show, Ike?" Tune asked. The fuel quantity gauge was on the instrument panel directly in front of the copilot.

"Two thousand seven hundred and eighty gallons," Flynn answered. They had a full set of tanks.

"Okay, then," Tune said. "Let's go."

Flynn continued reading the checklist. "Start engines—Fire extinguisher engine selector." Flynn answered this one also. "Checked."

"Energize."

"Energized."

"Mesh."

With his right hand, Tune reached for the ignition switches on the control panel. He flipped them confidently.

With a belch of white smoke from their cowlings, *Tail End Charlie*'s massive engines rumbled to life. As soon as the propellers completed one revolution, Tune flipped on the magnetos.

"Flight indicator and vacuum pressures," Flynn called out.

"Check."

Flynn looked back down at the checklist. "Radio," he said. This was another of the copilot's responsibilities. He turned it on. "On," he told Tune.

"Check instruments."

Jabbing at each gauge with gloved fingers, Tune and Flynn assured themselves that they were satisfied with the engine temperatures, oil pressures, voltages, and hydraulics. "Check," Tune told Flynn. "Check," Flynn responded.

"Crew report," Flynn said.

"Roger," Tune replied. He flipped his intercom to transmit to the crew. "Crew, report." In carefully measured tones, the responses flooded in, identifying each position and announcing, "check."

With the crew check complete, Flynn continued with the checklist. "Radio call and altimeter set," Flynn read. This time, Tune ignored him. A radio call would have been appropriate in peacetime, but the 2nd Bombardment Group was not going to break radio silence by calling the control tower for altimeter settings. Instead, he simply confirmed that the altimeter was set to the number that had been provided in the weather officer's briefing.

"All right. Engine run-up check," Tune announced to his copilot.

"Brakes set," Flynn replied, confirming the brakes were locked. "Trim tabs?" he added.

In response, Tune set all three of his trim tabs at the zero mark. "Set," he announced. A properly trimmed aircraft in flight made it much easier, but trying to take off with the bomber's trim already set could be disastrous for a bomb-laden Fortress heavy with a full tank of highly inflammable aviation fuel.

"Exercise turbos," Flynn said.

Tune reached for the throttles. Together, they formed a shovel handle-like device mounted on the control pedestal between him and Flynn. He pushed them forward and watched the engines' RPMs climb to 1500 on the tachometer. Then he ran the turbo controls and RPMs through their ranges. While he was doing this, he also checked the plane's generators and the pitot heater.

"Running up engines," Tune announced to Flynn. Starting with Engine No. 1, he opened that engine's throttle to a manifold pressure of 28 degrees and began flipping the magnetos back and forth. Flynn watched for unusual changes in engine RPM, while Tune kept a careful eye out the window on the engine cowling and nacelles. The RPM hovered around 2400.

"Okay," Tune thought. He pulled back on the throttle, reducing Engine No. 1's RPM back down to 1000. Then he proceeded with the run ups for the other three engines. By now, the noise at Amendola was deafening, and a yellow haze of dust rose from the dried grass behind the aircraft hard stands.

"There's the light," Flynn announced shortly after they finished running up Engine No. 4. He was referring to a flashing green Asdic light from the control tower. The light signaled clearance to taxi and line up on the runway for takeoff. Tune waved his arm out the cockpit's open window and signaled for the ground crew chief to drag away the heavy wooden chock blocks from *Tail End Charlie*'s massive wheels. "Tail wheel locked, Ike?" he asked.

"Locked," Flynn confirmed.

Satisfied, Tune reached for the throttle. He grasped it with his right hand, palm facing upward, and gently pushed it forward. The bomber eased out of its hard stand, across the taxiway, and onto the runway. By alternating power to the outboard engines, Tune maneuvered the heavy bomber, fighting the urge to use his brakes as he rolled onto the runway. Using brakes was a rookie mistake. Tune was not about to burn through his brakes at the beginning of the mission. Before he turned the bomber to the right, he spoke to Flynn again.

"Unlock tail wheel," he said. Flynn reached down to a parking brake-like lever on the floor beside the cockpit's lower control pedestal. He lowered the lever, unlocking the brake. A small red light on the instrument panel blinked on.

"Unlocked," Flynn confirmed. Tune manipulated the throttle again, sending *Tail End Charlie* into a slow smooth roll to the right. He let the bomber coast to a halt. Once his plane was stationary, Tune lifted his feet and planted both boots firmly on the brakes. He and Flynn slid their windows shut. Outside, the bomber's ground crew took positions alongside the runway, keeping a careful eye on the roaring engines and looking for telltale sign of flames or other trouble.

"Cowl flaps open?" Tune asked.

"They're open," Flynn confirmed.

Outside, the sky lightened from dark purple to light blue as a hazy summer dawn approached.

"There it goes," Flynn announced. Tune gave the control tower a quick glance and saw a green flare arcing through the sky—the signal for takeoff, right on time at 0615. Almost immediately, a B-17 piloted by Lieutenant Colonel Joseph S. Cunningham, 429th Squadron's commanding officer, began his takeoff run. Cunningham was flying as the group leader for the mission. In less than five minutes, all of the 429th's Fortresses were airborne. But before the 429th's last bomber had even cleared the end of the runway, the pilot in the 96th Squadron's first bomber accelerated into his own takeoff run. Once those seven bombers were airborne, the 49th Squadron followed suit. Tune's squadron, the last in the group, would be next.

With the bomber's brakes set, Tune progressively pushed all four throttles forward, alternating quickly but steadily between the right and left engines as he advanced them all. Reaching down, he twisted the throttle lock to keep them from creeping forward or back. The roar of engines seemed to threaten to shake the aircraft apart, but Tune held its position on the runway as the bombers in front of him began to take off. Then the last bomber from the 49th Squadron rolled away, accelerating down the runway. Tune gave it a 30-second head start. Then, before the other bomber had even left the ground, Tune released his brakes to follow its lead. *Tail End Charlie* began rolling forward.

"Tail wheel lock," he said to Flynn.

Flynn reached down and locked the tail wheel as *Tail End Charlie* gained speed. "Tailwheel locked—light out. Gyros."

Tune quickly reached forward and set the plane's gyros to confirm with the magnetic compass's heading.

"Gyros set," he announced.

"Generators," Flynn called out. When the RPMs reached 1500, Tune turned them on with his left hand.

Working the aircraft's rudder slightly, but keeping his ailerons in a neutral position, Tune let the bomber accelerate down the runway. Its wheels hummed on

the steep plate as it picked up speed. The group shared the airfield with the Royal
Air Force and, to Tune's right, a series of parked Halifax, Wellington, and Liberator bombers dissolved into a blur as *Tail End Charlie* raced toward the end of the
runway.

As the plane's indicated airspeed approached 110 knots, Tune pulled back slightly
on the control column. The nose lifted and, seconds later, the heavy B-17 struggled
ponderously into the air. In a flash, the bomber roared over the end of the runway
and, at treetop level, skimmed the tops of abandoned olive groves.

"Landing gear up," Tune instructed Flynn.

"Roger," Flynn replied. With his feet, he applied gentle pressure to the bombers' brakes to stop the wheels from continuing their rotation. Then he reached in
front of the throttles on the control pedestals and pushed the landing gear switch
forward.

A moment later, Tune glanced out of his window.

"Landing gear up left," he said.

"Landing gear up right," Flynn confirmed.

"Tail wheel up," offered the flight engineer. Flynn then flipped the landing gear
switch back down into the neutral position.

By now, the bomber's indicated air speed was registering 150 knots. Tune pulled
back on the throttles until the manifold pressure registered 35 inches. As he did,
Flynn reduced the engine speed back down to 2200 RPM. Pulling further back on
the control column, Tune began to climb to altitude. He held the bomber's rate of
climb at 500 feet per minute. Once he reached an altitude of 1,000 feet, he temporarily leveled out, allowing the other six B-17Gs of the squadron to rise into position to join him.

⌐∾

William Bullock, piloting a bomber bearing the aircraft serial number 44-6359
(in the airmen's shorthand vernacular, the bomber was known simply as 359) followed *Tail End Charlie* down the runway and into the air. Bullock was paired this
morning with Second Lieutenant Clarence B. Jackson, a native of Wilmington,
Delaware, as a copilot. Second Lieutenant John C. Quinn, of Flushing, Long Island, New York, was on board as their bombardier. Today's air raid would be Bullock's twenty-fifth.

Ed Smith sat at the bomber's navigator's table. Despite his recent unpleasant experience in the Adriatic following the last Ploesti raid, he was still flying the same
frenetic schedule in a squadron undermanned in trained navigators. He had already
accumulated 36 missions to his credit and had flown with over a dozen separate

crews. "Everyone of [those crews] was shot down before I was, except for the crew on my first mission," Smith recalled "That was their last mission (50). . . . I began to think of myself as a jinx."[18]

Smith's fellow crew members on board 359 that August morning included, in addition to his fellow officers, Jim Martin, the former sharecropper's son from Hollis, Oklahoma. Martin would again occupy the ball turret position on today's mission. Sergeant Morris M. Goldberg, from Philadelphia, and Staff Sergeant Joseph N. Laratta, from Brooklyn, manned the right and left waist guns respectively. Laratta was a new addition to the crew, replacing the regular left waist gunner who was still nursing wounds from a previous mission. Technical Sergeant Joseph N. "Whitey" Morien, the flight engineer and upper turret gunner, from Rockland, Michigan; Staff Sergeant Maurice E. Nelson, the tail gunner, from Roseau, Minnesota; and Technical Sergeant Wallace M. "Wally" Clayton, the radio operator, from Dallas, rounded out 359's crew.[19]

⤴

Next came *Snafuperman,* a B-17G more formally described in the 20th Squadron's ledgers with aircraft serial number 42-107118. Once again, "Mutt and Jeff," as Leo Zupan described his pilot and himself, would be taking to the air—Bill Garland sat next to Zupan in the pilot's seat. With 27 missions under their collective belts, Garland and Zupan were due for an R & R trip to Rome or the Isle of Capri. For the crew of *Snafuperman,* it had been a hard-flying two months. Some rest and relaxation was long overdue, and Zupan already had his beer and cigars laid out on his cot ready to take on the trip.

With Loy Dickinson pulling duty as the squadron's lead navigator on board *Tail End Charlie* with Bill Tune and Ike Flynn, Second Lieutenant Albert E. Novak, *Snafuperman's* erstwhile bombardier, manned the bomber's navigational charts and maps. Novak called St. Louis home, where his wife, Maxine, was waiting out the war back on Leola Street. With Novak pulling navigational duties, Staff Sergeant William G. Hayett, of Milwaukee, assumed the role of the bomber's bombardier. In such cases, crews called substitutes like Hayett "togglers." Rather than manipulate the complicated Norden bombsight, Hayett would simply watch for *Tail End Charlie* to begin dropping its payload and then immediately toggle and release his own cluster of bombs. At the time, Hayett was bouncing from crew to crew, trying to complete his requisite number of missions as soon as he could in hopes of making it home for Christmas. The mission to Moravska Ostrava would be his seventh mission in seven days.

Staff Sergeant Irving D. Katz, of Chicago, served *Snafuperman* as its flight engineer and upper turret gunner. Katz, like his fellow flight engineer Coogan on board *Tail End Charlie,* was Jewish. How a Jewish serviceman such as Katz would fare in the hands of Nazi captors was anybody's guess.

Staff Sergeant James Barker, of Quitman, Georgia, would occupy the ball turret as soon as the bomber left friendly airspace. Sergeant Ralph DeWitt was *Snafuperman's* right waist gunner, and Sergeant Russell I. Payne was the aircraft's left waist gunner. DeWitt's wife was home in Egan, Illinois; Payne's waited for him in Michellville, Maryland. Sergeant Robert C. Hoadley, the tail gunner, called Pasadena, California, home. Staff Sergeant Charles E. Griffin, of Hartsdale, New York, worked the bomber's radios.[20]

⤿

First Lieutenant Merrill A. Prentice's Flying Fortress rose into the air next. Like Bullock's, it was a relatively anonymous bomber that did not enjoy an irreverent nickname. Instead, the crew referred to the aircraft bearing serial number 42-31885 as simply 885. Prentice, a native of Astabula, Ohio, was flying only his fourth combat mission this month. On his three previous missions, he had flown as a copilot. Today, however, Prentice was flying as a pilot-in-command for the first time.

For this morning's mission, the squadron had teamed Prentice with Second Lieutenant Theo Heath, of Newport, New Hampshire. Charles McVey drew duty as their navigator for this particular mission. For some reason, the squadron's mission board had plucked him from his usual pairing with Robert McCloskey and Willard Netzley and plunked him down with Prentice and Heath. Second Lieutenant Robert A. Laux, from Amherst, Ohio, arrived at the aircraft with Norden bombsight in hand. He was 885's bombardier.

Another Buckeye, Sergeant Frank J. Balcerzak, of Toledo, manned the ball turret. Sergeant Herbert S. Goodstein, of the Bronx, served as the flight engineer and upper turret gunner. Sergeant Leroy E. Johnson, of Walnut Grove, Minnesota, manned the right waist gun; Sergeant Claude A. Petrey, of Shreveport, Louisiana, stood by the left gun. In the rear of the plane, Sergeant Robert E. Fitch, a native of Detroit, bore the lonely responsibility for the tail gun. Sergeant Kenneth W. Ellis, of Clayton, North Carolina, operated the radios.[21]

⤿

My Baby, inscribed with aircraft serial number 42-31473, was the fifth bomber flying in the squadron on this morning, with Second Lieutenant Robert McCloskey as its pilot. As a relatively inexperienced pilot, McCloskey had, to date, been relegated to flying in the "tail end charlie" position of the squadron. Today, however, he was happy to see he was flying in what he called the "coffin corner" slot.

Despite the ominous ring to it, most pilots found the rear left echelon position to be a better draw for an assignment in the formation than bringing up the rear.

Second Lieutenant Harold W. Helveston Jr., of Philadelphia, sat beside McCloskey as copilot on this particular mission. McCloskey's regular copilot was on sick call with a bad back and so Helveston, with only one combat mission under his belt to date, was filling in for the grounded aviator. Willard Netzley drew duty as *My Baby*'s navigator, filling in for Charles McVey, who, in the day's shuffle of crews, was flying with Prentice's bomber on this mission. Bombardiers were, in theory, at least, partially trained as navigators and, as far as the group was concerned, Netzley fit the bill. In the absence of a bombardier, Sergeant John J. Curran, of St. Paul, Minnesota, drew duty manning the bomber's nose guns, while Staff Sergeant James A. Jones, of Sheridan, Arkansas, served as *My Baby*'s flight engineer and upper turret gunner.

Below *My Baby*'s fuselage, Sergeant Luther L. Durrette, of Bowling Green, Kentucky, would occupy the cramped ball turret. Sergeant Charles A. Munden, of Dallas, manned the right waist gun. Behind him, Sergeant Harold Schirmer, of Southgate, Kentucky, stood by the left waist gun. Sergeant Elmer J. Pruitt Jr., of Clair Shores, Michigan, drew duty as *My Baby*'s tail gunner—filling in for the tail gunner who had shot himself shooting at lizards with his .45. Staff Sergeant Edwin R. Everett, of Scranton, Pennsylvania, operated the bomber's radios.[22]

When McCloskey arrived at the aircraft that morning following the air mission briefing, a doleful Everett met him under the bomber's wing. "Lieutenant, I forgot my dog tags," Everett said. But at that point, it was too late to retrieve them from the distant bivouac. Everett, McCloskey knew, would just have to hope that such identifying measures were not needed.[23]

A B-17G designated with aircraft serial number 42-32048, nicknamed *Ball of Fire* by its crew, came next. Jim Weiler, whose dreams of flying had led him from Burlington, Wisconsin, to the AAF, occupied *Ball of Fire*'s pilot's seat. Since early July, he had flown a dozen missions. Flight Officer Irving D. Thompson, of Poughkeepsie, New York, sat beside him as copilot. Like Donahue and Kirsch, he was a survivor of the previous month's Ploesti mission but now often found himself flying wherever needed. Second Lieutenant Robert L. Embry Jr., of Jackson, Mississippi, was the bomber's navigator, while Second Lieutenant Frank A. Sulkey, a native of Cleveland, Ohio, manned the Fortress's bombsight.

Technical Sergeant Lennie H. Bumgardner, of Thomasville, North Carolina, bore the twin responsibilities of flight engineer and upper turret gunner for *Ball of Fire*. Staff Sergeant Ernest W. Wagoner, of Macy, Indiana, was the bomber's ball turret gunner. Sergeant John H. Adair, of Italy, Texas, manned the right waist gun, while Staff Sergeant Loren E. Byam, of New Lisbon, Wisconsin, stood at the left waist gun position. The crew would depend upon Staff Sergeant George D. Dalcanale, of Caspian, Michigan, to ward off enemy fighters from the tail gunners' position. For radio communications, they looked to Staff Sergeant John J. Martin, of Walton, New York.[24]

⌒

Wichita Belle, a B-17G with aircraft serial number 42-38096, rounded out the 20th Squadron's seven bombers on this morning's mission. Ironically, despite the bomber's name, not a single crewmember called Kansas home. Second Lieutenant Thayne L. Thomas, the pilot, was from Spanish Fork, Utah. Copilot duties fell to Second Lieutenant Carl S. Goodman, of Concord, North Carolina. The navigator, Second Lieutenant William M. McDonough, hailed from Weymouth, Massachusetts. Second Lieutenant Richard P. Hartman, of Jacksonville, Illinois, was *Wichita Belle*'s bombardier.

Staff Sergeant Robert L. Brown, the upper turret gunner and flight engineer, was a native of Waseca, Minnesota. Nineteen year-old Sergeant Robert J. Flahive, the ball turret gunner, came from Seattle, Washington. Sergeants Jerome Bauman and James J. Johnson, of San Diego and Louisville, Kentucky, respectively, manned the left and right waist guns. Another native of San Diego, Sergeant William R. Mays, served as *Wichita Belle*'s radio operator, and Sergeant Dudley E. Standridge, of San Antonio, Texas, filled the tail gunner's position.[25]

⌒

As squadron leader, Tune's immediate responsibility was to form up the 20th Squadron's seven B-17s and join with the rest of the 2nd Group into a formation hopefully capable of resisting enemy aerial attacks. To that end, Tune put *Tail End Charlie* into a slow, steady, climbing spiral turn to the left. Behind him, Bullock gave him ten seconds and then followed him into the turn. Ten seconds later, Garland did the same.

Tune continued his climb, spiraling higher into the sky. He and Flynn kept their eyes carefully peeled for other aircraft. They knew that, short of combat, forming up was one of the most dangerous episodes of a flight, especially on a hazy, cloudy day like today.

A few minutes later, Bullock's B-17 pulled up on *Tail End Charlie*'s right echelon, 50 feet behind and to the right of Tune's plane.

"Bullock's in position," Flynn announced.

Tune looked over his left shoulder. Garland was a talented, experienced aviator. With calm assurance, he guided *Snafuperman* in so close to *Tail End Charlie* that their wings almost overlapped.

"So is Garland," Tune replied. These three planes would form the squadron's first element. Behind them and slightly beneath, forming another "V," a second element would be locking into place momentarily, followed by lonely Prentice—the true "tail end Charlie." In all, the 20th Squadron took on a diamond-like shape.

With the squadron's six other aircraft behind him, Tune pulled his planes into position at the end of the 2nd Bombardment Group. By now, Tune's wristwatch showed 0710, and the bomber's altimeter signaled that they were 10,000 feet over Amendola. The rocky plateau of the Gargano Massif rose to the north; the city of Foggia lay several miles to the west.

"Oxygen masks," Flynn reminded over the intercom. The crew obediently snuggled their rubber masks over their noses. The air inside *Tail End Charlie* was getting colder, and some of the crewmen began tugging on their leather flight pants and jackets. A long, cold flight to distant Czechoslovakia lay ahead of them. Outside, to Tune's left, front, and right, white contrails streaked the Italian skies, pointing like aerial lances toward the Third Reich.

Cry havoc. Once again, the Fifteenth Air Force had let slip the dogs of war.

As *Tail End Charlie* flew over Italy's coastline and cut across the Adriatic Sea, Marinello climbed down into the ball turret and occupied his uncomfortable post—curled into an almost fetal position on his back, his feet up in stirrup-like pedals level with his face. Once in place, he rotated his ball turret and tried his best to enjoy the panorama unfolding beneath him. His duty station was arguably the most unpleasant gun position in the bomber but, at times like this, it had the distinct advantage of providing an awe-inspiring view. Through breaks in the clouds, he watched whitecaps speckle the windy surface of the dark blue Adriatic Sea. It was still too early to really worry about enemy fighters. Nevertheless, when he received an order from Tune to test-fire guns, he jabbed the firing buttons on his guns' handle. The dual-mounted .50-caliber machineguns responded reassuringly with a staccato burst, sending a line of slugs toward the sea below. A jangle of spent shells, ejected out of a small opening in the turret, tumbled below them. Elsewhere in the bomber, other gunners test-fired their guns as well.

Meanwhile, *Tail End Charlie* continued to climb, clawing through the thinning air to lead the 20th Squadron to an altitude of 26,500 feet. As the squadron climbed, a half hour passed, and Cunningham, in the lead aircraft, banked slightly to the left. The group's 27 other pilots followed his lead. On each of those planes, navigators like Dickinson marked the time and, as necessary, reworked their route calculations. In the radio compartment, Kirsch called in his first position report back to Amendola and noted the time in his log. The other enlisted members of the crew, relatively unoccupied and unneeded at this point in the mission, cracked open their K-rations and shared a quick snack of crackers and cheese.

In the cockpit, Tune looked out his left window. With satisfaction, he noted that Garland was maintaining *Snafuperman*'s position well. With a similar glance to the right, Flynn confirmed that Bullock's bomber was locked in position also. Less reassuringly, however, Flynn noticed that the group as a whole seemed to be struggling to maintain position with the groups ahead of it.[26]

Below the bombers, however, trouble was brewing. A trio of white wakes marked the paths of three E-boats, the German version of a PT boat. If the Americans could see the E-boats, then the German sailors on board them could see the bombers overhead. From his bomber in the group's vanguard, Cunningham signaled to the Fifteenth Air Force's headquarters in Bari, Italy, warning the headquarters of the E-boats' presence.[27] But other than transmitting that message, there was little to do about the boats except soldier on.

Minutes later, Cunningham's formation of bombers crossed the rocky shore of Yugoslavia's Dalmatian coast. Now they were over enemy-occupied territory. The American bombers huddled together as best they could and cut north into the outer dominions of the Third Reich. Some remember thinking that the group was lagging behind the three other groups flying in the wing on the mission.

"I became increasingly concerned about the erratic pattern of the group lead plane," Flight Officer Duane Seaman remembered from the cockpit of 44-6369, a bomber flying in the tail-end charlie position of the group's 49th Squadron. His co-pilot, Ben J. Pastorino, was not only a fellow flight officer but, like Seaman, a native of New Jersey as well. "It was not a smooth, cohesive formation. The lead would surge forward and then ease back in an apparent effort to pull the group together which only added to the confusion."[28]

On board *Tail End Charlie,* Kirsch did not share Seaman's vantage point. Focusing on other matters, he dialed in a German radio station broadcasting Axis Sally. The German propagandist played a few popular tunes, which Kirsch piped over the bomber's intercom for the benefit of the other crewmen.

"Good morning to you men of the 2nd Bomb Group," Axis Sally announced unexpectedly during a break in the music. "Today's your lucky day. Today you will get shot down, but before you do get shot down, I want to play you a song." A second later, the tune "Franklin D. Roosevelt Jones" rolled across the airwaves.[29]

"You could have knocked me over with a feather when I heard that," Owsianik reported, suddenly reminded of his crew chief's dire warning.[30]

Undaunted, the formation lumbered over Croatia and into Hungary. Tune kept a steady pace, determined to keep the squadron's planes within the group's protective fold. As far as he could tell, he had the 20th Squadron locked in tightly behind the 49th Squadron's own "tail end charlie"—a bomber piloted by First Lieutenant John Fitzpatrick bearing the serial number 42-97915 and the nickname *Wolf Pack*.[31] Fitzpatrick, a former baggage handler for TWA back in Pittsburgh, had risen through the ranks from draftee to AAF bomber pilot.

Back in *Tail End Charlie,* Tune leaned forward and looked down through the clouds, catching a glimpse of Hungary's Lake Balaton shimmering in the summer sun below. He knew that Budapest was a scant 60 miles away. He also knew that three enemy fighter bases surrounded the lake.

At 0947, Marinello called Tune from the ball turret.

"Lieutenant Tune, it looks like we got some skulkers," Marinello warned over the intercom. With an electronic "whirring" of gears, he rotated his turret to face the interlopers. "Three of them—below and behind us." "Skulkers" was the airmen's slang for German fighters tasked with trailing a formation of enemy bombers. Matching the American's airspeed and maneuvers, they could radio vital information about the route and speed of the oncoming bombers to their *Luftwaffe* comrades lying in wait.

"Okay, Marinello. Just keep an eye on them," Tune said.[32] He knew that, like the E-boats, there was nothing to be done about their unwelcome companions.

Thirty minutes later, the bombers crossed the Danube River and soon rumbled over the Czechoslovakian town of Nove Zamky. In the distance, Tune could see the dark green mass of the Carpathian Mountains. He knew the group would find Moravska Ostrava just beyond them. They would be reaching the IP soon. Knowingly, *Tail End Charlie*'s crew pulled on their flak helmets and jackets and prepared for the bomb run.

In the cockpit, Tune worked to keep his squadron's formation as tight as possible with the aircraft of the 429th Squadron ahead of him. With nerves cooled by the experience of 47 prior missions, he stayed on *Wolf Pack*'s tail. Looking up, Tune could clearly see *Wolf Pack*'s ball turret gunner curled in his uncomfortable perch beneath the plane's fuselage.

Another ten minutes passed. Then Cunningham broke radio silence from the group's lead bomber.

"'Little friends' will be arriving in the next two to three minutes," Cunningham cautioned. "Little friends," as every bomber crewman knew, was the term of endearment for Allied escort fighters. "Tell your gunners not to fire on them when they pop out of the clouds."[33]

Tune relayed Cunningham's warning to his crew. He glanced at his wristwatch. It was now 1040, and they were approaching the Czech city of Trencin. They would be over Moravska Ostrava in 22 minutes.

At that moment, in *Wolf Pack,* Staff Sergeant James J. Delutes Jr., of Harrisburg,

Pennsylvania, called over the intercom to his pilot Fitzpatrick from his position in *Wolf Pack*'s tail.

"Tail gunner to pilot. A group of fighters is coming up on our tail. They look like the enemy," DeLutes warned.

"Copilot to tail. Don't fire. They could be our escort. But keep a close watch," ordered Second Lieutenant Charles H. McGhee from his copilot's seat.[34] The Briggsdale, Ohio, native knew that the P-38 fighters that had spearheaded their flight so far were due to be replaced by P-51 Mustangs for the final surge toward the target. From the front, the elegant Mustangs, with its inline engine, could be easily mistaken for German Bf 109s. Besides, as McGhee well knew, this was the crew's eighth mission in 11 days. He did not want a tired gunner firing on a friendly fighter.

Donahue, *Tail End Charlie*'s tail gunner, was also scanning the hazy skies and low layer of clouds above the formation for the telltale black specks that marked incoming fighters. Like Fitzpatrick's gunner, he spotted a foursome of fighters closing fast from the rear, flying in the four-abreast formation favored by the American escorts.

"Fighters coming up. Probably are friendly," Donahue called up to Tune.[35]

But before Tune could even reply, all hell broke loose in the skies over Czechoslovakia.

"No, no—they are not!" Donahue yelled, desperately correcting his earlier mistake.[36] On board *Wolf Pack,* DeLutes shouted a similar warning to Fitzpatrick and McGhee. But it was too late. A salvo of German wing-fired rockets slashed through the squadron, providing lethal punctuation to the tail gunners' shouted warnings.

Seconds later, waves of German fighters—Bf 109s and Fw 190s—speared straight toward the heart of the American formation from three different directions. As tail and waist gunners frantically yanked back on their guns' charging handles and the turret gunners swiveled to meet the oncoming onslaught, there was no time to count the enemy aircraft filling the sky. A later report placed as many as 70 *Luftwaffe* aircraft in the attack.[37]

With a blink of the eye, the German fighters scythed through Tune's squadron. Their wings winked evilly with the twinkle of firing machineguns as they roared past the lumbering B-17s. Then, with the sun glinting off their metal wings, they banked left and right for another pass. As Tune watched the Fw 190s and Bf 109s circle back around, a thought hit him like a punch to the stomach.

Maybe his luck was about to finally run out.

8
The Meat Grinder

While Bill Tune rued his sudden turn of fortune in the skies of eastern Czechoslovakia, his German adversaries embraced their own good luck. In the bloody summer of 1944, when the crushing press of the Combined Bomber Offensive was steadily taking its toll on the Third Reich's aerial defenders, such moments of opportunity were becoming increasingly rare for Germany's beleaguered corps of fighter pilots. If air superiority was not indisputably in Allied hands by that point in the war, it certainly seemed increasingly inevitable.

The path to the brink of such air superiority had not necessarily followed the course charted by Allied air strategists. Initially, it had been a basic tenet of faith of Operation Argument that certain critical components of Germany's aircraft production capacity represented a vital collection of key pressure points on Hitler's ability to mount an effective air defense. Such components included its aircraft factories, assembly airfields, and, to a lesser extent, its ball bearing plants. Knock those out, the reasoning went, and it would cripple Germany's "war potential."[1]

The Germans' industrial innovation and remarkable recuperative powers, however, shattered the Allies' illusions that such targets were Germany's Achilles heel. Two decades after the war's conclusion, Field Marshall Erhard Milch, Hitler's state secretary of aviation, lectured at the U.S. Air Force Academy and shared an anecdote that illustrated Germany's industrial resilience. He recalled a winter day in 1943, when American bombers raided a Junkers aircraft factory in central Germany that had been producing 50 Ju-88s per month. The raid totally destroyed all of the buildings, to include the factory heating installation—no small loss on a day when temperatures plummeted to zero degrees Fahrenheit. Milch arrived at the factory a half hour after the last bombs had fallen.

"I found one third of the work force engaged in extinguishing the fires, one third engaged in removing the debris, and the last one third repairing the damaged aircraft," Milch reported. "The entire sight was catastrophic and I asked the assembled workers how long, in their estimation, it would take until all the damage had been repaired."

"Their answer was," Milch relayed, "at the latest within a month! Actually on the tenth day of the following month the factory delivered the 50 aircraft scheduled for delivery during the previous month (when the attack had occurred); the 50 aircraft scheduled for delivery during the current month were also delivered before the end of that month."[2]

Broader statistics bear out Milch's conclusions. In February 1944, the *Luftwaffe* accepted 1,016 new single-engine fighters into its inventory. Four months later, despite enduring a concentrated assault on its factories, Germany's aircraft industry's delivery figures jumped to 2,177 fighters.[3] German daytime fighter strength actually peaked in November 1944.[4] In short, if there was a chokepoint in Germany's war potential, it did not seem to be its aircraft or ball bearing factories and, in his talk to the Air Force Academy's cadets, Milch identified it.

"Only in 1944 were long-standing German fears turned into reality," Milch concluded, "when the Allies began their systematic destruction of the oil and petroleum product refineries. As soon as the repair of a damaged refinery seemed to near completion, the Allies launched a new attack on the installation, destroying it again. These Allied successes were mainly due to daylight operations. They, in fact, delivered the real, decisive, death blow to Germany."[5]

Few would argue that Germany's plummeting fuel production bore the lion's share of blame for the Luftwaffe's woes in the summer of 1944. However, to take Milch's pronouncement at face value risks oversimplifying matters. In reality, a more complicated and intertwined cause-and-effect calculus was at play.

For one thing, throughout much of the war, fuel shortages dogged its pilot training program. Prior to June 1944, a typical German pilot received only half the training hours of an American pilot. For the remainder of the war, as the Allied raids on the Reich's oil facilities took their toll, the number of training flight hours shrank to one-third.[6] Similar problems hampered postflight school operational training, where *Luftwaffe* pilots received only 60–80 hours of training in their operational aircraft; a figure that compared poorly to the 225 hours of operational training averaged by AAF and RAF pilots.[7] For the Germans, the situation eventually deteriorated to such a point that, by August 1944, the *Luftwaffe* was restricted to only those missions flown in actual operations against the Allies.[8] After the war, the Strategic Bombing Survey went so far as to label the decline in quality of Germany's fighter pilots as the single greatest cause for the *Luftwaffe*'s defeat.[9]

Proper—or, as the case seemed to be, improper—employment of Germany's fighters further exacerbated matters. Germany's fighters were, as the *Luftwaffe* General Josef Kammhuber declared in a postwar assessment of the Reich's air defense, "the backbone of a home air defense system. . . . The basic problem of a day fighter command, when confronted with mass approach flights, is the employment of its fighters. It is still the old controversy: free or restricted combat; attack against the fighter escort or attack only against the bomber formation."[10]

Generalleutnant Josef "Beppo" Schmid, who ended the war as the last commander of *Luftwaffe* Command West, minced no words when he assessed the choice the *Luftwaffe*'s leaders made in response to that particular controversy—to attack only the bombers. It was, according to Schmid, "the capital mistake in the Air Defense of the Reich. . . . Assuming that the enemy bomber units would be the primary opponent, tactics of attack, equipment of aircraft, training, armament, and ammunition were designed for the exclusive use of fighting the bombers."[11]

Although perhaps logical at first blush, the focus on the bombers surrendered the initiative to the Allied fighter pilots. Freed of concerns regarding their German counterparts, Allied fighters could thus roam the skies at will and pick the time and circumstances to attack.[12] It was an abdication that had significant consequences on German fighter operations and on morale.

General Adolf Galland, inspector of fighter aviation for Germany, underscored that predicament in his postwar memoir, *The First and the Last.* "Our losses rose unrelentingly," Galland remonstrated. "Forced onto the defensive, our units forgot how to conduct a dogfight. Now it had come to banking and diving away. Naturally, any cohesion of the unit was lost, and singly our fighters were finished off by the enemy fighters who outnumbered us greatly."[13]

Inadequate training caused by increasingly scarce fuel supplies, coupled with questionable operational tactics, aggravated the underlying problem that increasingly tormented the German pilots—the brutal, grinding attrition of a war in which no magic number of missions would send a pilot home in safety. For Germany's fighter pilots, the equation was far simpler—fly in defense of the Fatherland until they were killed or the war ended. Operating in such an equation, survival became a statistical improbability. In the first half of 1944, German fighter pilot losses approached 99 percent, with replacements barely keeping pace with losses numerically but certainly not qualitatively.[14]

In the final calculus, it is no stretch to say that, by 1944, the air war had degenerated into a brutal Verdun-like slugfest in the skies of occupied Europe. "There were no decisive moments of clear-cut victories," concluded U.S. Air Force historian Williamson Murray. "Rather, the American pressure put the German fighters in a meat grinder battle of attrition both in terms of pilots and of material."[15]

The *Luftwaffe* fed *Unteroffizier* Willi Reschke into the meat grinder in June 1944. Born and raised in the town of Muhler an der Oder in eastern Germany, the activities of a resurgent *Luftwaffe* at a nearby airfield in the 1930s inspired him to become a fighter pilot. The outbreak of war with Poland solidified his ambition and, in February 1940, at the age of 18, he enlisted in the *Luftwaffe*.[16]

Reschke passed a frustrating year before he was finally called to duty. Even more frustrating, after his basic training, he spent a year on a technical team at the airbase at Konigsberg-Neumark. It was not until the spring of 1942 that he finally began his preflight training, based, for a time, on the *Monte Rosa,* a training ship anchored in Stettin harbor. The British and Canadians landings at Dieppe that summer, although recognized to be an almost unmitigated disaster for the Allies, at least succeeded in disrupting Reschke's training program. For a time, he and his classmates trained as infantrymen.[17]

By the fall of 1942, Reschke was back in flight school and learning to fly in winch-launched gliders. Then, in late winter and spring of 1943, he progressed to motorized aircraft, eventually earning his wings on June 27, 1943. Specialized fighter-pilot training followed, which Reschke completed the following February. Then fate delivered the eager Reschke another blow—he was left behind in Zerbst as a flying instructor.[18] A series of random assignments and circumstances enabled him to cobble together both experience as an instructor pilot and operational training as a potential night fighter pilot.

Finally, in June 1944, Reschke received his long-awaited orders to join an operational single-engine night fighter unit. The *Luftwaffe* called such units *Wilde Sau,* or "Wild Boar," units, and Reschke traveled by train to Gotzendorf, Austria, to join a unit designated I/JG 302 on June 20, 1944.[19] An eager pilot like Reschke easily understood the numeric designation—he was joining I *Gruppe* of *Jagdgeschwader* 302. He soon discovered, however, that such *Wilde Sau* units were increasingly serving as day fighters in the summer of 1944 in a desperate attempt to counter the surging operational tempo of the Allied daylight bombing raids.

Assigned to 1 *Staffel,* or the first squadron, of the *Gruppe,* Reschke found himself in the *Luftwaffe*'s iconic but increasingly dated standby—the Bf 109. Reschke was more fortunate than most. His assignment as an instructor pilot had at least provided him with a respectable number of flying hours. Nevertheless, on his first combat flight on June 26, 1944, when his *Gruppe* challenged a Fifteenth Air Force raid on Moosbierbaum, he barely survived a brush with a P-51 Mustang. "In addition to getting used to [the American fighters] numerical superiority, we had to cope with the obvious high level of training of the enemy pilots in the escort fighters," he admitted ruefully.[20]

A week later, on his third combat mission, Reschke downed his first enemy aircraft, a pair of B-24s. Following this fight, engine problems forced him to crashland in a clover field outside of Budapest, where he was almost assaulted by Hungarian civilians who mistook him for a downed American pilot.[21] Later, on July 6, while defending Munich, Reschke shot down a P-51, although the lack of a corroborating witness prevented him from receiving credit.[22] The next day, once again over Hungary, he jumped a B-24 straggling home. When his guns jammed, he made a split-second decision to ram the hapless Liberator. At the cost of his Bf 109, Reschke downed the B-24 and parachuted to safety, suffering nothing worse than a split lip.

"When I stepped off the train in Vienna in the early hours of the following morning, I was quite certain of one thing: as far as I was concerned, anyone who wanted to ram could do so, but for me this chapter was closed forever," Reschke declared. "The chances of escaping with one's life were minimal and were out of all proportion to the courage required to put such a plan into action."[23]

Despite such successes, Reschke's group was losing pilots faster than it could replace them. Even on July 13, when Reschke downed his first B-17, he still sensed the growing sense of desperation among the *Gruppe*'s shrinking ranks. "That night in the 1 *Staffel* mess, where the pilots of the 4 *Staffel* also gathered to discuss the *Gruppe*'s mission, there was a perceptible sense of helplessness among the men. Authorized strengths were constantly being lowered and replacement aircraft and especially pilots could not keep pace with the losses," Reschke admitted.[24]

The losses affected tactics as well as morale. "With scarcely more than fifteen aircraft, screening the 'Heavy Group' was far beyond the capabilities of the high-altitude *Staffel*," Reschke declared. "The steadily increasing number of [Allied] escort fighters reduced the chances of massed attack on the bomber formations."[25]

As the days passed, the *Unteroffizier* rued the *Luftwaffe*'s seeming inability to inflict losses on the bombers decisive enough to foil a single bombing raid. On the contrary, he noted, he and his fellow pilots increasingly fought on the defensive, simply trying to survive in a war against escort fighters whose numbers and radius of action grew steadily. "As a result," Reschke concluded, "the offensive nature of the fighter pilots came to mean little and losses became unbearable. None of this was able to crush the courage and fighting spirit of the pilots, however, and they continued to score to the end in spite of adverse conditions."[26]

Recognizing the strain that the daylight bomber missions were putting on Germany's fighter pilots, the AAF increasingly capitalized on the indirect value of its air raids. Such value found articulation in the euphemism "counter air defensive attacks," as the 5th Wing's operations order for the Moravska Ostrava raid used the term.[27] Confronted with the challenge of an oncoming bomber raid, the Germans would have no choice but to meet it with increasingly undertrained fighter pilots. In the ensuing dogfights with escort fighters and attacks on the disciplined, heavily armed bomber formations, some of those German fighters would fall. Even less experienced pilots, their training woefully inadequate due to fuel shortages, would rise to take their place. In such a manner, the Allies found themselves gaining air superiority, one downed German fighter at a time.

Nevertheless, German pilots such as Reschke could, when the rare opportunity presented itself, still rely on that first principle of warfare drilled into young officers throughout the world—the principle of mass. Mass at the right place at the right time, and unleash too many fighters against too few enemy bombers, and even a well-manned, well-flown, tight formation could be overwhelmed by sheer numbers. On August 29, 1944, Tune's squadron offered just such an opportunity.

The Germans had not simply relied on sheer luck to bring their overwhelming force to bear on Tune's beleaguered bombers. Standard German day fighter operational procedures, as related in postwar debriefings by *Luftwaffe* officers to their Allied captors, provide a sense of what might have brought about the events of August 29 to Tune and his comrades. One such debriefing was a report entitled "German Dayfighting in the Defense of the Reich from Sep. 15, 1943, to the End of the War," prepared by the former *Luftwaffe* leader Schmid.[28] As one U.S. Air Force historian cautioned, "On any given day, German tactics and procedures might deviate from the norm—it was a strength of the German general staff system that low-level initiative was not merely permitted, but encouraged."[29] Nevertheless, Schmid's retrospective on how Germany organized and implemented its air defenses provides a logical and likely context upon which today's historians can build.

According to Schmid, German air defense staffs facing an impending Allied bombing raid would, as an initial matter, appraise their own "air situation." Daily reports from subordinate units would advise upper echelons of the numbers and types of German aircraft ready for operation, as well as the names and ranks of combat formation leaders.[30] An initial assessment and evaluation of meteorological conditions also took place. Meanwhile, staff officers would gather and correlate intelligence regarding the oncoming fighters and bombers, eavesdropping on the radio communications between the fighters and their escort bombers. Here, the very massive nature of the gathering forces worked in the Germans' favor. The assembly of the bomber groups into formation and the subsequent rendezvous with their escorts could take several hours, thereby providing the Reich's air defenders with sufficient time for preparing their own defensive operation.[31]

"The approach of the bomber aircraft was as a rule ascertained," Schmid confided. Doing so with respect to bombers flying out of England, Schmid admitted, presented an easier task than discerning the routes of those flying out of the Italian bases. But once the American bombers began utilizing the pathfinder radar systems, even those formations were susceptible to tracking by Germany's own radar network. "Badly disciplined" radio traffic further aided the Germans' efforts. "Messages such as 'Crossing the enemy coast' or '30 minutes to target' or 'No clouds over target' could be picked up again and again."[32]

"As long as the enemy bombers were flying above the clouds during the day and were not using [pathfinder radar], the work of [our] radar sets was hampered, but never completely arrested," Schmid reflected. "Later, bearings taken on the [radar] sets in bomber aircraft and on the R/T traffic of fighter aircraft would always result in an exact picture of the air situation even in case of bad weather conditions."[33]

Such situational awareness would be meaningless, of course, without an equally adept operational system to capitalize on it. When possible, the Germans relied on a centralized control structure, particularly during the day.

"A centralized control structure," Schmid declared, "was of still greater importance for dayfighting than for nightfighting, because the relation of strength between friend and foe was always by far more unfavorable by day, and because, by day, it was more important to bring, if possible, all the forces available into effective simultaneous action in the same area."[34]

To do so, adequate preparations were paramount, starting with a preliminary situation briefing at daybreak every morning. Based on that briefing, commanders would shift units as needed to meet the prognosticated threat. Such shifts had to occur early in the morning, particularly during the long summer months. Otherwise, the units transferred would be ill prepared once the action began.[35]

Assuming the fighters had been shifted in time to the right location, the pilots were briefed, learning the types of aircraft that would comprise the combat formation, their leaders, and how and where the various units would rendezvous into their assembly area. Use of landmarks such as well-marked towns, river bends, or lakes helped to ensure accurate identification of the assembly areas; in the absence of such landmarks, antiaircraft batteries could fire smoke rounds to help in the navigational effort. The latest weather information would also be provided and updated as the pilots waited in one of either two states of readiness—"instant readiness," or *alarmbereitschaft,* which had the pilots actually sitting in their aircraft ready to start, or "10-minute readiness," with the pilots in their flying gear in the hangars or at the dispersal points. With any luck, the pilots would also learn the possible target of the developing air raid.[36]

In order for the fighters to accurately intercept the oncoming bomber stream, it was "most important," Schmid recalled, to "effect a most exact and foreseeing work of dead reckoning (*Koppelungsarbeit*), taking into consideration high altitude winds, speed of enemy aircraft, performance of own aircraft and own standard of training, weather, and high altitude visibility." A premature start to the interception would drain the fighters of their precious fuel before the enemy bombers appeared on the scene. Conversely, a late start ran the risk of being attacked by enemy fighters while still in the process of assembly.[37]

Schmid also recognized the importance of careful work of command and control at the headquarters of the individual *Jagddivisions,* or Fighter Divisions, which in turn were comprised of the individual *Jagdgeschwader,* or wings. "For a large part success depended on their ability and the quality of the Fighter Controllers in the Ops Rooms," he wrote. "At all day-fighter stations the enemy air situation had to be plotted carefully according to the divisional telephone reportage. Only then was it possible for fighters, flying their second mission for fighting the returning bombers, to contact the enemy."[38]

In his own postwar study, Kammhuber provided his captors with a detailed description of a typical air defense division headquarters. "The center of activity of a division headquarters was the position map," he wrote. "In division headquarters a large vertically placed position map, especially treated to prevent warping, was utilized. This map had a scale of 1:50,000 and its size, never smaller than six by six meters, depended upon the extent of the area to be covered. It was divided into grid squares, with designations such as AA, AB, AC—the so-called fighter grid network."[39]

"The first information which had to be indicated on this large position map was enemy targets," Kammhuber continued. "This could be accomplished by various methods. As long as the radar equipment was not jammed or as long as it could still give accurate information as to the positions of enemy targets, the position data of targets plotted by the *Wuerzburg Riese* [a parabolic, unidirectional, ground-based radar system] located at the night fighter stations was transmitted telephonically by the *Seeburg* plotting table."[40]

Light indicators, and later small light projectors, kept track of the movement of the enemy aircraft and their altitudes across the position map, with appropriately colored blue and red filters in front of the lens of the light indicator providing the color-coded identity of the targets. So-called eye-on aircraft reports—in other words, visual reports from aerial observation aircraft called "skulkers" by Allied airmen—complemented the radar data, as did information from radio intercepts. All of this information was fed onto the position map.

Kammhuber recognized that maintaining control of friendly air assets was no less important than identifying the position of the oncoming bombers. To that end, ten to 15 fighter aircraft control officers manned a row of control desks in front of the large position map. Each was equipped with a microphone to maintain radio contact with the fighter plane or fighter formation in the air and a telephone to maintain contact with the airfields at which the fighter aircraft were stationed.[41]

"Verbal radio communications," Kammhuber explained, "was carried out on either in conjunction with the *Benito* [ground radar] control system or, if this was not available, by a voice or key ground-to-air transmitter. If the *Benito* control system was used, the position data of friendly fighter aircraft . . . were projected by light point projectors onto the large position map, except that these light point projectors had been placed from the very outset on a raised gallery in front of the position map."[42]

Observing the movements of the blue and red dots of lights, the fighter control officers guided the friendly fighter planes up to the enemy targets. "The more accurate the picture on the position map, the better the chances of success," Kammhuber described. "For this reason the chief purpose of the entire division headquarters organization was to attain the greatest possible degree of accuracy in the picture of aerial operations."[43]

The aircraft reporting service occupied a special work area in the air defense division headquarters, capable of transmitting information to any external organization concerned with the unfolding operation. An antiaircraft artillery officer also claimed a work area, from which he could inform and direct his subordinate units.[44]

The commanding officer of the headquarters occupied his own work area. "He, of course, was in a position to choose any place he wanted in front of the large position map," Kammhuber explained. Some would sit "in the very front directly before the large position map; in other headquarters, his place was at the very back so that he could better survey the entire room. The most important thing about his place was that it commanded a good view of the large position map and had direct line communications to all the agencies whom it might be necessary to reach."[45] To that end, communication lines could be linked together, allowing conference calls that allowed for all concerned agencies to receive information, and orders, simultaneously.[46]

The division headquarters meteorologist's work area occupied the upper story of the command headquarters. Weather maps hung along the side walls of the large room, readily visible to the aircraft control officers. If those officers had any questions, they could contact the meteorologist on duty at any time by telephone from their desks. The meteorologist shared the upper story with another aircraft reporting station, capable of receiving reports which it tracked on its own small plotting table. If necessary, its information would be projected onto the division's large position map.[47]

To ensure self-sufficiency in their increasingly fragile wartime environment, all division headquarters boasted their own power plants, emergency power units, and special workshops. They were also equipped with lounges, messes, and restrooms, and, in at least one case, a subterranean emergency exit.[48]

Today, the identity of the division that plotted the attack on Tune's "tail end charlie" squadron remains a matter of some conjecture. In Germany's air defense scheme, 8 *Jagddivision,* based in Vienna, bore responsibility for the defense of southern Germany, Austria, Bohemia, and Moravia in the summer of 1944.[49] Consequently, that particular fighter division, which encompassed Reschke's *Jagdgeschwader* 302, is the likely suspect in the attack on Tune's squadron. At the time, *Oberst* Gotthardt Handrick, an officer of impressive professional pedigree, commanded 8 *Jagddivision.* Eight years earlier, at the Olympic Games in Berlin, he had captured the gold medal for Hitler in the pentathlon and, shortly thereafter, flew with Germany's infamous Condor Legion in the Spanish Civil War. In the Battle of Britain, however, Handrick's lackluster command of *Jagdgeschwader* 26 prompted Goering to sack him in August 1940 and replace him with the already legendary Adolf Galland. Nevertheless, by 1944, Handrick's career had recovered enough that Goering entrusted him with command of the *Jagddivision* defending the southern sweep of the Reich. Bearing the title *Jagdfuhrer Sud* ("Fighter Leader South"), Handrick operated under the code name *Rosenkavalier* ("Red Knight").[50]

In his memoirs, Reschke described a typical set of directions received when his *Staffel,* or squadron, scrambled from its airfield near Gotzendorf, Austria, for his first combat mission.

"*Rosenkavalier* checked in soon after our takeoff," Reschke recalled. "A very pleasant female voice transmitted information on the incoming bomber formations."[51]

"*Dicke Autos mit Indianer* (fat autos, meaning bombers, with Indians, meaning fighters) at *Hanni* (height) 7,000 meters in GO (a reference to the fighter defensive grid) approaching Vienna." the unseen female warned. "Climb to 8,000 meters, *Caruso* (course) 220 degrees," *Rosenkavalier* then directed.[52]

Once Reschke and the Red Knight's other fighters were in the air and being vectored toward the intercept of the bombers, various factors forced matters of aerial command and control to be kept as simple as possible. The single-engine German fighters had little room in their crowded cockpits for sophisticated radio sets and avionics packages and there seemed to be a dearth of such equipment anyway. Nor did the expertise of the signals specialists assigned to the day fighter units inspire much confidence. Compounding the problem was the ever-diminishing level of training of the German day fighter pilots.[53] In response, the *Luftwaffe* relied on such measures as well-qualified commanding officers of the formations, maximum careful preparation for operations on the ground, the use of "Y" aircraft (guide aircraft specially equipped with VHF radio sets), and flak indicator bursts and flak rockets to denote assembly areas and, in the case of bad weather, landing fields.[54]

Issues of command and control were, of course, only part of the Germans' problem. Putting their fighters in the right place at the right time was meaningless unless those fighters were capable of delivering a punishing blow to the American bombers. The increasing use of an operational method known as *Gefechtsverband* offered heartening encouragement to the fighters tasked with delivering such a blow. A *Gefechtsverband*, or "battle formation," would match a *Sturmgruppe* of heavily armed and armored Fw 190s with a pair of escorting Bf 109 *Gruppen*.[55] Together, they would strike the enemy bomber stream somewhere along its length, smashing into a bomber squadron with a force of approximately 90 fighters. Based on eyewitness accounts of the attack unleashed against the 20th Squadron, it seems reasonable to conclude that Tune and his comrades ran afoul of just such a *Gefechtsverband*.

It seems equally reasonable to defer to Kammhuber's description of how such an attack likely developed from the German perspective. The preferred procedure, he wrote, was "to have several fighters attack a heavy bomber simultaneously, in order to divert and thereby neutralize its defense so that the decisive burst of fire, which actually results in downing the plane, can be delivered from a fairly great distance away. The lowest ratio possible will be three fighter aircraft against each enemy bomber . . . for the fighter pilots it means developing a coordinated, threefold attack."[56]

"The combined attack of a group of three fighter planes against a heavy bomber might look like this," Kammhuber continued. "Two fighter planes keep the bomber's defensive weapons, the heaviest of which are located in the tail, engaged from behind or the sides, while the third fighter parallels the course of the enemy plane to the side and below it. The fatal burst of fire is delivered from below . . . Since, in this case, the entire length of the enemy machine offers a barn-door type of target which can hardly be missed and since the fire enters the non-armored parts of the plane, the enemy aircraft can usually be downed with very few exceptions."[57]

Clutching the flight controls of *Tail End Charlie,* Tune had no idea that he and his fellow airmen were the objects of such calculating, ruthless attention. But whether or not their bombers would be one of the "very few exceptions" to survive Kammhuber's tactics would, in the next few minutes, depend almost solely upon the .50-caliber machineguns wielded by the leather-gauntleted hands of the Fortresses' gunners.

1. A B-17G Flying Fortress bomber, of the type flown by the 2nd Bombardment Group. (Courtesy AFHRA)

2. Robert D. Donahue's B-17 crew during operational training in Ardmore, Oklahoma, April 14, 1944. *Front row, left to right:* Flight Officer Roswell P. Pierce; Flight Officer Irving D. Thompson; Lieutenant Thomas H. Hancock; and Lieutenant Arnold A. Witoff. *Back row, left to right:* Robert R. Kirsch; Charles C. Watson; John E. Butler; Joseph A. Bernard; William D. Winston; and Robert D. Donahue. (Courtesy Thomas Donahue)

3. William S. Tune's B-24 crew prior to overseas deployment in Topeka, Kansas. *Front row, left to right:* William S. Tune; Ralph T. Mooney; Leon H. Leigh; and Fred P. Markowitz. *Back row, left to right:* Paul J. Ryan; Rex V. Phinney; Lloyd H. Allen; Richard P. Rasmussen; Sergeant (first name unknown) Palmer; and Angelo Cirigliano. (Courtesy Bill Tune)

4. Prisoner of war Leo Zupan.
(Courtesy Leo Zupan)

5. William C. Bullock Jr. (Courtesy Nancy Crumpton)

6. Jim Weiler. (Courtesy Mary Huckstorff)

7. Loy Dickinson. (Courtesy Loy Dickinson)

8. Robert Donahue being awarded the Silver Star, Amendola, Italy. (Courtesy Thomas Donahue)

9. Downed airmen and other Allied personnel awaiting rescue in Slovakia, September 1944. Robert Donahue is in the bottom row, second from left. (Courtesy Thomas Donahue)

10. The Tune brothers. *From left to right:* Leon Tune, Tillman Tune Jr., and William S. Tune. (Courtesy Bill Tune)

11. Bill Tune (*top*) and his hut mates enjoying copies of the *Birmingham News* in Amendola. (Courtesy Bill Tune)

12. *Left to right:* Lieutenant Thayne Thomas, Jan Surovec, and Robert Donahue. (Courtesy Thomas Donahue)

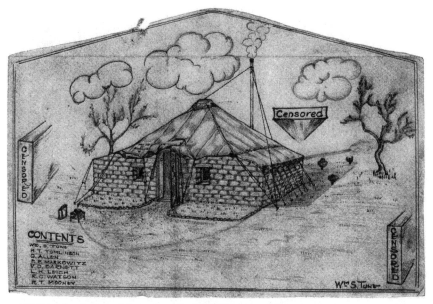

13. Bill Tune's hut in Amendola, as drawn by Tune. (Courtesy Bill Tune)

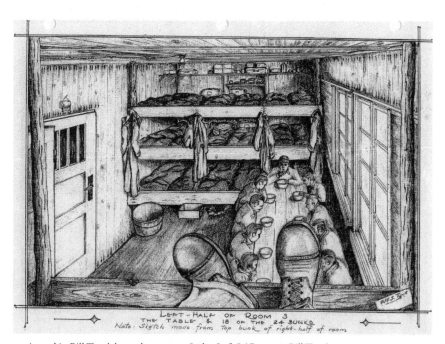

14. A meal in Bill Tune's barracks room at *Stalag Luft I*. (Courtesy Bill Tune)

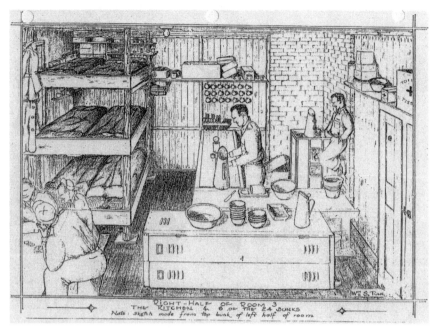

15. Preparing a meal at *Stalag Luft I*. (Courtesy Bill Tune)

16. A guard tower at *Stalag Luft I*. (Courtesy Bill Tune)

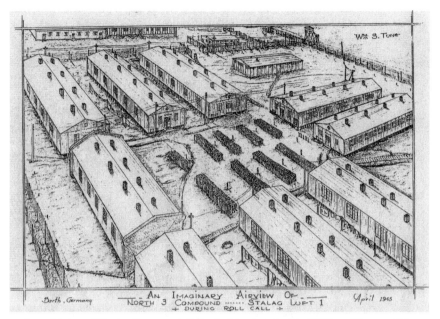

17. An aerial view of North 3 Compound, *Stalag Luft I,* as imagined by Bill Tune. (Courtesy Bill Tune)

9
"All Hell Broke Loose"

In the cramped cockpit of his Bf 109, Willi Reschke led his *Gruppe*'s aerial charge against Bill Tune's seven bombers. After two months of flying with *Jagdgeschwader* 302, Reschke had quickly become, like Tune, a seasoned and formidable pilot. Since June 28, he had survived two bail outs, a pair of crash landings, and the impetuous ramming of a B-24. He had downed at least 13 American aircraft in the process and, perhaps more important, was becoming an increasingly rare phenomenon—a survivor.

"The *Gruppe*'s pilots still got together in the evenings," Reschke reminisced, "but the optimistic cheerfulness of earlier days was gone. The gaps in the individual *Staffeln* could no longer be concealed. The *1. Staffel* was down to just six pilots, and the other *Staffeln* were not much better off."[1]

By 1944, a change in operational technique by the American escort fighters had further accelerated the depletion of the *Luftwaffe*'s pilots. In the early days of the air war in Europe, the AAF had kept its escort fighters on a tight leash, typically flying in sight and within easy reach of the bomber squadrons. But such an approach surrendered the initiative to the Germans. Shackling the escort fighters to the bombers allowed the *Luftwaffe* fighter pilots to pick the time and place of their attacks on the American formations.

As the air war over Europe progressed, however, American fighter and escort tactics evolved. The AAF began allowing its fighters to range ahead of the bomber stream to attack the enemy fighters as they took off or before they could form up for their attacks. "Clearing the air," it was called. In practice, the technique proved remarkably successful, contributing heavily to both the bombers' survival and the attrition of *Luftwaffe* fighter pilots, particularly as the training and quality of the German fighter pilots deteriorated.[2]

Despite its success, the "clearing the air" technique was not without its flaws. Foremost among them was its presumption that the Allied fighters ranging ahead of the bombers would intercept and destroy, or at least disrupt, the German fighter formations. If that presumption proved inaccurate, however, then the bomber streams—and particularly its trailing elements—would find themselves naked to enemy fighter attack.

Such was precisely the situation in which Bill Tune's vulnerable squadron now found itself. The escorting fighters of the 306th Fighter Wing were miles away. The Bf 109s and Fw 190s of Reschke and his comrades, however, were right on top of them. Whether through impeccable planning and coordination or sheer luck, the German pilots were precisely where they needed to be at precisely the right time. Like a pack of frenzied hounds that had cornered a hapless fox, their fighters tore into the 20th Squadron.

⌐

As Reschke's comrades roared in for the kill, Bill Tune clutched *Tail End Charlie*'s control column, his heavy leather gloves masking his white knuckles. In the lead aircraft, he quickly decided that he would try to hold a steady position for the six bombers behind him. But with waves of German fighters roaring past his cockpit's windows, it was a daunting prospect. Looking up, Tune saw that John Fitzpatrick's ball turret gunner in *Wolf Pack* was "practically sitting in my lap."[3] But the pilot from Carbon Hill, Alabama, held steady. Like a wagon train of settlers attacked by rampaging Indians, the Fortresses had to lager up and beat off the assault as best they could.

In Tune's left rear echelon, *My Baby* flew in the formation's aptly named "coffin corner." At *My Baby*'s controls, pilots Robert McCloskey and Harold Helveston did their best to survive the fighters' initial onslaught. Theirs was, however, a losing battle. When James Jones, the upper turret gunner, crumpled into a heap at the base of his turret behind the pilots' seats, McCloskey knew *My Baby* was in serious trouble. A flurry of tracers ripping past the cockpit's windshield underscored the point. For McCloskey's crew, the shout of "enemy fighters!" over the intercom had come far too late.[4]

"There were shells popping; the engines were burning as well as the panel; [we] had a flash oxygen fire; I think we had it all," McCloskey remembered.[5]

In the cockpit, McCloskey yelled at Helveston to help with the controls. Willard Netzley, the combination bomber-navigator for the mission, looked out the right-side windows and saw Fw 190s diving in "from 4:00 high, firing machine guns mounted in the wings and cannon shells through the propeller hub."[6]

John Curran, *My Baby*'s nose gunner, was also manning the .50-caliber guns that jutted out of both sides of the navigator's compartment. Stepping to the gun on the aircraft's right, he blasted at incoming fighters he identified as Bf 109s.[7] As they swooped past, he switched to the left side gun, firing at them until they flew out of range. The German pilots, however, circled around to the front for another run on *My Baby*. In response, Curran moved to the Fortress's chin turret gun and readied for another assault. Meanwhile, Netzley struggled to jettison their bombs. But with the bomb bay already burning, the jettison controls failed. The deadly cargo of 250-pound bombs remained hanging in their racks.

"Most systems were gone, auto pilot out, three engines out, and limited manual control," recalled McCloskey. "The only thing that seemed to be working was the intercom. Things seemed to be hopeless, so I gave the order to bail out."[8]

"Pilot to crew. Pilot to crew. Bail out! Bail out!" McCloskey shouted over the intercom.[9]

In the nose, Netzley and Curran reached for their parachute chest packs. In his haste, Curran started fastening Netzley's pack to his harness. When he realized his mistake, he handed it over obligingly to the bombardier. Snapping on his own pack, he followed Netzley out the nose hatch. Normally, they would have preferred to exit through the bomb bay doors, but that section of the plane was burning too fiercely to allow that avenue of escape.

Abandoning their controls in the cockpit, Helveston and McCloskey scrambled for the nose hatch. As they did, McCloskey tried to drag Jones's body with him. But with the cockpit empty and the autopilot ineffective, the Fortress spun into a flat spin. She whirled uncontrolled toward the ground like a falling leaf.

McCloskey, suffering from a severely burned face, scalp, and hands and a badly wounded left wrist himself, could not budge Jones against the centrifugal force of the spin. Realizing there was nothing he could do, he left Jones's body and followed Helveston through the nose hatch. Once outside, he bounced painfully off the aircraft but fell free and somehow managed to deploy his parachute. Seconds later, *My Baby* exploded, showering wreckage along the Moravian-Slovakian border near the town of Bosaca.

Nearby, in the bomber called 885—the squadron's true "tail end charlie"—the battle ended almost as quickly. A barrage of 20 mm cannon slugs ripped through 885's metal skin, with a fusillade smashing into the section of the nose where navigator Charles McVey and bombardier Robert Laux sat. Broken and splintered by the shower of German bullets, the .50-caliber ammo boxes stored in the nose began smoking. Within seconds, pilot Merrill Prentice ordered "Bail out!" across the aircraft's intercom.[10]

Only moments before, McVey and Laux had helped each other put on their heavy flak suits. Now, with a rip of a cord, McVey let it fall to the deck. His chest parachute had been hanging from one clip on his side, so he quickly clipped the other clip to his opposite side.

Snatching off his oxygen mask, McVey stepped down to the nose escape hatch and pulled on the hatch's emergency handle—to no avail. Prentice and the copilot, Theo Heath, crowded in next to him to try to work the door's regular handle. As McVey continued to tug on the emergency handle, he noticed that Laux was still half crouched near the end of the navigator's table. It occurred to McVey that the bombardier must be wounded; otherwise, he would have been directly behind McVey ready for the opportunity to jump.[11]

By that point, the bomber was completely out of control and bouncing McVey and his fellow officers around the crowded compartment. Struggling to stay upright, they began kicking the escape hatch in an effort to force it open.

"Just then another burst . . . tore much of the nose away and probably all of the plexiglass," McVey recalled. "I was partly stunned but realized I might get out through the blown-off nose better than the door, so I half turned to start to crawl out that way. The next thing I knew, I was falling through space."[12]

McVey did not know it at the time, but he was the only man to survive 885's demise. Robert Fitch, the tail gunner, managed to drop out of the escape hatch beneath his position but did not survive the descent to the ground. The bomber's other eight crewmen either died at the hands of German fighters in the air or perished when 885 slammed into a Czech farmhouse near Vyskovec. Prentice's, Laux's, Heath's, and five other bodies were discovered in the bomber's mutilated wreckage.

⌒

As McVey's Fortress tumbled out of the formation, tight arrowheads of *Luftwaffe* fighters smashed through the B-17 squadron like a series of aerial battering rams. Flashing past the surviving bombers, their machineguns twinkled while cannon and rocket fire coughed ugly puffs of smoke. Tracers, cannon shells, and rockets filled the sky. Too often, they found their mark, ripping through the bombers' thin aluminum skin or punching ugly holes in the cockpits' and windows' plexiglass.

On board *Ball of Fire*, pilot Jim Weiler watched the formation disintegrate around him. Abandoning his position in the center of the squadron's formation, he sought escape for his bomber by diving to a lower altitude. But Weiler's gamble failed. A quartet of Fw 190s jumped the bomber, mauling it mercilessly. Irving Thompson, the copilot, managed to bail out of the mortally wounded Fortress, but he was the only survivor. Moments after he slipped out, *Ball of Fire* smashed into the ground near the towns of Bojkovice and Krhov. Weiler's dreams of flying, nourished since the days of parochial school in Burlington, Wisconsin, ended in a Czech farmer's field.

⌒

Meanwhile, behind the controls of *Wichita Belle*, pilot Thayne Thomas struggled to survive in the squadron's right rear echelon position. In the unfolding confusion, he spotted a swarm of nearly 30 Bf 109s and Fw 190s materializing from behind a cloud. With remorseless detachment, they fired a devastating volley of rockets into the squadron's formation.

"The rockets started exploding all around us and then we were hit on the left wing near the No. 2 engine, which is next to the fuselage," Thomas recalled. The force of the explosion slammed Thomas's head against the cockpit's side window and hurtled his copilot halfway out of his seat. It also set fire to the number 2 engine, damaged the number 1 engine, and set the interiors of the bomber's nose compartment and the flight deck ablaze.[13]

Looking down into the nose compartment, Thomas could see that his navigator, William McDonough, and his bombardier, Richard Hartman, had been thrown to the compartment's floor. So had Robert Brown, *Wichita Belle*'s flight engineer and upper turret gunner. The whole nose compartment was a blazing shambles. Desperately, McDonough and Brown grabbed fire extinguishers and began to battle the flames.

In the cockpit, Thomas tried to call the bomber's other crewmembers over the intercom. It seemed dead. After another try, Thomas rang the emergency bell to signal "bail out." In response, McDonough, Hartman, and Brown interrupted their firefighting efforts and began to don their parachute packs. Once he had his chute on, Brown began walking toward the rear of the aircraft, presumably to make sure the other crewmen received the order to bail out. To reinforce that message, Thomas rang the bell once again.

"Suddenly, I was aware of very intense heat and a red flash of light," Thomas remembered. "The next thing I remember was the wind tugging at my mouth, eyes, nostrils, and body. I tried to grasp the 'D' ring on the chute to pull the rip cord but the wind was buffeting the chute and my body so hard I could not get a firm grip on it. I must have been within 1500 feet of the ground because I could look out horizontally and see that the mountain ridges were above me."[14]

Battling the slipstream, Thomas managed to place his left arm over the top of his chute pack. He pushed the pack downward with his left hand while simultaneously tugging at the pack's D-ring handle with his right. In response, the chute popped open explosively, snapping Thomas's left arm into his face.[15]

Numbed and dazed, Thomas floated earthward, oscillating violently beneath his chute. A burning fuel tank hurtled past him, followed by an unfortunate airman whose chute had failed to properly deploy. Like McVey, he was the only man to make it out of his bomber alive. It detonated in midair, showering the outskirts of the town of Sanov like a man-made meteor shower. Parts of the aircraft were still burning a day later.

⌐

By now, the carefully constructed formation of bombers, with their mutually supporting and interlacing fields of fire, was a shattered wreck. Like a breached dam, it broke wide open, scattering aircraft across the Czechoslovakian skies.

At the head of the formation, Tune clung grimly to *Tail End Charlie*'s controls, still trying desperately to provide a cornerstone around which the remnants of the squadron could build a defense. He pulled as close as he could to *Wolf Pack*, ahead of him, ignoring the danger of flying so close to the other bomber.

"I said [to myself] I have really screwed up royally because I have got our formation in too tight a position and I started to pull the throttles back," Tune remembered. "[But] I said, 'no, don't touch them and try to ride it out' because I would have caused all these poor fellows on the side to scatter."[16]

Regardless of Tune's own missgivings, William Bullock and Clarence Jackson, at the controls of aircraft 359, did not question their lead pilot's decision. They stayed loyally on his right wing. On the other side, Bill Garland and Leo Zupan did the same, keeping *Snafuperman* tucked in on the left.

Sitting beside Tune in *Tail End Charlie*'s cockpit, Frank Flynn remembered surviving the first wave of attackers and marveling at a *Luftwaffe* pilot streaking past the bomber's right wing a scant 30 yards away. "The sky was filled with white explosions, and our plane sustained more hits," the copilot remembered. "The right wing showed seven or eight holes, some with flames."[17]

In the bomber's radio room, Joe Owsianik had switched positions with Robert Kirsch, the radio operator, and started preparing his camera for the upcoming bomb run at the time of the attack. Then he heard the shouted warning: "There they are at six o'clock."[18] *Tail End Charlie* carried a .50-caliber mounted in the roof of the radio compartment, and Owsianik craned his head to look out through that gun position. To his dismay, he saw lines of German fighters racing from behind in a series of V-shaped waves. "They were stacked up like a flight of stairs, ten high," he remembered.[19]

Above him, Thomas Coogan's twin .50s in the upper turret began barking at the first wave of attackers as the flight engineer fought to protect his bomber. By the time Owsianik brought his machinegun into action, the second wave washed over them. He trained his gun on an incoming Fw 190 and poured a stream of tracers into it, the heavy machinegun recoiling like a jackhammer as it spat brass shell casings across the fuselage's floor. A burst of flames around the German fighter's fuselage signaled a hit.

There was no time to gloat, however, as the third wave of fighters swept in. A cannon shell punched through the radio bank and exited through the bomb bay doors, leaving a tunnel of bright sunlight to mark its passage. Another burst of gunfire wounded Owsianik, leaving his right arm torn and bleeding. Elsewhere in the aircraft, other machineguns still chattered angrily in response. As *Tail End Charlie's* gunners fired, they called out excitedly to one another, warning of incoming aircraft and claiming hits on others that swooped too close.[20]

Faced with such odds, however, *Tail End Charlie* was hopelessly outmatched. It shuddered and rattled constantly as it shouldered its way through the latticework of German tracers. "The incendiary shells were so thick it looked like you could walk on them," Tune recalled.[21] Then a burst of 20 mm cannon fire caught Russell Meyrick, the aircraft's bombardier, killing him instantly.[22]

With Meyrick dead, the bomb bay doors remained closed, leaving the bomber's deadly payload to hang menacingly in the racks. Rockets and cannon fire blasted holes "as large as washtubs" in the bomber's wings.[23] Within seconds, the No. 2 engine caught fire. Another cannon shell hit and blew up the oxygen tank on the plane's right flight deck wall, wounding both Flynn and Tune. With his aircraft ablaze and falling out of what remained of the squadron's formation, Tune signaled his crew: "Get ready to bail out. We're going down!"[24]

Owsianik took one look at the bomb bay racks full of bombs and decided it best to bail out from the waist hatch. On his way, he reached down and tried to crank up the ball turret. It was jammed—the nightmare of every ball turret gunner. For Joseph Marinello, trapped in the ball turret below the battered bomber, there was nothing that could be done. Trying not to think about the doomed ball turret gunner, Owsianik joined Joseph Sallings, the other waist gunner, and Kirsch by the waist hatch. Sallings pushed out the hatch and jumped, followed by Kirsch and Owsianik. From the tail, Robert Donahue also exited. Meanwhile, at the other end of the aircraft, Tune struggled to keep the bomber flying straight and level. He wanted to give his crewmen a fighting chance.

"While waiting for the crew to bail out," Tune remembered, "my life started whirling through my mind. I thought about, of all things, what a great time my three brothers and I had had growing up. The incident that stood out most was a simple one—what we did when I was six or seven years old—sliding down a pine straw-covered hill on barrel staves. I remember thinking about what fun and joy this had been."[25]

But as Tune sat faithfully at the controls, his copilot was struggling to follow Tune's orders to bail out. Flynn, with Dickinson's and Coogan's help, had reached the bomb bay doors but found them jammed shut. In desperation, he jumped on them, but to no avail. Defeated, Flynn finally just stood on the catwalk and stared dejectedly at them, "with the feeling I was going to meet my God. Suddenly the bomb bay doors started opening. As soon as I saw enough room to clear them, I jumped out."[26]

Unbeknownst to Flynn, Coogan and Dickinson had returned to the front of the aircraft. Although wounded himself, Coogan cranked the bomb bay doors open by hand using the crank by the pilot's seat. He had just enough time to get the doors open and jettison the plane's bombs before a shell exploded in the cockpit—in Flynn's empty pilot seat. The force of the explosion, or perhaps the lack of oxygen from the destroyed oxygen tanks, knocked Tune out cold.

As Tune slumped over the controls, Coogan and Dickinson dragged Tune out of his seat and down the ladder into the compartment below. Wasting no time, they pushed him out of the aircraft headfirst.[27] Caught in the slipstream, Tune's limp body flew back and smacked into the ball turret, breaking his leg. He bounced off the bomber and tumbled earthward.

With its fuel tanks burning brightly, *Tail End Charlie* staggered through the air as Coogan and Dickinson jumped clear. According to William Hayett, flying on board *Snafuperman* as its nose gunner, he could still see Marinello in the ball turret, blasting at German fighters. Hayett and Marinello normally flew together, and Hayett watched with dismay as a burning *Tail End Charlie* fell out of their makeshift formation and began a lethal, lazy curve toward the ground.

"He was still shooting his guns when I last seen [*sic*] him," Hayett reported to the AAF after the war. "He did shoot down one Fw 190 to my knowledge. Please send me info on this man," he added plaintively. "He *is* my best buddy. Thank you."[28]

Shedding chunks of aluminum and aircraft parts over the village of Nevsova, *Tail End Charlie* finally smashed into the ground near the small village of Rudimov, near the larger town of Rudice. German soldiers later found the bodies of Meyrick and Marinello in the wreckage.

⌒

The aerial action was not completely one-sided, however, and, even with numerical odds in their favor, the German pilots had a healthy respect for their adversaries. Reschke, flying in the first wave of fighters to wash over Tune's squadron, was no exception.

"The B-17s opened fire very early," Reschke remembered. "This first phase of the attack was always a test of nerves: the pilot sat crouched behind his sight, while the target grew larger and larger in the gunsight glass. But he had to wait until the B-17 filled the reticle before opening fire. These seconds always seemed like an eternity, and one's own nerves were stretched to the breaking point. It was always a relief when one's own guns began firing."[29]

Closing quickly with the formation of B-17s from behind, Reschke quickly picked one to attack. He fired his first burst of cannon fire at the Fortress's tail gunner, reasoning that the tail gunner possessed the widest field of fire to the rear and thus posed the greatest threat. From there, his fusillade of slugs chewed through the aluminum, working its way to the right across the bomber's wing and to the inner engine.

"The effects of the MK 108 [cannon] rounds were always staggering: immediately after the first strikes pieces of the wing structure flew off and the engine began pouring smoke," Reschke wrote. "This quickly turned to flames and the B-17 showed the first signs of dropping out of formation."[30]

But before Reschke could turn his attention to another bomber, he noticed, over his shoulder, a stream of tracers drawing nearer and nearer to his Bf 109. Somewhere behind him, amid the chaos of the unfolding air battle, one of his comrades was unleashing a string of machinegun bullets too close to Reschke's aircraft.

"Then the inevitable happened," the German reported. "There were several hard blows in the rear of my machine. I had been hit by one of my own people and I knew that I had to go down."[31]

Dropping away from the melee, Reschke looked behind him and saw that the "friendly fire" had chewed his tail surfaces to pieces. Now his Bf 109 was extremely nose heavy and dangerously slow to respond to his foot pedals. Efforts to adjust trim to compensate were only partially successful at keeping the damaged fighter flying straight and level. There was, he realized, no way he would make it to a friendly airfield.

"I had to decide whether to make a forced landing or bail out," Reschke recalled. "An inner voice told me not to bail out, for the damaged elevators might not produce sufficient force to catapult me from the cockpit. I searched in vain for a suitable place to land, losing altitude all the while."[32]

As Reschke drew closer to the green earth, he could see that the terrain was hilly, with swathes of dark green forest broken up by patches of farmers' fields and meadows. He spotted one of the latter and, working the Bf 109's sluggish controls, guided his wounded fighter toward it for a belly-landing. Cutting back his throttle, he flopped down into the meadow, plowing an ugly brown furrow through the green meadow as his plane slid downhill. The moment it slowed to a stop, Reschke shoved open the canopy and leaped out. The Bf 109 did not explode or catch fire, however, and, before long, a group of Czech police and firemen had arrived on the scene from the nearby town of Ungarisch-Brod. Reschke had crashed in eastern Moravia. Before the day was out, he was on a train heading back to rejoin his *Gruppe*.

⌇

As Reschke crashed in the Czech countryside somewhere below him, William Bullock kept 359 on Tune's right wing for as long as he could. Bullock was the head of a veteran crew. None of 359's previous three dozen missions, however, had prepared them for the chaos unfolding around them.

In the middle of the fuselage, radioman Wally Clayton was looking out his compartment's small window over the bomber's wings when the German fighters materialized from the surrounding clouds.

"[They] swarmed all over us, like bees around honey," Clayton remembered. "There were fighters all around us, [Bf 109s] and [Fw 190s]. The [Bf 109s] had cannons in the nose and were chewing us up. The attack was so fast we had little chance to fight back."[33]

"On our ship, we were all firing at attacking fighters," navigator Ed Smith added. "Then I noticed our right inboard engine, as I recall, was on fire. We had lost our ship's intercom system—apparently, it had been shot out. I stuck my head up in the navigator's astrodome, which is a short ways in front of the pilot's windshield, and looked at [Bullock]. He was gesturing violently with his head and mouthing the words 'get out.'"[34]

Smith needed no more encouragement. He signaled for the bombardier to do the same, tugged off his flak suit, and popped open the compartment's escape hatch. Fortunately, at the last moment, he noticed that he had clipped his parachute pack on his harness upside-down. He paused long enough to re-clip his parachute pack and then dove out the open hatch.[35]

In the bomber's radio compartment, the intercom system still seemed to be working. Through his headset, Clayton heard copilot Clarence Jackson yell, "Bail out, bail out, salvo bombs!" As the radio operator, he was responsible for visually confirming that all bombs had been jettisoned. Faithfully, he staggered back to make sure the bomb bay was empty. To his dismay, Clayton saw that the right rack, riddled with bullets and cannon shells, had jammed.

"Right bomb bay door jammed," Clayton called into the intercom.[36]

At that moment, a wave of German fighters began another pass at 359, lacing the Fortress with gunfire. A bullet smashed into Clayton's left leg, sending him staggering back into the radio compartment. Then a cannon shell punched through the fuselage, smashing into the radio beside the sergeant and shattering it. A piece of plastic shrapnel from the radio set rocketed into Clayton's nose, burrowing into his right eye and knocking him off his feet. Spread-eagled on the compartment's floor with a severed oxygen hose, the radio operator began to drift into unconsciousness.

Back at the waist gunner positions, gunner Morris Goldberg remembers his fellow waist gunner panicking at the sight of the incoming planes. "[He] was going crazy," Goldberg later described. "He was jumping up and down and flailing his arms about. I didn't know what to do, so I kicked him, and motioned for him to get back to work."[37]

But as soon as he had calmed down his fellow gunner, Goldberg's intercom died. Instinctively, he looked forward in the plane and, to his dismay, saw a sheet of flame blocking the radio room. Realizing that the Fortress was on fire, Goldberg decided it was time to bail out. He unhooked from his oxygen and turned for the waist door.

The other waist gunner was lying on the deck in front of the waist door. Apparently, in his frantic struggles to escape before being wounded, he had somehow managed to jam up the emergency release cable before being overcome from lack of oxygen.

"I started dragging him past the tail wheel," Goldberg recalled, "but I started getting dizzy from lack of oxygen so I had to let go of him. When I got back to the tail, there was Maurice [Nelson], slumped at his position and his tail door open. I pushed him out not knowing what his condition was and followed him out."[38]

Underneath the Fortress, in the painfully exposed ball turret, Jim Martin had a frightening front-row seat for the unfolding assault. "[The fighters'] wings winking at me was my first realization that we were being attacked by enemy aircraft," Martin remembered. "From the lower turret, it seemed like wave after wave of ME's and FW's were coming at us from below. Of course, down in the ball, I couldn't see what was going on above."[39]

As the first wave of enemy fighters crashed against the squadron's formation, a 20 mm shell punched through Martin's ball turret. It shattered against the steel plate behind him. Shrapnel filled the turret, flaying the gunner's right hand and the back of his legs. Once piece practically ripped off one of Martin's left toes. It would later be amputated.

With his turret out of action, Martin pulled himself painfully out of the turret and into the fuselage. He quickly snapped on his parachute pack to his harness and prepared to bail out. Then he spotted Clayton lying semi-unconscious, his left leg covered in blood, on the radio compartment floor.

Grabbing a handful of spent shell casings off the bomber's floor, Martin hurled them at Clayton. The rain of shells on Clayton's face woke the sergeant. Woozy from lack of oxygen, he sat up unsteadily and began crawling back toward the partially open bomb bay. There he met Whitey Morien, the upper turret gunner. Clayton nodded at Morien, signaling for him to jump. Morien needed no further encouragement. He bailed out, followed a split second later by Clayton. For his part, Martin made good his escape through the tail gunner's escape hatch.

As their crew abandoned the flaming bomber, the two pilots tried to do the same. Jackson left his seat and moved for the bomb bay, just as another shell struck the Fortress and detonated. The explosion knocked him out of the plane, but Bullock was not so fortunate. Some crewmen believe he was standing behind Jackson, waiting to bail out when the explosion rocked the bomber. Others reported him, wounded and bleeding profusely, still at 359's controls.[40] Regardless of such uncertainty, the fate of 359 was indisputable. Mortally wounded and out-of-control, it crashed to earth near Kasava.

⤺

Among the 20th Squadron's seven planes, *Snafuperman* lasted the longest. Piloted by the experienced team of Bill Garland and Leo Zupan, *Snafuperman* stayed locked terrier-like on *Tail End Charlie*'s left echelon for the entire flight. They were in that position when the German fighters first struck.

"All of the sudden, there were bursts of small flak bursting in front of us," Zupan recalled. "About that time, the tail gunner calls in 'fighters!' Then our radio and intercom system went dead. Fighters went screaming past us."[41]

"Suddenly, all hell broke loose," Garland remembered. "Enemy aircraft, [Bf 109s] and [Fw 190s], were all around, over and under us. We took a lot of hits. At the first hit, our radio intercom was knocked out. A [Bf 109] came in so close on his pass that I could see the pilot's features very clearly. Our engineer in the top turret [Frank Katz] was firing at him and as the [Bf 109] went down, I yelled in the radio, 'You got him, Katz!' but only silence answered—the radio was out."[42]

Tucked in on Tune's wing, Garland saw *Tail End Charlie* take a direct hit. He knew that his usual navigator, Loy Dickinson, was flying on board Tune's bomber on this particular mission. With smoke pouring out of *Tail End Charlie,* Garland yelled into the radio:

"Tune, you're on fire!"[43]

But, once again, only silence answered. The radio, like the intercom, was dead. Mortally wounded, its left wing a ball of flame, *Tail End Charlie* dropped away from *Snafuperman.* At that moment, only Garland and Lieutenant Bullock's crew, in 359, were left, and the two bombers huddled close to try to weather the enemy onslaught. But soon Bullock's bomber, trailing smoke and fire, banked away and exploded in midair.

With 359 gone, *Snafuperman* flew alone. It was a deadly predicament, as Garland and Zupan well knew. In the cockpit, Zupan pushed the throttles forward, coaxing as much power as possible out of the bomber's laboring engines. But first one, and then another, engine caught fire and had to be feathered. As Zupan and Garland knew, the remaining two engines would be hard pressed to keep *Snafuperman* in the group's protective fold.

Leaning over, Garland yelled at Albert Novak, their bombardier, to jettison *Snafuperman*'s bombs. The beleaguered bomber needed every bit of speed she could coax out of her Wright Cyclone engines. Novak put on an oxygen bottle and, accompanied by Hayett, managed to open the bomb bay doors. Nineteen of the 20 bombs tumbled free. The twentieth, however, stayed in the rack, its arming prop spinning furiously. In desperation, Hayett straddled the open bomb bay, reached up, and bent the prop to stop its spinning. The last thing the Fortress needed was an armed 250-pound bomb hanging in its innards. Meanwhile, with its load lightened, *Snafuperman* surged forward and pulled closer to the squadrons ahead.

As the group approached Moravska Ostrava, Garland began weighing his bomber's options. He knew that as soon as the group dropped its bombs its bombers would increase their speed—and when that happened, the crippled *Snafuperman* would not be able to keep pace. Garland also knew that, left behind and increasingly low on ammunition, the B-17 stood no chance of surviving the German fighters' exclusive attention.

"As all of this ran through my mind, it made the decision clear that we had to have the use of another engine to make it home," Garland decided. "So I unfeathered No. 4 engine and the fire broke out in it again. In desperation, I dove the plane hoping to snuff out the fire."[44]

"We thought maybe we had the fire put out," Zupan recalled. "Two fighters stayed with us, pass after pass, then the fire started up again in No. 1 engine and it spread into the wing. All of a sudden the control cables were severed and the plane could not be controlled manually. Bill switched on the automatic pilot and we were flying it with the knobs."[45]

At that moment, a Bf 109 ripped in from one o'clock, its wing-mounted machine guns winking evilly at Garland and Zupan.

"He was so close I could see the pilot's face," Zupan remembered. "Then he zoomed over our bomber. To this day, I don't see how he missed."[46]

Garland put the Fortress into a right spiraling glide, descending through 18,000 feet. With only one engine still working and *Snafuperman* beset by fighters, he gave up all hope of making it back to Amendola.

Moments later, a terrific explosion rocked *Snafuperman*'s cockpit. A 20 mm shell had smashed into it just behind Garland's seat, blasting out the side of the aircraft and the oxygen tanks. "The only thing that saved my life," Garland recognized, "was the piece of armor plate behind the pilot's seat. A few more inches toward me and I would not be writing this today."[47]

"Acrid, cloudy smoke filled the cockpit," Zupan added. "The plane shuddered and shook like a wounded animal. We were lucky. Twelve inches forward would have taken Bill's and my heads off."[48]

By now, the left wing was burning so badly that Zupan could see its skeletal wing ribs. *Snafuperman* had fought a gallant fight, but the end was obviously moments away.

"Let's get the hell out of here!" Zupan shouted to Garland.[49] Garland needed no further encouragement. Leaving Zupan, he headed for the back of the aircraft to tell the rest of the crew to bail out.

For his part, Zupan tugged at Sergeant Katz's leg above him in the upper turret and motioned the flight engineer toward the nose hatch. Rather than squeeze through the narrow hatch, Katz elected to jump through the bomb bay doors. Novak and Hayett followed, with Zupan close behind. Recognizing the risk of hitting the ball turret after he exited the aircraft, Zupan dove out headfirst.

"It was just like a big 'swoosh,'" he remembered. "I went tumbling, and then straightened out, like I was swimming. On my back, I fell through the sky toward the ground below."[50]

Meanwhile, Garland worked his way back through the aircraft. Daylight shined through the holes that now peppered *Snafuperman*'s fuselage. At the waist gunners' position, a bloodied crewman greeted him. At first, Garland did not recognize Charles Griffin, the bomber's radio operator. When the wounded tail gunner, Bob Hoadley, pulled himself out of the tail without his parachute, Griffin had ignored his own wounds and crawled back to retrieve the tail gunner's chute.

Alongside Hoadley and Griffin, Garland found Jesse Barker and Ralph DeWitt.

The two men were laboring to fasten a parachute onto Russell Payne, one of the waist gunners. Payne had been shot in the back by a 20 mm shell that had exited his stomach. Hemorrhaging and coughing blood, he was lying helpless on the bloody deck.[51]

Barker later described the scene in a report to AAF authorities:

"Unable to converse with the forward part of the ship, I left the ball turret after seeing my guns helplessly jammed and the left wing afire. I found [Payne] lying unable to move but conscious. With the help of [DeWitt] who had been manning his gun we restored oxygen to [him]. The tail gunner and the radioman had also been wounded but were able to help themselves. [Hoadley] helped me pull [Payne] to the waist door after [DeWitt] had secured a spare chute for [Griffin] whose chute had been badly damaged. We had secured the safety strap to [Payne's] rip cord . . . when the pilot came back to the waist."[52]

Assessing the crowded, chaotic scene, Garland moved quickly, motioning the men out of the bomber through the rear door. But as the last one exited, disaster struck. The crewman tripped on the safety strap that had been fastened to Payne's rip cord, causing the chute to pop open inside the aircraft. Garland scrambled to wrap the loose chute around Payne's limp body. As he did, Payne stirred, opened his eyes, looked at his pilot, and went limp. There was nothing Garland could do but roll him out of the door. Then it was Garland's turn.

"With all the crew out, I sat down at the rear door intending to roll out," he remembered. "At the last minute, I looked down and my parachute harness was not buckled. There was a buckle you sat on and it was very uncomfortable and we did not buckle up until we approached the target." As soon as he did, he scooted out the bomber's rear door, leaving the burning bomber in his tumbling wake.

"I tried to roll back into the plane but with the slipstream on my legs and with the lack of oxygen, I could not get back into the plane. Then I looked out at the wing, the aluminum had burned off of the outer wing and the Tokyo gas tanks were afire. I realized the plane could blow up at any minute and this provided the incentive to roll back into the plane and buckle up my harness."[53]

Meanwhile, as he floated to earth, Hoadley looked up and saw *Snafuperman* explode in midair. Flaming chunks of wreckage showered the fields near the Czech town of Metylovice. The Fortress's fall, after 20 minutes of desperate aerial battling, marked the complete destruction of the squadron's aircraft aloft that August day. But in the meantime, the 2nd Group soldiered on toward Moravska Ostrava.

10

Time on Target

Flight Officer Duane Seaman had a front-row view of the disaster that swamped the 20th Squadron and that, in the end, overwhelmed his B-17 crew as well. Seaman, a native of Newark, New Jersey, piloted a bomber identified as 44-6369. It occupied the tail-end charlie position of the 49th Squadron, which flew in the echelon right forward of the 20th Squadron. A sergeant named Timothy J. Reidy, of Belmont, Massachusetts, manned the bomber's ball turret and, like the gunners of the 20th Squadron, initially mistook the onrushing Bf 109s for friendly P-51 Mustangs.[1] But not for long.

"Then all hell broke loose," Seaman recalled. "We were hit by furiously attacking enemy fighters. In what seemed like a matter of seconds there was a huge hole between engines 1 and 2 and flames were shooting out of the burning gas tanks eight feet high. No. 3 engine was hit and had a runaway propeller with oil running over the wing."[2]

In 369's upper turret, Technical Sergeant John A. Nigborowicz, of Gallitzin, Pennsylvania, battled back as best he could, returning fire with his pair of .50-caliber machineguns. Then a 20 mm shell struck the turret, knocking out the glass and cutting both its oxygen and its power. Amid the rush of frigid wind pouring through the hole, Nigborowicz groped for a portable oxygen bottle. In the cockpit, Seaman and Pastorino did the same.

Despite the beating his bomber had taken, Seaman managed to keep it under control. Staying in formation, however, was another matter. The stricken bomber simply could not keep up with the rest of the squadron. With a gentle turn of the yoke, Seaman banked his Fortress off to the right. For a few moments, he tried to join up with the mangled survivors of the 20th Squadron and ride out the attack with them.

Looking outside, Nigborowicz realized Seaman's plan would not work. He spotted the skin on the left wing melting away from the tremendous heat of the burning fuel tanks. Seaman saw the same sight. He pushed the bomber into a dive, hoping to blow out the flames. The maneuver failed. Soon the entire wing was a blazing pyre.

"Bail out!" Seaman called out over the intercom. A moment later, he repeated the command. But Nigborowicz and the bomber's nose gunner, Staff Sergeant Donald B. Hausler, of Cleveland, Ohio, needed no such encouragement. Nor did navigator/bombardier Flight Officer Robert E. Mickadeit, a Native American of Nebraska's Winnebago tribe. The three men hopped out the nose hatch while other crewmen dropped through the bomb bay or out the waist hatch.

In the lonely tail gunner position, Staff Sergeant Marty Childress slipped out of his flak gear, snapped on his parachute pack, and pulled the lever on the tail section's emergency hatch. The Texan expected it to fly open. It didn't. Alarmed, Childress aimed a solid kick at the hatch. This time, it gave way and tumbled free. Childress wasted no time plunging after it. Behind him, the burning Fortress wobbled on.

Once the crew was out, Seaman and Pastorino abandoned the cockpit and hurried for the bomb bay. With a quick look over his shoulder to make sure Pastorino was behind him, Seaman dropped through the open bomb bay doors. Pastorino followed closely behind him. All ten of Seaman's crew managed to escape the burning bomber alive and rode out the rest of the war in German POW camps.

⌐

Directly ahead of Tune's 20th Squadron flew John Fitzpatrick's *Wolf Pack*, the bomber more formally known as 42-97915 and the unlucky occupant of the 429th Squadron's tail-end charlie position. Although Tune's squadron bore the brunt of the German attacks, the 429th endured a number of aggressive passes by the enemy and, at the back of the formation, *Wolf Pack* was particularly vulnerable.

"German fighters were all over the sky," remembered Staff Sergeant Vincent Contrada, a former high school student from Norfolk, Virginia, now flying as *Wolf Pack*'s left waist gunner and struggling to deal with the elusive fighters diving in "from every conceivable direction." "Hell broke loose," Contrada declared. "It was impossible to remember details in all that excitement."[3]

Curled in the ball turret beneath *Wolf Pack,* Staff Sergeant Vincente Martinez, of Vallectos, New Mexico, may well have questioned his luck at this particular moment. He was a last-minute addition to *Wolf Pack*'s crew, added only to replace a sick crew member. Or he may have simply spun into action as he had on so many other missions. Regardless of his internal thoughts, his actions were clear. Whirling in the motorized turret, he blasted at first one fighter and then another.

In the face of such resistance, one Bf 109 pressed its luck too far. Catching the fighter in their sights, Martinez and another gunner sawed off one of its wings with a long burst of their machineguns. But then another Bf 109 pulled up alongside *Wolf Pack* and opened fire with his cannon. The bomber lurched "like a car hitting a curb" from the impact, but Martinez had a golden opportunity with the enemy fighter cruising in point-black range. With a quick turn of the turret, he framed the enemy fighter squarely in his sights.

"He's mine," Martinez thought. "I have him. I'm going to put this right between his eyes." With a grim sense of satisfaction, he pulled his guns' triggers.

Nothing.

Martinez pulled the triggers again. Again, there was no result. Instead, he only heard the solenoids clicking that should have been activating the guns' trigger mechanisms. He was out of ammunition. Unaware of his fortunate reprieve, the Bf 109 banked away while Martinez stayed in the ball turret and continued to swivel back and forth, tracking incoming fighters. Perhaps, he thought, he could bluff the enemy into thinking the bottom of the bomber was still protected with his twin .50-caliber machineguns. Other gunners, running out of ammunition themselves, did the same.[4]

Meanwhile, in the chaos of the *Luftwaffe*'s onslaught, confusion reigned. The tail gunner, Staff Sergeant James J. DeLutes Jr., of Harrisburg, Pennsylvania, remembered *Wolf Pack* taking hits from four separate German fighters as it lumbered stubbornly through the tracer-streaked sky.[5]

DeLute's fellow crewmen, however, recall a different version of events. In *Wolf Pack*'s cockpit, copilot Second Lieutenant Charles H. McGhee, of Briggsdale, Ohio, spotted the tail gunner of the B-17 to their echelon right front firing wildly and taking out the number 3 and 4 engines. *Wolf Pack*'s bombardier, Second Lieutenant Paul Sumner, a former school teacher from Denver, Colorado, later remembered an equally wild waist gunner shooting up another one of *Wolf Pack*'s engines. *Luftwaffe* pilots, Sumner maintained, deserve credit for knocking out two of the other engines.

Regardless of who was to blame, *Wolf Pack* was in serious trouble, and Fitzpatrick and McGhee knew it. Both the number 3 and 4 engines were inoperable and spewing fuel and oil. Fitzpatrick tried but failed to feather the number 3 engine, which left the bomber with a propeller that had "the same effect as a ten foot square sheet of plywood," in McGhee's words.[6] Unable to keep up with the rest of the squadron, *Wolf Pack* banked to the left and dropped out of formation and tried to form up with the remnants of Tune's battered force. But with its stricken engines trailing white smoke, *Wolf Pack* simply couldn't keep up. Discouraged, Fitzpatrick jettisoned its bombs, made a futile call for a fighter escort, and turned for home. With a quick call over the intercom, he confirmed that at least all his crewmen had survived the German attacks unharmed.

The B-17's troubles, however, persisted. With every passing minute, the bomber dropped lower and lower. Then it blundered over a German flak training camp. Dark ugly puffs of smoke exploded around *Wolf Pack* as the flak crews opened fire on the wayward Fortress. Without hesitating, Fitzpatrick nosed the bomber into a dive, trading altitude for speed as he dashed for safety. The gambit paid off, but only temporarily. Now *Wolf Pack* was flying even lower—and still losing precious altitude. It clawed its way southward over the White Carpathian Mountains, but just barely, before eventually crashing into a Hungarian wheat field. Fitzpatrick and his crew survived, only to be rounded up by Hungarian soldiers and later turned over to the Germans. Like Seaman's crew, they would spend the rest of the war behind barbed wire.

⌐

As the 20th Squadron and its unfortunate comrades succumbed to the enemy assault, the rest of the 2nd Group pressed on for Moravska Ostrava. But the German fighters were not content to let them slip away. In their first pass, they had swept through Tune's squadron and let their momentum carry them, guns and cannon blazing, into the rear of the 2nd Group's three squadrons. Although denied the success they enjoyed at the 20th Squadron's expense, the *Luftwaffe* pilots did not leave those squadrons unscathed.

In the 96th Squadron, Staff Sergeant John A. Lamb crouched in the tail gunner position for a B-17 bearing the tail number 161. He caught an exploding 20 mm shell in his face and shoulders, severely wounding him and badly damaging his bomber. With the aircraft's mechanical and electrical linkage rods to the bomb racks shot out, the plane's bombardier, Staff Sergeant James O'Grady, had to jettison each bomb by hand. It was a chore that lasted until the Fortress crossed back over into Yugoslavia. In the middle of the squadron's formation, Second Lieutenant Henry Wallet's bomber took a hit as well. His bomber, number 379, labored on with a two-foot hole in the tail.[7]

Meanwhile, at the head of the group's formation and in the lead of the 429th Squadron, Lieutenant Colonel Cunningham found himself the object of much of the German's unwanted attention. A series of 20 mm shells rocked his Fortress, blasting off the left elevator and the left wing's aileron and flaps. Cunningham also sustained damage to his number 2 engine. Buffeted by the barrage of cannon fire, he came close to inadvertently looping the massive bomber. The other aircraft in the squadron banked and dove away, fearful of a midair collision. But the experienced Cunningham managed to regain control and the other pilots quickly swooped back in alongside him. With rampaging German fighters on the prowl, they had to keep the formation together.[8]

With Cunningham back in control, the American bomber pilots forged ahead. Of the 19 aircraft left in the group, six were damaged. Four of those planes, to include Cunningham's, were severely damaged. Nevertheless, their gunners managed to take their toll on the attacking Germans.

Sergeant Melvin E. Leppo, curled into the ball turret of aircraft 198, was one such gunner. With Fitzpatrick's *Wolf Pack* out of position, Leppo's bomber had slipped into the tail-end charlie position of the 429th Squadron. The pilot of a Bf 109, thinking he had an opportunity to pounce on another straggler, came in low from the 5:00 position, its machineguns and cannon firing. It was the last mistake the German pilot ever made. Leppo, a former dairy farmer who had enlisted from central Pennsylvania, allowed his adversary to get within 400 yards of his ball turret. Then the patient Leppo opened fire with his twin .50-caliber machineguns. The fighter curved away, swooping within 300 yards of the B-17. Keeping his thumbs on the firing levers, Leppo poured what he estimated were 200–250 rounds into the Bf 109. Suddenly, it was as if the enemy fighter had run into a buzz-saw. It literally disintegrated in midair. The triumphant whoops of 198's right waist gunner punctuated the kill.[9]

Meanwhile, Leppo's tail gunner, Sergeant Gilmer Hawkins, of Hood River, Oregon, tore into another Bf 109. He registered a "probably destroyed." Elsewhere, three other gunners downed a pair of Bf 109s and an Fw 190, while three other Bf 109s were eventually reported as "probably destroyed." Two other enemy aircraft—a Bf 109 and an Fw 190—were reported damaged.[10] In addition to whatever downed aircraft Tune's men would have been able to claim had they returned to Amendola, the Group in total shot down three Bf 109s and an Fw 190. Another four Bf 109s were probably destroyed, with another pair of fighters damaged.[11]

For 20 minutes, the group weathered the German storm. Finally, as 1100 approached and the Fortresses angled in for their bomb run on Moravska Ostrava, a flight of five P-51 Mustangs streaked down past the group's formation. They managed to catch one Bf 109, damaging it badly enough to force its pilot to bail out near Slavicin. The rest of the German fighters disappeared as suddenly as they arrived, leaving Cunningham and his pilots to try their luck with the flak gunners of Moravska Ostrava.

Today, the city appears simply as Ostrava on today's maps of the modern Czech Republic. Tucked into the northeastern corner of the country, it first gained prominence in the Middle Ages as a small town that guarded the so-called Moravian Gate, the entrance to the Moravian lowlands. Its location near the junction of the Oder and Ostravice Rivers, coupled with rich anthracite and bituminous coal and iron ore deposits, helped propel the city in the late nineteenth century to prominence as the nation's third-largest, and arguably most industrialized, city. At the outbreak of the war, some 125,000 people called it home.[12]

Prior to World War II, the noted travel author Joseph Wechsberg, who would later find fame writing for *The New Yorker,* grew up in Moravska Ostrava. He remembered a city where "large coal pits were located almost in the center of the business district and the theater and the opera house was but a stone's throw from the [slag] heaps."[13] But despite the heavy press of industry—or perhaps because of it— the city had a reputation as a hard-partying metropolis. It was a "fast-living, fast-spending town," according to Wechsberg, where, in the prewar days, "people got drunk so they could boast the next day that they had been drunk" and the girls enjoyed the reputation of having "by far the best legs of all the girls in Moravia."[14]

"It was all very F. Scott Fitzgerald, though of course no one in town had ever heard of him," Wechsberg reported. "No doubt our town had the dimmest-lit bars, the noisiest "American" jazz bands, the most daringly gypping headwaiters, and a very special blend of racketeers who traded in saccharine, frozen potatoes, 'Persian' rugs from Slovakia, 'original English' woolens from the Brno textile mills, and 'old' paintings which were new paintings in old frames."[15]

Wechsberg left Moravska Ostrava in 1938, the same year Hitler's legions rolled into the Sudetenland and only months before they proceeded to occupy the rest of Czechoslovakia. The Germans created the *Reichsprotektorat Böhmen und Mähren*— the Protectorate of Bohemia and Moravia—and encouraged Czechoslovakia's eastern half to break away and form the Nazi puppet state of the Slovak Republic. In both states, the ruling fist of Berlin steadily tightened over the next six years, quashing nationalist dissent while persecuting a steadily dwindling indigenous Jewish population.

But until August 29, 1944, the war had not yet visited Moravska Ostrava. On this particular Monday, however, Cunningham's bombers brought the global conflict home to the city with a vengeance. On Cunningham's first pass, coming in from the south, his group found the Privoser Oil Refinery and the marshaling yards obscured by smoke and clouds. Temporarily foiled, the lieutenant colonel led his remaining three squadrons north past Moravska Ostrava and into Poland. Then, wheeling around, they came back in for a second pass over the city, this time using their PFF pathfinder radars. Heavy-caliber flak burst around them. Undistracted, Cunningham's bombardiers spotted their target and, as soon as they could, released a total of 22 tons of bombs on the Czech city below.

Later that day, the intelligence section of the 5th Wing would complete its "Final Strike Assessment Report" for the day's raids. Compiling the day's results, First Lieutenant C. B. Hearn, one of the wing's staff officers, noted that the impact of the 2nd Group's bombs, which were intermingled with the efforts of the 454th Bombardment Group's B-24s, was difficult to assess. "Bombs fell on industrial, residential buildings and in open fields," he wrote. "Two or three explosions were visible and numerous fires lit; it is impossible to place their origin. One explosion was in a marshalling yard. Any definite assessment is impossible due to cloud, smoke, and the mixed nature of the bombing."[16]

A "definite assessment," however, was probably far from the minds of the 2nd Group's survivors. Over four hours of hard flying still separated the group from the Foggia airfields. Determined to keep his damaged bombers with him, Cunningham flew low and slow. Twice flak batteries opened fire on them, but no more fighters challenged their withdrawal. Leaving the ugly black bursts of flak behind them, the crews of the surviving bombers blessed their good luck, tended to their wounded, and pressed on for home.

⌒

Meanwhile, back at Amendola, a replacement B-17 crew had completed a long journey that took it from Lincoln, Nebraska, through Grinier Field, New Hampshire, Gander, Newfoundland, the Azores Islands, French Morocco, Tunisia, and finally into Amendola. Staff Sergeant Melvin W. McGuire, of Hatch, New Mexico, was the new Fortress's left waist gunner. Years later, in his memoir *Bloody Skies,* he recalled the scene as the green crew arrived to join the 20th Squadron.

"Army 428, turn right and taxi to a hard stand in the parking area," Amendola's control tower radioed. The new crew was less than impressed with their new home's control tower—"I've built a tree house bigger and better than that," one of McGuire's crewmates commented—but the bomber's pilot quickly obeyed. No sooner had he cut the engines and the crew popped the plane's hatches when a weapons carrier roared up in a cloud of dust. An older man eased out and limped hurriedly to McGuire's aircraft. He wore no rank or identifying insignia, not even a cap.

"All right, everybody get his personal gear and leave everything else just where it's at," the man said. "Do you have any tools in there?"

"And who are you?" McGuire responded, unimpressed with their reception thus far.

"I'm Bernie Cohen, and I'm the line chief. We need this airplane pretty quick and need to start working on it. So, get your stuff and clear the airplane."[17]

McGuire and his crewmates began pulling their gear from their bomber. As they worked, they could not help but notice the grim faces of the ground crew around them. In quiet knots and clumps, they stood on the empty aircraft hard stands. Some of them even had tears in their eyes. Finally, someone asked one what had happened. An hour earlier, the man said, the group had radioed back the news of the 20th Squadron's demise. Seventy men were missing.

Before the conversation could continue, a truck arrived to take McGuire and his crew the few miles to the olive grove that cloaked their squadron's headquarters. There they met Tiny Atkerson, the squadron's first sergeant.

"Welcome to the 20th Bomb Squadron, Second Bomb Group," the first sergeant said. "We're upset and grieving over the loss of that squadron. Normally, new crews are not greeted and handled as you have been. We're not yet prepared for you. We haven't cleaned out your tents yet as we have just received word that the 20th was wiped out today."[18]

"We're sorry," Atkerson continued, "but you'll have to use the tents in their present condition. The personal effects and uniforms of the previous occupants are still there. We'll get you new blankets before you proceed to your tent. Drop off your bags and then return here for additional briefings."[19]

McGuire and his enlisted comrades quickly found their tent, a makeshift affair placed against a stone wall at the end of an olive grove and patched with scores of colorful swathes of cloth and canvas. Inside, the unmade bunks looked as if the occupants had just left. Personal effects such as rings, wristwatches, fountain pens, and cash were piled on the bunks, waiting for the return of their owners. With a gulp, McGuire realized that those piles would remain uncollected.

A series of other hurried briefings followed. With the loss of seven crews, one officer warned the new arrivals that they would soon be going into battle. Sobered by the warning, McGuire trekked to the mess hall for a late lunch. They found it almost deserted. Its few occupants were gathered in small groups, talking quietly in subdued voices. Upon a closer look, McGuire noticed that several—including an otherwise grizzled crew chief—were wiping tears from their eyes. A few cried openly. Even the Italian prisoners of war tasked with assisting the cooks were clearly upset.[20]

As McGuire grabbed a tray and went through the mess line, a cook looked at him quizzically.

"You're new guys, aren't you?" he asked.

"Yes," McGuire answered.

"Tough luck today with the outfit. Just eat everything you want because we got too much. We got seventy missing tonight, so there's plenty of everything."[21]

⌒

As McGuire and his crew were completing their briefings and eating lunch, Cunningham and the group's survivors approached Amendola. By now it was approximately 1515. The weary B-17s fell into a circling formation over the airfield. Two of them fired flares, signaling to the ground that they needed an ambulance to meet them as soon as they landed. One by one, they began landing.

On the ground, the 20th Squadron's ground crew, which would have normally been abuzz with activity, simply stood idly on their empty hard stands and watched the other squadrons' planes land. Across the runway, as Cunningham cut his engines and pulled himself out of his bomber, a ground crewman approached.

"Colonel, what happened?" he blurted out.

"Well, I left with twenty-eight airplanes this morning and I only brought nineteen home. The Second Bomb Group took ninety-two casualties today. Everybody in the 20th went down."[22]

⌒

As dusk approached, another B-17 arrived at Amendola, this one piloted by Second Lieutenant Ed Bender. Bender had shepherded his crew from the States across the Atlantic by the same route as McGuire's bomber. He shared another trait with McGuire's crew—his crew also contained a future author. Six decades later, Bender's bombardier, Second Lieutenant Jack Myers, would pen *Shot At and Missed: Recollections of a World War II Bombardier*.

After landing at Amendola, Bender, Myers, and the rest of the crew were told to park their bomber and stand by their aircraft. An hour passed and then a jeep arrived, driven by Major Charles Shepherd. "Welcome to the 20th Squadron," Shepherd, the unit's commanding officer, said simply.[23]

The major took Myers and the other officers on to the Officers' Club for a dinner, while another jeep deposited the enlisted men at their quarters. In Myers's estimation, his new commanding officer was a pleasant enough individual but not very talkative. It was a bouncy jeep ride of several miles from the end of the runway into the low-lying hills where, amid a grove of olive trees, Myers spotted a veritable shantytown of tents, huts, and other assorted buildings in the gloom. They had arrived at the group's bivouac area.

By now, it was almost 2000, and, upon arriving at the Officers' Club, they found that the cooks had left for the night. A couple of Italian waiters hustled up bread and jam for sandwiches and, after giving the new arrivals a chance for a quick bite, Shepherd drove them to their new quarters. Pulling up alongside a cluster of tents and canvas-roofed stone huts, the major told Myers and the others to pick one out.

Climbing out of the jeep, Myers stepped inside the nearest hut. Inside, he found four canvas cots, footlockers, a table, and a pair of homemade chairs. Clothes and other personal effects were scattered throughout it.

"Someone lives here," Myers called out to Shepherd.

"They were shot down on today's mission," the squadron's commander replied. He paused for a moment, then continued. "In fact, we lost the whole squadron. They're empty."[24]

The next day, in the wake of the catastrophe, the 2nd Bomb Group "stood down" for a day without flying to rest from the catastrophe. But that day was anything but restful for the necktie-clad men of the army's local Graves Registration Unit. Two businesslike men from the unit arrived at McGuire's new tent just after breakfast.

"We need the personal effects from the crew that was there," they told McGuire and his tent mates.[25] Then they spread six white sheets outside the tent—one for each bunk. As they started packing the missing men's gear, they asked the tent's new occupants to go through the gear and remove anything their families should not see, such as letters from girlfriends, pornography, or classified material. With lists in hand, the two men checked them against the effects left for each man. Then they stepped back outside the tent. McGuire followed.

Outside, McGuire looked at the tents in the area.

"It was scary," he recalled. "Every tent had six bundles in front of it, filled with personal effects. The men finished wrapping up the sheets and loaded them from each tent into a truck. When they left, the truck was almost full."[26]

Within a week, McGuire, Myers, and their crews would be flying their first combat missions, falling into a routine that would have seemed numbingly familiar to Tune and his squadron mates. But for those men of the 20th Squadron still missing in action, their war had veered off onto a frightening new course.

"For You the War is Over"

Blasted from *Tail End Charlie,* Bill Tune regained consciousness 6,000 feet above Czechoslovakia. Facing skyward, with his hands instinctively clutching his parachute pack, he hurtled toward the unseen ground below. Once again, Tune's thoughts returned to childhood memories of Carbon Hill. "The wind going by felt like riding in an open truck with your back in the direction of travel," he recalled.[1]

As he plummeted through the sky, Tune glanced at his hands. His right hand seemed uninjured, but the left one was bleeding badly. At the moment, though, he knew that his injured hand was not his immediate priority. Somewhere behind him, Europe rushed to meet him. Unless he did something soon, it would be a catastrophically violent encounter. He had to open his chute.

With his right hand, Tune clawed for his parachute pack's D-ring handle. Swiping frantically against the canvas, he dragged his hand along the pack's side. He found no handle. In increasing desperation, he forced himself to feel methodically along the right side of the pack. Once again, he found no handle. And with every second, he knew Czechoslovakia loomed ever closer.

Craning his head forward, Tune examined the sides of his parachute pack. With a grimace, he realized that he had buckled it on upside down. That explained the missing D-ring. It faced left rather than right. Reaching across with his uninjured right hand, Tune grabbed the handle and yanked it. With an explosive snap of silk and canvas, his chute billowed open and jerked him upright. In an instant, the deafening roar of wind was replaced with an almost eerie silence.

Suspended beneath his chute, Tune oscillated gently. He knew he was descending, but at that altitude there was no sensation of downward movement. For a moment, he seemed peacefully suspended above the Czech countryside.

A pair of German fighters streaking below quickly dispelled that illusion. Back in Foggia, Tune had heard many tales of vengeful *Luftwaffe* pilots machinegunning parachutists. Regardless of the truth of those stories, he now watched the pair of enemy fighters with fearful eyes. Tune knew his vigilance was an exercise in futility. Hanging beneath this white parachute, there was nothing he could do if the two Germans came after him.

Fortunately, the fighters took no notice. Apparently, they had wreaked enough havoc for one day. Within a matter of seconds, they scooted out of sight and left the battered lieutenant to try to collect his thoughts.

With the German fighters gone, Tune examined his bloody hands more closely. He realized that his left hand was badly injured. In fact, as he would discover later, it had been peppered with numerous shell fragments when the fighters had strafed *Tail End Charlie*. His left leg, he suspected, was in worse shape. It felt odd. He surmised that the torn holes in his trouser legs marked even more wounds.

Beyond his dangling legs, Tune saw the green earth drawing ever closer. Normally, a parachutist could, to some extent, guide his descent by pulling down on some combination of his chute's so-called risers, the long canvas straps that connected the parachute harness to the silk canopy. By tugging and holding a handful of risers on his right, for example, a parachutist could slip through the sky to the right. However, such manipulation of the risers required two good hands and a considerable amount of upper body strength. With his left hand practically useless, Tune knew he had little control over where he would land.

As Tune descended through 1,000 feet, the illusion of motionless floating evaporated. Now the ground came rushing toward him. It was a series of hills, blanketed with a checkerboard of light green farm fields, an occasional white-walled, red-tiled village, and dark evergreen woods. To land in the woods would be disastrous. Images of being skewered on a dead tree trunk or crashing into a heavy bough flashed through Tune's mind as he tried to judge where his chute was taking him.

In the last few seconds of his descent, Tune realized that his luck was holding. A grassy field opened beneath him and, with a gentle wind filling his chute's canopy, he managed a comparatively soft landing while favoring his injured leg. As his canopy collapsed on the ground behind him, he quickly unbuckled his chute. He had no desire to be dragged across the ground in his current state.

Sitting up, Tune tried to establish just what that current state might be. His left hand was still bleeding profusely and his left leg was numb. Prodding it with his right hand, he succeeded in sending jolts of pain coursing through his body. As he feared, it was broken.

"Tune, you are in a pickle now," he said to himself.[2] Looking at his mangled hand and broken leg, Tune realized that there was little point in futile heroics. Nor was he going to outrun anyone in a footrace. Accordingly, he ejected the magazine from his .45 caliber pistol, tapped it on his uninjured leg, and shook the bullets out onto the ground. He then scooped them up with his good hand and hurled them into the tall grass. If anyone discovered him, he knew he would likely be caught and he did not want to be shot with his own gun.

With his bullets disposed, Tune pulled his scarf from around his neck and tied a tourniquet around his left arm. Limited to the use of his right arm, he found it an awkward exercise. Nevertheless, the makeshift dressing seemed to stem the bleeding, although he worried uneasily about how often he should ease the tourniquet to keep his hand alive.[3] He had no ready answer and so he turned his attention to his left leg.

As he struggled to find a way to splint his broken leg, Tune heard a series of whistles in the distance. Was it a German patrol tracking downed fliers? The idea of being hunted down sent his pulse pounding once again.

Moments later, a group of teenage boys, strung out in an orderly line at 100-foot intervals, crested a nearby hill. They were obviously looking for survivors. With a wave of his arm, Tune signaled to one of them. The teenager reacted by blasting on his whistle. In response, the entire line ran forward.

The boys surrounded Tune in a close circle, staring down at the wounded lieutenant. He handed over his pistol to an older boy, eliciting a series of seemingly impressed comments. The Czechs exchanged a few words and folded Tune's parachute into a rough triangle. Grabbing Tune under the arms, they pulled him gently onto the makeshift stretcher. Then, clutching handfuls of silk, the boys began dragging Tune across the field. They tried to be gentle, but each bump sent flashes of pain coursing through Tune's body.

As his left side throbbed with pain, Tune could not help but compare his current situation to that of a half hour ago. Then, he had been the master not only of his destiny but the fates of 69 other men. Now he was being dragged across a Czechoslovakian field by a gaggle of teenagers to an uncertain future. He wasn't even sure if the boys were rescuers or captors.

After the boys had dragged Tune a quarter mile, they encountered a group of adults. These were Czech foresters, each armed with a shotgun. Tune realized that the forest guards wanted to claim him for their own. Tune could not understand the language but it was apparent to him that one man, brandishing his shotgun angrily, even wanted to shoot him on the spot. He began threatening the teenagers surrounding the wounded American flier. One teenager in particular bore the brunt of the shouted threats. Nevertheless, the unarmed boy obstinately refused to back down, even as the argument grew more heated. After several moments of shouting, the teenagers somehow prevailed. Tune did not know it at the time, but the angry forester was the stubborn boy's father. A Nazi sympathizer, the elder Czech would pay for his misplaced loyalties with six years in prison after the war.[4]

The defeated foresters slunk away and the triumphant boys started to drag Tune once again. Another quarter mile passed. Tune gritted his teeth in pain with every bump and jolt. Rolling his head to the left, he spied an unlikely sight. A girl, wearing a red swimsuit, was running down the hillside toward them. In her hands she carried a cot. Breathlessly, she presented it to Tune's captors. It was such a surreal sight that, for a moment, Tune wondered if he was hallucinating. But he was not, and the boys lifted Tune off the chute and onto the cot. It provided a much sturdier stretcher for him. Tune's pain, however, grew steadily worse, even with the improvement in his means of transportation.

Before long, Tune's group reached the village of Luhacovice. As the boys paraded down the little town's main street with their prize, pub owners stepped out of their establishments. Clutching dark bottles, they offered Tune small glasses of plum brandy. By now, he was in too much pain to accept their offerings.

A small hospital stood at the edge of Luhacovice. The boys carried Tune to its door, where they sat his cot gently on the ground. A team of young white-coated doctors and orderlies descended on Tune, transferred him to a gurney, and wheeled him inside. Within moments, they were dressing his wounds and splinting his broken leg. Had Tune understood Czech, he would have heard that his leg's tibula and fibula bones were fractured in several places.

After the Czech doctors finished their ministrations, they placed their patient in a waiting area—to wait for the arrival of the Germans, Tune presumed. But his first visitor was a Czech woman who looked to be in her forties. She seemed to be the same age as his mother. Taking Tune's right hand in hers, she gently mopped his brow with a cool wet cloth. Back in flight school, at the air base in Italy, or even in the air, Tune had never given much thought to what kind of reception he would find on the ground if he ever bailed out. He had certainly never allowed himself to hope for so much kindness and to be treated with such dignity. This would change, he suspected, once the Germans arrived.

The Germans were not long in coming. A squad of *Wehrmacht* soldiers, clad in their *feldgrau* trousers and blouses, trooped into the hospital and quickly found

Tune's room. As Tune watched them enter his room and surround his bed, he realized that, after months of combat, this was the first time he had confronted a German face-to-face.

The Germans seemed less philosophical. They moved quickly and efficiently. Wheeling the wounded American out of the hospital, they loaded him onto a truck and drove him to a nearby school building that they had commandeered as a gathering point for captured airmen. It already contained several other fliers.

Evening arrived at the schoolhouse, but it failed to bring dinner with it. With his stomach growling and his leg aching, Tune drifted off to sleep on his first night of captivity. He did not know it at the time, but he was faring far better than some of his fellow crewmates. At least he had survived.

‿

Joe Owsianik had exited *Tail End Charlie*'s waist door when Tune ordered his crew to bail out. Determined to put as much distance as possible between himself and the mangled, burning bomber, the waist gunner plummeted some 10,000 feet before tugging his ripcord. With a violent snap, the chute opened, leaving Owsianik dangling above the Czech countryside.[5]

Immediately, he saw he was in trouble. A German Fw 190 fighter, engulfed in flames, was bearing down on him. A machinegun attack or midair collision seemed unavoidable. But at the last minute, the burning fighter roared past him, leaving a thick trail of smoke across the sky. It passed so closely that the parachutist could feel the heat on his face. The doomed plane's slipstream buffeted Owsianik's chute. For a moment, the canopy buckled, and Owsianik's stomach flipped as he plunged downward once again. But after a few ominous flaps, it filled once more. He continued downward at a more accommodating pace.

As he descended, Owsianik looked for a suitable landing spot. He saw that he seemed to be heading toward a farmer's field of some kind speckled with small trees. To his dismay, he spotted several people running across the ground and converging on the same spot. Owsianik doubted their intentions were friendly, and he tried to scout out a likely escape route from his temporary vantage point.

Moments later, Owsianik smacked down into the field with a heavy thud. It was a cabbage field, he realized, full of ripening cabbages almost ready for the autumn harvest. A random assortment of apple trees peppered the field. His chute draped the lower branches of one of them.

Still on his back, Owsianik popped the risers from his parachute harness. Standing up, he unbuckled his parachute harness as quickly as he could and then broke into a run toward a patch of nearby woods. From what he had seen in his descent, the woods were the best place for him to hide.

"Halt, halt," a voice cried out behind him. He had barely even managed a few steps. So much for his escape, he thought. Resigned to capture, he stopped and turned to face his captors.

They were a group of seven or eight Czech civilians. They did not seem armed, but the sergeant knew he could not outrun them in his heavy flight boots. Besides, his right arm was bleeding from a wound he had received during one of the fighter attacks on his bomber. Surrender seemed the only option.

The Czechs, however, acted more like friends than captors. One ripped a length of silk off his parachute canopy and tied a loose tourniquet around his upper right arm. It slowed the bleeding, and he soon removed it. In the meantime, the Czechs began pointing at the woods. "Comrade, comrade," they told Owsianik. With the civilians leading the way, Owsianik entered the woods. Another Czech civilian stepped out of the trees and led the band to another downed airman. Owsianik recognized his copilot, Lieutenant Francis Flynn.

Immediately, Owsianik could tell that Flynn was badly injured. An ugly wound ripped along his back, and the back of his uniform blouse was soaked in blood. With handfuls of torn parachute cloth, he tried unsuccessfully to staunch the bleeding. After a few moments, he realized that his rudimentary first aid was not going to help the wounded lieutenant. Flynn needed a doctor. In simple English, he asked the Czechs for a stretcher. With a quick nod, a pair of the civilians broke away, slipping through the woods to a nearby village. They returned a short time later with a stretcher.

Owsianik and the Czechs eased Flynn onto the stretcher and carried him into a nearby village. As the reached it, a villager stepped forward to join them.

"Hey, Joe!" he called out to Owsianik in perfect English. Startled, Owsianik stopped in his tracks.

"Hey, Joe, where are you from?" the villager asked.

"Uh, New Jersey," Owsianik replied.

"Oh, yeah, well, I am from Patterson," the Czech said, naming a New Jersey town. "Come on with me," he offered. "I'll get you a bite to eat and some whiskey."[6]

What a small world, Owsianik marveled. But he knew he had to stay with Flynn. Politely, he declined his new acquaintance's invitation and pressed on with the stretcher party to the next village, a small hamlet called Petruvka.

In Petruvka, the Czechs carried Flynn to the village's church, where they placed him in the entrance to a small room off the main sanctuary. With the lieutenant reasonably secure, Owsianik sat down at a small table, pulled out his rudimentary escape maps, spread them out across the table, and tried to determine his present location. The civilians crowded around, trying to help as best they could. Owsianik remembered that the group's intelligence officer had suggested they try to make it to Romania if they were shot down. But finding Romania on the map was one thing. Pinpointing where this particular church's position was quite another.

As Owsianik mulled over his maps, the door to the church burst open. A group of young German soldiers stormed into the room, followed by their sergeant. "*Raus, raus!*" the sergeant shouted. The Czechs had been under Nazi occupation long enough to understand "get out, get out." In a mad scramble, they poured out of the church as the German soldiers leveled their rifles at the American sergeant.

"*Pistolie, pistolie!*" the sergeant yelled, demanding Owsianik's pistol. Owsianik held up his empty hands, indicating that he was not carrying a sidearm. But the sergeant was not convinced. Drawing his own pistol, he shoved its barrel into Owsianik's mouth. "*Pistolie, pistolie!*" he shouted again.

"I have no pistol. I have no pistol," Owsianik said as best he could, trying not to gag on the German pistol.[7] The sergeant stepped back, allowing his soldiers to grab their captive and start ripping his clothes off. Soon Owsianik stood naked in the church, surrounding by glowering Germans.

The sergeant snapped a command at his men, and two of them grabbed Owsianik, allowing him to shove the pistol back in the sergeant's mouth once again. Tiring of Owsianik's gagging, the sergeant pulled it out and smashed him over the head with it. A flash of pain exploded across Owsianik's skull, and he felt himself being bent over. With probing fingers and coarse, guttural comments, the German soldiers subjected the airman to a thorough and humiliating full-body search.

After they finished with him, one of the soldiers motioned for Owsianik to put his trousers back on. As soon as he did, another told him to empty his trouser pockets into his undershirt lying on the floor. Wincing from the pain reverberating in his head, Owsianik dropped his wallet, cigarettes, and even his dog tags onto the shirt. His captors searched his wallet and pack of cigarettes, gave his dog tags a quick look, and tossed them back to him. Owsianik slipped them around his neck.

"I guess this is it," Flynn mumbled from the stretcher on the floor. Owsianik did not answer. With his legs wobbling from the pistol blow, he was struggling to even stand. Before he fell, a pair of soldiers grabbed him and guided him to the church door.

"Goodbye, lieutenant," Owsianik muttered forlornly to Flynn as he was led out of the church.[8]

Outside the church, the Germans walked Owsianik down a gravel path to the parish's cemetery. Spying the ancient tombstones, Owsianik feared the worst. Obviously, his captors meant to shoot him. Trembling with fear, and still weak from the blow to his head, he stumbled and fell. Two of the soldiers pulled him to his feet and shoved his undershirt in his hands. Holding that makeshift bag of belongings in his hands, he shuffled along with the Germans out of the village and through a wooded area.

As the group marched on, Owsianik realized that now, more than ever, he could really use a cigarette. After a half hour had passed, he summoned his courage and mimed smoking a cigarette to his captors. To his surprise, they stopped, pulled out his pack of cigarettes from his undershirt bundle, and gave the pack to Owsianik. With shaky hands, Owsianik tapped out one for each his guards and one for himself. A German offered a lighter, and the group of men lit their cigarettes. After a few drags, Owsianik allowed himself to hope that the worst was over. But with a nudge, the Germans indicated that the march was not over.

A few minutes later, the band reached a clearing in the woods. A lone building sat in the clearing. Owsianik assumed mistakenly that it was a POW facility. Instead, as he quickly discovered, the building was a barracks for a detachment of soldiers and Hitler Youth. Its inhabitants took all of Owsianik's belongings from him and tossed him into a cell. Nursing his sore head, the sergeant stretched out on the cell's rough cot and waited for dinner. None came. With his stomach rumbling, he eventually drifted off uneasily to sleep.

After leaping from *Tail End Charlie,* Loy Dickinson enjoyed a relatively peaceful descent to the ground after escaping from the burning B-17. A few moments later, with a crackling crash of branches, the navigator landed unceremoniously in a thicket of bushes near a Czech farmhouse.

A moment later, a young man, Mojmir Baca, stepped out of the house to investigate the commotion. To his surprise, Baca found the 19-year-old Californian struggling out of his parachute harness. Without a moment's hesitation, he signaled for Dickinson to come with him. By noon, the downed aviator was sitting down with the Baca family for lunch. Later, the Bacas stashed Dickinson in their loft. Safe from prying eyes, the navigator fell fast asleep.

His night, however, did not pass uninterrupted. News of the American passed quickly among the Bacas' neighbors. Throughout the night, visitors climbed into the loft to take a look at the downed aviator.

"As I recall," Dickinson reported, "only one visitor could speak any English and he wanted to know about 'gangsters' in Chicago."[9]

Waking the next morning, Dickinson made a quick but difficult decision. Despite the apparent security of his surroundings, he did not want to expose the Baca family to the danger of harboring an American flier. After breakfast, Dickinson managed to explain to his hosts that he intended to walk to Slovakia. Biding them farewell, he began walking east toward the town of Slavicin.

A few minutes into his trek, however, Dickinson spotted a young man and an elderly police officer coming down the road toward him. Caught in the open, the navigator realized that there was no escape. He surrendered to the two men, learning later that the younger was a local doctor named Turcinek. Dr. Turcinek and the policeman escorted Dickinson the rest of the way into town, where they deposited him with the local police station.

"*Pistolie?*" the Czech police officers demanded. To their surprise, he was not carrying a firearm. They were equally surprised to learn that their captive was only 19. "They are flying children in this war," one man chided in heavily accented English.[10]

Later that afternoon, the Czechs handed Dickinson over to the German garrison in Slavicin, where the navigator gratefully accepted a bowl of hot soup unexpectedly provided by his captors. "It was probably the best meal I had had in my young life," he recounted. "It was delicious, welcomed, and unexpected all in one."[11] The following day, the Germans transported Dickinson first to Zlin and then, by bus, to Brno.

In Brno, Dickinson joined a party of other POWs for a train ride to Vienna. While the POWs and their guards waited, a few cautious conversations began among captors and captives. After a few moments, one of the guards offered to buy a round of beers at a nearby *biergarten* with the POWs' dollars. He made good on his end of the bargain but a German officer chanced upon the unlikely scene after only the first few sips. "The incipient comradeship came to an abrupt halt," Dickinson remembered dolefully.[12]

From Vienna, Dickinson and the others rode through the night to Frankfurt. There, on the outskirts of the city in a camp known as the *Dulag,* Dickinson's first real brush with German interrogators awaited—and it was unlikely to involve the sharing of a friendly *bier.*

↶

After buckling his parachute pack at the last moment, Bill Garland rolled out of *Snafuperman*'s rear door. Seconds later, the flaming bomber he had piloted moments earlier exploded in midair. But although Garland had fallen free in the nick of time, he knew he was not safe yet. Garland fought the urge to open his chute and instead free-fell through the sky. Only when the trees began to take shape below did he deploy his chute. It opened with an ear-shattering, spine-cracking snap at a height Garland estimated to be 4,000 feet.

"After falling for some distance, it is quite a shock to the body when that chute opens," the pilot reported.[13]

Garland's parachute carried him into a farmer's field, where he endured a rough landing. He injured his ankle, making him a relatively easy catch for the Czech police. After apprehending Garland, they turned him over to Germans.

A German officer soon subjected Garland to a quick interrogation and informed him that both Russell Payne, one of *Snafuperman's* waist gunners, and Irving Katz, the flight engineer, were dead. When he spoke of Katz, the officer disparagingly tapped on his nose and muttered "Yiddish." Garland tried to explain that Katz was simply of Polish descent but the officer ignored him. For years to come, Garland would fear that his flight officer had been killed by his German captors once he landed on the ground.[14]

Leo Zupan hurled himself out of *Snafuperman's* bomb bay as the bomber dropped through 18,000 feet of altitude. "The left wing was burning so badly that the wing ribs were exposed," he remembered.[15] He plummeted for several thousand feet before pulling his rip cord at 3,500 feet. For the copilot, it was a textbook bail out from an aircraft—certainly everything for which he could have hoped. Nevertheless, his flawless technique did not prevent him from being apprehended quickly by German troops once he landed on Czech soil. "A few minutes later, I became a guest of the Third Reich," he reported sardonically.[16] And thinking back to the stash he had left on his cot back in Amendola in preparation of his pending R & R trip to Rome, he added, "I wonder who the lucky guy was that got my beer and cigars?"[17]

Ed Smith, the navigator for 359, escaped from the B-17 though the escape hatch in the navigation compartment. He knew that the bomber was flying at approximately 22,000 feet and that, at that altitude, the lack of oxygen could prove fatal if he deployed his chute too early. Resisting the urge to do so, he fell through the air, tumbling head over heels as he caught quick, blurred glimpses of the ground below. When he judged he was at an appropriate altitude, he decided it was time to pop his chute. With his right hand, he reached for his rip cord's handle—only to discover that it was not on the right side of his pack. Instead, in the heat of battle, he had clipped his parachute onto his harness upside down. For the briefest of moments, Smith wondered what the result would be when he deployed the improperly attached chute. But the rapidly approaching ground did not provide him with the luxury of much time to consider his dilemma. Resigned to his fate, Smith tugged his rip cord to the left.[18]

In response, the chute snapped open—"it felt like I was on the end of a 'crack-the-whip-line,'" he recalled—and Smith realized that he was 12,000 feet or so above the earth. "The ride down was beautiful," he reflected. "It was absolutely quiet and you had a wonderful view of the countryside. You had no sensation of falling until you got close to the ground."[19]

Within a matter of moments, Smith was indeed close to the ground—and sinking into a thick, green forest. Remembering his limited parachute training, which consisted merely of a set of lectures, he crossed his legs as he plunged through the leafy boughs. He lacked the time, however, to uncross them and ready to hit the ground. Instead, he smashed awkwardly into the dirt, badly spraining his left foot and ankle in the process.

Despite the injury, Smith quickly slipped out of his parachute harness. His chute, hung up in the tree branches above him, defied his efforts to pull it down and bury it. Instead, he left it hanging where it was and quickly limped off to put as much distance between the incriminating chute and himself as possible. But hobbled by his injured ankle, Smith struggled to cover much distance. Pausing by a small creek, he pulled off his heavy flight boots, slipped on his GI boots, and, limping along for a short distance, found a dense thicket. Dropping to his hands and knees, he crawled into its center to hide.

Shortly thereafter, Smith heard unseen people moving through the nearby woods. Moments later, a series of excited shouts convinced him that they had found his chute. He hunkered down in his thicket and, to his surprise, heard someone whistling "Yankee Doodle" walking down the forest path past his hiding place.

"I have always wondered if this was a trick of some German or if it was some local trying to make contact with me," Smith said. "I never responded to the whistle," he added.[20]

Smith's caution paid dividends—at least initially. He avoided capture that first day and, despite his sprained ankle, managed to evade the Germans for the next week as well. Mile by mile, he hiked to the southeast. One night, he took refuge in an old farm shed, where he fell victim to a vicious swarm of fleas. The next morning, he paused from his travels long enough to strip naked and to try to pick the fleas out from his clothes one by one. It was a hopeless and ultimately unsuccessful endeavor.[21]

The downed navigator eventually covered some fifty miles on the ground. As he walked, he found himself wondering if he had misinterpreted Bullock's signal to bail out. After all, he never saw any other chutes as he floated to the earth. "I kept wondering if my crew was back in Italy wondering why I bailed out."[22]

Eight days into his trek, Smith was battling a bad cold and shuffling along on terribly blistered feet. When he stumbled into a group of German soldiers outside the town of Piestany, he was in little shape to evade them. Instead, he was taken prisoner and quickly bundled onto a train to Vienna.

Jim Martin, the ball turret gunner on board 359, did not even remember actually bailing out of the bomber. Roused from unconsciousness by the sound of a barking dog, he woke up sprawled across a cobblestone street in Zlin, a city in southeastern Moravia, with a rifle muzzle in his face.[23] Badly wounded by shrapnel in his right hand and the backs of his leg, he could only look up at the number of soldiers and civilians crowding around him.

"For you the war is over," one soldier advised him in English.[24]

Martin's captors quickly delivered him to the local hospital, where doctors amputated one of his toes. Wally Clayton, a fellow crew member from 359, joined him there. The radio operator was also seriously wounded and had lost an eye in the air battle. Together, they were destined to spend the next several days in Zlin recuperating from their wounds before being transferred to prisoner-of-war camps to spend the duration of the war. But for some of Martin's and Clayton's fellow aviators in the 20th Squadron, the war was not quite over yet.

12
Evasion

Robert Donahue, *Tail End Charlie*'s tail gunner, escaped the plane without injury. The order to bail out, however, had caught him in the middle of changing from his clunky leather flight boots to his GI brogans. In response, he leapt out of the stricken Fortress leaving both pairs of shoes behind. When he landed in a plowed field a few short minutes later, his olive-drab socks hit the dirt first. Thirty yards away, two farmers stared incredulously at the shoeless American who had just dropped out of the sky. Donahue waved at them. The two men, slack-jawed with amazement, waved back.

Donahue had no time to seek further introductions. Looking across the fields, he saw a company of men charging toward him a quarter mile away. He gathered his parachute, walked hurriedly for 30 yards into nearby woods and, once concealed, broke into a run. After a few minutes, he stopped, hid his parachute as best he could, and began running once again. Plunging through the trees, Donahue encountered a forest path and raced down it. He spied a dense thicket of undergrowth and, dropping to his hands and knees, squirmed into it. Five minutes later, as he lay flat on his stomach, Donahue heard his pursuers rushing down the same path and fanning out through the woods around him.

"I thought for sure they could hear my heart pounding," Donahue remembered years later.[1]

The woods were full of such searchers, and capture seemed inevitable. But after a few minutes, the search party moved further into the forest. As Donahue's heart rate slowed, he decided to stay in the thicket for a few more hours.

As the hours passed, Donahue pulled out his escape kit. It contained a compass, a map, and eight dollars. As the aircraft's tail gunner, he was not blessed with particularly good information as to his current location. He knew, however, that Germany lay to the northwest and west. That was enough for Donahue. He would, he decided, strike out for the east.

For the rest of the day, Donahue picked his way carefully along the path through woods and fields. Occasionally, he stopped to drink from streams. As dusk descended, he traversed a creek and, as he pulled himself up the opposite bank, encountered a small dog. It began barking at him. In the gathering gloom, someone called out in Czech for the dog and began walking toward the creek.

Hearing his approach, Donahue flopped to the ground and crawled behind a pile of dirt. Peering around it, he saw the dog's owner arrive. Apparently, he was a farmer, ready to go home after a long day in the field. The man called the dog to his side and kept walking. Relieved, the sergeant watched him fade into the dusky darkness.

The plop of a raindrop on Donahue's neck interrupted his observations. Above, the sky opened up in a late summer rainstorm. Looking around, Donahue spied a large haystack in a nearby field. He sprinted over to it and crawled into it. For the moment, he simply intended to plan his next move, but the warmth and security of the hay were too much to resist. Almost immediately, he collapsed into a deep sleep.

Donahue slept soundly throughout the night in his makeshift burrow, waking the next morning to continue his hike. As he walked, he formulated a plan. He would keep moving through the day and then, at nightfall, approach a farmhouse for help.

At noon, however, his plans suddenly changed. Walking along a forest path, he crested a wooded hilltop and surprised two teenagers gathering firewood. Donahue estimated that they were 15 years old. Realizing that he had been spotted, and deciding that fortune would favor the bold, he walked up to them, pulled out a pack of cigarettes, and offered them each one.

"I'm an American," Donahue said.

In response, they only looked at him quizzically.

"English?" one finally said, pointing to him.

"Yes, English," he responded.[2]

Donahue's response visibly excited the pair of boys. Smiling, they crowded around him and tried to explain the best route for him to take. Following their pantomimed advice, the sergeant continued down the path.

A short distance later, Donahue encountered an elderly couple riding in a horse-drawn cart. The old man driving the cart pulled up on his reins and slowed to a stop, allowing Donahue to come up alongside him. Through a series of gestures, the downed aviator explained that he was an American and had parachuted from an airplane.

Apparently, the couple understood Donahue's crude explanation. The man's wife climbed down off the cart and, reaching into a pocket in her dress, pulled out a piece of bread and offered it to Donahue.

"This was probably her lunch for the day," Donahue reflected. "This was typical of how [the] people treated me. There are no better people anywhere."[3]

The woman then climbed back onto the cart and her husband motioned for Donahue to join them. Together, they turned the car around and rode into a nearby village where the farmer introduced Donahue to the village's mayor. Although he searched the flier for weapons, he immediately invited him into his office afterward, where he shared his own lunch with the village's newest guest. As soon as they finished, another man arrived and escorted Donahue to a house on the outskirts of the village. There, Donahue tried to convince the villagers he had already eaten but, in the end, forced himself to consume a third lunch—"I did not want to offend them," he explained.[4]

While he ate, Donahue pulled out his escape map. With a series of hand motions, he sought his hosts' advice as to where he was located. He also indicated that he wanted to move on rather than put them at risk. Politely but firmly, the house's occupants prevented him from leaving. Soon, Donahue learned why.

The front door to the cottage opened and an old man walked in. His eyes widened in surprise as he saw the uniformed aviator sitting at the villagers' table.

"Jesus Christ—an American!" he exclaimed, reaching out to hug Donahue.[5]

Donahue was as surprised as his visitor but soon learned that the man had previously emigrated to the United States, lived there for 23 years, and then returned to his native Czechoslovakia. In fact, he had only lived 20 minutes away from Donahue in Pittsburgh. The two men quickly fell into a long conversation.

"People are going to help you," the man told Donahue. "Listen to them and they will get you to a safe place."[6]

As they talked, a young girl offered Donahue a pair of shoes for his bare feet, asking that he be sure to return them. The sergeant barely had time to thank her before being hustled onto a nearby truck and driven to the Slovakian city of Trencin, an ancient city on the Vah River dominated by an eleventh-century castle overlooking the city's white-walled, red-tiled buildings. In Trencin, the truck pulled alongside a warehouse, where another helpful Czech handed him a pair of work shoes. From there, the truck took him to a military barracks. Donahue's escorts walked him inside and instructed him to wait there for further instructions.

Over the course of that afternoon and the next morning, a random collection of other downed American aviators joined Donahue in the barracks, including the remnants of a crew from a B-24H Liberator, *Rough Cobb,* assigned to the 737th Squadron and bearing the serial number 42-52313. The bedraggled Americans included *Rough Cobb's* badly injured pilot, First Lieutenant Billy R. Ray, of Chappell, Nebraska. Ironically, the day's mission was Ray's fiftieth. It proved to be Ray's last, but not in the manner in which he had hoped. Knowing that his pilot was flying his last mission, Staff Sergeant Oscar "Bud" Thielen Jr., of Cincinnati, Ohio, had volunteered to fly the mission as his ball turret gunner—a fateful act of friendship and loyalty for Thielen. First Lieutenant Louis Stromp, the plane's navigator, from Irvington, New Jersey, had also volunteered to fly for Ray and now found himself imprisoned alongside him.

Other survivors from *Rough Cobb* included First Lieutenant Louis F. Leon, the bombardier, a former marine from Hoboken, New Jersey; William F. Anderson, the tail gunner, from Farson, Wyoming; and Ferris Joyner, the bomber's radio operator, a former truck driver from Richland County, South Carolina. Confined to the barracks, the Americans huddled together, nursed Ray as best they could, and wondered what the next few hours would bring.[7]

~

When Willard Netzley's chute opened, the fierce snap of silk ripped his GI boots out of his clutches and even knocked one of his fur-lined leather flying boots off his feet. *My Baby's* bombardier floated down into a grove of pine trees, where his chute caught in the branches and left him dangling above the ground. Netzley unhooked from his harness and fell painlessly onto the soft carpet of pine needles below. Then, remembering his limited training for such situations, he pulled his chute down out of the trees, buried it to prevent it from giving away his position, and began to trot away from where he had landed.

A few hundred feet later, Netzley realized belated that he should have kept the parachute, or at least part of it, to help him stay warm. Chagrined, he tried to retrace his steps but, in the gloom woods, had no luck. He had done such a good job burying it that he could not find it.[8]

Frustrated, Netzley moved further into the forest and hid in the underbrush until dusk approached. Then, in the fading light, he checked his maps and began to move south toward distant Yugoslavia. As he worked his way down a forested hillside, it began to rain. Rather than continue, he decided to stop for the night and covered himself with leaves to stay warm.

"Down in the valley there was a blue-stucco, thatched-roof cottage with the lights on in the house and someone was playing a concertina," Netzley remembered. "Their dog, who knew someone was up on the hill, was barking. I was one lonely young American airman."[9]

The next morning, Netzley moved further down into the valley. Finding a dry creek bed running through a six-foot-deep gully and concealed by heavy brush, he took the opportunity to disrobe and hang up his wet clothes to dry. But as he waited, he heard a rustle in the nearby brush. Someone was approaching along the creek bed and there was scarcely time to react.

A second later, the interloper stepped into view. It was Charles McVey, who had served as the navigator on Netzley's regular crew. "No two guys were ever happier to see each other," Netzley declared.[10]

⤿

While on board 885, McVey had been thrown out of the ragged hole ripped in the front of the bomber's nose by German cannon fire. The only injury he suffered was a severe scratch across the bridge of his nose. It was a small price to pay for escaping 885; McVey was the bomber's only survivor.

Hurled from the mangled Fortress, an oxygen-starved McVey plummeted toward the ground, struggling groggily to find his rip cord. By the time he recovered and pulled it, he was already close to the ground. The chute opened, barely giving him enough time to realize that he was descending into a large clearing amid a forest of trees. He assumed that a billowing chute in the middle of a field would be readily visible and so, pulling on his chute's risers, he managed to side-slip into the trees on the edge of the clearing. Here, however, the chute caught in the branches of a massive pine, leaving the downed aviator to dangle 40 feet above the ground.[11]

McVey pulled up on the shroud lines and began to pendulum back and forth. He finally swung over to a tree limb, where he slipped out of his harness and climbed down to the ground. Wearing a set of electrically wired coveralls and a pair of similarly wired slippers, he struck out cross-country to put some distance between himself and his parachute.

As night fell, McVey found a hedgerow and squirmed into it. A light rain began to fall and, as the night wore on, he became more miserable by the minute. Leaving the hedgerow, he found a farmer's haystack and wormed into it, pulling the hay in behind him to keep out the rain and keep in his warmth.

The next morning, McVey breakfasted on a pair of potatoes from the farmer's garden plot, eaten raw and later complemented by the few berries that he found on his trek through the meadows and woods of the Czech countryside. For the moment, McVey actually found himself enjoying his latest adventure.[12]

Before long, however, a Czech farmer spotted McVey. Recognizing him to be a downed Allied airman, the farmer motioned for McVey to follow him to his farmhouse. The navigator complied and, as a guest of the farmer and his wife, enjoyed a meal of fried bread dough covered in warm goat's milk. With lunch finished, McVey motioned farewell to his hosts and continued his journey. Shortly thereafter, while walking up a dry creek bed, he encountered Netzley.

The two men, after quickly swapping stories of their escapes from their bombers, left the gully and walked on. Cresting a grassy hill, they stumbled into a trio of Slovak soldiers lounging on the ground. The three soldiers, rising to their feet, calmly signaled for McVey and Netzley to come with them. Noting that the soldiers each had a rifle slung over his shoulder, the two airmen obeyed. Together, the five men trekked across the White Carpathian foothills before eventually arriving in the small town of Drietoma, on the Moravian-Slovak border. There, the soldiers turned their captives over to the town's chief of police.

In Drietoma, McVey and Netzley faced extensive questioning—particularly since a jettisoned American bomb had landed in the backyard of one of the citizens of the town, leaving an immense hole. As fate would have it, the homeowner was a lady who had formerly lived in Chicago and spoke English quite well. The two Americans assured her that the bombing of her backyard was purely accidental.[13]

Their investigation into the wayward bomb concluded, the police loaded McVey and Netzley in a small car that evening and drove them into Trencin. There, they joined Donahue and the other survivors. By now, the downed Americans were beginning to realize that they were not so much prisoners of war as pieces of human flotsam in an increasingly dangerous political maelstrom.

Five years earlier, in the wake of Hitler's seizure of the Sudetenland and faced with the impending emasculation of Czechoslovakia, Slovakia declared its own independence under the leadership of Jozef Tiso. Immediately thereafter, Nazi Germany invaded the remaining regions of Czechoslovakia—Bohemia, Moravia, and Silesia—and established a protectorate. Although subsequently recognized by some 25 other countries, most considered the authoritarian, one-party Slovak Republic to be a vassal state of the Third Reich. Some Slovaks, however, after centuries of chaffing under foreign domination, welcomed any modicum of national self-determination, even if it was in the shadow of the Swastika.

By 1944, however, there was growing dissatisfaction with the Slovak Republic's German overlords and Tiso's regime. Democratic forces had long chaffed under

Tiso's dictatorial regime while massive losses by the Slovak Army Group fighting alongside the *Wehrmacht* on the Eastern Front had further cooled ardor for the Axis cause. Allied successes on the battlefield, and particularly the Red Army's advance through southern Poland and toward the Dukla Pass on Slovakia's northeastern border, underscored the deteriorating situation for the Axis.

As the summer drew to a close, attacks by partisan units in the mountains of north-central Slovakia became more frequent. Meanwhile, dissident members of the Slovak army, supported and encouraged to varying degrees by the Soviets, the British Special Operations Executive, and the American Office of Strategic Services, made preparations for a general uprising.

Coincidentally, the Slovak National Uprising began on August 29, 1944—the same day as the 20th Squadron's ill-fated mission to Moravska Ostrava. The same ill luck that plagued the squadron's raid seemed to settle on the Slovaks as well. On the first day of the revolt, a fast-acting German *panzer* unit managed to disarm two divisions of the Slovak army before they could join the uprising, depriving the uprising of a major, well-disciplined force to resist the angry Germans. Meanwhile, a number of units of Slovakia's air force opted to fly east and defect to the Soviets rather than cast their lots with the rebels. In the cities of Bratislava, Nitra, and Trencin, the garrisons also refused to join the uprising. As columns of determined German troops poured into Slovakia, it became clear that the Slovakian resistance—the Military Revolutionary Command, or VRV, according to its Slovak initials—had failed to achieve a *fait accompli*. Rather, it looked as though the length and breadth of Slovakia would soon become a battlefield.

Fortunately for the downed American fliers detained in the military barracks in Trencin, the local situation remained confused. One friendly young Slovak, Jan Surovec, envisioned opportunity amid the chaos. He spoke English well and invited the Americans to join him and some others in a pending escape north from Trencin. To a man, McVey, Netzley, Donahue, and the others all agreed to go. Looking out the barracks' window and noticing that a unit of German soldiers was gathering in the streets, Donahue wondered if they were already too late. Alarmed, he warned Surovec.

"Do not worry," Surovec assured him. "They do not know you are here."[14]

The next morning, as they finished breakfast, Surovec told the American fliers that they would be leaving.

The next afternoon, however, a civilian walked into the barracks. Drawing a pistol, he shouted, "*Raus mit du!*" to the gathered airmen. Thinking it was a joke, Netzley, who was reclining on a nearby bunk, only laughed. Unfortunately for him, the intruder was a local Gestapo agent. A split-second later, a squad of German soldiers poured into the room, rounded up the Americans, shoved them out into the street, and began to march them to the town's airport.[15]

Two German soldiers, accompanied by a sergeant carrying a Luger pistol, led the way. The airmen came next, followed by an open-topped Mercedes with a machinegun mounted on it. Groups of Slovak townspeople lined the streets, silently watching the bedraggled procession.

After a short, unhappy march, the prisoners reached the local airport, where the German's placed them under guard to await a flight. But as McVey, Netzley, and the others gathered their thoughts, they realized that not all of their comrades from the barracks were present. Remarkably, someone had apparently managed to escape.

↩

Donahue, as it turned out, was the fortunate escapee. Seconds before the Gestapo agent and the squad of soldiers had burst into the room, he had stepped down the hall to use the nearby toilet. It may have been the luckiest bathroom break of his life.

When he returned, he found the room in turmoil. Not a single American remained. Obviously distraught, Surovec grabbed Donahue and pulled him to the window. Outside, Donahue could see his friends being marched off by the Germans. But there was no time for regret. Surovec led Donahue quickly to the building's basement, where he gave him the uniform of a Slovak soldier. Donahue donned it and then accompanied Surovec out of the building. Stepping into the open street, they walked along boldly, saluting other soldiers as they passed.

Determined to put some distance between his remaining charge and the Germans, Surovec escorted Donahue to another town outside of Trencin. Leaving the sergeant on a street corner and asking him to stay there, Surovec darted into a doorway. The American obeyed, presuming that his Slovak benefactor was seeking further directions.

But while Donahue waited, a local man, apparently taken in by Donahue's disguise, asked him a question. Naturally, Donahue had no idea what the man was saying. He tried to ignore him, but to no effect. The Slovak began shouting and, within seconds, a crowd of ten men surrounded Donahue, pushing and shoving him.[16]

For a moment, things looked grim for Donahue. But then Surovec appeared, pushing his way through the throng and rattling off an explanation. It apparently had the intended effect—"I got a lot of hugging and kissing," Donahue reported.[17]

After their brush with trouble on the street corner, the pair continued their journey. Stopping in a nearby house, Surovec exchanged Donahue's Slovak uniform for civilian clothes. They then managed to grab a few hours of sleep.

In the middle of the night, however, Surovec shook Donahue awake. A car waited on the darkened street outside, and Surovec placed him in its back seat. Donahue slipped in next to another passenger. To his delight, he realized that it was Lieutenant Thayne Thomas, the former pilot of the *Wichita Belle* and the bomber's only survivor. As the two men compared their experiences, they rode further into the dark countryside.

The car delivered them to a beautiful estate owned by an elderly couple. Apparently, the couple allowed the underground to use it as a safe house for downed fliers from time to time. Donahue and Thomas appreciated their kindness but, by the next morning, they were on the road once more. Later, Donahue heard that the couple's activities had been discovered by the Nazis and that they died at the hands of a German firing squad.[18]

The fugitive airmen's car soon joined unlikely company—the convoy of a Czech general and his entourage. Despite the events of recent days, stealth and secrecy seemed forgotten as the general's motorcade rolled through the countryside. The fields and woods of Moravia gave way to spectacular mountains and valleys as the cars picked their way east. At every village, his caravan would stop, allowing the bombastic general to summon the inhabitants and deliver a speech. Before long, word spread ahead that the general counted two downed American fliers among his guests. At an afternoon stop, villagers swarmed Donahue and Thomas, shaking their hands and wishing them well while the general met with the village's mayor.

Late that afternoon, the motorcade reached its destination, the Slovak city of Banska Bystrica. Banska Bystrica was an old mining town nestled in the foothills of the Lower Tatra Mountains, surrounded by difficult, wooded terrain. In the wintertime, it was a popular base for recreational skiers. Now, however, it had become the bastion of Slovak resistance operations by the so-called Czech Forces of the Interior, or CFI.

The motorcade deposited the general and the two Americans at the city's military headquarters, a four-story building complete with carpeted floors, buzzing phones, wall-mounted maps, and bustling orderlies. Thomas and Donahue waited in the local commander's foyer while the commander met in his office with the general. A few moments later, the general emerged, pale and extremely agitated. A squad of grim-faced Slovak soldiers surrounded the officer and hustled him quickly past the two American fliers. Moments later, a crackle of gunfire echoed across the garrison. Thomas later learned that the CFI soldiers had executed the general for alleged collaboration with the Nazis.[19]

If the general's demise bothered the Slovak commander, he did not show it. Instead, after joining them in the foyer, he welcomed them warmly and dispatched them to his finance officer to draw some local currency. Once they finished with the finance officer, partisans showed them to their beds and toilet facilities. In his postwar recollections, Thomas remembers retiring for the evening.

Donahue, however, has a more colorful memory—"a great memory," in fact, to use his words. He also remembers meeting up with two other downed fliers that first evening—Lieutenant Walter Leach and Sergeant Clayton Miller.[20]

"The first evening we ate with the top brass," Donahue remembered. "After dinner, a few of the junior officers stayed with us. At the time we had no money but they sent out for bottles of alcohol which we heartily consumed, while Miller played the piano and tried to sing their songs while we tried to sing theirs. Hours later, one of their higher officers came in and gave them all kinds of hell for keeping people awake. We all left together walking across the parade ground with our arms around each other."[21]

Soon thereafter, the two Americans met a middle-aged man named Tomas. Tomas's parents had returned to Czechoslovakia when he was 12 but, nevertheless, he retained not only his American citizenship but also a ready grasp of American-style English. Coupled with Surovec, he was a welcome addition to their team.[22]

In the meantime, the Americans enjoyed a bracing round of Slovak hospitality. Given a free rein to explore Banska Bystrica, they walked its streets, stopped in at the local barbershop for a daily shave, and frequented its sidewalk cafes and restaurants. Local families extended countless invitations for lunch and dinner in their homes—so much so that they could not accept them all. In all, it was almost a surreal experience. The culinary experience alone was strikingly unique, particularly after months of mess hall food back in Amendola. *Kapustnica,* a thick cabbage soup full of smoked pork sausage and mushrooms, was a mainstay. Entrees included pork chops and roasts, stuffed trout, duck, and venison, often accompanied by various sauerkraut dishes or potato pancakes. Crepes were a popular dessert, while the local plum brandy, *Slivovice,* provided a powerful kick to most meals.[23]

Almost every day more Americans filtered into the rebel town. Before long, Clarence Jackson, who had flown on board 359 with William Bullock, Ed Smith, and Jim Martin, joined the group. Meanwhile, Thomas resisted the *Slivovice* and capitalized on Tomas's excellent English to coordinate efforts by the CFI to transmit the identities of downed fliers back to the Fifteenth Air Force Headquarters in Bari, Italy. He sensed that some sort of plan was afoot to airlift the Americans out of Banska Bystrica. He had no idea about any details, however, or even when such a rescue might occur.

An answer came on Sunday, September 17. By midmorning, the skies over the Slovak city suddenly filled with the roar of fighter planes. Looking up, Thomas assumed they must be Soviets. Then he recognized them to be P-51s. Two of the Mustangs made a low pass at 500 feet directly over the city's main square, much to the delight of the cheering Americans below. At the time, Thomas and the others did not realize it, but 41 P-51s had escorted two B-17s dispatched that morning from Bari, Italy, to deliver an OSS team and supplies and, it was hoped, to retrieve any downed aviators.

Nevertheless, Thomas was astute enough to recognize that rescue could well be at hand. He quickly commandeered a military truck and drove it up and down the square, yelling for and collecting his fellow Allied airmen. He intercepted Donahue and one group en route to an ice cream shop. Jackson also climbed on board. In total, Thomas rolled out of the city and toward Tri Duby airport with 13 Americans, two escaped Australian POWs, and Tomas. Tri Duby was some six miles south of the city, in a valley surrounded by low-lying hills, and their truck seemed to make agonizingly slow progress.[24]

Thomas's truck reached the grass airfield just as the two B-17s were taxiing across the grass. Fearing they would take off without them, Thomas directed the truck's driver to cut across the field and cut off the bombers. He did, and the two Fortresses braked to a stop. Thomas and the others leaped out of their truck and ran to board the waiting bombers. Within moments, they were all airborne.

As the B-17 winged its way back home, both Donahue and Thomas reflected on the bravery of the Slovakians who had helped them survive. They knew that the penalty for aiding an Allied flier was death. To have so many men and women risk their lives for them was a sobering thought, and it lingered in their minds long after the Fortress touched down safely in Italy. "The people of Slovakia are as kind a people as you will find anywhere," Donahue later declared.[25]

⌒

Although Thomas's, Donahue's, and Jackson's experiences with the Slovak rebels seemed the stuff of a Hollywood screenwriter's imagination, the experiences of Joseph Sallings seemed to prove that truth could be stranger the fiction. Sallings passed away in 1972, back home in his native Union County, Tennessee, taking the full story of how he managed to survive eight months in German-occupied Czechoslovakia with him to the grave. A collection of material from various sources, however, hints at what would have been, regardless of the actual details, a remarkable adventure.

According to the Sallings family, a Czech family offered to harbor the downed airman. Accepting their courageous invitation, Sallings adopted the guise of the family's deaf-and-dumb brother, using his split tongue to aid in the deception. For their part, the family loyally stood by their unexpected guest, nursing him back to health when he caught pneumonia and shielding him from discovery by the Germans or their Czech allies.[26]

The authors of *Defenders of Liberty*, upon interviewing Drahomer Brzobohaty, the curator of the Slavicin Museum, provided more information. Sallings, they wrote, "landed in the forest and was soon found by friendly Czechs, and taken to a small village where he was hidden with the large family of the local smith. He lived with the family for eight months under great danger and stress. At the time, aiding and sheltering the enemy was punishable by death of the family and sometimes the whole village."[27]

"Sallings learned a little bit of the language," the authors continued, "and melted [*sic*] in with the family so well that on one occasion he played cards with a German soldier. The village was liberated in May of 1945 but Sallings stayed on for another month."[28]

Eventually repatriated home, Sallings shared his story with the *Knoxville Journal*. "I've got some good friends over there in Czechoslovakia but I don't think I'll ever see them again. All I want to do is stay in Tennessee the rest of my life."[29]

13
Dulag

While men like Thomas and Donahue began the first evasive steps that would take them back to Allied lines, and while Sallings hunkered down with his friendly Czech hosts, Bill Tune awoke on August 30 to begin his second day of captivity in Luhacovice. Later that morning, his captors transferred him to a nearby *Luftwaffe* hospital. There, military doctors examined the wounded pilot and, on his admittance form, estimated his wounds would take ten weeks to heal. They then placed Tune in a room of his own. Later that evening, a German brought the new prisoner a plate of food covered with a large cabbage leaf. Intrigued, Tune pulled the leaf aside, only to reveal a huge green fly.

"I suppose they were hoping I would eat it," Tune reflected, "but I just put the food over on the bedside table and left it."[1]

The next morning, the Germans loaded Tune into an ambulance. To his delight, he discovered it already contained Francis Flynn and five other Americans. Tune's former copilot had received little medical attention from his German captors and was nursing a badly infected leg. The ambulance delivered Tune and Flynn to another hospital, where orderlies placed Tune and Flynn in a locked room. They eventually learned that they were in the Moravian city of Bruenn. Today, it is known as Brno, the second-largest city in the Czech Republic.

Meanwhile, the population of Bruenn seemed to keep growing, one American aviator at a time. The next day, September 1, another captured airman arrived. From their beds, the two pilots could see that the unconscious American was suffering from a terrible head wound. There seemed to be nothing, however, that the

German doctors could do for him. Two days later, their comrade died without ever regaining consciousness. Flynn later identified the man as Harold Helveston, the copilot for 473.[2]

The doctors fared better with Tune. They reset his leg, cleaned his wounds, removed the shrapnel from his leg, and stitched the cuts and slashes on his head and hand. Flynn, suffering from a back wound that stubbornly refused to heal, also underwent a series of operations. As the days passed, the two pilots learned that the doctor treating them was an Austrian whose own wife had been killed in an Allied bombing of their hometown, reportedly by a low-flying B-24. But if the doctor harbored any animosity for them, he never showed it—"a fine gentleman," in Tune's memory.[3]

The hallways of the hospital provided another personal glimpse of the war Tune and Flynn had not yet witnessed. They were the only two Americans in the hospital and, as they rolled to and from the operating room, they passed dozens of horribly wounded men. "I saw German soldiers with no arms and no legs," Tune recalled, "just like logs lying in the beds."[4]

After several days at the hospital had passed, the staff began leaving the door to the captives' room unlocked. One evening, the door handle turned. A young German soldier stepped in and closed the door quietly behind him. He pulled up a chair beside Tune's bed and sat cautiously in it. In stilted English, he asked Tune "to tell him about America and cowboys."[5] Cowboys were few and far between in their hometowns of Carbon Hill, Alabama, and Dunkirk, New York, but Tune and Flynn were happy to try to oblige. The three men spent several evenings talking. Later, a maid began sneaking slices of apple strudel into their room at night as well.

"Flynn and I did not care if she was hiding them under the wash rags in her bucket or not because they were so good," Tune remembered. "She always brought one for each of us."[6] For a couple of prisoners of war, life could certainly have been much worse.

Unfortunately, the hospital staff did not overlook the unlocked door for long. They began locking it once more, effectively bringing an end to Tune's chats with the young soldier and the nocturnal deliveries of pastry. It was another reminder that the Germans were clearly in control. Tune was at the mercy of their slightest whim.

Genèrally, however, there was little of which to complain in Bruenn. Tune and Flynn remained in the hospital for three months as they recuperated from their wounds. For Flynn, it was an arduous process. The wounds in his back refused to heal properly, but he was eventually able to walk. As for Tune, his fractured leg healed enough so that he could hobble along with the aid of a cane.

On November 29, 1944, Tune's and Flynn's sojourn at the hospital ended. An armed soldier arrived at their room in the hospital and, in broken English, told them to collect their few belongings. Before the sun set, Tune, Flynn, and the guard were on a train bound for the German city of Frankfurt am Main.

Rolling across Czechoslovakia, Bavaria, and central Germany, the two Americans had a front-row look at the devastating effects of the Allied bombing campaign. Some of the cities they transited seemed completely destroyed by the bombs. As they approached Frankfurt, their guard became noticeably more stressed.

"Be careful in Frankfurt," he warned them. "The people are not friendly."[7]

When they pulled into the Frankfurt *Bahnhof*, they could see why. "The city was in complete rubble," Tune remembered. "The buildings were piles of brick and the train station roof was almost gone from bomb hits."[8] The nervous guard and his prisoners shuffled through a gauntlet of hostile stares and quickly boarded a train for a rehabilitation camp at Meiningen.

After letting Tune stay a few days at Meiningen, the Germans decided that he had recuperated enough. As Tune collected his meager belongings for another train journey, he bid Flynn farewell. His copilot was still ailing from his injured back and was not yet ready for more travel. He would eventually find a more permanent home in a holding camp for wounded POWs near Nuremberg. Tune, however, had no such luck. His captors transferred him to a camp north of Frankfurt known as *Durchgangslager der Luftwaffe*. Its English translation was "Transit Camp of the *Luftwaffe*." Although the camp's official title was *Auswertestelle West* (Evaluation Center, West) its inhabitants simply called it *Dulag Luft* (although the term was, admittedly, also applied freely by POWs to other camps, such as the transit facility located in Wetzlar).

Dulag Luft served as an intelligence clearinghouse for captured Allied airmen, where some 60 German interrogators coddled, coaxed, and coerced information out of the downed pilots and airmen. The camp, built on a level patch of ground, sprawled across 500 acres in the Frankfurt suburb of Oberursel. Two concentric fences, overlooked by watch towers and machinegun emplacements and patrolled by guard dog teams, surrounded the facility. Large white rocks spelled out "Prisoner of War Camp" across the length of the camp's front lawn to deter errant Allied bombing missions. Its occupants had painted the same phrase on the roof of practically every building.

Today, the pilots and aircrews of the United States Air Force receive formal training regarding what to expect and how to act should they be downed behind enemy lines or captured. In modern military parlance, this battery of training is known as SERE—"Survival, Evasion, Resistance, and Escape." But during the

Second World War, pilots and their crews received little information and even less training as to how they should avoid capture, survive on the ground, or behave in captivity. For the most part, they were simply told to give only their name, rank, and service serial number. As a concession to the Germans' preferential treatment to officers and noncommissioned officers, the Air Corps made sure that all of its crewmen were at least sergeants. But other than that, precious little prepared a downed airman for survival on the ground behind enemy lines or in a POW camp.

This lack of training was an unfortunate oversight for, according to July 1944 figures released by the U.S. War Department, there were 28,867 U.S. prisoners of war in German hands; 16,593 of those were airmen.[9] The Germans housed these prisoners in nearly 60 camps (*Offizierlagers* for officers, and *Stammlagers,* or *Stalags,* for other ranks), smaller satellite facilities, and hospitals. Captured naval officers and sailors were kept in camps known as *Marinelagers.* As the war progressed, however, the Germans struggled to maintain the rank distinctions, and many officers ended up in *Stalags.* Altogether, there were eight major *Stalags.* The *Wehrmacht* ran three of the larger *Stalags* that imprisoned U.S. Army officers and soldiers. The *Luftwaffe,* as a nod to Herman Goering's paternalism for his fellow aviators, ran five large *Stalags* for captured airmen.

For most captured aviators, the route to their eventual *Stalag* ran through the *Dulag Luft.* Morris J. Roy, a B-17 pilot based in England and shot down over northern Germany on February 21, 1944, wrote of the *Dulag Luft* immediately after the war in his memoir *Behind Barbed Wire.* In it, he described airmen crammed together into small waiting rooms, where unseen microphones waited to record careless conversations. He also described the interrogation room.

"The contents of the room fairly took [my] breath away," he wrote. "The latest American navigation instruments, complete in every detail, were on a desk to [my] right. Maps of every description adorned the walls; the exact location of each Allied Group was marked. And [I] was shown files containing records of each flight, squadron, and group. The room resembled a well-equipped operations office in England, but with much more detail."[10]

Working out of such rooms, patient German interrogators threatened, tricked, or cajoled information out of their captives. Casually proffered cigarettes and kind words alternated with sudden strip searches, meager rations, and hard bunks in solitary confinement as the interrogators sought to keep their subjects off balance. The amazing amount of information that the Germans possessed seemed to be particularly disconcerting to the POWs. Outright torture seemed to play no part in the interrogation process, however, and most airmen were soon on their way to more permanent lodgings. As Roy noted, the axiom he had heard back in England held true: "The longer one stays at Dulag, the surer he may be that he is giving military information."[11]

At the *Dulag,* the Germans put Tune into solitary confinement in a small cell that measured only seven feet long by four feet wide. One tiny window provided a modicum of illumination and ventilation, but there was no sink or toilet. Before his first day in his oppressive new surroundings had passed, the guards pulled him out for his first interrogation.

"The interrogator spoke perfect English and told me that he had lived in Miami, Florida, before the war," Tune recalled. "When the war started he told me he had come back to Germany to help Hitler. After his introduction he began asking questions about my war service and I would only answer with name, rank, and serial number. This procedure continued for about ten days with the same answers and the same results—back to solitary confinement. On the tenth day he surprised me."[12]

"If you are not going to answer my questions, let me tell you what I know," the interrogator began. "This turned out to be almost everything—my life history, and what happened," Tune admitted. Happily, the one-way conversation marked the end of Tune's interrogations.

Released from the rigors of solitary confinement, Tune joined the general population of the processing camp. During his first evening of relative freedom, while visiting a nearby latrine, he had the remarkable luck to bump into Tommy Tomlinson, his old friend from pilot training and his former hut mate back in Amendola. Tomlinson had been shot down that summer over Budapest but had worked in a hospital for the first six months of his captivity. Like Tune, Tomlinson had just arrived at *Dulag Luft* and Tune was overjoyed to see a familiar face.

Several days later, the Germans prepared to ship Tune out of the *Dulag* to his next destination. As preparations unfolded, Tune happily noted that Tomlinson was among the small group of transients. The Americans spent the better part of a day traveling northward in their train, chugging at one point through a railway marshaling yard that had been bombed less than an hour before. "Not a bomb had hit the target and the railroad was still intact," Tune noted dolefully.[13]

Eventually, Tune's and Tomlinson's train pulled into the town of Barth, on Germany's windy Baltic coast. A detail of guards and a truck met the train and quickly delivered the Americans to their new home. For the rest of the war, the two men would call *Stalag Luft I* home.

⌐

Loy Dickinson, Tune's navigator, had passed through the *Dulag* in Oberursel in early September. Upon his arrival, guards separated him from his traveling companions and put each of them in separate cells—"my guess of size would be 8' x 10', possibly smaller. [My] memory [is] not clear but [I] believe we were fed twice a day, [with] food delivered to the room—a form of room service," Dickinson wrote.[14]

Dickinson faced interrogation at the hands of a German officer who spoke fluent English and who claimed to have been in the lumber business in Memphis, Tennessee, before the war. With stubborn persistence, the German prodded Dickinson for more information than simply his name, rank, and serial number— "What was your target? Who was the commanding officer?"—"to most of which, the honest answer was 'I don't know,'" the navigator admitted.[15]

"My feeling was that the interviewer was able to deduce from the body language what he needed to know," Dickinson surmised. "Also, it was clear even to this 19 year old, that the Germans knew at this stage that the war was over and they might well have been going through the motions. But being the efficient 'race' they are reputed to be there was never any hint that duty would not be performed in the prescribed manner."[16]

"In the long hours of the day and night there was literally nothing to do," he continued. "There was no communication with other prisoners, much less the captors. The only scheme that I could manage was to count the nails. The nails in the floor board, the walls and the ceiling. I never will know how many times I may have done this, nor do I recall the numbers arrived at as the actual count."[17]

On the fifth day of his confinement, Dickinson's captors pulled him out of his cell for a second interrogation. "It was a much different atmosphere," Dickinson recalled. "The [interrogator] did all of the talking. He recounted in great detail the composition of the Bomb Group, how many had been captured, and the like. He even told me that Captain Charles Shepard and his crew had taken the week of leave that our crew was scheduled for at Capri (I had flown with Captain Shepard three times previously)."[18]

Later that day, the Germans put Dickinson, in the company of another shipment of POWs, on a train bound for the transit and processing camp located at Wetzlar, a medieval Hessian town perched on the banks of the Lahn River. "It turned out to be quite a civilized place," Dickinson admitted. The Germans seemed sensitive to the health of their prisoners, perhaps because of a Red Cross presence that monitored such issues and ensured the issuance of adequate clothing. Dickinson even had an opportunity to write a post card home to Berkeley.[19]

Dickinson spent slightly less than a week in Wetzlar before yet another train ride took him east, this time through Berlin and on north to Barth. He, like Tune, would spend the rest of the war behind *Stalag Luft I*'s barbed wire.

৵

Joe Owsianik's route to the *Dulag* was a less pleasant one. Back in Czechoslovakia, he endured three days in solitary confinement in his lonely barracks cell. Other than water, he received no food. On the third day, however, good luck finally visited Owsianik's cell. Unexpectedly, it came in the form of a *Luftwaffe* fighter pilot. "I am the pilot who shot down your plane," the pilot proclaimed in halting English. Looking carefully at Owsianik, he added, "When did you last eat?"

"Three or four days ago," Owsianik answered. Clearly, this surprised the pilot. His face darkened and he stormed out of the cell. In the hallway beyond the door, Owsianik could hear him shouting angrily. Then he returned and sat down on the cell's cot beside Owsianik.

"So, you fly the B-17," the German commented. "It is a good airplane. Of course, the Fw 190 is better." Having shared that observation, he pulled out a pack of cigarettes, lit one for Owsianik, and gave him the others to keep.

"When the blonde Czech girl brings you your meals, you should ask her to light the others," he advised.[20]

At that point, the cell door opened. A guard stepped in carrying a plate of pork chops, potatoes, and bread and a cup of coffee. Satisfied the pilot motioned for Owsianik to eat it. Standing up to leave the airman to his meal, the German clicked his heels and, raising his right hand in the Nazi salute, declared, "Heil Hitler!" Owsianik put down his plate, stood up, and snapped his right hand to his forehead to return the salute. The two men then shook hands and the German left the cell. Owsianik never saw him again.

As the days dragged on, Owsianik came to believe that he was the only prisoner being held in the barracks. Only the occasional meal of cabbage and bread broke the monotony. But one day, the guards pulled him from his cell and escorted him to the barracks' courtyard. There stood Thomas Coogan, *Tail End Charlie's* flight engineer. When he spied Owsianik, his face broke into a nervous grin.

"Let me have one of your dog tags," Coogan whispered conspiratorially to Owsianik. "I'm Jewish," he explained. "I want a Christian tag."[21]

It made sense to Owsianik. He carefully slipped Coogan one of his two tags. Shortly thereafter, the Germans transported them under guard by bus to Bruenn. There, they boarded a train for first Vienna and then Frankfurt. From there, Owsianik had his own appointment with the interrogators of the *Dulag Luft*.

At the *Dulag*, Owsianik endured several days in solitary confinement, interrupted only by a German interrogator quizzing him about his mission, his unit, and his aircraft. Each time, Owsianik responded with merely his name, rank, and serial number. A number of those sessions occurred and, as far as the sergeant knew, he was keeping the Germans in the dark about his unit and its activities.

But one day, Owsianik's interrogator visited his cell a final time. In a calm voice and in near-perfect English, he addressed the captured sergeant.

"Joe, you are a good soldier," he said, "but I will tell you a little about yourself.

You were a cameraman in the 2nd Bombardment Group, Fifteenth Air Force. Your unit was based in Foggia, Italy. Isn't that right, Joe?"

Stunned, Owsianik blurted out, "My name is Joseph P. Owsianik. My serial number is 32254463 and, according to the Geneva Convention, that is all I have to say." He then braced for whatever retribution this futile defiance might bring.[22]

But there was none. The interrogator took his remaining dog tag, verified his name, and returned it to Owsianik. Guards then escorted him to another room, took his photograph, and gave him a German POW identification tag. Owsianik glanced at it and saw that he was now Prisoner No. 3164. With a resigned shrug, he put the POW tag onto the chain around his neck with his American dog tag. Now, the reality sank in—he was officially a prisoner of war.

Shortly thereafter, the Germans placed Owsianik in a sealed boxcar bound for more permanent residence. "There must have been eighty of us in there," Owsianik remembered. "We had to take turns standing up and sitting down. We'd use the corner of the car for our latrine."[23]

Several days later, the train reached Berlin, where the guards intended to overnight. The RAF's night bombers struck that evening, however, blasting the rail yard where the prisoners' boxcars had been sidetracked. For Owsianik and his fellow POWs, it was a terrifying experience.

"The blasts from the bombs rocked the car," Owsianik recalled. "It teeter-tottered back and forth and almost fell on its side. 'Don't move! Don't move!,' everyone yelled each time it tottered to the side."[24]

In the end, the prisoners' train survived the raid, but the rail yard was devastated. With the surrounding tracks destroyed, the train was trapped within the shattered yard for four days. Sealed in the cars, Owsianik and his comrades were reduced to begging for water from the guards.

On the fifth day, enough tracks had been repaired to allow the train to continue on its journey and, on the fourteenth day after leaving Frankfurt, Owsianik's train pulled into the small Pomeranian village of Kiefheide, in the northeastern recesses of Germany. The guards pulled the POWs from the boxcar, tied them together, and hustled them down the road in a shuffling run-walk. A little over two miles later, they reached the town of Gross Tychow and plunged through the front gates of their new home—*Stalag Luft IV.*

14
Kriegies

Joe Owsianik's new home, *Stalag Luft IV*, was a relatively new POW camp. *Oberst-leutnant* Aribert Bombach, a short, thin-faced officer and staunch Nazi, lorded over the *Stalag* and its inhabitants.[1] By some estimates, the camp held 8,500 prisoners of war, mainly Americans but with approximately 800 RAF POWs also. The American ranks included several other survivors from the 2nd Group's raid on Moravska Ostrava—Thomas Coogan, the flight engineer from *Tail End Charlie;* Jim Martin, the Oklahoma sharecropper's son who had flown as William Bullock's and Ed Smith's ball turret gunner on board aircraft 359; and Vincent Contrada, the young Virginian who had manned one of *Wolf Pack's* waist guns.

In the slang of the day, Owsianik and his comrades were now "*Kriegies,*" short for *Kriegsgefangen,* or prisoners of war. A smaller group of Russian and Polish prisoners were also imprisoned at *Stalag Luft IV* as what amounted to slave labor for the Germans. Owsianik did not know it at the time, but the *Stalag* already had a rough reputation—an initial rumor had it that the camp was a secret facility run by the Gestapo and shielded from the Red Cross. The rumor was false but indicative of the camp's reputation as "a byword for brutality," to quote some historians.[2]

The Germans had constructed *Stalag IV* in a forest clearing approximately one and a half miles square. Two barbed-wire fences, ten feet high, completely surrounded the camp. Set at close intervals along the fence line, guard towers kept watch with machineguns and searchlights. Within the perimeter itself, 50 feet from the interior fence, ran the so-called warning wire. Crossing that wire would trigger a fusillade of bullets from one of the watch towers. Questions, if any, would be asked later.

New *Kriegies* such as Owsianik encountered a roughly efficient organizational machine. First came a close search by their captors, who then forwarded the new arrivals to a reception committee of American prisoners. That committee subjected the camp's new guests to a thorough questioning in an effort to ensure that they were indeed captured Americans and not German plants. The committee also sought information about general war news. Once satisfied, it issued the new *Kriegies* blankets, a toothbrush and toothpaste, a towel, underwear, pants, and a shirt. Owsianik also received a surplus British army jacket, although he was also warned that, rather than receiving a weekly Red Cross parcel, the prisoners were only receiving one parcel per month.

After finishing with the reception committee, the new prisoners were escorted to their new homes. Within the wire, Germans had divided the camp into four compounds, or lagers. Each lager held ten barracks, built on stilts three feet off the ground to foil efforts at tunneling. Each of the barracks contained a central hallway lined with ten rooms, each with eight double bunk beds equipped with straw mattresses. A single 25-watt light bulb dangled in the middle of the room, casting a weak light on the room's table, pot-bellied stove, and collection of rough benches. To supplement the weak illumination, the prisoners crafted oil lamps out of tin cans, lard, and bed webbing.[3]

In theory, eight bunk beds per room meant that each room should have held 16 men. In reality, some rooms were at nearly double occupancy. The extras had to sleep on the table, benches, or the floor. Bathing in the barracks' washroom could prove equally uncomfortable—with one bath a week that relied on a self-dousing of a bucket of frigid water. During the day, the *Kriegies* relied on a set of outdoor latrines. For nocturnal calls of nature, they relied on an unlit, two-hole latrine in the washroom in the back of the barracks.[4]

Generally, conditions were equally grim as the winter of 1944–1945 unfolded into one of the coldest in European memory. Each building garnered only one lump of coal per man per day for the barrack's pot-bellied stove, while the prisoners battled influenza, dysentery, and malnutrition as they suffered through a daily routine of increasingly mind-numbing boredom. That routine typically started between 0730 and 0800, when the guards would unlock the barracks doors and assemble the prisoners for the morning roll call. The POWs would line up in rows of fours to be counted. Mistakes in arithmetic seemed inevitable, and the prisoners would stand in formation until the guards were satisfied with their head count. Once the roll call was completed, it was time for breakfast. Each lager housed a mess hall, from which the guards distributed the prisoners' food—which, for breakfast, usually consisted of a thin slice of German black bread from a prisoner's weekly ration of one-eighth of a loaf, complemented by a cup of black ersatz coffee.

"It was so foul it took a few weeks for our stomachs to become accustomed to the shock," Contrada later wrote of the coffee. He was no more complimentary of the bread. "It was good for almost everything: doorstops, sculpting, an anvil, etc. I read where it was 50% bruised rye grain, 20% sliced sugar beets, 20% tree flour (sawdust), and 10% minced leaves and straw." Lunch was scarcely better—usually a half cup of thin soup made of dehydrated vegetables, tasteless and cold and often garnished with cooked bugs. At the end of the day, supper consisted of a half cup of boiled potatoes, mixed sparingly with watered-down powdered milk.[5]

Such meager rations required precious little time to consume, which meant that Contrada and his comrades had long hours to fill within the confines of the barbed wire. At first, his initial thoughts were to dispatch mail home to relieve the worries of his parents back in Norfolk. As a POW, he was allowed to write four cards and two letters a month.

"At first, the number seemed inadequate, but as the months passed and no mail was received, mail writing lost its interest," Contrada recalled. "However, we all looked forward to mail call with undying hope even though there were repeated disappointments. The fortunates who received mail usually read their letters to all of us. We were starving for news from home, but the lack of mail broke down the morale of the *Kriegies* faster than any other single factor."[6]

After breakfast, Contrada typically walked around the compound for an hour and a half with a friend, sharing memories of home and mulling over the possibilities of their future. A small library of Red Cross–provided books provided further distraction, and Contrada made a habit of reading through the collection for a couple of hours every morning. "I can remember the names of only two books: *The Biography of Charles Darwin* and *Lord Jim*," Contrada remembered. "I didn't like *Lord Jim* when I tried to read it in high school, and to this day I have never finished *Lord Jim*."[7]

The Red Cross had also provided equipment for softball and football games. Contrada avoided the touch football games—"the guys were too big and mean for me—they played for keeps," he remembered—but he did play softball "with a ball that had been hit so much it was as soft as a pillow." For the big barracks-against-barracks games, bookies conducted a brisk business in gambling. For the POWs, cigarettes were the main currency.[8]

Even within the confines of the *Stalag*, some of the prisoners performed semi-official duties, usually on one of the camp's numerous committees. A "News Committee" distributed information culled from a secret radio built from parts obtained from bribing German guards. A "Nuisance Committee" worked to make the supervision of the POWs as difficult as possible for their guards—hiding prisoners to disrupt head counts, imitating the sound of radio broadcasts from certain barracks to keep the Germans looking for nonexistent radios, and even, in one case, setting fire to a barracks. An "Escape Committee" vetted prisoners' ideas for escaping and, through a series of subcommittees, supported such endeavors with tunnels, maps, personal documents, civilian clothes, and travel plans.[9]

To foil such escape efforts, the guards, or "goons," as the *Kriegies* called them, maintained a steady pressure on their prisoners. Most were middle-aged men seemingly unfit for combat, sometimes accompanied on their rounds by the so-called ferrets—those guards, often with leashed dogs, tasked with sniffing out contraband, hidden storage spaces, or tunnels. As a countermeasure, POWs would announce every move of the guards within a compound or a barracks. Shouts of "Goon's up!" "Goon entering barracks!" "Goon entering room number 5!" would echo across the compound.

For the most part, the guards were an omnipresent and irritating presence. Even within that oppressive environment, a hulking, middle-aged guard the POWs called "Big Stoop" managed to carve out a reputation for himself. Patrolling the compounds with a whip, the massive guard would swing it menacingly at the POWs. At other times, he took great delight in tearing up the prisoners' rooms in furious searches, scattering food, Red Cross parcels, and personal belongings across the floor. If a prisoner warranted his personal wrath, Big Stoop would cuff him violently on the side of the head with his cupped hands. Sometimes, the resulting pressure would puncture the unfortunate prisoner's ear drums.[10]

Even without the abuse of guards like Big Stoop, life in *Stalag Luft IV* was miserable. "The days were very long. The nights were longer," Contrada remembered. "I slept on my back, on two benches with all my clothes, and it was so cold. You could hear a rat run across the floor, then somebody cursing at it trying to scare it to another part of the room only to hear another curse in the dark. And you could hear the dogs scurrying under the barracks."[11]

For Contrada, Christmas brought a welcome respite from the drudgery of prison life. "We were permitted to put on a vaudeville show in our little meeting room," Contrada recalled. "Bill Meiselbar, probably the oldest *Kriegie,* who owned a paint and wallpaper store in Ft. Wayne, Indiana, was asked to decorate the place and asked me to assist him. From the Red Cross stockpile, the Germans gave us a bunch of crepe paper, which Bill used to camouflage the dreary place into a festive hall."[12]

"It was probably ugly," Contrada admitted, "although all of us thought it was beautiful. The show was a typical amateur production. Volunteers did their best to entertain us. We loved it. We laughed and laughed. It was a happy time." Afterward, an English priest, who had been captured at Dunkirk five years earlier, celebrated a Christmas Eve Mass at midnight for his fellow *Kriegies*—the only religious service in the compound. Fearful of escape attempts should so many prisoners be out of their barracks after dark, the Germans relented only after the POWs' leaders promised nobody would try to escape during the service. No one did.[13]

Soon after Christmas, the weather took a turn for the worst. But despite the bitter weather, the promise of liberation began to warm the spirits, if not the bodies, of the *Kriegies*. At night, in the distance somewhere over the eastern horizon, the low rumble of Soviet artillery offered hope that their days of captivity were drawing to a close. The Germans, however, had no intention of allowing their prisoners to fall into the Red Army's hands. In late January, they warned the *Kriegies* that they would be marched out—destination unknown, or at least unspecified.

Almost immediately, the somnolent camp erupted into confused bedlam. Prisoners hastily prepared for whatever the next day might bring, scraping together provisions for the march. Then the POWs learned that the injured POWs would be evacuated west by train. Martin, still nursing shrapnel wounds on his right hand and legs, was among those who drew a space on the evacuation train. When the Germans realized that extra space was available, they randomly selected healthy prisoners to join them. To Contrada's delight, his name was on the list.

On January 29, 1945, Contrada marched out of the *Stalag*'s gates and on to the train station, where he saw a long line of "40&8" cattle cars. According to accepted military logistics, 40 men or eight horses could be transported in such cars. The guards, however, crammed Contrada and 52 other POWs in a single car. The POWs quickly scrambled for the best spots and, as the scramble degenerated into a round of pushing, shoving, and cursing, realized that they would have to take 20-minute turns sitting and standing if they were all to fit in the crowded quarters. With a quick vote, they elected a leader to arbitrate disputes and to call the time. Even sitting required a level of organization.

"The first man sat down and pulled his legs up to his butt, then the next man sat the same way with his back up against the legs of the first man," Conrada recalled. "The third and fourth man sat the same way but facing the first two. So there were four men in a row tightly squeezed together for the length of the boxcar."[14]

Three hours passed before the train began to move and, as Contrada and his fellow passengers well knew, Germany's railways had become a prime target for aggressive Allied pilots. Each time the men heard aircraft engines, they retreated into silent prayer. Meanwhile, the train continued on a slow, seemingly haphazard, start-

and-stop journey that eventually lasted nine days and nights. Contrada and his comrades endured nine days and nights in the locked box car. "It was hell," he declared simply. "When I returned home, every time I was in a crowded bus, streetcar or subway, I would always say, 'Vince, now stay like this for nine days.' . . . [It] was an absolutely miserable, painful, frightening, hungry, thirsty, dirty, nine-day trip."[15]

Trapped in their own filth, Contrada and his fellow passengers soon suffered from rampant diarrhea. With no toilet paper available, the misery was absolute as the prisoners passed a pair of empty water buckets back and forth as makeshift toilets. "There were constant cries of 'Hurry up!' 'I can't hold it any longer,' 'Pass the bucket, damn it!'" Contrada recalled. "Needless to say, the bucket filled up quickly. You held the bucket on your lap after you used it until the next person called for it. As the bucket was passed, it usually spilled on a few guys, and the cursing really erupted."[16]

"Men began to urinate against the wall so the water would trickle out," he continued. "Those who were sick to their stomachs vomited on themselves and others. For the few we thought were dying, we tied the ends of a blanket to the roof with shoelaces to make a hammock. The long nights almost drove us crazy."[17]

Two days into the trip, the guards finally let Contrada and his fellow passengers out for a brief respite. After tumbling out of the stinking car and down a snowy hillside, the sergeant dropped his pants and squatted in the snow. Then he looked up the hillside—only to see "fifty rear ends defecating." "It was an ugly sight," he added unnecessarily.[18]

As the journey progressed, the POWs quickly realized that the lack of drinking water presented a major problem. Contrada remembered going without water for nearly three days during one grim stretch. On the infrequent rest stops, the prisoners collected as much clean snow as possible, hording their precious caches for as long as possible. "You felt like crying when your cache of snow melted," Contrada remembered.[19]

It took Contrada's train four days to cover 100 miles and reach Szczecin, Poland, an inland port that the Germans called Stettin. That night, the RAF paid the city a visit, bombing the railway yards where the train was waylaid. Contrada's boxcar rocked from the concussions while, inside, its occupants prayed for deliverance. As soon as the bombing ceased, a mob of civilian refugees demanded space on the prisoners' train. A near riot ensued, and the guards struggled to beat them off. Only the arrival of German army troops succeeded in dispersing the crowd.[20]

Leaving Szczecin behind, Contrada's train continued north for the Baltic coast. Five days of miserable travel remained before the train deposited the POWs in the medieval town of Barth. A short hike through the cobblestone streets brought Contrada, Martin, and the others to their new home within the barbed wire of *Stalag Luft I.*

⏤

Despite the misery of their train ride, Contrada and Martin should have counted themselves among the lucky evacuees of *Stalag Luft IV.* Owsianik was not so fortunate. There would be no train to take him to the relative safety of a new camp. Instead, he was destined to endure a forced 330-mile march of almost epic proportions. As he and his fellow prisoners marched out of the camp's gates, a German guard shoved Red Cross parcels into their hands. The parcels' contents included a half pound of sugar cubes, one pound of powdered milk, one pound of margarine, seven ounces of crackers, half a pound of cheese, two bars of chocolate, four ounces of powdered coffee, six ounces of jam, five packages of cigarettes, twelve ounces of corned beef, twelve ounces of Spam, six ounces of pate, and six and a half ounces of tuna or salmon.[21] After the chronic food shortages of life behind the wire in *Stalag Luft IV,* it almost seemed like largesse—at least until Owsianik and the others realized how long their impending march would last.

"It was a march of great hardship," Dr. Leslie Caplan, one of the camp's captured doctors, later testified to a war crimes investigator after the war. "For 53 days we marched long distances in bitter weather and on starvation rations. We lived in filth and slept in open fields or barns. Clothing, medical facilities, and sanitary facilities were utterly inadequate. Hundreds of men suffered from malnutrition, exposure, trench foot, exhaustion, dysentery, tuberculosis, and other diseases. No doubt many men are still suffering today as a result of that ordeal."[22] Caplan witnessed at least seven men dying "as a result of neglect" on the march and he stressed that "it is likely that there were other deaths that I do not know about."[23]

Owsianik shared Caplan's memories. "I can say that there were life-threatening times [as a POW]—the box car rides, the marching, back and forth, which I made. The guards telling us that we were going into the ovens at Luckenwalde as we looked at them through a fence. We were forced to march again at 1:00 a.m. and then shot at by P-51s as we marched by. [The mission against Moravska Ostrava] really did a number on me and has affected my life ever since."[24]

Ferris Joyner, the former South Carolina truck driver who had served as a gunner on board the B-24 nicknamed *Rough Cobb,* and now shared the rigors of the winter march from *Stalag Luft IV* with Owsianik. After the war, Joyner jotted down a rough itinerary of the prisoners' march. His notes from the first week of the march reflected the mounting challenge: "1st day—February 6—walked 15 kilometers—slept in barn. 2nd day—February 7—walked 32 kilometers—slept in barn. 3rd day—February 8—walked 20 kilometers—slept in barn. 4th day—February 9—rested—received some potatoes from Russian workers on farm. 5th day—February 10—walked 24 kilometers—snow melting—mud and water. 6th day—February 11—walked 20 kilometers—mud, snow, ice and water. 7th day—February 12—rest—Red Cross food very low."[25]

The further the men marched, the further the food supplies dwindled. At times, the POWs endured two or three days without food and, when food was provided, it was rarely more than three or four small potatoes. They marched through snow, sleet, and cold rain, sometimes ending a grueling day's march with only the cold, wet ground upon which to sleep. Nevertheless, those that reached such rude accommodations counted themselves lucky. They had passed too many of their comrades lying prostrate in roadside ditches during the day to consider themselves otherwise.

By the thirtieth day of the march, the men reached the town of Beckendorf. Some days they had only moved one kilometer; on others, they covered 28 on a journey that seemed to have no clear destination or route. As far as food was concerned, Joyner's notes reveal an uneven diet of spuds, soup, and the occasional fragment of a Red Cross parcel. Sometimes they slept in barns; other times, in open fields. Fifty-one days into the trek, Owsianik, Joyner, and a ragged collection of their comrades caught a ride on boxcars that deposited them, two days later, on March 30, 1945, at *Stalag IIB* in Fallingbostel. There they were welcomed with two-thirds of a can of barley and carrot soup. The camp itself was filthy, consisting primarily of large, lice-infested tents into which the POWs were crowded. They slept on the ground side-by-side in those tents. For a latrine, they relied on a foul-smelling ditch used by hundreds of other prisoners. Liberation of *Stalag IIB* would eventually come, but, when it did, it would not be a moment too soon.[26]

⌒

Compared to the prisoners of *Stalag Luft III* and *Stalag IIB*, Bill Tune and his comrades fared well when fate, in the winter of 1944, brought them to *Stalag Luft I*. Nevertheless, an unsettling feeling descended on Tune as he passed through the front gate of the *Stalag* for the first time. The camp was a maze of low, unpainted wooden barracks. Barbed wire, mounted on double fences with tangle wire curled between the posts, encircled the camp, while a menacing collection of guard towers, equipped with spotlights and machineguns, dotted the fence's perimeter.

Once inside the camp, Tune received a set of prisoner ID tags—in his case, No. 02345—and a brief opportunity to send a card home to the States notifying his family where he was imprisoned. But shortly thereafter, guards pulled Tune from the camp's general population and took him to the camp infirmary for further treatment. A recently constructed addition to the camp's existing 30-bed hospital provided Tune with a clean berth, while two British doctors and six orderlies promised competent care.

"I'll save you a bunk," his friend Tomlinson assured him as an orderly helped Tune limp into the infirmary.[27]

Tune spent some two months in the camp's hospital. As he lay in his bunk, he watched an American officer assigned to a nearby barracks pace around an enclosed pen that barely measured 20 feet by 60 feet. Tune soon learned that the restless lieutenant colonel was none other than Francis S. Gabreski—the AAF's leading ace in Europe. "Before I was discharged he had worn a rut in the ground where he walked," Tune remembered.[28]

Gabreski was not the only one bored with his confined surroundings. According to Tune, one of his doctors was "about to climb the wall in order for something to do." Tune's arrival—and his semi-paralyzed injured left hand—promised a welcome distraction for the doctor. Chuckling gleefully, the doctor informed Tune that he would operate and see if he could connect the severed nerves back together. A day-long operation soon followed. "Neither of us felt he was successful," Tune reflected, "but what a good time he had."[29]

As he recuperated from his various injuries, Tune had ample opportunity to survey his new surroundings. By that point in the war, *Stalag Luft I* was over two years old. The *Luftwaffe* had placed the prison camp on the immediate outskirts of Barth, a small community sheltered on a bay on Germany's Baltic coast. From within the camp, POWs could see the town's most prominent feature, the tall, red-stone church spire of St. Marienkirche, a massive edifice that dated back to the fourteenth century.

In the spring of 1944, *Stalag Luft I* housed some 3,400 prisoners.[30] By the time Tune limped in several months later, the camp had grown from its original two compounds to a total of five, forming a rough L-shape that opened onto a marshland fronting the sea. In the winter of 1944, the camp was home to approximately 6,000 prisoners.[31] Those numbers were destined to grow even higher thanks to both the Germans' Christmas counteroffensive in the Ardennes, which bagged a fresh catch of POWS, and the arrival of previously incarcerated prisoners who were being evacuated from camps threatened by the advancing Red Army.

In such circumstances, Tune might have been hard-pressed to find a place to sleep. Upon being discharged from the infirmary, however, he found that Tomlinson had kept his promise to save him a bunk. Tune joined Tomlinson in North 3 Compound, taking a vacant bunk in Room 3, Barracks 306. The average barrack quartered 200 men and was divided into rooms of various sizes. Tune was in one of the larger rooms with 23 other occupants. He drew a berth sleeping on a straw-filled mattress side-by-side with another POW on a triple-decker bunk bed. A square, coal-fired metal stove, food pantry, rough wooden table, a collection of stools, and a pair of benches filled the limited floor space between the beds. Makeshift shelves made of bed boards and empty Red Cross parcel cartons lined the walls, while laundry hung from interior clotheslines.[32]

"We were 24 men to a room, sleeping on thin straw pads, with little food [but] I do not believe there was ever a tense moment from attitude or stress," Tune wrote. "Three men had the talent to make the cooking vessels we used from powdered milk cans, using a bolt head that we had removed from the building as a hammer. [It was] proof that American ingenuity is great."[33]

Despite Tune's stoicism, it was difficult to deny the camp's shortcomings. "A communal dayroom was set aside in almost every barracks, but equipment was negligible," the Military Intelligence Service's postwar report on the *Stalag* declared. "Light was inadequate throughout the camp, and since the Detaining Power required the shutters to remain closed from 2100 to 0600, ventilation was entirely insufficient. . . . Stoves for heating and cooking varied in each compound [and] facilities in all compounds were inadequate. Many of the buildings were not weatherproof, and the extremely cold climate of northern Germany made living conditions more difficult for the PW."[34]

"Both the number of stoves and the amount of fuel issued were insufficient to maintain good health," the Service continued. "Upper respiratory diseases were a source of concern to the medical staff"—which, until the arrival of an American captain in March 1945, consisted of the two British doctors and their orderlies— "and this became a great danger when the Germans required the shutters to remain closed during the night. Small ventilators were allowed open but offered insufficient air under the circumstances."[35]

Three of the compounds, to include Tune's, only contained barracks. However, two of the compounds, North 1 and West, boasted a kitchen-barrack, theater room, chapel room, library, and study room. During the day, prisoners could circulate among the compounds to take advantage of those amenities, such that they were. Within the larger camp, the U.S. and British prisoner contingents were organized into provisional units for command, control, and disciplinary purposes. They remained autonomous of one another, although there was close cooperation and coordination.

For their part, the Americans were concerned; they organized into a four-group Provisional Wing. Tune's arrival coincided with that of a new senior Allied officer to command the wing. Colonel Hubert Zemke, a famed P-47 Thunderbolt ace who commanded the 56th Fighter Group, had bagged 28 German aircraft before falling victim himself in December 1944.

Although *Stalag Luft I* did not have a reputation as a particularly brutal *Stalag*—in fact, one pair of historians described it as a camp with "a good reputation to be in: the facilities were fair, as was the regime, and morale was generally high"—leaders like Zemke faced a challenging time nevertheless.[36] Maintaining order within the wire was only one of their worries. Their main concern was convincing, coercing, and cajoling their captors to comply with the strictures of the Geneva Conventions, or at least ensuring that visiting representatives from the International Red Cross and neutral nations like Switzerland and Sweden—the so-called Protecting Powers—were at least aware of the problems. They were not always successful, particularly as the spring of 1944 passed to summer and then to autumn.

During that time, the German guards, perhaps becoming increasingly jittery about the intensifying Allied air raids, ordered the POWs to immediately return to their barracks as soon as an "immediate warning" air raid siren sounded. The penalty for failing to do so was to be shot on sight. In May 1944 alone, three slow prisoners found themselves dodging bullets as the sirens sounded. A new guard policy regarding the use of deadly force to avenge "insults to German honor" further heightened the tension, as did the Germans' increasing willingness to throw prisoners into isolation—the "cooler"—for minor infractions of German disciplinary regulations and to deny them their weekly Red Cross parcels.[37]

Personal hygiene was another challenge faced by the POWs behind the *Stalag*'s wire, and the Military Intelligence Service identified "very poor sanitation" as the "most serious detriment to the health of the [POWs]. . . . One bath-house containing ten shower-heads represented the only facilities for over 4,000 officers to bathe, and it was also used as a delousing plant for new arrivals or for any outbreaks of body-crawling insects. Early in 1945 an additional bathhouse was completed which contained ten shower-heads."[38]

"Insufficient quantities of wash basins and soap made laundering difficult, and no arrangements were made to care for the men's laundry outside of the camp," the Service continued. "Bed linen was theoretically changed once a month, but this period was greatly extended with the influx of new PWs. No facilities existed for the disposal of garbage not cared for by incinerators, and latrine and wash drains were so unsatisfactory that the areas around the barracks were frequently flooded."[39]

Adequate nutrition also posed a challenge for the POWs. The German rations of potatoes, turnips, bread, and cabbage—sometimes complemented by horse meat—

were inadequate for sustenance, causing the prisoners to rely on their weekly Red Cross parcels to survive. Such parcels typically contained tins and packets of jam, cheese, powdered milk, meat, sardines, margarine, raisins, chocolate, coffee, sugar, and crackers, although the effort to get such parcels to *Stalag Luft I*'s inhabitants was increasingly hampered by the accelerating collapse of Germany's transportation network. Accordingly, the POWs tried to cultivate small vegetable patches in which they grew lettuce, radishes, beets, onions, and tomatoes, but with minimal results. Meanwhile, a simple calculus developed for distinguishing between a good mess manager and a bad one: "a good mess manager would tell you there were worms in the food. A bad mess manager wouldn't tell you."[40]

Nevertheless, the *Stalag* did boast some limited amenities. West and North 1 compounds contained full-sized football and baseball fields, equipped with an impressive array of sports equipment. Two Catholic priests and three Protestant chaplains ministered to the spiritual needs of their captive congregations, while a pair of bands earned well-deserved reputations.[41]

The quality of the music and the sports equipment was not, however, enough to convince all of the POWs imprisoned at *Stalag Luft I* to remain content with waiting out the war behind its barbed wire. Escape attempts occurred, although they were rarely, if ever, successful. Once, for example, a group of six soldiers dressed one of their number in a stolen German uniform and, with him serving as an "escort," four of the others carried the sixth man out of their compound on a stretcher. They managed to bluff their way through two gates before being finally stopped at a third. The effort earned the audacious crew two weeks in the cooler.[42]

A more successful—at least initially—group simply "planked" a walkway across the wire with a large, hand-held board. Eight POWs bridged the wire in such a manner, dropping into an unenclosed area of the camp one night and making their escape. Although they were later apprehended, their example provided a thrilling inspiration to their fellow POWs dreaming of freedom beyond the wire.[43]

Other escape attempts were more spontaneous. One POW managed to slip into the battery box of a truck that had been allowed into the camp to make a delivery. The truck rolled out of the gate without being checked and, as soon as darkness fell, he slipped out of his cramped hiding place and headed for the distant Allied lines.[44] Despite his initial success, however, he was eventually caught as well.

For many others, tunneling under the wire seemed a safer course of action, even though the sandy soil and the high water table—approximately six feet below the ground surface—presented formidable obstacles. Nevertheless, in April 1944, 30 POWs managed to complete a tunnel and were on the verge of a mass escape when an alert guard patrolling outside of the wire stumbled across the first of the would-be escapees pulling himself out through the topsoil. With rifle in hand, the guard apprehended one prisoner at a time as they popped up out of their tunnel.[45]

Despite such failures, the POWs continued with their tunneling. As the months passed, however, so many tunnels collapsed and caved in that a zone radiating out from the barracks to the fences became lumpy and took on the appearance of a giant washboard. One prisoner estimated that some 140 tunnels were eventually dug at the *Stalag*.[46]

To foil such efforts, the guards had originally placed the barracks buildings on small foundation posts eight to twelve inches off the ground. They also dug trenches across such crawl spaces, which allowed eavesdropping guards or sniffing guard dogs to worm under the barracks. The dogs, vicious and poorly fed, were particularly feared. Led by handlers, they patrolled the compounds at night. Woe to any POW caught outside of a barracks—or even sticking his head outside of a window for a quick breath of fresh air—should any of those dogs catch him.

The twice-a-day roll calls were another means to keep tabs on the POWs. Summoned by the guards' shouts, the POWs would line up in formations five men deep and await the completion of the guards' tally. Oftentimes, simple counting errors caused the guards to think a prisoner had escaped. Although the spectacle of frantic guards was an amusing one, such miscounts also forced the prisoners to endure hours of standing in formation while fruitless searches took place.[47]

An important remedy to such boredom came with the surreptitious publication and distribution of an underground camp newsletter, the *POW-WOW*, which reportedly stood for "Prisoners of War Waiting on Winning." Its writers obtained news from a small radio set, built from parts smuggled in by German guards in exchange for cigarettes and hidden in a barrack wall in the South Compound. Listeners would transcribe notes on toilet paper, stuff the transcript into a hollow wristwatch, and dispatch it to Barracks 9, North Compound. Other news came from friendly guards who passed information from radio broadcasts out of Copenhagen and Oslo to the prisoners.[48]

In Barracks 9, editors checked the various news reports against secret maps while two typists quickly hammered out enough copies of the 2,000-word newsletter to be forwarded to each of the other barracks in the camp, where they were read and quickly destroyed. "The only truthful newspaper in Germany," the newsletter's masthead boasted.[49]

Thanks to the *POW-WOW*, the prisoners kept abreast of the pace of the war. "Invasion!—Yanks-British Land in Europe!!!" the June 6, 1944, edition trumpeted. "Allies Inside Germany," declared the September 16, 1944, edition. Its editors took pride in scooping their stateside civilian counterparts, claiming that they had reported the news of D-Day a full two hours before any New York paper reported the invasion of France. Those editors' ranks included Lowell Bennett, an International News Service correspondent who had been shot down while flying on a night bomber mission with the RAF.[50]

For his part, Tune passed the time putting his artistic talents to use while he penciled scenes of camp life—"I drew in order to have something to do," he remembered simply.[51] He hammered one of the metal Red Cross parcel tins into a makeshift scrapbook album cover, entitled it "The Uninvited Guests," and began to fill it with meticulously detailed sketches of guard towers, his compound, and the interior of Room 3. He also penned postcards—marked "Lager-Bezeichnung Stalag Luft I"—home to his parents and to his fiancée Fran, trying to put on a cheerful face for the folks back home.

"Dearest Fran," he wrote to her back in Canon, Georgia, on January 26, 1945. "All is still going along as usual—still well, healthy and getting fat—but I don't get about too much. Virgil Colson is here and we get a kick out of talking together. I wish that I could hear from you and Mother but I will not for awhile. A hello to your Mom and Dad. Love, Billy."[52]

Elsewhere in the camp lived other survivors of the raid on Moravska Ostrava. Loy Dickinson had grown up in sight of San Francisco Bay; now he looked through the barbed wire at the gray expanse of water that separated Barth from the Darss Peninsula. He began his internment in the compound known as North 2, only to be moved in December to North 3.

"Since the war I have seen photos of the mess arrangement in the two older compounds," Dickinson reported. "We had nothing as elaborate. I vaguely remember taking part in the revolving kitchen duties. . . . We also had no theater, rec room or any athletic gear to speak of. [Roll call] was a dreary activity but one that no one was excused from. Morning and evening without fail. It was only dismal in the coldest days of the winter."[53] By the time Dickinson arrived in the camp, the Allies were rolling across northern Europe. Accordingly, he recalled little interest in escaping. "One statement I remember that purported to be from Eisenhower to the effect that 'All friends of Freedom, stay put,'" Dickinson recalled. "In essence, if you get out into the open, you will endanger your life if you get caught in a battle situation. This I understood to have been the case after D-Day in June."[54]

For Dickinson, food was, understandably, a preoccupation. Nevertheless, having been brought up with two younger sisters and two younger brothers during the Great Depression, he enjoyed a certain degree of perspective regarding hunger. "We didn't starve by any means [at *Stalag Luft I*]," Dickinson reflected, "but we ate a lot of coleslaw and meatloaf."[55]

That was not to say, however, that Dickinson failed to seize upon the happy opportunities for more food that occasionally presented themselves. Once, he and a fellow *Kriegie,* John Birkenmeir, spotted another POW inexplicably toss a round of cheese into a garbage pit. After exchanging a look of disbelief with each other, Birkenmeir and Dickinson scrambled into the pit like a pair of rats. "We returned to our barrack to be greeted as heroes in our little room of 16 men," Dickinson reported.[56]

Ed Smith, the navigator from Bill Bullock's 359, was imprisoned in North Compound 2. "We had no physical mistreatment," Smith recalled simply. "Food was the main problem."[57] In the compound, he reunited with John Quinn, his bombardier from the ill-fated mission. Like Tune, he realized it was a small world indeed.

Leo Zupan had also ended up in the coastal *Stalag.* It was certainly not the kind of vacation he had in mind when he had carefully laid out his beer and cigars for his post-mission R & R to Rome. Bill Garland was there as well, along with Charlie McVey. As the sole survivor of 885, Charlie McVey was simply glad to be alive, even if he had now progressed from TVA to AAF to POW. Like the other POWs, McVey was hard-pressed to remember any specific acts of mistreatment by the German guards, although he admitted having to survive on "very strict rations of food and fuel. We were allowed seven briquettes of coal each day for each room of about twenty airmen for cooking and heating."[58]

The food, in McVey's memory, was equally modest—mostly potatoes, rutabagas, and black German war bread the guards called *Kriegesbroten,* complemented by Red Cross parcels. He entered the camp weighing 155 pounds; he would lose 30 of them by the time the war was over.[59]

Duane Seaman, the flight officer who had piloted the B-17 downed from the 49th Squadron, the 20th's sister unit, also landed in *Stalag Luft I.* "I have to say, it was a hum-drum way of life," Seaman reflected. "It was so basic—almost like you were living 200 or 300 years ago. All you had was your barracks. There were 20 prisoners to a room, on double beds stacked three high. The barracks were up off the ground and were drafty, particularly in the wintertime. The food was poor—I dropped from 148 pounds to 118 pounds."[60]

Williard Netzley also joined Seaman and the others at *Stalag Luft I.* "Twenty-four of us lived, cooked, ate and slept in a room about fifteen feet square," he remembered. "We had a coal stove but no electricity. We slept two wide and three deep in bunk beds. Food, which we prepared ourselves, consisted of what the Germans gave us, and our Red Cross parcels."[61] As far as such meals were concerned, he remembered so-called purple passion (red cabbage and horsemeat which turned purple upon boiling), "green death" (ground-up dried vegetables, to include stems, leaves, and silage—when boiled, it turned a sickly green color), pumpernickel bread "with sawdust and slivers in it for fiber," and giant turnips and potatoes.[62]

"When we got our Red Cross parcels they contained, among other things, ascorbic acid (Vitamin C) pills," Netzley continued. "We would mix these with cooked turnips and make 'applesauce' or slice the turnips and fry them for pancakes spread with 'applesauce.' When you are hungry enough, almost anything tastes good. I smile when I think this diet is recommended today—low on meat, dairy products and sugar [but] high in vegetables and fiber. We were young and tough and in good health when we were shot down and were optimistic."[63]

Education provided an intellectual outlet for Netzley and his fellow POWs. "We had fellow prisoners who were teachers or college students of every subject, so we could arrange a class in architecture, Spanish, history, Composition English, or whatever. Some of us would bring a bench and a lump of coal. Our 'teachers' were knowledgeable, did a good job, and we all had plenty of time. So, in my resume, I can truthfully say that I have studied abroad."[64]

As the winter of 1944–1945 wore on, an influx of prisoners from the *Stalags* evacuated in eastern Germany conspired to push conditions at *Stalag Luft I*— and Netzley's good humor—to their limits. Food, already in short supply, became even scarcer as more and more POWs crowded into the camp, often sleeping on the barracks' rough floors. But the refugees also brought with them the promise of impending liberation and the hope of an end to the seemingly interminable waiting—if the prisoners could survive the inevitable chaos that liberation would likely bring.

15
VE

In at least one way, the POWs awaiting liberation in the *Stalags* were the lucky ones. Whether ensconced in camps like *Stalag Luft I* or caught up in the sheer misery of the winter evacuations from camps in eastern Germany and Poland, they at least knew that, if they woke up in the morning, they were still alive. That certainty, despite the dysentery, the lice, the cold, and the hunger pangs that accompanied it, was worth something.

For their loved ones back home, however, no such assurance existed. In 1944, when the fastest form of communication available to a serviceman usually came in the form of a Western Union telegram, it took families days to learn that their husbands and sons had been shot down. For many, the arrival of such news—sometimes preceded by a note from a helpful squadron mate—marked only the beginning of what seemed like an interminable period of waiting, wondering, and worrying.

⌐

The Netzley family first received word that their son Willard was missing in action at 9:30 on Sunday evening, September 10, 1944, when Robert McCloskey's mother called from Porterville to warn them that she had been notified that McCloskey was missing in action. As the families knew, McCloskey was the pilot on Netzley's crew.[1]

Fifteen minutes later, a Western Union telegram from Major General James A. Ulio, the adjutant general of the United States Army, arrived. "The Secretary of War desires me to express deep regret that your son Flight Officer Willard P. Netzley has been reported missing in action since twenty-nine August over Czechoslo-vakia," the telegram declared. "If further details or other information are received you will be promptly notified."[2]

"Public prayer for young Netzley is being offered Sunday at the Christian Church in Covina and at the Baptist Church in Pomona," the local newspaper reported. "Private Richard Netzley, brother of the flyer, arrived home Monday from Fort Sill, Oklahoma, to comfort his parents," the paper added. "Another son, Earl, is serving with the Army Air Corps in England."[3]

A month later, a letter dated October 10, 1944, and penned by Bob Jackson, one of Willard's friends in Amendola, arrived carrying reassuring news.

> Dear Mr. and Mrs. Netzley. I went over to Willard's old squadron this morning and got some good news. It's unofficial but I'm sure it is authentic. He went down on the 29th of August on a raid up to Czechoslovakia. It was a pretty rough target and his whole squadron was wiped out. Most of his crew, I understand, bailed out successfully and Willard, McVey, and another boy made their way to a farm house. While there this other fellow stepped out of the house and while he was gone the Germans came in and captured Willard and McVey. This other fellow finally made it back to this base. So as far as anyone knows, [Willard] is 'sweating out the war in a prison camp.' I'm glad to be able to tell you this. I hope that you won't worry about him. Probably you will hear from him soon or the War Department will notify you of his status.[4]

A subsequent telegram arrived on November 2, confirming Jackson's letter. "Report just received through the International Red Cross states that your son Flight Officer Willard P. Netzley is a prisoner of war of the German government," the telegram stated. "Letter of information follows from Provost Marshal General."[5]

The following month, Robert Donahue wrote to the Netzley family, explaining that he had flown with Netzley on the mission to Moravska Ostrava, albeit on a different aircraft. Donahue explained that he and Charles McVey had, along with Netzley, been sheltered initially by friendly Slovak soldiers and that only he had escaped eventual capture.

"I am sure Willard will be alright and I hope that it will be very soon when you hear from him again. This war can't last much longer and I hope that it will be but a short time when he will be home again. If there is anything else I can tell you, let me know and I will be only too glad to do it."[6]

William Bullock's family in North Carolina first received word that he was missing via a Western Union telegram. Major General Nathan Twining followed with a letter to Bullock's father on September 26, 1944, assuring him that the War Department would provide the family with further details as they became available.

"While he was with this air force Bill proved that he had all those qualities which are associated with our best flying personnel," Twining stated. "He was respected and admired for the manner in which he carried out his duties as the pilot of his ship. In recognition of meritorious achievement he has been awarded the Air Medal and one Oak Leaf Cluster. I extend sincere sympathy."[7]

For the Bullock family, five months of painful uncertainty followed, only to end on February 23, 1945, with the arrival of another Western Union telegram. "Report now received from the German government through the International Red Cross states your son First Lieutenant William C. Bullock, Jr., who was previously reported missing in action, was killed in action on twenty-nine August nineteen forty-four over Czechoslovakia. The Secretary of War extends his deep sympathy. Confirming letter follows."[8]

For Fran Beggs, her first indication that her fiancé, Bill Tune, was still alive came in December 1944 thanks to a telegram from Tune's father, Tillman. "Have telegram Billy is Prisoner of War of Germany," the telegram read. "Letter will follow. Mr. Tune."[9]

Shortly thereafter, Fran received word directly from Tune in the form of a postcard from the *Stalag* dated December 30, 1944. "Dearest Fran," Tune wrote. "Christmas 1944 is over and I only hope that yours was as good as ours. We enjoyed a turkey dinner with all the trimmings—thanks to the American Red Cross. Fran, we are only allowed to write three letters and four cards a month but I will write as often as possible. Note my POW number is 6543. Love, Billy."[10]

The Fitzpatrick family, in their home on Sarah Street in McKees Rocks, Pennsylvania, also learned of their son John's failure to return via a Western Union telegram. Later in September, a letter from Major General Nathan Twining, the commander of the Fifteenth Air Force, arrived as well.

"Dear Mr. Fitzpatrick," General Twining wrote, "I know that you will want the details, however meager, on the last flight of your son, Second Lieutenant John F. Fitzgerald, 0-761067, who has been carried as missing in action since August 29, 1944, when his Flying Fortress failed to return from a high altitude bombing mission over the Privoser oil refineries in Czechoslovakia."

"Unfortunately," he continued, "the extent of our knowledge is that John's plane was hit by flak while making its bomb run, and it is believed to have gone down in the general vicinity of the target. The bomber did not remain within the vision of our other crews for any length of time, and we are unable to report whether any parachutes were used. Those are the details as we have them at present. In due time, we should receive definite word concerning the loss of the plane, but until that information is actually at hand, we can only hope that your son was able to reach the ground safely."

"John has made a fine record during combat participation with us," Twining concluded. "He has seen action requiring the utmost skill and courage and has contributed greatly to our many recent successes in this theater. In recognition of his fine record he has been awarded the Air Medal and one Oak Leaf Cluster."[11]

At the time, Fitzpatrick's wife, Dorothy, was living in San Francisco with her sister. In California, working as a delivery room nurse, she tried to keep her mind off of her husband's fate. "I was devastated when I learned that he was a POW," she said. "I couldn't even think much about it, and for the longest time we didn't even know where he was being held. His father stayed in touch with the service and did his best to keep up with him. But it was rough."[12]

⌒

Twining's hopes were well founded—Fitzpatrick had indeed reached the ground safely. His captors eventually imprisoned him at *Stalag Luft III* and then *Stalag VIIA*. Other men, and other families, were not so fortunate.

On September 9, eleven days after the ill-fated raid on Moravska Ostrava, Russell Meyrick's family back in West Springfield, Massachusetts, received a telegram warning them that Meyrick was missing. A month later, on October 8, Meyrick's wife, Ellie—who had married him shortly before he shipped out overseas and was awaiting her husband's return back on Cottage Street—received a letter from Vic Kreimeyer, Meyrick's regular copilot.

"We are all very optimistic as to Russ' safety," Kreimeyer wrote. "I know you have faith and share our optimism. None of us were on the raid of the 29th with Russ. Had we been someone would be writing our wives the same sort of letter I am writing you now."[13]

"I realize what a shock it must have been to you and his folks," he continued. "We couldn't believe it when we heard the report that a squadron failed to return. I want to do everything possible that will help you in any way. Now we must pray and have faith in God. Many of us in combat have found that only in him can we have confidence in our future."[14]

"Do not give up your faith or optimism under any circumstances," he advised.

"Worry as little as possible, because that will only destroy your own hope as well as health. Many wives and parents have undergone the same situation, and many with less to look forward to than you. So be of good faith, then, regardless of what happens. Sincerely, Vic."[15]

A second telegram received on December 2, however, proved Kreimeyer's hopes to be futile. Citing reports from the German Red Cross, it informed the Meyrick family that their son, and Ellie's husband, had been killed in action.[16]

After her own son Loy returned safely home to Berkeley and told her of his mission to Moravska Ostrava, Pearl Dickinson wrote to Meyrick's mother in Massachusetts. "I know how great your loss is and my heart goes out to you for we are so very thankful to have our son with us," she wrote. "The cost of our American freedom and peace, when it comes, is far too great. God bless you."[17]

⌒

The Weiler family, back in Burlington, Wisconsin, was also destined to wait many months before eventually receiving tragic news regarding their son Jim. At the time, the Weilers' other three sons were also serving in the military. Harold "Doc" Weiler was a naval lieutenant stationed at Corpus Christi; Joseph Weiler was a sergeant with an armored regiment in France; and their youngest, Philip, was in the naval reserve awaiting orders to report for training at Great Lakes Naval Training Base.

"Our service flag was full—our house, empty," wrote Weiler's sister Mary, referring to the red-bordered white flag displayed in the family's front window. The flag boasted four blue stars, one for each of the Weiler sons serving in the military. Meanwhile, Mary's father kept a large world map tacked on the wall in the kitchen. With brightly colored tacks, he tracked each of his son's progress through the global conflict.[18]

For his son Jim, the tacks on the map stopped in Italy.

First, a Western Union messenger delivered a telegram on September 9, 1944, warning the Weilers that Jim was missing in action.[19] A letter from General Nathan Twining, the commanding officer of the Fifteenth Air Force, soon followed, but then nearly another year passed before any more definitive information could be learned. Such information came in the form of another telegram on August 10, 1945, when the War Department informed the Weiler family that their son's copilot, Irving Thompson, had been liberated and confirmed that he was the only survivor of the bomber's crew.[20]

Shortly thereafter, Robert Ellis, who had served with Weiler on his original combat crew that formed and trained in the United States, wrote to Weiler's parents.

"Jim's life was short, but it was magnificent," Ellis declared. "He was youthful, strong, bubbling with energy, clean, wholesome, and above all Christian. He lived, fought, and died for the ideals he believed in. He was a good leader and a good pilot until the end. He holds a proud record, which you and I will do well to imitate."[21]

With Jim's fate determined, the Weilers quietly exchanged one of the four blue stars on the family's service flag for a new star—this one colored gold.

⸺

Even after receiving the official news of Weiler's death from the War Department, his family still did not know where, or even if, he had been buried. In fact, the lieutenant, along with 27 of his downed comrades, had been interred in a mass grave in distant Slavicin.

In the wake of the mission to Moravska Ostrava, German soldiers scoured the Czech countryside, following the telltale plumes of black smoke to the downed bombers and their dead crewmen. By the end of the day on August 29, they had located 27 bodies. Manhandling them with disdain, they stacked the bodies in the morgue at Slavicin's cemetery. The next day, they deposited another, bringing the total to 28. They had no intention of allowing the local townspeople to attend a memorial service but they nevertheless summoned Father Frantisek Manak, the local Catholic priest, to arrange the impending burial. They ordered the priest to arrange for a mass grave of specified dimensions to be dug.[22]

Realizing what was about to occur, Manak asked to be allowed to perform appropriate funeral services; he was denied. The German officer in charge explained that these were "enemy terrorists." Later that evening, Manak revisited the issue with him and, this time, the officer relented. Townspeople, however, were still prohibited from attending.[23]

Late on the morning of August 31, the burials began. Initially, the German soldiers, wearing gas masks to shield them from the odor of the bodies—some badly burned—on the hot August morning, carefully laid the bodies side-by-side into the grave in groups of three. As the day wore on, the Germans decided to use a coffin cart and a wheelbarrow to speed up the process. Unceremoniously, they dumped the remainder of the bodies into the grave, filled it with dirt, and covered it with sod.[24]

In addition to Father Manak, there was one other observer of the burials. Technical Sergeant Robert Kirsch, the radio operator from *Tail End Charlie* who had been turned over to the Germans by a Nazi collaborator, watched as well.

"He asked me how long I thought the war would last," Kirsch recalled. "I told him three months, which turned out to be wishful thinking."[25] That was particularly the case for Kirsch, who was destined to spend the rest of the war in *Stalag IXC* near Bad Sulza, Germany.

The Germans put a simple wooden plaque on the grave. It read "28 American fliers. Died August 29, 1944. Buried August 31, 1944." They also dispatched the town crier to walk the streets of Slavicin, beating his drum and warning the townspeople against any shows of commemoration at the gravesite. The Germans' prohibition, however, only survived as long as their occupation of Slavicin. As soon as the last *Wehrmacht* soldier departed, Slavicin's residents began bringing flowers to the grave.[26]

⤺

Meanwhile, as winter passed to spring and the shattered Third Reich splintered beneath the onslaught of the hard-charging Allied armies, the imprisoned survivors of the mission to Moravska Ostrava prepared for one final challenge—surviving the chaos that would likely accompany their impending liberation. Imprisoned at Moosburg's *Stalag VIIA,* John Fitzpatrick, the former pilot of *Wolf Pack,* was fortunate enough to fall directly into the hands of his countrymen. At the *Stalag,* a brief firefight erupted as diehard guards resisted the Sherman tanks of the U.S. 14th Armored Division. By the end of the morning, however, the camp was in American hands. At that point, however, more uncertainty set in as the POWs pondered their next steps. The American combat troops were ill equipped to handle the needs of 80,000 liberated POWs. In response, the camp's former inhabitants began to wander the countryside, scrounging food and exploring their surroundings.

Fitzpatrick was one of those men, strolling along a quiet Bavarian road on the outskirts of Moosburg when a jeep pulled to a stop alongside him with a happy shout. The jeep's driver, Sergeant Eddie Kramer, recognized Fitzpatrick from their shared childhood in their hometown of Pittsburgh.

"Sgt. Kramer and his pals took Lt. Fitzpatrick to their home, which was a farmhouse which had been abandoned by its owners," the *Pittsburgh Post-Gazette* reported. "There he was treated royally and given a meal of good American ham and eggs, his first in over a year."[27]

⤺

Joe Owsianik was another POW lucky enough to be liberated by U.S. forces. On April 24, 1945, he was on the march once again—this time part of a bedraggled column of POWs encamped in the town of Dommitzsch. A flight of P-51 Mustangs spotted the POWs along the western banks of the Elbe River and signaled their location to American troops. Two days later, U.S. soldiers moved into town shortly after dawn and liberated the POWs. Owsianik was, finally, a free man.[28]

⤺

Meanwhile, at *Stalag Luft I,* Vincent Contrada awoke on May 1, 1945, stepped outside of his barracks, and discovered that Americans were in the guard towers.

The realization of what their presence in the towers meant was staggering. "The morning of May 1, 1945, was an amazing day," Loy Dickinson agreed. "No Germans around. They had completely vanished."[29]

Later, Contrada and Dickinson learned that Colonel Hubert Zemke and the other senior Allied officers in the camp had weathered a late-night showdown with their German captors the previous evening. The Germans had been ordered to evacuate the camp and march its occupants to the west; in response, Zemke calmly informed the camp commandant that the POWs had no intention of evacuating the camp. Furthermore, the Germans should consider themselves *his* prisoners until they provided Zemke's men with access to keys, guns, ammunition, short-wave radios, records, and the locations of booby traps and minefields. In the end, the Germans acquiesced and, eager to quit the scene before the impending arrival of the Red Army, disappeared over the western horizon.[30]

The Soviets were not long in coming. First came what seemed to be Cossack irregulars, riding hell-bent-for-leather on foaming horses in galloping columns. A train of wagons, pulled by equally exhausted horses, followed close behind. The wagons were piled high with a remarkable array of booty—including antique clocks, kitchen equipment, and bicycles—plundered from German homes.

"As the Russians left a house, a soldier on the outside lobbed a hand grenade through the window, regardless of whether or not there were people inside," Ross Greening, an American POW, recalled. "Quite a number of houses were blown up this way. The carnage was something to behold."[31]

"My only recollection was of Russian troops with little or no uniforms straggling through the town," Dickinson added. "One donkey-driven cart had wheels which were not round. It was unreal in that they appeared to be near savages and probably were close to it."[32]

Amid the barely contained chaos, the Soviet commanding officer arrived to pay his respects to Zemke, who met him at the camp's gate. The Soviet officer asked Zemke why his men were still behind barbed wire; Zemke responded that he had received orders from his superiors to keep POWs together because planes were being sent to evacuate the men.[33]

Surprised, the Soviet insisted the men should be free. Zemke, in response, refused, which in turned sparked the other officer to draw his revolver and, at gunpoint, order Zemke to release the prisoners. At that point, chaos erupted. Some POWs began tearing down the fences, allowing hundreds others to stampede across the open fields beyond the camp's perimeter.

"It was complete pandemonium," Greening wrote. "A number of men left because they went berserk at the prospect of freedom. To the best of our knowledge, there were twelve that never were accounted for. One poor lad was blown to pieces by a land mine. We couldn't identify him; there weren't enough pieces left."[34]

Willard Netzley recalled a more benign series of events. "The Russian commanding officer told our commanding officer how lucky we were to be liberated and that if we didn't tear up the place to show our appreciation, they would," Netzley wrote. "So we tore down the guard towers and made tripods—stuffed German uniforms with straw—and set them on fire. The Russians were pleased and their band held a concert for us; each musician had a machine gun slung over his shoulder as he blew or banged away."[35] Meanwhile, as the guard towers burned, scores of their fellow POWs bolted into the falling twilight.

The next day, many of those same POWs returned sheepishly to the camp, realizing belatedly that it represented the most likely prospect for security, shelter, and food. With regard to the latter, the Soviets obliged the former POWs by rustling up many cattle and herding them into the camp for the POWs to butcher.

Nevertheless, not every prisoner gave up on escaping to the Allied lines. "Some ran to the docks hoping to steal a boat and sail across the Baltic to freedom," Contrada recalled. "A few men commandeered a train and ran into trouble over the complicated tracks and switches in the yard. A couple pilots went to the airport, stole a single engine plane, and were going to fly to safety. The plane was booby-trapped."[36]

As the days passed, the POWs became increasingly uneasy about well-founded rumors that Roosevelt, Churchill, and Stalin had agreed at the Yalta Conference that Allied prisoners of war liberated by the Soviets were to be transported to Odessa, on the Black Sea, for shipment home. In the face of such a 1,500-mile detour home, Zemke and the other officers pressed for an alternate plan as the camp's awkward calm devolved into an uneasy stalemate. A series of formal dinner banquets between the higher ranking POW officers and the Soviet commanders managed to preserve some feeling of collegiality, as did less formal, but equally festive, parties between their lower-ranking counterparts—all fueled by copious amounts of vodka. "The Russians and the Allies had a joint party one night," Charles McVey, the sole survivor from aircraft 885, remembered. "The Russians performed their Cossack dances and the Americans danced the jitterbug!"[37] Nevertheless, despite such distractions, as the days wore on, boredom grew and tension mounted as to when the POWs would be repatriated to their own forces.

"The few remaining days of their stay were the longest spent by the Kreigies," wrote Morris Roy in his 1946 account of his stay at *Stalag Luft I*. "Though daily reports persisted that planes would arrive at any moment, the skies remained empty. From May 5 until May 12, the monotony of waiting was broken only by the arrival of a few jeeps containing American officers and G.I.'s, and by the entertainment provided by the Russians."[38]

On May 12, 1945, the roar of approaching multiengine aircraft signaled that the stalemate's end, and imminent evacuation, was at hand. "We saw a B-17 appear over the trees, and a cheer went up," Contrada recalled. "A general and his small coterie of officers flew in with the rescue planes. We were so out of whack with military regulations [that] we hardly paid any attention to them. . . . He was just a human being like us. We sat on the ground and greeted him. The officers were not disturbed at all as they must have realized we had been prisoners for so long we had forgotten how to be military. They smiled pleasantly as we chatted with them."[39]

Four hundred miles away, another general received a far less congenial reception. Russian general Andrei Vaslov had fallen into German hands in 1942 and, turning against Stalin, recruited a 50,000-man strong Russian Liberation Army from Soviet POWs to fight alongside the Germans. Ending the war in Czechoslovakia, he surrendered there to the Americans. Stalin, however, soon agitated for the renegade general to be turned over to the Soviets for trial and punishment. The U.S. Army finally relented, delivering Vaslov to the vengeful Soviets at 2:30 P.M. on May 12. An hour later, the Soviets allowed the first American bomber to land at Barth. At least one historian contends the chain of events was linked.[40]

Greening surmised a different reason for the breakthrough in negotiations with the Soviets. At the time, future U.S. senator Harry P. Cain, who had left his job as the mayor of Tacoma, Washington, to join the AAF, was serving with the Eighth Air Force in England. Cain had badgered his Soviet counterparts in London to pressure Moscow to allow an aerial evacuation of *Stalag Luft I*. Impatient for an answer, he eventually arranged for the flights to begin regardless.[41]

Whatever the true rationale for the arrival of the B-17s might have been, such issues were well beyond the scope of interest of the POWs on the ground. They simply wanted to get out of Barth. Fortunately, the full-blown aerial evacuation soon began. Planes landed, picked up 30–35 prisoners, and took off in a continuous flow of aircraft that lasted for the next three days. Finally, on May 15, 1945, on a beautiful spring day, the evacuation was completed.

"The pilot of our B-17 purposely took us on a tour of the Ruhr Valley to show us the destruction we had caused to Germany," Contrada remembered. "Every city we flew over was gutted. It was impossible to fathom how Germany would ever recover. This wasn't devastation like the path of a tornado one sees on TV. These were major cities totally destroyed."[42]

Contrada's plane landed on a short runway outside of Reims, France, where he and the other liberated prisoners were trucked to a temporary camp set up to feed incoming POWs. Medical personnel, who apparently knew in which prison camp the formers POWs had been incarcerated and the nature of their diets there, stood on each side of the feeding line. They subjected each man to a quick examination before warning them to "go easy" on the amount they ate.

"The first thing everyone commented on was the fresh baked white bread," Contrada recalled. "It tasted like cake! Our meal consisted of steak, mashed potatoes with gravy, fresh vegetables, and ice cream for desert. It was the best meal any of us could remember."[43]

After eating, Contrada and his comrades boarded a train in Reims bound for the town of St. Valery, on the English Channel, outside of the city of Le Havre. There, as a so-called Recovered Allied Military Personnel, or RAMP, Contrada found a temporary home in the sprawling tent city known as Camp Lucky Strike (maintaining a tradition of naming the transient camps around Le Havre after cigarettes—other camps were known as Camp Chesterfield, Camp Old Gold, Camp Twenty Grand, and Camp Philip Morris, among others). Other former inhabitants of *Stalag Luft I*—men like Dickinson, McVey, Netzley, Bill Tune, and Ed Smith—were already there and processing through the camp.

"We were told to shed our clothing, were deloused, and had a chance to shower and shave before our new uniforms were issued," Contrada reported. "Later we were given instructions on where to report for a medical exam the next day and the location of S-2 (Intelligence), where we had an appointment to be debriefed. Soon after, we were told we could write a short message to our parents. I don't remember my message but it dealt with love, happiness, and 'see you soon.'"[44]

Contrada eventually made his way to England, where he managed to secure a place on the *Queen Elizabeth* for passage home from Southhampton to the United States. The once luxurious cruise ship had spent the war as a converted troop ship. Two-passenger cabins now berthed soldiers swaying in a dozen hammocks as the liner zigzagged westward through the Irish Sea and across the Atlantic Ocean. The war in Europe was over but her captain was unwilling to take any chances on a renegade U-boat captain. Six days later, the ship reached New York City. "What a thrill to see the Statue of Liberty," Contrada remembered. "I thought of my Dad who came to America all alone when he was 14 years old."[45]

For the *Queen Elizabeth*, the six-day voyage to New York marked her first trip to the United States to return victorious U.S. troops since VE Day, and in Contrada's words, "New York was expecting us. All the ships in the harbor blew their horns. Fire boats shot water into the sky as they cruised along beside our ship. It was like the newsreels when some big celebrity was coming to town. A band was playing John Phillip Sousa's music. Dancing girls were rolling and shaking their hips on the docks. Reporters, radio commentators, newsreel cameramen, still photographers, and politicians were all there."[46]

A bus took Contrada from the docks to Fort Dix, New Jersey. There, a briefing officer informed him that orders were being cut for transportation to his next base—one near his home where he could receive the balance of his accrued pay and orders for a sixty-day leave and a subsequent two-week sojourn to an R & R center. Contrada tried to call home to Norfolk but quickly realized that the fort was incapable of handling so many outgoing calls. Nevertheless, he was home in Norfolk the next day, walking up the sidewalk to 363 West Princess Anne Road once more.

"When I arrived home," Contrada remembered six decades later, "I can't describe the emotion of hugging my mother and father and the rest of my family at that moment. All cried. God was good."[47]

⌒

In the meantime, other survivors of the mission to Moravska Ostrava steamed home in a far more mundane manner. After a month-long stay at Camp Lucky Strike, Netzley, along with Charles McVey, boarded the *Admiral Butner* and sailed for Newport News, Virginia. They arrived seven days later after a week of smooth sailing.

From there, for Netzley, it was "onto a coal-burning 'G.I. Pullman' (a boxcar) with the doors on the side, to California and home with my family in Glendora.... I was home and still on leave on August 6, 1945, when Colonel Paul Tibbits and the crew of the Enola Gay dropped the atomic bomb on Hiroshima, Japan. On August 9, 1945, the U.S. dropped a second atomic bomb, this time on Nagasaki."[48]

"The war with Japan ended September 2, 1945," Netzley recited. "I have a personal reason why I'm glad it did. As an experienced bombardier who was shot down before he completed his tour of duty, I expected to be assigned to the crew of a B-29 and sent to bomb Japan."[49]

Fate, however, had another future in store for Netzley, and the end of the war in Japan marked the end of his military career. The raid on Moravska Ostrava was destined to be the last combat mission he ever flew. In that regard, Netzley recorded no complaints.

⌒

Bill Tune also greeted the end of his military career with no complaints. Flown out from Barth on board a B-17, he processed through Camp Lucky Strike and secured a berth on a transport ship bound for New York City. In all, it was a lengthy process and it was not until July 1945 that he was able to send a telegram to Fran back in Georgia that simply read: "Dearest Fran. Will arrive there Tuesday by auto or bus. Love, Billy."[50]

That Tuesday, Fran waited patiently for Tune as long as she could stand it. Late that afternoon, when he had still not arrived, she could, in her words, "stand it no longer." Fran and her father drove down the highway, hoping to intercept him en route, and succeeded in meeting him as he drove toward them in a car he had borrowed from a friend.

"There was dancing on that Georgia road when we met," Fran laughed six decades later.[51]

Epilogue

Hometown Men

As military historians penned their postwar histories, the Fifteenth Air Force's mission to Moravska Ostrava scarcely merited a footnote when cast into the broader perspective of the Second World War. The 5th Wing's after-action report hints at some success for the raid—to wit, a series of explosions and fires, to include at least one in the railroad marshaling yard—but clouds and smoke defied a more detailed assessment. One can only surmise, therefore, as to the impact that the raid had on the German's immediate war effort.

It might be useful, therefore, to attempt to juxtapose the Moravska Ostrava raid into the larger context of Germany's Eastern Front in the late summer of 1944. The chaos of that front's collapse as erstwhile Romanian, Hungarian, and Bulgarian allies wavered and crumbled makes even a casual analysis difficult. At any rate, it is hard to imagine that an air raid on Moravska Ostrava—whether a complete success or a complete failure—adjusted the calculus of Germany's unfolding catastrophe in Romania one way or the other. At the same time, however, it is difficult to argue that the loss of even a single gallon of fuel or a single rail car failed to make the German's desperate efforts to hold onto Slovakia and Hungary that much more difficult. The same could be said for the loss of the German pilots lost in their confrontation of the 20th Squadron and the 2nd Bombardment Group in the skies over Czechoslovakia.[1]

Nevertheless, in terms of military accomplishment, one struggles to justify or, for that matter, to criticize the mission against Moravska Ostrava. Such a failure, however, is not necessarily a bad thing because, in order to do so, one would be relying on the benefit of hindsight that was not enjoyed by the air mission planners of the Fifteenth Air Force. Furthermore, reveling in such hindsight today would ignore the immediate context of the planning—and brutal acceptance of costs—of those same missions in 1944.

Consider, for example, that the 20th Squadron's sacrifice was soon eclipsed by an even more disastrous mission—the 445th Bombardment Group's raid on Kassel, Germany, on September 27, 1944. A navigational error caused the group to miss Kassel and to press on, without fighter escort, against the alternate target of Gottingen instead. The group had faced negligible opposition in the skies over occupied Europe since February of that year. Perhaps they flew into Germany's skies cursed with an unfortunate degree of overconfidence.

But this time the Germans were ready, well organized, and well prepared to give battle. They pounced on the opportunity and hurled over 100 fighters against the lone group. In the wake of the vicious air battle that followed, only four B-24s managed to make it back to their airbase in Tibenham, England. The loss of 25 bombers from the group marked it as the greatest operational loss suffered by an AAF unit in the history of the war.[2]

In the end, therefore, it is difficult to rank the mission to Moravska Ostrava in terms of mighty military achievement or to even declare it a mighty disaster of historic scale. At the same time, however, that very same uncertainty and anonymity regarding the mission's place in history perhaps underscores its most valuable lesson. That lesson was that, in the summer of 1944, young American airmen were in their second year of a bloody war of attrition in Europe's skies so mercilessly brutal that the destruction of an entire bomber squadron scarcely merited notice outside of Amendola, Italy—or outside of Carbon Hill, Alabama, or Berkeley, California, or Burlington, Wisconsin. It was, therefore, a mission mighty in sacrifice alone, tucked within a massive bomber campaign that, fortunately, was mighty in achievement as well as sacrifice.

Few men who survived the mission to Moravska Ostrava, however, entertained such lofty analysis of their role in the Second World War. Almost to a man, they returned to their homes after rescue or liberation and, in the time-honored tradition of America's citizen soldiers, quietly resumed the lives they had left behind.

Vincent Contrada—"Everybody wanted to hear about my experiences in combat and prison camp, but my mother and father tried to play it down," Contrada wrote of his immediate homecoming in Norfolk. "I believe they had instructed the family not to ask me a lot of questions about the war believing they would depress me. The talking didn't bother me. I was happy to be home and alive."[3]

"Neighbors I hardly knew invited me to dinner," the former waist gunner from

the 429th Squadron's *Wolf Pack,* continued. "Relatives went out of their way to entertain me. I was treated with a great deal of respect and honor. Those old school-
boy friends, who had also returned, got together in the evenings to share stories and
a lot of beer. Everybody was so nice. They made it easy for me to get accustomed
to returning to civilian life."[4]

Contrada received an honorable discharge from the army on October 23, 1945, at
Maxwell Field, Montgomery, Alabama, after logging two and a half years of military service. Making a career in education, he eventually retired as the superinten-
dent of the Toledo, Ohio, school district. He then moved to Naples, Florida, where
he enjoyed 23 years of retirement playing golf and investing in real estate before
passing away on April 14, 2003.[5]

Loy Dickinson—Dickinson returned to Berkeley, California, where he discovered that, in his absence, his 42-year-old mother's hair had turned completely white.
Shortly thereafter, he visited his former crewmate Thomas Coogan, the flight engineer from *Tail End Charlie,* at Letterman Hospital, on the Presidio at San Francisco. The date was August 14, 1945, and Dickinson had a date later that afternoon
with Alice Craig, a friend from Berkeley who worked for the IRS on McAllister
Street, near the downtown area. After bidding goodbye to Coogan, Dickinson left
to meet his date.

"On the streetcar trip back to town we turned east off of Van Ness onto McAllister. There were people out on the street waving their arms and yelling," Dickinson remembered. "It was VJ Day! After another block or two the streetcar couldn't
go any further and everyone got off. Surveying the situation I realized that I was
not going to catch up with Alice. Twenty minutes later, walking, literally down the
middle of Market Street in a crowd of at least half a million people, we ran into
each other. Needless to say we were able to keep what turned out to be a very special date."[6]

Dickinson spent 60 days on R & R leave. "Languishing on the deck at Fallen
Leaf Lake and playing the tables on the Nevada side of Lake Tahoe cured me of the
idea of pursuing an appointment at West Point," he later wrote.[7] He entered the
freshman class at UC Berkeley in the fall of 1945, where he pledged Phi Gamma
Delta and was elected freshman class president with the slogan "Loy Is Your Boy."
Majoring in city management, he graduated in June 1948. Reflecting on his college
education, Dickinson declared, "The GI Bill of Rights was the greatest thing our
Congress did aside from the Marshall Plan in the 20th Century."[8]

After a fellowship with The Coro Foundation, Dickinson took a position as the
executive director of the Oakland Better Business Bureau. "This was so because

the Bureau was broke and could not afford to hire anyone who knew what he was doing," Dickinson later joked.[9] In 1950, he took a sales job with Moore Business Forms. Today, Dickinson resides in Parker, Colorado. He served as the president of the 2nd Bombardment Group Association and still stays in close touch with the descendants of the Baca family who originally sheltered him when he parachuted into Czechoslovakia on August 29, 1944.

Robert Donahue—After being flown out of Slovakia and back to Italy, Donahue returned to the United States, where the former tail gunner of *Tail End Charlie* spent the rest of the war training to be an aerial gunnery instructor. The war ended, however, before he taught his first student. Leaving the service, Donahue returned to Pittsburgh, where he worked as a letter carrier, became president of the mail carriers union in the city's North Side, and also worked for fifteen years as a floor manager for Gimbel's Department Store in downtown Pittsburgh. He succumbed to a heart attack in 2003.[10]

John Fitzpatrick—Fitzpatrick, Contrada's pilot on board *Wolf Pack,* enjoyed a particularly happy homecoming. Arriving in San Francisco to reunite with his wife, Dorothy, in June 1945, he found her holding a special surprise for him—his three-month-old son John Jr. Ten other children would eventually follow. "John was so excited," his wife recalled. "He wanted so much to have a large family. Being an only child in an Irish-American Catholic family, I think he saw all of his cousins and their families and thought he was missing out on something. Well, he certainly accomplished that!"[11]

Returning to work for TWA, Fitzpatrick later worked for a smaller airline before moving to Arizona. There, he pursued a number of business ventures before succumbing to a brain hemorrhage in 1970. Dorothy, however, still attends the 2nd Bombardment Group's reunions. "John was always proud that he did not lose a man on that mission," she recalls.[12]

Bill Garland—After liberation and his return to the United States, Garland, the former pilot of *Snafuperman,* returned to Phoenix, Arizona, where he resumed his work with Western Pipe & Steel. In 1950, he formed his own company, Garland Steel, which he successfully operated for over two decades. In the meantime, he served on Phoenix's city council, as its vice mayor, and spent 15 years on Arizona's Public Service Commission before eventually moving to Sedona. In Sedona, his family now operates Garland's Oak Creek Lodge and several local businesses. "I am now retired in Sedona with three children and eight grandchildren living there," Garland wrote. "They manage to keep me busy."[13] He died on May 25, 2008.

Ferris Joyner—Joyner returned to South Carolina, married his girlfriend, Thelma

Greene, on September 17, 1945, a week after he was discharged from the military, and resumed hauling freight for his former employer Simon Faust. He later took a job with RC Motor Lines, where he worked until he retired.

"He was not only my uncle but one of the best friends I ever had or hoped to have," his niece Jeanette Ross remembered. "He was a very witty person and very giving. He enjoyed planting a huge garden every year and gave most of it away to neighbors and friends. During the last 20 years or so of his life, he was very devoted to church work and was a highly respected church member." Joyner passed away in 1998.[14]

Jim Martin—Martin, who had flown on board 359 with William Bullock as the bomber's ball turret gunner, reunited with his wife, Judy, in California. "She was an exceptional person," Martin wrote of his wife, who had spent the war working in a defense plant outside of Los Angeles and who passed away in 1985. "She took everything in stride."[15] After 62 days of leave, he served at an AAF training camp near Delano, in California's San Joaquin Valley. Discharged from the service in November 1945, Martin completed an on-the-job training program in agriculture and worked on a 6,000-acre grape farm. He became a foreman, stayed in the agriculture business, and rose to a position in produce processing. When he retired, he moved to Parks, Arkansas, where he resides today.

Charles McVey—McVey, the navigator on board 885, returned to Nashville, Tennessee, after liberation. There he met his infant son Charlie Jr. for the first time. McVey's wife, Mildred, had given birth to their son on March 29, 1945, while he was imprisoned in *Stalag Luft I*. In Nashville, he resumed his work for the TVA, attended college at Vanderbilt University on the GI Bill, and eventually graduated *summa cum laude*. Staying with TVA but moving to Chattanooga, he rose to become the company's manager of investments, an elder of the Brainerd Church of Christ, and a board member of the Boyd-Buchanan School. "Dad wasn't one to just chat about any of his war experiences," his son remembered, "however, when we asked him questions he was very willing to [talk to] us about things in great detail. He wasn't much for cooking, but always liked to cook fried potatoes and corned beef 'hashed' together—he said it reminded him of the best meals he had as a POW."[16] McVey passed away in 2003.

Willard Netzley—In Netzley's words, "Thank God for the G.I. Bill of Rights! In late 1945, or early 1946, I enrolled in pre-law at the University of Southern California, was later admitted to USC's School of Law, graduated with a Juris Doctor degree in 1950, passed the California Bar [exam] on the first try, and joined Lance D. Smith in the law firm of Smith and Netzley in La Puente, California, where I practiced law for 50 years."[17]

Netzley married Cathryn "Kati" Cordelia Thomas two years after he graduated from Law School. "I have had a good life. I am having a good life," *My Baby*'s former bombardier wrote in 2004. "I love my family, my country, and the dear Good Lord." After living in the city of Rowland, in California's San Gabriel Valley, the Netzleys moved to Banning, California, in 2002, where he remained active in his community and also, at the age of 79, took up his first hobby—watercolors. Netzley passed away in 2006 after a two-year battle with cancer.

Joseph Owsianik—Owsianik, one of the former waist gunners on board *Tail End Charlie,* was discharged from the service in St. Petersburg, Florida, on September 23, 1945, and returned to New Jersey, where he resumed his job as a milkman. Later, he took a job as a floor mason, installing tile floors. Today, he is retired but, like several of the other survivors, has stayed in contact with the Czechs whose paths he unexpectedly crossed in the late summer of 1944. In 2005, he returned to the Czech Republic and visited, among other places, the gravesite of Russell Meyrick and Joseph Marinello. Warmly welcomed by his Czech hosts, he returned two years later with his grandson.[18]

Joseph Sallings—After leaving his Czech friends and making his way back to American lines, Sallings returned to Union County, Tennessee, after the war. Like his father, he became a farmer but, despite the wartime economic boom, life remained hard in the hills of eastern Tennessee for Sallings, his wife, Imogene, and their four boys. When the American grandson of Sallings's Czech benefactors visited the family shortly after the war ended, he found the Sallingses struggling financially. Returning to New York, the Czech sent the family a package of clothes in a gift of generosity the family still recalls.[19] The former waist gunner from *Tail End Charlie* passed away in 1972, at the age of 50.

Duane Seaman—Back in New Jersey, the former pilot of the 49th Squadron's 369 attended Seton Hall for three years at night. He became an automobile salesman and eventually a sales manager for a local Cadillac dealership. Retiring in 1980, he moved to Arizona, where he resides today.[20]

Ed Smith—The AAF honorably discharged Smith, the bombardier from 359, in the fall of 1945. He returned to Ohio, married, and attended the University of Michigan's Forestry School. Earning first an undergraduate and then a master's degree, Smith joined the United States Fish & Wildlife Service in 1950. Jobs of increasing responsibility with Wisconsin's Department of Conservation and the Bureau of Land Management followed. Smith retired in 1987 and currently lives in Springville, Virginia.[21]

Paul Sumner—Sumner, who flew as the navigator on board John Fitzpatrick's *Wolf Pack,* returned to Colorado after the war. He resumed his teaching career as an industrial arts teacher at Denver's North High School, retired in 1980, and still lives in Colorado.[22]

Bill Tune—The former pilot of *Tail End Charlie* married Fran Beggs on March 10, 1946. He worked in Birmingham, Alabama, for a period of time before attending Alabama Polytechnic Institute (today's Auburn University), where he earned a degree in architecture. The Tunes lived in Birmingham and Gadsden, Alabama, for a brief time before they finally settled in Florence, Alabama, where Tune embarked upon a successful career as an architect, eventually settling in a home overlooking Wilson Lake, on the Tennessee River, in a house Tune designed.[23]

Six decades after they flew their final mission together, Frank Flynn wrote to Tune on November 22, 1994. "The main thing I wanted understood," Flynn wrote, reflecting on a recent reunion, "is that I feel that neither you as leader of the 20th Squadron or I as your co-pilot could have done no more than what was done at the time. What happened, happened. Period. . . . I never or rarely even think of our last flight. . . . To me it is over. We were just young men at the time doing the job we were trained to do, and I think we did it."[24] Tune passed away in the autumn of 2008.

Leo A. Zupan—Garland's former copilot on board *Snafuperman* returned to Oregon, where he worked first as a traveling salesman and then as a real estate salesman. Finding success in the latter field, Zupan rose to become the president of Windermere/Van Vleet & Associates, one of the largest real estate firms in southern Oregon.[25]

Notes

Prologue

1. Thomas Donahue, telephone interview by James L. Noles Jr., May 15, 2005.
2. William S. Tune and Loy A. Dickinson, interview by James L. Noles, October 14, 2003.
3. Ibid.
4. Captain George B. Sweeney, "Consolidated Eye-Witness Description Composed by Investigation Officer" (August 30, 1944) (accompanies Missing Air Crew Report 8110) (hereafter referred to as Sweeney Report).

Chapter 1

1. William S. Tune, interview by James L. Noles, August 4, 2003.
2. Ibid.
3. Ibid.
4. For information on Carbon Hill during the Great Depression, visit "A New Deal for Carbon Hill: A Photographic Document" by William C. Pryor, at http://newdeal.feri.org/carbonhill/index.htm (accessed August 15, 2006).
5. William S. Tune, interview by James L. Noles, August 15, 2006.
6. Ibid.
7. Donahue, interview.
8. Frank C. W. Pooler to Pittsburgh Chamber of Commerce, May 23, 1940, copy in authors' possession.
9. Loy Dickinson, email correspondence with James L. Noles Jr., July 1, 2004.
10. Loy Dickinson, email correspondence with James L. Noles Jr., July 15, 2004.
11. Loy Dickinson, email correspondence with James L. Noles Jr., September 15, 2004.
12. Loy Dickinson, email correspondence with James L. Noles Jr., July 1, 2004.

13. Mary Huckstorff, telephone interview by James L. Noles Jr., April 14, 2004.

14. Ibid.

15. Mary Huckstorff to James L. Noles Jr., April 18, 2005, letter in possession of the authors.

16. Ibid.

17. Leo Zupan, telephone interview by James L. Noles Jr., August 24, 2004.

18. Ibid.

19. Ibid.

20. Ibid.

21. Ibid.

22. William Bullock, telephone interview by James L. Noles Jr., April 29, 2004.

23. Ibid.

24. Albert E. Smith, telephone interview by James L. Noles Jr., July 12, 2005.

25. Walter Havighurst, "The Miami Years: 1809–1984," at www.lib.muohio.edu/my (accessed July 12, 2005).

26. Willard P. Netzley to James L. Noles Jr., January 15, 2006, letter in possession of the authors.

27. Ibid.

28. Willard P. Netzley, "War and Willard" (unpublished memoir, 2004), 10 (hereafter cited as "War and Willard"), copy in authors' possession.

29. Charles McVey Jr., email correspondence with James L. Noles Jr., July 19, 2005.

30. James R. Martin, telephone interview by James L. Noles, June 20, 2006.

31. Ibid.

32. Ibid.

33. Bill Garland to James L. Noles Jr., July 8, 2006, letter in possession of the authors.

34. Ibid.

35. Joe Owsianik, telephone interview by James L. Noles Jr., September 6, 2004.

36. Ibid.

37. Ibid.

38. Ibid.

39. Ibid.

40. Ibid.

41. Fern Wagner, telephone interview by James L. Noles Jr., March 25, 2005.

42. Elizabeth Meyrick Reed, telephone interview by James L. Noles Jr., July 26, 2006.

43. Ibid.

44. Ibid.

45. National Archives' Electronic Army Serial Number Merged File, circa 1938–1946 (Enlistment Records), "Meyrick, Russell F."

Chapter 2

1. Wesley Frank Craven and James Lea Cate, eds., *The Army Air Forces in World War II*, Vol. 1, *Plans and Early Operations, January 1939 to August 1942* (Washington, D.C.: Office of Air Force History, 1983), 104.

2. Tami Davis Biddle, *Rhetoric and Reality in Air Warfare: The Evolution of British and American Ideas about Strategic Bombing, 1914–1945* (Princeton, N.J.: Princeton University Press, 2002), 155.

3. Ibid.

4. Organizational History Branch, Air Force Historical Research Agency, "The Birth of the United States Air Force," at http://www.au.af.mil/au/afhra/wwwroot/rso/birth.html (accessed August 26, 2004).

5. Ibid.

6. Rebecca Hancock Cameron, *Training to Fly: Military Flight Training 1907–1945* (Washington, D.C.: United States Air Force, 1999), 300.

7. William N. Hess, *Great American Bombers of World War II* (Osceola, Wisc.: MBI Publishing Company, 1998), 7.

8. Ibid.

9. Edward Jablonski, *Flying Fortress: The Illustrated Biography of the B-17s and the Men Who Flew Them* (New York: Doubleday & Company, 1965), 6.

10. Ibid.

11. Ibid., 16–18.

12. Hess, *Great American Bombers of World War II,* 15.

13. Craven and Cate, *The Army Air Forces in World War II,* Vol. 1, 105.

14. Cameron, *Training to Fly,* 309–310.

15. Doris Kearns Goodwin, *No Ordinary Time: Franklin and Eleanor Roosevelt—The Home Front during World War II* (New York: Touchstone, 1995), 313.

16. Smithsonian National Air and Space Museum, "Boeing B-17G Flying Fortress," at http://www.nasm.si.edu/research/aero/aircraft/boeing_b17g.htm (accessed December 5, 2007).

17. Jablonski, *Flying Fortress,* 37.

18. Bill Gunston, *Aircraft of World War II* (New York: Crescent Books, 1980), 43; Hess, *Great American Bombers of World War II,* 15.

19. Ibid.

20. Ibid.

21. Jablonski, *Flying Fortress,* 38–39.

22. Cameron, *Training to Fly,* 309. The twenty-four–group plan envisioned five heavy bomber groups, six medium bomber groups, two light attack bomber groups, and only nine fighter groups—an illustrative glimpse of the prewar Air Corps's lack of emphasis on providing its bombers with escort fighters. Ibid. at 376–377.

23. Ibid.

24. Ibid., 309–310.

25. Ibid., 310.

26. Ibid.

27. Ibid., 313, 375.

28. Franklin D. Roosevelt, "On Progress of the War," radio broadcast delivered February 23, 1942 (available at http://www.fdrlibrary.marist.edu/022342.html) (accessed October 15, 2004).

29. Cameron, *Training to Fly,* 375.

30. Ibid.

31. William S. Tune, personal notes, n.d., notes in possession of the authors (hereafter "Tune notes").

32. Kenneth Fieth, "The Army Air Forces Classification Center," at http://prodigy.net/nhn.slate/nh00018.html (accessed December 2, 2004).

33. Tune notes.

34. Cameron, *Training to Fly,* 384.

35. Tune notes.

36. Ibid.

37. William S. Tune, interview with James L. Noles, August 4, 2003.

38. Cameron, *Training to Fly*, 392.

39. William S. Tune, interview with James L. Noles, August 4, 2003.

40. Cameron, *Training to Fly*, 325.

41. Tune notes.

42. Wright Patterson Airbase Air Force Museum website, "Beech AT-10 Wichita," at http://www.wpafb.af.mil/museum/early_years/ey23.htm (accessed December 14, 2004).

43. Tune notes.

44. Ibid.

45. Army Air Forces Pilot School (Specialized Four-Engine) Maxwell Field, Alabama, Pilot Transition Training Record: Tune, William S.

46. Ibid.

47. Tune notes.

48. Ibid.

49. Ibid.

50. Ibid.

51. Leo Zupan, telephone interview by James L. Noles Jr., September 2, 2004.

52. Ibid.

53. Ibid.

54. Ibid.

55. Jim Bertao, The California State Military Museum, "Historic California Posts: Eagle Field," at http://www.militarymuseum.org/EagleField.html (accessed November 27, 2004).

56. Smithsonian National Air and Space Museum, "Fairchild PT-19A Cornell," at http://www.nasm.si.edu/research/aero/aircraft/fairchild_pt19.htm (accessed December 8, 2004).

57. Leo Zupan, telephone interview by James L. Noles Jr., September 2, 2004.

58. Ibid.

59. Ibid.

60. Ibid.

61. Ibid.

62. Ibid.

63. Ibid.

64. Ibid.

65. Bill Garland to James L. Noles Jr., July 8, 2006, letter in possession of the authors.

66. Ibid.

67. Leo Zupan, telephone interview by James L. Noles Jr., September 2, 2004.

68. Ibid.

69. Bill Garland to James L. Noles Jr., July 8, 2006, letter in possession of the authors.

70. Leo Zupan, telephone interview by James L. Noles Jr., September 2, 2004.

71. Bill Garland to James L. Noles Jr., July 8, 2006, letter in possession of the authors.

72. Ibid.

73. Leo Zupan, telephone interview by James L. Noles Jr., September 2, 2004; Bill Garland to James L. Noles Jr., July 8, 2006, letter in possession of the authors.

74. Leo Zupan, telephone interview by James L. Noles Jr., September 2, 2004.

75. Bill Garland to James L. Noles Jr., July 8, 2006, letter in possession of the authors.

76. Ibid.

77. Leo Zupan, telephone interview by James L. Noles Jr., September 2, 2004.

78. Ibid.

79. Ibid.

80. *Burlington Free Press*, May 27, 1943.

81. Cameron, *Training to Fly,* 422.

82. Ibid., 334.

83. Ibid., 448.

84. Ibid., 385–386.

85. Loy Dickinson, telephone interview by James L. Noles Jr., January 18, 2005.

86. Ibid.

87. Ruben E. Ochoa, "Hondo Army Airfield," *The Handbook of Texas Online,* at www.tsha.utexas.edu/handbook/online/articles/print/HH/qch2.html (accessed December 2, 2004).

88. Loy Dickinson, telephone interview by James L. Noles Jr., January 18, 2005.

89. Ibid.

90. Bill Garland to James L. Noles Jr., July 8, 2006, letter in possession of the authors.

91. Ed Smith, telephone interview by James L. Noles Jr., July 12, 2005.

92. Ibid.

93. Ibid.

94. Ibid.

95. Ibid.

96. Ibid.

97. Ibid.

98. Ibid.

99. Cameron, *Training to Fly,* 334.

100. Ibid., 346.

101. Vic Kreimeyer, telephone interview by James L. Noles Jr., May 19, 2005.

102. Ibid.

103. Ibid.

104. Willard Netzley to James L. Noles Jr., January 15, 2006, copy in possession of the authors.

105. Ibid.

106. "History of Deming Army Airfield," at http://www.zianet.com/kromeke/ArmyAirField/DAF10.htm (accessed April 26, 2006).

107. Netzley.

108. Ibid.

109. J. H. MacWilliam and Bruce D. Callander, "The Third Lieutenants," *Air Force Magazine* (March 1990), at www.afa.org/magazine/1990/0390third.asp (accessed April 27, 2004).

110. Netzley.

111. Ibid.

112. Daniel Markus, "Miami 1941–1945: From VIP Suites to GI Barracks," Historical Association of Southern Florida *Update* 8, 4 (November 1981).

113. Ibid.

114. Robert D. Donahue, personal statement, January 6, 1995, in possession of the authors.

115. Ibid.

116. Ibid.

117. Cameron, *Training to Fly,* 447.

118. Stephen Vaughn, *Ronald Reagan in Hollywood: Movies and Politics* (Boston: Cambridge University Press, 1994), 113.

119. Donahue.

120. Ibid.

121. Joseph Owsianik, email correspondence with James L. Noles Jr., April 15, 2005.

122. Ibid.

123. Fern Wagner, telephone interview by James L. Noles Jr., March 25, 2005.

124. Owsianik.

125. James R. Martin, telephone interview by James L. Noles, June 20, 2006.

126. Ibid.

127. Ibid.

Chapter 3

1. William S. Tune, interview by James L. Noles, November 25, 2005; AAF Orders 370.5 #297 (135–31) (March 19, 1944), copy in possession of the authors.

2. Ibid.

3. Ibid.

4. AAF Orders 370.5 #297 (135–31) (March 19, 1944), copy in possession of the authors.

5. William S. Tune, notes, n.d., copy in possession of the authors.

6. Ibid.

7. Ibid.

8. Ibid.

9. Ibid.

10. Ibid.

11. Ibid.

12. Leo Zupan, telephone interview by James L. Noles Jr., October 17, 2004.

13. Ibid.

14. Ibid.

15. Joseph Owsianik, telephone interview by James L. Noles Jr., September 7, 2004.

16. Inscriptions on photograph, circa 1944, provided by Thomas Donahue. Copy in possession of the authors.

17. Ibid.

18. Willard Netzley to James L. Noles Jr., January 15, 2006, copy in possession of the authors.

19. Mary Huckstorff, telephone interview by James L. Noles Jr., April 14, 2004.

20. Ed Smith, telephone interview by James L. Noles Jr., July 12, 2005.

Chapter 4

1. *The Army Air Forces in World War II: Combat Chronology, 1941–1945* (Washington, D.C.: Office of Air Force History, 1973).

2. Craven and Cate, *The Army Air Forces in World War II,* Vol. 1, 146.

3. Stephen Budiansky, *Air Power: The Men, Machines, and Ideas That Revolutionized War, from Kitty Hawk to Gulf War II* (New York: Viking, 2004), 287. Dr. Richard Muller, a professor of military history at the USAF Air Command and Staff College, correctly points out, however, that "AWPD/1 was no more an example of 'chutzpah' than the Army's 90-division plan, or the Navy's blueprint for vast fast carrier task forces." Richard Muller to James L. Noles Jr., email correspondence, April 25, 2005.

4. Alfred M. Beck, ed., *With Courage: The U.S. Army Air Forces in World War II* (Washington, D.C.: Government Printing Office, 1994), 74.

Notes to pages 61–70 / 247

5. Ibid., 75.

6. Ibid. at 75–76. Arnold's planning staff, led by Lieutenant Colonel Harold L. George, had estimated that the destruction of AWPD/1's target list would require 6,800 aircraft—3,740 heavy bombers, 1,060 medium bombers, and 2,000 fighters. Returning to Budiansky's claim of "sheer chutzpah," it is worth noting that the AAF only had some 700 bombers in its total inventory at the time.

7. Stephen L. McFarland and Wesley Phillips Newton, "The American Strategic Air Offensive against Germany in World War II," in *Case Studies in Strategic Bombardment,* ed. R. Cargill Hall (Washington, D.C.: U.S. Government Printing Office, 1998), 189.

8. Beck, *With Courage,* 131.

9. Craven and Cate, *The Army Air Forces in World War II,* Vol. 1, 597–598.

10. Ibid.

11. McFarland and Newton, "The American Strategic Air Offensive against Germany in World War II," 241, n. 3.

12. Budiansky, *Air Power,* 318.

13. McFarland and Newton, "The American Strategic Air Offensive against Germany in World War II," 189.

14. Ibid., 190.

15. Ibid.

16. Paul Sumner, telephone interview by James L. Noles Jr., December 20, 2004.

17. Beck, *With Courage,* 198.

18. McFarland and Newton, "The American Strategic Air Offensive against Germany in World War II," 192–194.

19. Stephen F. Ambrose, *The Wild Blue: The Men and Boys Who Flew the B-24's against Germany* (New York: Simon & Schuster, 2001), 114. Other counts tally the losses as 53 aircraft lost, 55 damaged, 440 airmen killed or wounded, and 79 interned in neutral countries. James L. True Jr., "The Tourniquet and the Hammer: A New Look at Deep Interdiction," in *Air University Review* (July–August 1981), available at http://www.airpower.maxwell.af.mil/airchronicles/aureview/1981/jul-aug/true.htm (accessed May 1, 2006).

20. Ibid., 192–194.

21. Beck, *With Courage,* 207.

22. Biddle, *Rhetoric and Reality in Air Warfare,* 228.

23. Ibid.

24. McFarland and Newton, "The American Strategic Air Offensive against Germany in World War II," 212.

25. Ibid., 213.

26. Ibid., 216.

27. Ibid.

28. Beck, *With Courage,* 225.

29. McFarland and Newton, "The American Strategic Air Offensive against Germany in World War II," 220.

30. Ibid., 221.

31. Budiansky, *Air Power,* 300.

32. Beck, *With Courage,* 232.

33. Biddle, *Rhetoric and Reality in Air Warfare,* 236.

34. Wesley F. Craven and James L. Cate, *The Army Air Forces in World War II,* Vol. 3, Europe, *Argument to V-E Day, January 1944 to May 1945* (Washington, D.C.: Office of Air Force History, 1983), 281.

35. Beck, *With Courage,* 232.

36. Richards, *The Second Was First,* 259.

37. 450th Bombardment Group, Unit Citation, April 5, 1944.

Chapter 5

1. The four squadrons were the 429th, the 49th, the 96th, and the 20th Squadron. Of the group's fifty-eight bombers, ten were classified as unserviceable—"two had wing changes; one for engine change; one for lack of casing; one radio equipment being repaired; four in service squadron and one being tested after engine change." Headquarters, Second Bombardment Group (H), "Unit history of the 2nd Bomb Group (H) for the period 1 to 30 April 1944, inclusive," 2, 4.

2. Robert F. Amos et al., *Defenders of Liberty: 2nd Bombardment Group/Wing 1918–1993* (Paducah, Ky.: Turner Publishing Co., 1996), 52.

3. Ibid., 106.

4. Ibid., 187.

5. Office of the Flight Surgeon, Headquarters, Second Bombardment Group (H) (June 1944), 22. Usually, the squadrons would have been dispersed to protect their men in case of an air raid. Given the distance of the bivouac area from the flight line, however, such precautions were deemed unnecessary at Amendola, thereby allowing for the operation of a consolidated group hospital.

6. William S. Tune, interview by author, December 9, 2005.

7. Ibid.

8. Loy Dickinson, email correspondence with author, June 18, 2005.

9. "War and Willard," 13.

10. Jack R. Myers, *Shot At and Missed: Recollections of a World War II Bombardier* (Norman: University of Oklahoma Press, 2004), 107.

11. Office of the Flight Surgeon, Headquarters, Second Bombardment Group (H) (June 1944), 33–34.

12. Ibid., 34–35.

13. "Unit History of the 2nd Bomb Group (H) for the Period 1 to 30 April 1944, Inclusive" (April 30, 1944), 5.

14. Ibid.

15. "War Diary," 20th Bombardment Squadron, 2nd Bomb Group (H), For Month of April 1944."

Chapter 6

1. Office of the Flight Surgeon, "Medical History," Headquarters, Second Bombardment Group (H) (June 1944), 23.

2. Ibid.

3. Ibid.

4. Bill Tune, interview by James L. Noles, December 9, 2005.

5. "Reggio Emilia, Italy—Mission No. 189," "History, Second Bomb Group (H)," 445.

6. Bill Tune, interview by James L. Noles, May 6, 2005.

7. Ibid.

8. Headquarters, Second Bombardment Group (H), "Historical Records-Unit History 1–31 May, 1944, dated 31 May, 1944."

9. William S. Tune, Flight Log.

10. Office of the Flight Surgeon, Headquarters, Second Bombardment Group (H) (June 1944), 21.

11. Amos et al., *Defenders of Liberty,* 237.

12. "July 4," War Diary, 20th Bomb Sqdn, 2nd Bomb Group (H), For Month of July 1944, 1.

13. William S. Tune, interview by James L. Noles, December 9, 2005.

14. Amos et al., *Defenders of Liberty,* 239.

15. Richards, *The Second Was First,* 292.

16. Ibid., 240. See also Veterans Administration "Nationwide Graveside Locator," available at http://gravelocator.cem.va.gov.

17. "History—Second Bombardment Group (H) for August 1944," 6.

18. "War and Willard," 14.

19. Willard Netzley to James L. Noles Jr., January 15, 2006.

20. Ibid.

21. Willard Netzley to parents, August 25, 1944.

22. Ibid.

23. "Tennessee Farm Boy Fought With Tito's Czech Guerilla Forces," *Knoxville Journal* (n.d.)

24. Ibid.

25. Donahue, interview.

26. Ibid.

27. Ibid.

28. Richards, *The Second Was First,* 286.

29. Albert E. Smith, telephone interview by James L. Noles Jr., July 12, 2005.

30. Ibid.

31. Ibid.

32. Richards, *The Second Was First,* 324.

33. Ibid.

34. Ibid., 325.

35. Ibid.

36. Ibid.

37. Ibid. at 327.

38. Ibid.

39. Ibid.

40. Loy Dickinson, email correspondence with James L Noles Jr., January 12, 2006.

41. Richards, *The Second Was First,* 315.

42. Ibid.

43. Loy Dickinson, email correspondence with James L. Noles Jr., January 12, 2006.

44. Loy Dickinson, email correspondence with James L. Noles Jr., November 16, 2007.

45. Loy Dickinson, email correspondence with James L. Noles Jr., January 12, 2006.

46. Craven and Cate, *The Army Air Forces in World War II,* Vol. 3, 298.

47. "History, Second Bombardment Group (H) for August 1944," 4.

48. Amos et al., *Defenders of Liberty,* 246.

49. Ibid.

Chapter 7

1. William S. Tune, interview by James L. Noles, October 14, 2003.

2. *Birmingham News,* August 29, 1944.

3. Ibid.

4. Myers, *Shot At and Missed,* 270.

5. A-2 Section, HQ, Fifth Wing, Annex to Operations Orders No. 680 for 29 August 1944, 1–2.

6. William S. Tune, interview by James L. Noles, October 14, 2003.

7. 2nd Bomb Group (H) Mission Report, August 29, 1944.

8. A-2 Section, HQ, Fifth Wing, Annex to Operations Orders No. 680 for 29 August 1944, 2.

9. Headquarters, Second Bombardment Group (H), Office of the Operations Officer—Operations Orders Number 263.

10. A-2 Section, HQ, Fifth Wing, Annex to Operations Orders No. 680 for 29 August 1944, 2.

11. Headquarters, Second Bombardment Group (H), Office of the Operations Officer—Operations Orders Number 263.

12. William S. Tune to Eleanor (Sheridan) Meyrick, July 12, 1945, copy in possession of the authors.

13. Amos et al., *Defenders of Liberty,* 180.

14. William S. Tune, interview by James L. Noles, October 14, 2003.

15. This and the following checklist items, as well as items of in-flight procedures and conversations, are derived from the following sources: B-17 flight manual checklists reproduced in Jablonski, *Flying Fortress;* William S. Tune, interview by James L. Noles, June 22, 2004; and James L. Noles Jr.'s correspondence with Ray Fowler, current pilot of the restored B-17 *Liberty Belle.*

16. Loy A. Dickinson, Frank Pindak, and William S. Tune, *Mission No. 263: Second Bombardment Group, Fifteenth Air Force, August 29, 1944* (Denver, Colo., and Florence, Ala.: Loy Dickinson and William S. Tune, 1997), 35.

17. Identities of crewmen and their hometowns are derived from their individual aircraft's Missing Air Crew Reports, commonly abbreviated as MACR. The Air Force Historical Research Agency maintains a file of MACRs at its facility at Maxwell Air Force Base, Alabama. Each MACR is numbered; in *Tail End Charlie*'s case, its relevant MACR number is 8763.

18. Richards, *The Second Was First,* 324.

19. MACR 8083.

20. MACR 7987.

21. MACR 8099.

22. MACR 8109.

23. Richards, *The Second Was First,* 344.

24. MACR 8098.

25. MACR 8110. *Mission No. 263* identifies the aircraft as *Wichita Belle. Defenders of Liberty,* however, states its nickname as *Big Time.*

26. Amos et al., *Defenders of Liberty,* 247.

27. Robert Hadley and Melvin W. McGuire, *Bloody Skies: A 15th AAF B-17 Combat Crew: How They Lived and Died* (Las Cruces, NM: Yucca Tree Press, 1993), 100.

28. Dickinson, Pindak, and Tune, *Mission No. 263,* 72. Their book also reported Flynn's statement that "the 2nd Bomb Group began to lag behind the other three groups." Ibid., 33.

29. Ibid., 35.

30. Ibid.

31. Ibid., 53. Bill Tune convincingly expressed his view regarding his squadron's position in the course of several interviews with the authors and, perhaps tellingly, none of the surviv-

ing pilots or copilots—the men with arguably the best vantage points to judge the squadron's position—reported Tune's squadron as straggling. Fellow pilot Duane Seaman, for example, reiterated in an interview on July 4, 2005, that the group as a whole seemed to be struggling to keep up with the groups ahead of it.

32. William S. Tune, interview by James L. Noles, June 22, 2004.

33. Ibid.

34. Dickinson, Pindak, and Tune, *Mission No. 263,* 79 and 82; Hadley and McGuire, *Bloody Skies,* 105.

35. William S. Tune and Loy A. Dickinson, interview by James L. Noles, October 14, 2003.

36. Ibid.

37. Captain George B. Sweeney, "Consolidated Eye-Witness Description Composed By Investigation Officer" (August 30, 1944) (accompanies Missing Air Crew Report 8110) (hereafter referred to as Sweeney Report).

Chapter 8

1. McFarland and Newton, "The American Strategic Air Offensive against Germany in World War II," 207.

2. Erhard Milch, "The Allied Combined Bomber Offensive: Two German Views (Part I): Field Marshal Erhard Milch," presented at the Second Military History Symposium, USAF Academy, 1968. This document is available on-line at http://www.au.af.mil/au/awc/awcgate/cbo-afa/cbo.05.htm (accessed January 13, 2005).

3. Craven and Cate, eds., *The Army Air Forces in World War II,* Vol. 3, 288.

4. McFarland and Newton, "The American Strategic Air Offensive against Germany in World War II," 236.

5. Milch.

6. McFarland and Newton, "The American Strategic Air Offensive against Germany in World War II," 248 n. 103.

7. Williamson Murray, *Strategy for Defeat: The Luftwaffe, 1939–1945* (Maxwell Air Force Base, Ala.: Air University Press, 1983), 278.

8. McFarland and Newton, "The American Strategic Air Offensive against Germany in World War II," 227.

9. Ibid., 237.

10. Josef Kammhuber, "Problems in the Conduct of a Day and Night Defensive Air War," USAF Historical Study No. 179, October 1, 1953, 30.

11. Josef Schmid, "German Dayfighting in the Defense of the Reich from Sep. 15, 1943, to the End of the War," Appendix VIi, File No. 519.601B-4, Section IVB, Vol. 3, December 10, 1945, 10.

12. McFarland and Newton, "The American Strategic Air Offensive against Germany in World War II," 217.

13. Adolph Galland, *The First and the Last,* trans. Mervyn Savill (New York: Henry Holt, 1959), 250.

14. Murray, *Strategy for Defeat,* 240.

15. Ibid., 255.

16. Willi Reschke, *Jagdgeschwader 301/302 "Wilde Sau": In Defense of the Reich with the Bf 109, Fw 190, and Ta 152* (Atglen, Pa.: Schiffer Military History, 2005), 7.

17. Ibid., 8.

18. Ibid., 10.

19. Ibid., 85.

20. Ibid., 90–91.

21. Ibid., 98.

22. Ibid., 104.

23. Ibid., 108.

24. Ibid., 115.

25. Ibid.

26. Ibid.

27. A-2 Section, HQ, Fifth Wing, Annex to Operations Orders No. 680 for 29 August 1944, 1–2.

28. Schmid, 1.

29. Richard R. Muller, USAF School of Advanced Air and Space Studies, email correspondence to James L. Noles Jr., September 16, 2006.

30. Schmid, 1.

31. Ibid., 2.

32. Ibid.

33. Ibid.

34. Ibid., 3.

35. Ibid.

36. Ibid., 4.

37. Ibid., 5.

38. Ibid.

39. Kammhuber, 206.

40. Ibid.

41. Ibid., 210.

42. Ibid.

43. Ibid., 211.

44. Ibid.

45. Ibid., 211–212.

46. Ibid., 212.

47. Ibid.

48. Ibid., 212–213.

49. Schmid, Section IV B. Vol. II, Appendix 2.

50. Reschke, *Jagdgeschwader 301/302*, 77.

51. Ibid., 89.

52. Ibid.

53. Schmid, 6.

54. Ibid., 6–7.

55. Price, 51.

56. Kammhuber, 103.

57. Ibid., 104–105.

Chapter 9

1. Reschke, *Jagdgeschwader 301/302*, 141.

2. MacFarland and Newton, "The American Strategic Air Offensive against Germany in World War II," 211–212.

3. William S. Tune, interview by James L. Noles, June 22, 2004.

4. Dickinson, Pindak, and Tune, *Mission No. 263,* 60.

5. Ibid., 59.

6. Ibid., 60.

7. Ibid., 61.

8. Ibid., 59.

9. Ibid., 60.

10. Charles H. McVey, Casualty Questionnaire, in Missing Air Crew Report 8099.

11. Dickinson, Pindak, and Tune, *Mission No. 263,* 68.

12. Ibid.

13. Ibid., 63.

14. Ibid.

15. Ibid., 63–64.

16. William S. Tune and Loy A. Dickinson, interview by James L. Noles, October 14, 2003.

17. Dickinson, Pindak, and Tune, *Mission No. 263,* 33.

18. Ibid., 35.

19. Joseph Owsianik, email correspondence with James L. Noles Jr., April 15, 2005.

20. William S. Tune and Loy A. Dickinson, interview by James L. Noles, October 14, 2003.

21. Dickinson, Pindak, and Tune, *Mission No. 263,* 29.

22. Frank Flynn, Casualty Questionnaire, Missing Air Crew Report 8763.

23. Ibid.

24. Dickinson, Pindak, and Tune, *Mission No. 263,* 35.

25. Ibid.

26. Ibid.

27. Thomas C. Coogan, Casualty Questionnaire, Missing Air Crew Report 8763.

28. William G. Hayett, Casualty Questionnaire, Missing Air Crew Report 7987.

29. Reschke, *Jagdgeschwader 301/302,* 146.

30. Ibid.

31. Ibid.

32. Ibid., 146–147.

33. Richards, *The Second Was First,* 347.

34. Dickinson, Pindak, and Tune, *Mission No. 263,* 54.

35. Richards, *The Second Was First,* 345.

36. Ibid., 347.

37. Dickinson, Pindak, and Tune, *Mission No. 263,* 57.

38. Ibid.

39. Ibid., 56.

40. Albert E. Smith, Casualty Questionnaire, Missing Air Crew Report 8083; Amos et al., *Defenders of Liberty,* 256.

41. Dickinson, Pindak, and Tune, *Mission No. 263,* 49.

42. Ibid., 45.

43. Ibid.

44. Ibid.

45. Ibid., 49.

46. Ibid.

47. Ibid., 45.

48. Ibid., 49.

49. Ibid.

50. Leo Zupan, telephone interview by James L. Noles Jr., December 29, 2004.

51. Jesse Barker, Casualty Questionnaire, Missing Air Crew Report 7987.
52. Ibid.
53. Dickinson, Pindak, and Tune, *Mission No. 263,* 47.

Chapter 10

1. That mistake was understandable, at least to some of those crewmen's fellow veterans. Melvin McGuire flew as a waist gunner in a B-17 with the 20th Squadron, joining the unit the day of the Moravska Ostrava mission. As he recalled, "It is almost impossible, under hazy conditions, to distinguish between a P-51 and a Me-109. About the only visible difference at that angle is the very small radiator hanging below the belly of a 109 that is different from the air scoop of a P-51." Hadley and McGuire, *Bloody Skies,* 105.

2. Dickinson, Pindak, and Tune, *Mission No. 263,* 72. The accounts of Nigborowicz and Childress, which follow, are also recounted in *Mission No. 263.*

3. Ibid., 82.
4. Hadley and McGuire, *Bloody Skies,* 111.
5. Dickinson, Pindak, and Tune, *Mission No. 263,* 85.
6. Ibid., 78.
7. Hadley and McGuire, *Bloody Skies,* 109.
8. Ibid., 110.
9. Combat Claim Form of M. E. Leepo (August 29, 1944), completed by Captain James M. McCoid.
10. Transmittal of Combat Claims, August 29, 1944, by Major Norman E. Annich, Group S-2.
11. Headquarters, Second Bombardment Group (H), "Special Narrative Report, Mission: 29 August 1944–Privoser Oil Refinery, Czechoslovakia."
12. Joseph Wechsberg, *Homecoming* (New York: Alfred A. Knopf, 1946), 7.
13. Ibid., 57.
14. Ibid., 39.
15. Ibid., 39–40.
16. Final Strike Assessment Report, HQ 5th Wing (August 29 1944), prepared by C. B. Hearn.
17. Hadley and McGuire, *Bloody Skies,* 82–83.
18. Ibid., 83.
19. Ibid., 84.
20. Ibid., 85–86.
21. Ibid., 86.
22. Ibid., 115.
23. Myers, *Shot At and Missed,* 36.
24. Ibid.
25. Hadley and McGuire, *Bloody Skies,* 86.
26. Ibid.

Chapter 11

1. Dickinson, Pindak, and Tune, *Mission No. 263,* 30.
2. Ibid.
3. Ibid.
4. Ibid., 8.

5. Ibid., 36.

6. Ibid.; Joseph Owsianik, telephone interview by author, September 6, 2004.

7. Ibid.

8. Ibid.

9. Richards, *The Second Was First*, 342.

10. Loy Dickinson, email correspondence with James L. Noles Jr., September 18, 2006.

11. Ibid.

12. Ibid.

13. Dickinson, Pindak, and Tune, *Mission No. 263*, 47.

14. Bill Garland to James L. Noles Jr., July 8, 2006, copy in possession of the authors. In later years, conversations with local Czechs would convince Garland that Katz's chute had simply failed to open.

15. Dickinson, Pindak, and Tune, *Mission No. 263*, 49.

16. Ibid., 50.

17. Richards, *The Second Was First*, 341.

18. Dickinson, Pindak, and Tune, *Mission No. 263*, 54.

19. Ibid.

20. Ibid., 55.

21. Ibid.

22. Ibid.

23. James Martin, telephone interview with James L. Noles, June 20, 2006.

24. Dickinson, Pindak, and Tune, *Mission No. 263*, 57.

Chapter 12

1. Dickinson, Pindak, and Tune, *Mission No. 263*, 38.

2. Ibid., 39.

3. Ibid.

4. Ibid.

5. Ibid.

6. Ibid.

7. Ibid., 93.

8. Ibid., 61.

9. Ibid.

10. Ibid.

11. Ibid., 68–69.

12. Ibid., 69.

13. Ibid.

14. Ibid., 40.

15. Ibid., 70.

16. Ibid.

17. Ibid.

18. Ibid., 66.

19. Ibid.

20. Ibid., 40. In Thomas's memory, they meet Leach and Miller the second night, and Miller's first name was Delos. Ibid., 66.

21. Ibid., 40.

22. Ibid., 66. Jim Downs identifies him alternatively as both Nick Tomas and Emil Tomas.

Jim Downs, *World War II: OSS Tragedy in Slovakia* (Oceanside, Calif.: Liefrinck Publishers, 2002), 45, 59.

23. Downs, *World War II,* 62.

24. Ibid., 59.

25. Ibid., 41.

26. Fern Wagner, telephone interview by James L. Noles Jr., March 25, 2005.

27. Amos et al., *Defenders of Liberty,* 254–255.

28. Ibid., 255.

29. "Tennessee Farm Boy Fought With Tito's Czech Guerilla Forces," *Knoxville Journal* (October 23, 1945). Admittedly, Tito was a Yugoslavian, and not a Czech, guerrilla leader.

Chapter 13

1. Dickinson, Pindak, and Tune, *Mission No. 263,* 31.

2. Frank Flynn, Casualty Questionnaire, Missing Air Crew Report 8763.

3. Tune notes.

4. Dickinson, Pindak, and Tune, *Mission No. 263,* 32.

5. Ibid., 31.

6. Tune notes.

7. Ibid.

8. Ibid.

9. John Nichol and Tony Rennell, *The Last Escape: The Untold Story of Allied Prisoners of War in Europe, 1944–1945* (New York: Penguin Putnam, Inc., 2002), 31. By the end of the war, the Germans were holding approximately 30,000 GIs and 26,000 airmen prisoners in northwestern Europe. Stephen Ambrose, *Citizen Soldiers* (New York: Touchstone, 1998), 357.

10. Morris J. Roy, *Behind Barbed Wire* (New York: Richard R. Smith, 1946), n.p.

11. Ibid.

12. Ibid.

13. Tune notes.

14. Loy Dickinson, email correspondence with James L. Noles Jr., September 18, 2006.

15. Ibid.

16. Ibid.

17. Ibid.

18. Ibid.

19. Ibid.

20. Dickinson, Pindak, and Tune, *Mission No. 263,* 37.

21. Ibid.

22. Ibid., 37–38.

23. Joe Owsianik, telephone interview with James L. Noles Jr., September 6, 2004.

24. Ibid.

Chapter 14

1. Nichol and Rennell, *The Last Escape,* 121.

2. Ibid., 30.

3. Contrada Memoirs, 27–28.

4. Ibid.

5. Ibid., 29.

6. Ibid., 30.

7. Ibid.

8. Ibid.

9. Ibid., 31.

10. Leslie Caplan, "Perpetuation of Testimony of Dr. Leslie Caplan," December 31, 1947.

11. Contrada Memoirs, 33.

12. Ibid.

13. Ibid.

14. Contrada Memoirs, 34.

15. Ibid.

16. Ibid., 35.

17. Ibid.

18. Ibid.

19. Ibid.

20. Ibid., 35–36.

21. Notes by Ferris Joyner, n.d., provided to James L. Noles Jr., by Jeanette Ross, copy in possession of the authors.

22. Caplan, "Perpetuation of Testimony of Dr. Leslie Caplan," 3.

23. Ibid.

24. Dickinson, Pindak, and Tune, *Mission No. 263,* 38.

25. Notes by Ferris Joyner, n.d., provided to James L. Noles Jr., by Jeanette Ross.

26. Ibid.

27. Tune notes.

28. Ibid.

29. Ibid.

30. Military Intelligence Service—War Department, "American Prisoners of War in Germany: Stalag Luft I," November 1, 1945, 2.

31. Ibid.

32. One of the sketches drawn by Tune during his imprisonment lists his fellow prisoners in Room 3. There are, in addition to Tomlinson and himself, M. S. Adler, J. F. Baer, R. A. Brautigam, K. J. Busse, W. P. Davis, F. L. Dunham, C. H. Enes, J. L. Hamilton, E. J. Holzer, R. E. Johnson, C. W. Lundsberg, R. H. McKenn, H. E. Munson, W. F. Nettekoven, J. H. Nugent, A. F. Pelka, D. A. Schulman, W. N. Shearer, J. C. Shields, W. J. Swigart, S. C. Wifree, and R. R. Woodward. Roy's *Behind Barbed Wire* also provides a description of a typical barracks room.

33. Tune notes.

34. Military Intelligence Service, "American Prisoners of War in Germany: Stalag Luft I," 2.

35. Ibid.

36. Nichol and Rennell, *The Last Escape,* 248.

37. Military Intelligence Service, "American Prisoners of War in Germany: Stalag Luft I," 3–4.

38. Ibid., 5.

39. Ibid.

40. *Stars & Stripes,* "Nazi Camp Held Galaxy of U.S. Aces," n.d.

41. Military Intelligence Service, "American Prisoners of War in Germany: Stalag Luft I," July 15, 1944, 5.

42. C. Ross Greening, *Not As Briefed: From the Doolittle Raid to a German Stalag* (Pullman: Washington State University Press, 2001), 180.

43. Ibid., 187.

44. Ibid.
45. Ibid., 181.
46. Ibid., 184–185.
47. Ibid., 182–183.
48. Roy, *Behind Barbed Wire,* n.p.
49. Ibid.
50. Ibid.
51. Tune notes.
52. William S. Tune to Frances Beggs, postcard, dated January 26, 1945, in possession of William S. Tune.
53. Loy Dickinson, email correspondence with James L. Noles Jr., September 11, 2006.
54. Ibid.
55. Ibid.
56. Ibid.
57. Dickinson, Pindak, and Tune, *Mission No. 263,* 56.
58. Ibid., 71.
59. Ibid.
60. Duane Seaman, telephone interview by James L. Noles Jr., July 4, 2005.
61. "War and Willard," 16.
62. Ibid., 17.
63. Ibid.
64. Ibid.

Chapter 15

1. "Willard Netzley Missing Over Czechoslovakia," newspaper clipping, n.d., copy in possession of the authors.
2. James A. Ulio to Florence Netzley, telegram, September 10, 1944, copy in possession of the authors.
3. "Willard Netzley Missing Over Czechoslovakia," newspaper clipping, n.d., copy in possession of the authors.
4. Bob Jackson to Mr. and Mrs. Netzley, October 10, 1944, copy in possession of the authors.
5. James A. Ulio to Florence Netzley, telegram, November 2, 1944, copy in possession of the authors.
6. Robert Donahue to Mrs. Netzley, December 5, 1944, copy in possession of the authors.
7. Nathan F. Twining to William C. Bullock Sr., September 26, 1944, copy in possession of the authors.
8. James A. Ulio to William C. Bullock Sr., February 23, 1945, copy in possession of the authors.
9. Telegram from Tillman Tune to Frances Beggs Tune, n.d. (telegram in possession of William S. Tune).
10. Letter from William S. Tune to Frances Beggs Tune, December 30, 1944 (letter in possession of William S. Tune).
11. Nathan Twining to James F. Fitzpatrick, September 22, 1944, copy in possession of the authors.
12. Dorothy Fitzpatrick, telephone interview by James L. Noles Jr., September 20, 2006.

13. Letter from Vic Kreimeyer to Eleanor S. Meyrick, October 8, 1944.

14. Ibid.

15. Ibid.

16. *Springfield Republican,* "Obituary: Body to Arrive—Lt. Russell W. Meyrick," May 8, 1949.

17. Letter from Pearl Dickinson to Kathryn Meyrick, n.d., copy in possession of the authors.

18. Mary E. Huckstorff, "Four Stars in the Window," n.d., copy in possession of the authors.

19. *Burlington Free Press,* "Lt. James A. Weiler Reported Missing While in Action," September 14, 1944.

20. *Standard Democrat,* "Death of Lt. James Weiler Established," August 17, 1945.

21. Ibid.

22. Dickinson, Pindak, and Tune, *Mission No. 263,* 15.

23. Ibid.

24. Ibid.

25. Ibid., 41.

26. Ibid., 16.

27. "Local Soldiers Meet Overseas," *Pittsburgh Post-Gazette,* n.d.

28. Joe Owsianik, telephone interview with James L. Noles Jr., September 6, 2004.

29. Contrada Memoirs, 37; Loy Dickinson, email correspondence with James L. Noles Jr., September 11, 2006.

30. Ibid. See also Nichol and Rennell, *The Last Escape,* 248–249.

31. Greening, *Not As Briefed,* 219.

32. Loy Dickinson, email correspondence with James L. Noles Jr., September 11, 2006.

33. Contrada Memoirs, 39–40.

34. Greening, *Not As Briefed,* 220.

35. "War and Willard," 19.

36. Contrada Memoirs, 40.

37. Dickinson, Pindak, and Tune, *Mission No. 263,* 71.

38. Roy, *Behind Barbed Wire,* n.p.

39. Contrada Memoirs, 42.

40. Nichol and Rennell, *The Last Escape,* 250.

41. Greening, *Not As Briefed,* 224.

42. Contrada Memoirs, 42.

43. Ibid., 43.

44. Ibid.

45. Ibid., 46.

46. Ibid.

47. Ibid., 47.

48. "War and Willard," 19.

49. Ibid.

50. William S. Tune and Frances Tune, interview by James L. Noles, July 31, 2006.

51. Ibid.

Epilogue

1. For a comprehensive sense of the challenges facing the German military on the Eastern Front in the late summer of 1944, see John Erickson, *The Road to Berlin: Stalin's War with Germany* (New Haven, Conn.: Yale University Press, 1999).

2. For more information on the 445th's fateful mission, visit The Kassel Mission Historical Society's website at www.kassel.com. The mission also receives treatment in John Nichol and Tony Rennell, *Tail-End Charlies: The Last Battles of the Bomber War, 1944–1945* (New York: Thomas Dunne Books, 2006) and elsewhere.

3. Contrada Memoirs, 47.

4. Ibid.

5. Ibid.

6. Loy Dickinson, email correspondence to James L. Noles Jr., July 16, 2006.

7. Loy Dickinson, email correspondence to James L. Noles Jr., September 19, 2006.

8. Ibid.

9. Ibid.

10. Donahue, interview.

11. Dorothy Fitzpatrick, telephone interview by James L. Noles Jr., September 20, 2006.

12. Ibid.

13. Bill Garland to James L. Noles Jr., September 22, 2006.

14. Jeanette Ross, email correspondence to James L. Noles, Jr., December 14, 2004.

15. James E. Martin to James L. Noles Jr., n.d., copy in possession of the authors.

16. Charles McVey Jr., email correspondence to James L Noles, Jr., July 19, 2005.

17. "War and Willard," 20.

18. Joseph Owsianik, email correspondence to James L. Noles Jr., December 12, 2007.

19. Fern Wagner, telephone interview by James L. Noles Jr., March 25, 2005.

20. Duane Seaman, telephone interview by James L. Noles Jr., July 4, 2005.

21. Ed Smith, telephone interview by James L. Noles Jr., September 25, 2006.

22. Paul Sumner, telephone interview by James L. Noles Jr., December 28, 2004.

23. William S. Tune, interview by James L. Noles, July 31, 2006.

24. Francis Flynn to Bill Tune, November 22, 1994, copy in possession of the authors.

25. Leo Zupan, telephone interview by James L. Noles Jr., December 29, 2004.

Bibliography

Primary Sources

Interviews

Contrada, Charles. Telephone interview by James L. Noles Jr., December 22, 2004.

Dickinson, Loy. Telephone interview by James L. Noles, January 18, 2005.

Donahue, Thomas. Telephone interview by James L. Noles Jr., May 15, 2005.

Fitzpatrick, Dorothy. Telephone interviews by James L. Noles Jr., December 12, 2005; December 21, 2005; and September 20, 2006.

Huckstorff, Mary. Telephone interview by James L. Noles Jr., April 14, 2004.

Kreimeyer, Vic. Telephone interview with James L. Noles Jr., May 19, 2005.

Martin, James E. Telephone interview by James L. Noles, June 20, 2006.

Owsianik, Joseph. Telephone interviews by James L. Noles Jr., September 6, 2004, and September 7, 2004.

Reed, Elizabeth Meyrick. Telephone interview by James L. Noles Jr., July 26, 2006.

Seaman, Duane. Telephone interview by James L. Noles Jr., July 4, 2005.

Smith, Albert E. Telephone interviews by James L. Noles Jr., July 12, 2005, and September 25, 2006.

Sumner, Paul. Telephone interviews by James L. Noles Jr., December 20, 2004, and December 28, 2004.

Tune, William S. Interviews by James L. Noles, August 4, 2003; October 14, 2003; June 22, 2004; May 6, 2005; November 25, 2005; December 9, 2005; July 31, 2006; and August 15, 2006.

Wagner, Fern. Telephone interview by James L. Noles Jr., March 25, 2005.

Zupan, Leo. Telephone interviews by James L. Noles Jr., August 24, 2004; September 2, 2004; October 17, 2004; and December 29, 2004.

Letters and Telegrams

Bonner, Lane, to Burnett Maybank, September 12, 1944, copy in possession of the authors.

Bresee, Howard F., to Mary Joyner, March 23, 1945, copy in possession of the authors.

Delegate, International Committee of the Red Cross, to Burnett Maybank, September 18, 1944, copy in possession of the authors.

DiNapoli, Albert, to Mary Joyner, August 29, 1944, copy in possession of the authors.

Donahue, Robert, to Mrs. Netzley, December 5, 1944, copy in possession of the authors.

Flynn, Francis, to Bill Tune, November 22, 1994, copy in possession of the authors.

Garland, Bill, to James L. Noles Jr., July 8, 2006, letter in possession of the authors.

Huckstorff, Mary, to James L. Noles Jr., April 18, 2005, letter in possession of the authors.

Jackson, Bob, to Mr. and Mrs. Netzley, October 10, 1944, copy in possession of the authors.

Johnston, Olin, to Mary Joyner, June 9, 1945, copy in possession of the authors.

Joyner, Ferris, to Mrs. James A. Joyner, December 7, 1944, copy in possession of the authors.

Kreimeyer, Vic, to Eleanor S. Meyrick, October 8, 1944, copy in possession of the authors.

Martin, James E., to James L. Noles Jr., June 29, 2006, letter in possession of the authors.

Netzley, Willard, to James L. Noles Jr., January 15, 2006, letter in possession of the authors.

———. To parents, August 25, 1944, letter in possession of the authors.

Ourn, James, to Mary Joyner, August 29, 1944, copy in possession of the authors.

Parsons, Bill, to William S. Tune, October 10, 2005, copy in possession of the authors.

Pooler, Frank, to Pittsburgh Chamber of Commerce, May 23, 1940, copy in possession of the authors.

Ray, Billy, to Mr. and Mrs. Joyner, May 9, 1945, copy in possession of the authors.

Shotton, Margaret, to Home SVC ARC, May 28, 1945, copy in possession of the authors.

Solock, Miss I. W., to Mary Joyner, April 30, 1945, copy in possession of the authors.

Todd, Mrs. John, to Mary Joyner, October 16, 1944, copy in possession of the authors.

Tune, Tillman, to Frances Beggs Tune, telegram, n.d., telegram in possession of William S. Tune.

Tune, William S., to Frances Beggs, December 31, 1944, in possession of William S. Tune.

———. To Frances Beggs, January 26, 1945, in possession of William S. Tune.

———. To Eleanor (Sheridan) Meyrick, July 12, 1945, copy in possession of the authors.

Twining, Nathan F., to William C. Bullock Sr., September 26, 1944, copy in possession of the authors.

———. To James F. Fitzpatrick, September 22, 1944, copy in possession of the authors.

Ulio, James A., to William C. Bullock Sr., February 23, 1945, copy in possession of the authors.

———. To Florence Contrada, September 10, 1944, copy in possession of the authors.

———. To Mary Joyner, telegram, September 10, 1944, copy in possession of the authors.

———. To Mary Joyner, telegram, October 24, 1944, copy in possession of the authors.

———. To Florence Netzley, telegram, September 10, 1944, copy in possession of the authors.

———. To Florence Netzley, telegram, November 2, 1944, copy in possession of the authors.

Email Correspondence

Dickinson, Loy. Email correspondence to James L. Noles Jr., July 1, 2004.

———. Email correspondence to James L. Noles Jr., July 15, 2004.

———. Email correspondence to James L. Noles Jr., September 15, 2004.

———. Email correspondence with James L. Noles Jr., June 18, 2005.

———. Email correspondence to James L. Noles Jr., July 16, 2006.

———. Email correspondence to James L. Noles Jr., September 18, 2006.

———. Email correspondence to James L. Noles Jr., September 19, 2006.

McVey, Charles, Jr. Email correspondence to James L. Noles Jr., July 19, 2005.

Owsianik, Joe. Email correspondence to James L. Noles Jr., April 15, 2005, and December 12, 2007.

Ross, Jeanette. Email correspondence to James L. Noles Jr., December 14, 2004.
———. Email correspondence with James L. Noles Jr., December 27, 2004.

Unpublished Memoirs and Personal Notes of Participants

Contrada, Vincent. "Vincent A. Contrada, United States Air Force World War II, April 3, 1943–October 23, 1945," August 1, 2002, copy in possession of the authors.
Donahue, Robert D. Personal statement, January 6, 1995, copy in possession of the authors.
Huckstorff, Mary E. "Four Stars in the Window," n.d., copy in possession of the authors.
Joyner, Ferris. Notes, n.d., copy in possession of the authors.
Netzley, Willard. "War and Willard," July 2004, copy in possession of the authors.
Tune, William S. Flight Log, copy in possession of the authors.
Tune, William S. Notes, n.d., copy in possession of the authors.

National Archives

National Archives' Electronic Army Serial Number Merged File, circa 1938–1946, (Enlistment Records), "Meyrick, Russell F."

Air Force Historical Research Agency, Maxwell Air Force Base, Alabama

A-2 Section, HQ, Fifth Wing, Annex to Operations Orders No. 680 for August 29, 1944.
Annich, Norman E. Transmittal of Combat Claims for Second Bombardment Group, August 29, 1944.
Final Strike Assessment Report, HQ 5th Wing, August 29, 1944.
Headquarters, Second Bombardment Group (H), "Historical Records-Unit History 1–31 May, 1944, 31 May, 1944."
Headquarters, Second Bombardment Group (H), Office of the Operations Officer—Operations Orders Number 263.
Headquarters, Second Bombardment Group (H), "Special Narrative Report, Mission: 29 August 1944—Privoser Oil Refinery, Czechoslovakia."
Headquarters Second Bombardment Group (H), "Unit history of the 2nd Bomb Group (H) for the period 1 to 30 April 1944 , inclusive," August 30, 1944.
"History—Second Bombardment Group (H) for August 1944," n.d.
Leepo, M. E. Combat Claim Form, August 29, 1944.
Missing Air Crew Report 7950.
Missing Air Crew Report 7987.
Missing Air Crew Report 8083.
Missing Air Crew Report 8084.
Missing Air Crew Report 8099.
Missing Air Crew Report 8109.
Missing Air Crew Report 8110.
Missing Air Crew Report 8763.
Missing Air Crew Report 11544.
Office of the Flight Surgeon, "Medical History," Headquarters, Second Bombardment Group (H), June 1944.
2nd Bomb Group (H) Mission Report, August 29, 1944.
Sweeney, George B. "Consolidated Eye-Witness Description Composed By Investigation Officer," August 30, 1944.
"Unit History of the 2nd Bomb Group (H) for the Period 1 to 30 April 1944, Inclusive," April 30, 1944.

"Unit History of the 2nd Bomb Group (H) for the Period 1 to 31 May 1944, Inclusive" May 31, 1944.

"Unit History of the 20th Bombardment Squadron (H) for the period 1 May 1944 to 31 May 1944," May 31, 1944.

"War Diary," 20th Bombardment Squadron, 2nd Bomb Group (H), For Month of April 1944.

"War Diary," 20th Bombardment Squadron, 2nd Bomb Group (H), For Month of July 1944.

Miscellaneous Materials

AAF Orders 370.5 #297 (135-31), March 19, 1944, copy in possession of the authors.

Army Air Forces Pilot School (Specialized Four-Engine) Maxwell Field, Alabama, Pilot Transition Training Record: Tune, William S.

Caplan, Leslie. "Perpetuation of Testimony of Dr. Leslie Caplan: For the War Crimes Office, Civil Affairs Division, WDSS—In the Matter of the Mistreatment of American Prisoners of War at Stalag Luft #4 from November 1944 to May 1945," December 31, 1947.

450th Bombardment Group, Unit Citation, April 5, 1944.

Gibeau, Raymond C. Affdavit in Support of Ferris Joyner's Disability Claim. September 3, 1982.

Military Intelligence Service—War Department, "American Prisoners of War in Germany: Stalag Luft I," July 15, 1944, 1, available at http://www.merkki.com/images/ scamp1.gif (accessed August 26, 2006).

Military Intelligence Service—War Department, "American Prisoners of War in Germany: Stalag Luft I," November 1, 1945, 2, available at http://www.merkki.com/images/scnv2.jpg (accessed August 26, 2006).

Roosevelt, Franklin D. "On Progress of the War," radio broadcast delivered February 23, 1942, available at http://www.fdrlibrary.marist.edu/022342.html (accessed October 15, 2004).

Secondary Sources

"A New Deal for Carbon Hill: A Photographic Document," at http://newdeal.feri.org/carbonhill/index.htm (accessed August 15, 2006).

Ambrose, Stephen F. *Citizen Soldiers.* New York: Touchstone, 1998.

———. *The Wild Blue: The Men and Boys Who Flew the B-24's against Germany.* New York: Simon & Schuster, 2001.

Amos, Robert F., et al. *Defenders of Liberty: 2nd Bombardment Group, 1918–1993.* Paducah, Ky.: Turner Publishing, 1996.

Beck, Alfred M., ed. *With Courage: The U.S. Army Air Forces in World War II.* Washington, D.C.: U.S. Government Printing Office, 1994.

"Becoming Americans Again." Virginia Historical Society, at http://www.vahistorical.org/sva2003/americans_again.htm (accessed December 22, 2004).

Bertao, Jim. "Historic California Posts: Eagle Field," at http://www.militarymuseum.org/EagleField.html (accessed November 27, 2004).

Biddle, Tami Davis. *Rhetoric and Reality in Air Warfare: The Evolution of British and American Ideas about Strategic Bombing, 1914–1945.* Princeton, N.J.: Princeton University Press, 2004.

Boiten, Theo, and Martin Bowman. *Jane's Battles with the Luftwaffe.* New York: Harper Collins Publishers, 2001.

Budiansky, Stephen. *Air Power: The Men, Machines, and Ideas That Revolutionized War, from Kitty Hawk to Gulf War II.* New York: Viking, 2004.

Burleigh, Michael. *The Third Reich: A New History.* New York: Hill and Wang, 2000.

Callander, Bruce, and J. H. MacWilliam. "The Third Lieutenants." *Air Force Magazine,* March 1990, at www.afa.org/magazine/1990/0390third.asp (accessed April 27, 2004).

Cameron, Rebecca H. *Training to Fly: Military Flight Training, 1907–1945.* Washington, D.C.: Air Force History and Museums Program, 1999.

Craven, Wesley F., and James L. Cate, eds. *The Army Air Forces in World War II,* Vol. 1, *Plans and Early Operations, January 1939 to August 1942.* Washington, D.C.: General Printing Office, 1983.

———. *The Army Air Forces in World War II,* Vol. 2, *Europe, Torch to Pointblank, August 1942 to December 1943.* Washington, D.C.: General Printing Office, 1983.

———. *The Army Air Forces in World War II,* Vol. 3, *Europe, Argument to V-E Day, January 1944 to May 1945.* Washington, D.C.: General Printing Office, 1983.

———. *The Army Air Forces in World War II,* Vol. 6, *Men and Planes.* Washington, D.C.: General Printing Office, 1983.

Davis, Richard G. *Bombing the European Axis Powers: A Historical Digest of the Combined Bomber Offensive, 1939–1945.* Maxwell Air Force Base, Alabama: Air University Press, 2006.

Dickinson, Loy A., Frank Pindak, and William S. Tune. *Mission No. 263: Second Bombardment Group, Fifteenth Air Force, August 29, 1944.* Denver, Colo., and Florence, Ala.: Loy Dickinson and Williams S. Tune, 1997).

Downs, Jim. *World War II: OSS Tragedy in Slovakia.* Oceanside, Calif.: Liefrinck Publishers, 2002.

Durand, Arthur A. *Stalag Luft III: The Secret Story.* Baton Rouge: Louisiana State University Press, 1988.

Fieth, Kenneth. "The Army Air Forces Classification Center," at http://prodigy.net/nhn.slate/nh00018.html (accessed December 2, 2004).

Frisbee, John L. "A Rather Special Award." *Air Force Magazine,* Vol. 73, No. 8 (August 1990), accessed at http://www.afa.org/magazine/valor/0890valor.asp (December 8, 2005).

Galland, Adolph. *The First and the Last.* Trans. Mervyn Savill. New York: Henry Holt, 1959.

"Gary Air Force Base," *Handbook of Texas Online,* at http://www.tsha.utexas.edu/handbook/online/articles/GG/qcg2_print.html (accessed November 20, 2005).

Goodwin, Doris Kearns. *No Ordinary Time: Franklin and Eleanor Roosevelt—The Home Front during World War II.* New York: Touchstone, 1995.

Greening, C. Ross. *Not As Briefed: From the Doolittle Raid to a German Stalag.* Pullman: Washington State University Press, 2001.

Gunston, Bill. *Aircraft of World War II.* New York: Crescent Books, 1980.

Hadley, Robert, and Melvin W. McGuire. *Bloody Skies: A 15th AAF B-17 Combat Crew: How They Lived and Died.* Las Cruces, NM: Yucca Tree Press, 1993.

Havighurst, Walter. "The Miami Years: 1809–1984," at www.lib.muohio.edu/my (accessed July 12, 2005).

Hess, William N. *Great American Bombers of World War II.* Osceola, Wisc.: MBI Publishing Company, 1998.

"Hill Aerospace Museum—A Short History of Hill Air Force Base," at http://www.hill.af.mil/museum/history/hafb.htm (accessed December 30, 2004).

"History of Deming Army Airfield," at http://www.zianet.com/kromeke/ArmyAirField/DAF10.htm (accessed April 26, 2006).

Jablonski, Edwards. *Flying Fortress: The Illustrated Biography of the B-17s and the Men Who Flew Them.* New York: Doubleday & Company, 1965.

Kammhuber, Josef. "Problems in the Conduct of a Day and Night Defensive Air War." USAF Historical Study No. 179, October 1, 1953.

Kirschbaum, Stanislav J. *A History of Slovakia: The Struggle for Survival.* New York: Palgrave Macmillan, 2005.

Markus, Daniel. "Miami 1941–1945: From VIP Suites to GI Barracks." Historical Association of Southern Florida *Update* 8, 4 (November 1981).

McFarland, Stephen L., and Wesley P. Newton, "The American Strategic Air Offensive against Germany in World War II." In *Case Studies in Strategic Bombardment,* ed. R. Cargill Hall, 183–252. Washington, D.C.: U.S. Government Printing Office, 1998.

———. *To Command the Sky: The Struggle for Air Superiority over Europe, 1942–1944.* Tuscaloosa: University of Alabama Press, 2006 (third revised edition).

Milch, Erhard. "The Allied Combined Bomber Offensive: Two German Views (Part I): Field Marshal Erhard Milch." Presented at the Second Military History Symposium, USAF Academy, 1968, available at http://www.au.af.mil/au/awc/awcgate/cbo-afa/cbo.05.htm (accessed Jan. 13, 2005).

Miller, Donald L. *Masters of the Air: America's Bomber Boys Who Fought the Air War against Nazi Germany.* New York: Simon & Schuster, 2006.

Murray, Williamson. *Strategy for Defeat: The Luftwaffe, 1939–1945.* Maxwell Air Force Base, Alabama: Air University Press, 1983.

Myers, Jack R. *Shot At and Missed: Recollections of a World War II Bombardier.* Norman: University of Oklahoma Press, 2004.

Neilland, Robin. *The Bomber War.* Woodstock: Overlook Press, 2001.

Nichol, John, and Tony Rennell. *The Last Escape: The Untold Story of Allied Prisoners of War in Europe, 1944–1945.* New York: Viking, 2003.

Ochoa, Ruben E. "Hondo Army Airfield." *The Handbook of Texas Online,* at www.tsha.utexas.edu/handbook/online/articles/print/HH/qch2.html (accessed December 2, 2004).

Organizational History Branch, Air Force Historical Research Agency. "The Birth of the United States Air Force," at http://www.au.af.mil/au/afhra/wwwroot/rso/birth.html (accessed August 26, 2004).

Overy, Richard J. *The Air War, 1939–1945.* New York: Stein and Day, 1980.

———. *Why the Allies Won.* New York: W. W. Norton & Company, 1996.

Perret, Geoffrey. *Winged Victory: The Army Air Forces in World War II.* New York: Random House, 1993.

Price, Alfred. *The Last Year of the Luftwaffe.* London: Greenhill Military Paperbacks, 2001.

Reschke, Willi. *Jagdgeschwader 301/302 "Wilde Sau": In Defense of the Reich with the Bf 109, Fw 190, and Ta 152.* Atglen, Pa.: Schiffer Military History, 2005.

Richards, Charles. *The Second Was First.* Bend, Ore.: Maverick Publishing, Inc., 1999.

Roy, Morris J. *Behind Barbed Wire.* New York: Richard R. Smith, 1946.

"Santa Ana Army Air Base," at www.costamesahistory.org/index.php?page=saaab_main (accessed November 27, 2004).

Schmid, Josef. "German Dayfighting in the Defense of the Reich from Sep. 15, 1943, to the End of the War." Appendix VIi, File No. 519.601B-4, Section IVB, Vol. 3 (December 10, 1945).

Smithsonian National Air and Space Museum. "Fairchild PT-19A Cornell," at http://www.nasm.si.edu/research/aero/aircraft/fairchild_pt19.htm (accessed December 8, 2004).

———. "Focke-Wulf Fw 190A-8," at http://www.nasm.si.edu/research/aero.aircraft/focke_190f.htm (accessed July 15, 2004).

———. "Messerschmitt Bf 109G-6," at http://www.nasm.si.edu/research/aero/aircraft/me109.htm (accessed July 15, 2004).

Steinhoff, Johannes. "The German Fighter Battle against the American Bombers." Presented at the Second Military History Symposium, USAF Academy, 1968, available at http://www.au.af.mil/au/awc/awcgate/cbo-afa/cbo.10.htm (accessed January 13, 2005).

Taylor, Michael J. H., ed. *Jane's Encyclopedia of Aircraft,* Vol. 3. Danbury, Conn.: Grolier Educational Corp., 1980.

———. *Jane's Encyclopedia of Aircraft,* Vol. 4. Danbury, Conn.: Grolier Educational Corp., 1980.

True, James L., Jr. "The Tourniquet and the Hammer: A New Look at Deep Interdiction." *Air University Review* (July–August 1981).

United States Air Force. *The Army Air Forces in World War II: Combat Chronology, 1941–1945.* Washington, D.C.: Office of Air Force History, 1973.

Wechsberg, Joseph. *Homecoming.* New York: Alfred A. Knopf, 1946.

Wright Patterson Airbase Air Force Museum. "Beech AT-10 Wichita," at http://www.wpafb.af.mil/museum/early_years/ey23.htm (accessed December 14, 2004).

Zentner, John J. "The Art of Wing Leadership and Aircrew Morale in Combat." The Cadre Papers, No. 11, n.d.

Index